Praise for The *Financial Times* Guide to Wealth Management, second edition

'Few books have its clarity and none its scope. It simplifies complex issues and shows you not only how to make your money work for you and your family but also how to enjoy it.'

David Kilshaw, Private Client Partner, Ernst & Young LLP

'A brilliant book, written in an accessible manner to help you understand the importance of life goals and values in the wealth management process. It is the best book I have ever come across on wealth management.'

Dr Lien Luu, Senior Lecturer in Financial Services, Northampton Business School; certified and chartered financial planner

'Many people's lives would be significantly enhanced by having a great relation-ship with a financial adviser. Jason's impeccably researched guide is an insight into how the best financial advisers do business and could help you re-evaluate your relationship with your money.'

David Jones, Head of Financial Adviser Services EMEA, Dimensional Fund Advisors

'This book, from one of the UK's leading financial planners, provides the essen-tial knowledge that investors need to help them think about and plan for their financial future.'

Steve Gazzard CFP^CM, Chief Executive, Institute of Financial Planning

'A practical, easy-to-read guide that provides a framework to help us all achieve our financial goals. This book is essential reading for investors.'

Cynthia Poole, Director, Raymond James Investment Services

THE FINANCIAL TIMES GUIDE TO WEALTH MANAGEMENT

PEARSON

At Pearson, we believe in learning – all kinds of learning for all kinds of people. Whether it's at home, in the classroom or in the workplace, learning is the key to improving our life chances.

That's why we're working with leading authors to bring you the latest thinking and best practices, so you can get better at the things that are important to you. You can learn on the page or on the move, and with content that's always crafted to help you understand quickly and apply what you've learned.

If you want to upgrade your personal skills or accelerate your career, become a more effective leader or more powerful communicator, discover new opportunities or simply find more inspiration, we can help you make progress in your work and life.

Pearson is the world's leading learning company. Our portfolio includes the Financial Times and our education business, Pearson International.

Every day our work helps learning flourish, and wherever learning flourishes, so do people.

To learn more, please visit us at www.pearson.com/uk

The Financial Times

With a worldwide network of highly respected journalists, *The Financial Times* provides global business news, insightful opinion and expert analysis of business, finance and politics. With over 500 journalists reporting from 50 countries worldwide, our in-depth coverage of international news is objectively reported and analysed from an independent, global perspective.

To find out more, visit www.ft.com/pearsonoffer/

THE FINANCIAL TIMES GUIDE TO WEALTH MANAGEMENT

· ·

HOW TO PLAN, INVEST AND PROTECT YOUR FINANCIAL ASSETS

SECOND EDITION

JASON BUTLER

Harlow, England • London • New York • Boston • San Francisco • Toronto • Sydney
Auckland • Singapore • Hong Kong • Tokyo • Seoul • Taipei • New Delhi
Cape Town • São Paulo • Mexico City • Madrid • Amsterdam • Munich • Paris • Milan

Pearson Education Limited
Edinburgh Gate
Harlow CM20 2JE
United Kingdom
Tel: +44 (0)1279 623623
Web: www.pearson.com/uk

First published 2012 (print and electronic)
Second edition published 2014 (print and electronic)

© Pearson Education Limited 2012, 2015 (print and electronic)

The right of Jason Butler to be identified as author of this work has been asserted by him in accordance with the Copyright, Designs and Patents Act 1988.

Pearson Education is not responsible for the content of third-party internet sites.

ISBN: 978-1-292-00469-3 (print)
         978-1-292-00470-9 (PDF)
         978-1-292-00471-6 (ePub)
         978-1-292-00518-8 (eText)

British Library Cataloguing-in-Publication Data
A catalogue record for the print edition is available from the British Library

Library of Congress Cataloging-in-Publication Data
Butler, Jason (Financial planner)
  The Financial Times guide to wealth management: now to plan, invest and protect your financial assets / Jason Butler. -- Second edition.
     pages cm
  ISBN 978-1-292-00469-3 (softcover)
  1. Finance, Personal. 2. Investments. I. Financial times (London, England) II. Title.
  HG179.B8768 2014
  332.024--dc23
                              2014034252

The print publication is protected by copyright. Prior to any prohibited reproduction, storage in a retrieval system, distribution or transmission in any form or by any means, electronic, mechanical, recording or otherwise, permission should be obtained from the publisher or, where applicable, a licence permitting restricted copying in the United Kingdom should be obtained from the Copyright Licensing Agency Ltd, Saffron House, 6-10 Kirby Street, London EC1N 8TS.

The ePublication is protected by copyright and must not be copied, reproduced, transferred, distributed, leased, licensed or publicly performed or used in any way except as specifically permitted in writing by the publishers, as allowed under the terms and conditions under which it was purchased, or as strictly permitted by applicable copyright law. Any unauthorised distribution or use of this text may be a direct infringement of the author's and the publishers' rights and those responsible may be liable in law accordingly.

All trademarks used herein are the property of their respective owners. The use of any trademark in this text does not vest in the author or publisher any trademark ownership rights in such trademarks, nor does the use of such trademarks imply any affiliation with or endorsement of this book by such owners.

Contains public sector information licensed under the Open Government Licence (OGL) v2.0. www.nationalarchives.gov.uk/doc/open-government-licence.

ARP Impressions 98
Printed in Great Britain by Ashford Colour Press Ltd

Cover image: travellinglight/ Alamy
Print edition typeset in 9pt Stone Serif Pro by 30

NOTE THAT ANY PAGE CROSS REFERENCES REFER TO THE PRINT EDITION

CONTENTS

PART 4
WEALTH TRANSFER AND SUCCESSION   387

ABOUT THE AUTHOR

Jason Butler is qualified as a Chartered Wealth Manager, Certified Financial Planner and Chartered Financial Planner and has been a wealth management professional since 1990. In 2001 he was awarded the Tony Sellon Memorial Prize for outstanding contribution to the development of the financial planning profession. He is a visiting lecturer on financial planning and an honorary Fellow of Northampton University. Jason is the founder and chief executive of Bloomsbury Wealth Management, a multi-award-winning wealth management and financial planning firm based in London. He lives in Suffolk with his wife, two daughters, two dogs and two horses.

ACKNOWLEDGEMENTS

I would like to thank all of my colleagues at Bloomsbury Wealth Management for the great job they do looking after our clients, which enables me to bury myself away researching and writing about private wealth planning.

Particular thanks to my colleagues Carolyn Gowen, Charles Wood and Robert Lockie, who kindly reviewed several of the chapters and offered useful feedback. A special thanks to Robert for creating many of the graphs and charts based on my spidery handwritten sketches. Thanks also go to my long-serving assistant Elaine McErlean for all that she does to support me.

Thanks also to the following individuals for reviewing various chapters: Jaskarn Pawar, David Lane, Jane Lee, Karen Barretto, Alan Pink, Sam Adams and Gavin Francis.

Special thanks to Tim Hale of Albion Strategic for allowing me to reproduce a number of graphics and insights from the research reports that he prepares for my firm, and for his assistance in sourcing data.

I would like to thank the following organisations for providing research, data or other resources: Barclays; Canada Life International; CEG Worldwide Inc; Dimensional Fund Advisors Inc; Finametrica Pty; FTSE; Fitz Partners; Morningstar; Raymond James Investment Services Limited; and Vanguard Group.

I would like to thank my editor Chris Cudmore for commissioning the second edition of this book and Lucy Carter, Melanie Carter and their colleagues at Pearson Education for pulling together this edition.

I would also like to acknowledge the families with whom I have had the privilege to work over the past 25 years and who put their trust in my firm to help them make good financial decisions. Those experiences gave me the motivation to write this second edition.

As always, any errors and omissions in this book are mine, but any value that is created from its contents is yours.

Jason Butler
September 2014

PUBLISHER'S ACKNOWLEDGEMENTS

We are grateful to the following for permission to reproduce copyright material:

Tables

Table 1.1 adapted from the Kinder Institute of Life Planning, which trains Financial Life Planners all over the globe using the EVOKE client process. Reproduced by kind permission of George Kinder and the Kinder Institute of Life Planning, **www. kinderinstitute.com**; Table 1.2 reproduced by kind permission of Maria Nemeth, Founder and Executive Director of the Academy for Coaching Excellence; Tables 2.1 and 6.3 courtesy of Morningstar, Inc. All Rights Reserved. Reproduced with permission. The information contained herein: (1) is proprietary to Morningstar and/or its content providers; (2) may not be copied or distributed; (3) does not constitute investment advice offered by Morningstar; and (4) is not warranted to be accurate, complete or timely. Neither Morningstar nor its content providers are responsible for any damages or losses arising from any use of this information. Past performance is no guarantee of future results. Use of information from Morningstar does not necessarily constitute agreement by Morningstar, Inc. of any investment philosophy or strategy presented in this publication; Table 6.2 from Dimson, E., Marsh, P. and Staunton, M., *Credit Suisse Global Investment Returns Yearbook 2014*, reproduced with kind permission of the authors; Table 7.1 from Big Society Capital Outcomes Matrix 2013, developed in partnership with New Philanthropy Capital, the SROI Network, Triangle Consulting and Investing for Good; Table 7.2 courtesy of Blue & Green Investor; Tables 9.1, 9.4, 12.2, 12.3 and 12.4 courtesy of Albion Strategic; Table 10.2 courtesy of the FTSE Group; Table 11.1 courtesy of the Association of Investment companies; Table 12.1 from Barclays Capital Equity Gilt Study 2014; Table 19.1 courtesy of Laing & Busson; Table 18.6 courtesy of London and Colonial; Table 21.2 courtesy of Canada Life; Table 23.1 from 'Payback Time? Student Debt and Loan Repayments: What Will the 2012 Reforms Mean for Graduates?', Institute of Fiscal Studies, April 2014 , **http://www. ifs.org.uk/publications/7165**

Figures

Figure 1.1 is excerpted from Bill Bachrach's Values-based Financial Planning book. It is provided courtesy of Bill Bachrach, Bachrach & Associates, inc., www. BillBachrach.com © 1996–2011 Bill Bachrach. All rights reserved; Figure 2.1 courtesy of Finametrica; Figure 3.4 courtesy of KMD Private Wealth Management; Figure 4.5 copyright © 2014, Financial Planning Standards Board Ltd. All rights reserved; Figures 4.7, 4.8, 4.9 and 4.10 courtesy of CEG Worldwide; Figure 5.1 courtesy of the Moneyfacts Group; Figure 5.2 reproduced by kind permission of Dr Jean-Paul Rodrigue, Department of Global Studies and Geography, Hofstra University; Figures 5.7, 6.12, 6.13, 8.2 and 12.1 from Barclays Equity Gilt Study 2014; Figures 5.17, 6.3, 6.10, 6.19, 6.24, 9.1, 9.4, 9.5, 10.8, 12.3, 12.4, 12.5, 12.6, 12.7, 12.8 and 23.5 courtesy of Albion Strategic; Figures 6.5, 6.6 and 6.9 courtesy of the FTSE Group; Figure 6.11 from Vazza, D., Kraemer, N., Gunter, E., *Default, Transition and Recovery: 2011 Annual US Corporate Default Study And Rating Transitions*, 23 March 2012. Published by Standard & Poor's Ratings Services, a division of The McGraw-Hill companies, Inc. Standard & Poor's Financial Services LLC (S&P) does not guarantee the accuracy, completeness, timeliness or availability of any information, including ratings, and is not responsible for any errors or omissions (negligent or otherwise), regardless of the cause, or for the results obtained from the use of ratings. S&P GIVES NO EXPRESS OR IMPLIED WARRANTIES, INCLUDING, BUT NOT LIMITED TO, ANY WARRANTIES OF MERCHANTABILITY OR FITNESS FOR A PARTICULAR PURPOSE OR USE. S&P SHALL NOT BE LIABLE FOR ANY DIRECT, INDIRECT, INCIDENTAL, EXEMPLARY, COMPENSATORY, PUNITIVE, SPECIAL OR CONSEQUENTIAL DAMAGES, COSTS, EXPENSES, LEGAL FEES, or LOSSES (INCLUDING LOST INCOME OR PROFITS AND OPPORTUNITY COSTS) IN CONNECTION WITH ANY USE OF RATINGS. S&P's ratings are statements of opinion and are not statements of fact or recommendations to purchase, hold or sell securities. They do not address the market value of securities or the sustainability of securities for investment purposes, and should not be relied on as investment advice; Figure 7.4 courtesy of Blue & Green Investor; Figure 7.5 courtesy of the World Economic Forum; Figure 7.6 courtesy of Carbon Tracker; Figure 7.8 courtesy of Worthstone Limited; Figure 7.9 courtesy of Big Society Capital; Figures 9.2 and 9.3 courtesy of Savills Research; Figures 10.1 and 10.2 courtesy of The Vanguard Group; Figures 11.1, 11.4 and 11.6 courtesy of the Association of Investment Companies; Figures 11.2 and 11.10 courtesy of Fitz Partners; Figure 11.3 courtesy of ETFGI; Figure 17.2 courtesy of TAP Assist Limited, Auto Enrolment consultants www.SimplyEnrolment.co.uk; Figure 20.2 courtesy of the Independent Schools Council; Figure 21.4 courtesy of Speechly Bircham; Figures 21.9 and 21.10 courtesy of Canada Life ; Figure 22.4 courtesy of Octopus Investments; Figure 22.6 courtesy of London and Colonial.

Articles

Article on page 76 by Dunkley, E. (2014), 'Management fees are high and still rising', Financial Times, 21 June 2014; © The Financial Times Limited 2013. All Rights Reserved; article on page 156 by Cohen, N. (2013), 'Making good and doing good', Financial Times, 23 March 2013; © The Financial Times Limited 2013. All Rights Reserved; article on page 222 by Dunkley, E. (2014), 'Investment trusts gear up before rate rise', Financial Times, 12 April 2014; © The Financial Times Limited 2014. All Rights Reserved.

Other

The publishers wish to thank Dimensional Fund Advisors for permission to use their data in Figures 6.17, 8.1, 10.3, 10.4 and 10.5 and the FTSE Group for their permission to use data in Figures 6.6, 8.1, 10.3 and 10.4.

Figures 4.6, 6.1, 15.5–7, 18.3–7, 21.11–16, 22.3, 22.5, 22.7 and Tables 5.3, 15.1 and 18.2 were created by Bloomsbury Wealth Management for the purposes of this book.

Unless otherwise stated, all other figures and tables were created by the author.

In some instances we have been unable to trace the owners of copyright material, and we would appreciate any information that would enable us to do so.

The material in this book is based on the author's understanding and interpretation of current UK legislation and practise (as at September 2014), both of which are subject to change. No material in this publication should be construed as financial advice as defined by the Financial Services and Markets Act 2000 (and as subsequently amended). You are strongly recommended to take independent and personalised advice from a suitably qualified and authorised financial adviser.

INTRODUCTION

The first edition of this book was published in late 2011, just as we were emerging from the depths of a global financial crisis. So much has changed in the wealth planning arena in the past few years that this second edition is almost a new book. As well as radical changes to many of the chapters, there are five new chapters: socially responsible and impact investing; property, land and woodlands; single-premium investment bonds; non-trust structures; and young people and money.

This book is set out in four main sections. Part 1 covers strategic wealth planning issues, including the importance of developing and maintaining a proper overall wealth plan that is in tune with your personal mission, vision, values and goals. This edition explores behavioural finance and the impact of emotions on decision making and financial outcomes. In addition, I have explained the role of guidance and advice and when and how to choose suitable professionals to work with, as well as the negative impact that the media can have on your financial wellbeing.

Part 2 deals with wealth preservation, including a condensed and 'elegantly simple' investment framework that is likely to form the core of your wealth plan, as well as an expanded chapter on the role of insurance. While there are many investment-related books that go into forensic detail, I've tried to explain the subject matter on the basis of what matters and, more importantly, what works. My view is that the simpler you can make your investment approach, the more likely it is to be effective.

Part 3 focuses on wealth enhancement, with an overview of tactical planning issues including general tax, portfolio tax and pension planning.

Part 4 deals with wealth transfer and succession, including later life issues, trusts, young people and money, philanthropy and life purpose.

Some of these subjects are complicated and wide ranging, so I've tried to cover what I think will be the most important issues to the majority of readers. I could easily have written three times as much material, so bear that in mind when reading those chapters, and if necessary seek additional reading.

Don't feel that you have to read the whole book from beginning to end. You might prefer to read random chapters that take your fancy, or read one whole section. If you read this book in small chunks, you might get more out of it than thinking you need to absorb every word. The language is as jargon-free and clear as I could make it, bearing in mind the complexity of some of the subject matter.

I do not think there is a definite 'right way' to manage personal wealth, but my approach has been shaped as much by my 25 years of practical experience of working with families on private wealth matters as it has by the thousands of hours spent studying, training and updating my technical knowledge. I would hope that this book becomes your trusty companion along life's financial highway and that it gives you the inspiration, understanding and confidence to make good decisions about your wealth or to hold to account professionals whom you engage to manage it for you.

If you spend less time and effort worrying about your money and more on living your life to the full then it will have been worth the effort.

PART 1
WEALTH PLANNING

CHAPTER 1
KNOW WHERE YOU ARE GOING AND WHY

'Happiness is not having what you want, but wanting what you have.'

Hyman Schachtel, US rabbi

Many people go about planning and managing their wealth in a haphazard and random manner. They have a vague idea of what they want, gain some information and go from one financial solution to the other, without any real plan or context. Over the years I've answered many readers' questions for the *Financial Times* and other weekend newspapers and a common question is: 'How should I invest my capital?' This is the same as asking: 'How long is a piece of string?' The answer is: 'It depends.'

Viktor Frankl, in his classic book *Man's Search for Meaning*,[1] wrote about his observations of human motivation when he was held in a Nazi concentration camp. His central observation was that 'a man can always find the "how" if he knows the "why"'. Before you can go about making good financial decisions you need to know your 'why'.

The key to a successful wealth plan is setting personal life goals and objectives in the context of your money values. In addition, agreeing and articulating overarching financial planning principles will assist with future decision making.

Money values

Abraham Maslow was a psychologist who developed the theory of 'the hierarchy of needs', which provides a basic framework for all human motivation and associated

---

[1] Frankl, V.E. (2004) *Man's Search for Meaning: The classic tribute to hope from the Holocaust*, New Edition, Rider.

actions. At the bottom of the ladder are basic needs such as food, shelter, sex, etc. Once these basic needs have been met the individual will seek to fulfil higher-level needs that serve to meet their wider personal desires, such as friendship, love, material possessions and status. Once these intermediate needs have been met, an individual will seek much higher-level needs, which at their highest level are known as 'self-actualisation'. These needs generally relate to wider society and the desire of the individual to find their real meaning or place in the world.

The self-actualisation stage is where real meaning and contentment can be found. For many people this concept of self-actualisation can appear a bit woolly or vague, even frightening. We can adapt Maslow's ideas to help us make decisions that are in tune with our 'money values'. Money values are overarching beliefs that you have about money and these follow a progressive hierarchy. The 'values

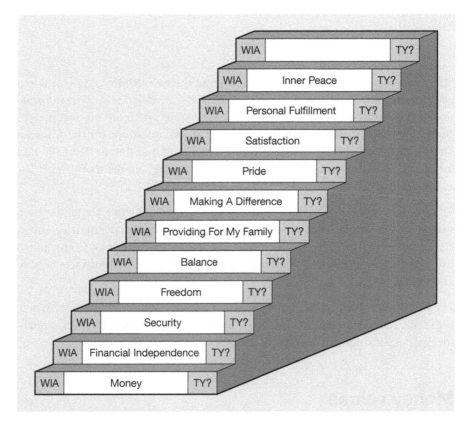

Figure 1.1 The values staircase: what's important about money to you?

Source: The Values Conversation® and The Values Staircase® were excerpted from Bill Bachrach's *Values-based Financial Planning* book. It is provided courtesy of Bill Bachrach, Bachrach & Associates, Inc., **www.BillBachrach.com** ©1996–2011 Bill Bachrach. All rights reserved.

conversation', as it is known, starts with asking the question: 'What's important about money to you?' (See Figure 1.1.) This approach was pioneered by Bill Bachrach in his excellent book *Values-based Financial Planning*[2] and this forms the basis of the training that his company provides to progressive financial planners.

Usually the first response to the question 'What's important about money to you?' will be general and basic answers such as 'financial security', which is a perfectly reasonable response. However, if you keep following this line of questioning with 'And what's important about financial security to you?', it will allow you to discover more deep-seated values. It is this process of self-actualisation that helps us to find real meaning and purpose for the future wealth plan. Some people find this process a bit uncomfortable as it requires a level of reflection and contemplation about money that we rarely give to it. However, this reflection can be highly liberating and might allow you to develop a better sense of priorities and objectives.

Life planning can give deeper meaning to goals and dreams

Over the years I've met many financially successful people who have stopped dreaming. They have 'switched off' from identifying real meaning, purpose and authenticity in their life. It is not uncommon for a business owner to work hard for years, sell their business for a significant sum and then lose all purpose in their life. This is because their central focus, their business, has been taken away. They then drift along slowly losing motivation and purpose. Other times they jump straight from the sale of their business to 'investing' some of their hard-won capital into a new business venture, only to see the business, and their hard-earned capital, slowly dwindle to nothing.

When I was looking for ways to help my clients to envisage a better future and to articulate their life goals and objectives, as well as to improve my own happiness and life meaning, I discovered life planning. In essence, life planning is about living life on purpose, whatever that means to you. George Kinder is considered by many to be the father of life planning and his ground-breaking book, *The Seven Stages of Money Maturity*,[3] sets out a radically different way of approaching managing wealth. I attended a training workshop during one of George's regular trips to the UK a few years ago, and I found it very enlightening as it made me question a

---

[2]   Bachrach, B. (© 2000–2011) *Values-based Financial Planning: The art of creating an inspiring financial strategy*, Aim High Publishing.

[3]   Kinder, G. (2000) *The Seven Stages of Money Maturity: Understanding the spirit and value of money in your life*, Dell Publishing Company.

number of my principles and ideas about my life and the role that money played in it. A consequence is that eventually I realised how much was 'enough' and what was really important to me.

The three difficult questions

A key element of the Kinder approach is to ask yourself three difficult questions.

- **Question one.** I want you to imagine that you are financially secure – you have enough money to take care of your needs, now and in the future. The question is, how would you live your life? What would you do with the money? Would you change anything? Let yourself go. Don't hold back your dreams. *Describe a life that is complete, richly yours.*

- **Question two.** This time, you visit your doctor who tells you that you have five to ten years to live. The good part is that you won't ever feel sick. The bad news is that you will have no notice of the moment of your death. What will you do in the time you have remaining to live? *Will you change your life and how will you do it?*

- **Question three**. This time, your doctor shocks you with the news that you have only one day left to live. Notice what feelings arise as you confront your very real mortality. Ask yourself: 'What dreams will be left unfulfilled? What do I wish I had finished or had been? What do I wish I had done? What did I miss?'

The purpose of these questions is to help uncover your deepest and most important values. Equally important is uncovering what is standing in the way of leading the life that is truly the one you want to live. In this context, another home or expensive car might not be the answer.

What's really important?

Kinder sets out a framework for helping us identify what is really important in life. The values grid, as it is known, determines between 'heart's core' – what really matters; 'ought to' – things that you feel obliged to do; and 'fun to' – irreverent things that aren't really important but nevertheless are possible goals. (See Table 1.1.)

Life can seem complicated, things get in the way and we sometimes do things we would rather not do and don't do the things that we would rather do. Maria Nemeth is a clinical psychologist and a Master Certified Coach. Maria asks her clients: 'Would it be OK if life got easier?' Maria has developed a useful tool called the Life's Intentions Inventory and this is reproduced in Table 1.2. Why not take some time now to go through the inventory and score the relative importance of each of the intentions. You might find it quite enlightening and it might make you rethink what's important to you and why.

Table 1.1 The values grid

	Possible uses of your wealth	Heart's core	Ought to	Fun to	N/A
In the adjacent table, you will find a number of possible uses to which you could put your current or future wealth. For each one, please place an 'X' in one of the four boxes to the right based on the following definitions. Heart's core: a deeply held core value of yours, as to how the wealth should be used. This is a value that you 'stand for'. Ought to: something you feel obligated to do, based on a commitment you may have made or a belief held by your family, someone outside your family or society in general. Fun to: the 'icing on the cake'. Doing this would add zest or spice to your life, is not an obligation you feel and is not truly a deeply held core value, but it sure would be fun!	Providing for my family's ongoing needs (Note: this involves day-to-day living expenses, mortgage and car payments, holidays, funding children's education, etc.)				
	Supporting parents, siblings and other family members in need				
	Providing an inheritance for my children				
	Adjusting selected elements of current lifestyle (a second home, a boat, an aeroplane, travelling, an 'expensive hobby', etc.)				
	Supporting a major change in my work and career				
	Actualising a very different direction for my life				
	Charitable giving/ philanthropy				
	Other(s) please specify				

Source: Adapted from the Kinder Institute of Life Planning, which trains Financial Life Planners all over the globe using the EVOKE Client Interview process. Reproduced by kind permission of George Kinder and the Kinder Institute of Life Planning. **www.kinderinstitute.com**

Table 1.2 The life's intentions inventory

Life's intentions represent underlying purposes that give meaning to our goals and dreams. **Please rate the intentions that are currently important to you. Use 1 for Relatively Unimportant and 5 for Very Important. This is only a snapshot in time, reflecting where you are today. How you rate your intentions could change at a later date.** **My intentions are to be:**	
Financially successful	
Physically fit and healthy	
A successfull painter or sculptor	
A successful musician or composer	
A successful author, playwright or poet	
A contributor to my community	
A visionary leader	
Spiritually developing	
A loving family member	
A trusted friend	
A well-respected professional	
An effective manager	
An effective teacher	
Well educated	
An effective coach	
A successful business owner	
An effective mediator	
Well travelled	
An effective mentor	
A successful entrepreneur	
An adventurer	
Politically active	
A successful communicator	

Source: Reproduced by kind permission of Maria Nemeth, Founder and Executive Director of the Academy for Coaching Excellence.

Financial planning policies

Once you have uncovered your purpose, motivations and money values, you can then use these to help you to formulate financial planning policies. Financial planning policies are tools for making good decisions in the face of financial uncertainty. They transcend the current situation by expressing, in general terms, what you plan to do and how you are willing to do it in terms not limited to the current circumstances. Such policies are broad enough to encompass any novel event that might arise, but specific enough so that we are never in doubt as to what actions are required. We'll see the value of having planning policies in Chapter 12 when we discuss withdrawal rates from an investment portfolio.

Examples of financial planning policies include:

- I will give 10% of my gross annual income to charity.
- I will only do work that I love.
- I will maintain sufficient life insurance to cover my children's education costs.
- We will provide family members with financial literacy support but will not give them money.
- I will not invest in any investment or tax planning that I do not understand.
- I will invest only in 'positively screened' ethical investments.
- I will delegate everything in relation to my finances either that I do not enjoy doing or that can be done by someone else at lower cost, taking into account the value of my time to be able to do other things.
- I will always maintain a minimum of one year's living costs in cash and if my portfolio falls more than 20% in a 12-month period then I will reduce the amount of regular withdrawal I take to 50% for up to 2 years.
- I will invest only in socially responsible funds.

Financial policies are the anchor points of your strategy to help decision making in difficult times or where there are competing objectives. Think of the policies as the keel of your financial boat, keeping you from capsizing in rough financial seas.

Clear goals

There is something incredibly enabling about defining and writing down clear life goals. Notice that I refer to life goals, not financial goals. My view is that people don't have financial goals, they have life goals that have financial implications.

In 1961 President Kennedy set the incredible goal of sending a man to the moon and safely returning him before the end of the 1960s. He didn't tell the NASA people to see what they could do in space over the next few years and come back to him with a few achievements; Kennedy was specific about what he wanted and had a clear timeline. In my experience, people who have clear and realistic life goals tend to make better financial decisions.

Life goals that will be common to everyone are maintaining financial independence and staying fit and well. This means being able to fund your desired lifestyle until you die, regardless of your desire or ability to work, and that your money lasts a lifetime, including a time when paid work is optional as you have enough financial resources available to fund your desired lifestyle. If you work for money, you do so because you want to, not because you have to. The term 'financial independence' is much more meaningful to people today than the concept of 'retirement' and is something worthwhile to aim for. This is because, unlike retirement, which for some people means a time of doing nothing but playing golf or gardening, financial independence means you have the choice of doing whatever you wish.

The four key factors that will affect this objective are how long you live, how much you spend, the return you achieve on your capital and the rate at which the cost of living rises. We'll cover these issues in more depth in Chapter 3 and determine what are reasonable assumptions to use when formulating your overall plan.

Clearly, your lifestyle, genetics and sense of purpose will play a large part in determining your standard of health, but if or when your health deteriorates, you'll want to make sure that you can afford any additional costs for health and long-term care and continue to enjoy a good quality of life. With people living longer and continual advances in medical treatment, the importance of planning for declining health will affect more and more people. Life expectancy in the UK has been rising for many years and some commentators have described 90 as the new 70. But life expectancy isn't the only issue that you need to factor into your plans – quality of that life is also important because it can have significant cost implications.

Other goals

There may be any number of other goals that are important to you. The following are real-life examples that I have come across in my work with clients. Some have more of a financial implication than others, but it is important to get the goals written down so that you can get excited about pulling together your wealth plan:

- funding part or all of the education costs of a child, grandchild or other family member or friend
- leaving a specific legacy to an individual or charity
- funding the cost of your child or your adult child's wedding
- taking up a hobby, such as sailing, shooting, scuba-diving or flying, which has a cost implication
- taking up further study or further education at a university or college
- mentoring young businesses and possibly providing development funds
- indulging an interest in culture such as opera, ballet, musicals or performance art at home and abroad
- learning a foreign language and staying in the relevant country for some time
- buying a second home in the UK or abroad
- moving abroad to live permanently
- helping your children or other family members to buy their first home
- setting up a small 'lifestyle' business such as a country pub, restaurant or shop
- travelling around the world to indulge an interest in historical buildings and/or interesting places
- learning a new skill such as dancing, martial arts or rock climbing
- buying a boat, classic car or plane
- collecting art or other items
- buying an expensive musical instrument
- visiting relatives more often, particularly those living overseas
- writing a book (take it from me, it's not easy).

While setting clear life goals is essential to developing a wealth plan that works, not all goals are of equal importance. I have found it helpful in my own planning and when working with clients to categorise goals in order of importance. Goals are therefore 'required', 'desired' or 'aspirational'.

Required goals

The 'required' goals are the most important and must be met come what may – they are non-negotiable – and will usually revolve around maintaining financial independence throughout your lifetime and remaining fit and well or obtaining treatment and care to enable you to have a high quality of life. You should state the minimum annual lifestyle cost that you would be prepared to accept – your basic financial independence target – in the event that things such as taxes, investment returns or inflation turn out worse than you expect. There may be other goals like funding school fees, which are equally important and must be met but for which you could substitute a cheaper option as a base scenario.

Desired goals

'Desired' goals are important but not at the expense of the required goals. You might, for example, wish to fund a slightly more expensive lifestyle than that assumed under the required goals. Examples of other typical desired goals might include making regular gifts each year to individuals, a trust or charity; preserving assets for your children; investing in a new business; or funding a holiday home. In essence, desired goals are important and broadly reflect the middle values in the values staircase in Figure 1.1. They usually, but not always, reflect a desire to help the wider family.

Aspirational goals

'Aspirational' goals are essentially those goals that you wish to achieve if everything else has been catered for and perhaps investment returns have been consistently above those assumed or you've spent less than anticipated. Such goals often reflect the desire to help wider society. Such 'aspirational' goals might be giving money, time or both to good causes in your lifetime or after death. The point is that if the investment strategy has produced returns below the original assumption, it is the aspirational goals that take the back seat, not your core lifestyle expenditure.

Philanthropy is a possible example of an aspirational goal, although it may be the quantum of philanthropy rather than the act. For example, you might have a 'required' goal to support a charity or cause with time or modest financial gifts, whereas you might have an 'aspiration' to give much more substantial amounts of money if you are able to do so.

Example

The unhappy surgeon

Many years ago, at a financial planning conference in the United States, I heard the following story that illustrates how we can think differently about work and 'retirement', sometimes with life-changing consequences.

A well-respected and ostensibly successful surgeon, let's call him Mr Jones, visited a financial planner. During the initial goal-setting discussion the planner gently asked Mr Jones what his key concerns were. Mr Jones revealed that he really didn't enjoy his job any more; his relationships with his wife and 13-year-old daughter were under strain; he had high blood pressure and suffered bouts of depression, for which he was on medication. In addition, Mr Jones, despite earning a high salary and having built significant wealth, didn't feel wealthy or successful.

Mr Jones' plan was to work hard for the next five years and earn as much as he could so that he could afford to 'retire' to Florida and have enough time for both his wife and daughter and his other hobbies like fishing and cycling, neither of which he currently had time to pursue. The planner took all this in and suggested that Mr Jones come back in a few weeks, once the planner had been able to run the numbers and see whether this would work.

Mr Jones duly returned a few weeks later. The planner showed a picture of Mr Jones' overall wealth and confirmed that the numbers did seem to support the strategy that Mr Jones was currently pursuing. However, the planner pointed out that with the current approach Mr Jones would continue to be unhappy over the next five years and possibly find that he might not survive long enough to enjoy his life when he stopped work.

The planner then showed another picture of Mr Jones' wealth that was also sustainable. In this alternative scenario Mr Jones would actually work about half his current hours, with immediate effect, but instead of stopping work in five years he would work at the new reduced rate for the next ten years and an even more reduced sum for the following five years. The planner explained that the benefits of this approach were that Mr Jones could do surgery, which he really enjoyed, he would have enough time to spend with his wife and daughter and pursue his hobbies *now*, and he would be able to schedule exercise and rest. Mr Jones had not considered this alternative approach and cautiously agreed to give it a try.

At the progress meeting with the planner about a year later, Mr Jones explained that he was really enjoying his work again, and the paradox of making himself less available meant that his value went up and he was almost earning the same income working 2.5 days a week as when he was busting a gut working 6 days a week. His blood pressure was now under control and he had lost about a stone in weight. His relationship with his wife had improved considerably and while no amount of planning could change the fact that his daughter was a typical teenager, with all the usual associated challenges, he felt much more able to understand her and flew off the handle far less.

The message here is that thinking differently about the big-picture plan could, quite literally, save a life.

Time horizon

Different goals will require different approaches based on whether they are short-, medium- or long-term goals. Funding a wedding or house in a couple of years will mean that the need is to avoid the potential for capital loss; inflation is less of a concern. Funding your long-term lifestyle, however, means that inflation will be more of a threat and therefore you could accept some risk to capital in return for the potential of generating real returns over the long term.

Current/desired lifestyle expenditure

The clearer you can be about what your current and future lifestyle costs are, the better your overall plan and associated financial decisions will be. This is because funding your lifestyle will have an influence on your investment strategy, tax planning and wealth succession planning. In my experience, the vast majority of people rarely have a clear idea of the cost of their current or desired lifestyle and they consistently underestimate how much they are spending. Sometimes this is because they feel guilty about how their expenditure. In other cases the attributes of their personality that helped them create their wealth may not be those required to manage it well. Entertainers are a classic example of individuals who have high earning capabilities but often have poor financial judgement. Elvis Presley was well known for being generous and gave Cadillacs to strangers. Who knows how much Elton John has spent on flowers over the decades?

Over the years I've had clients tell me: 'This was an exceptional year for spending.' Every year seems an exceptional year! Do remember to account for things such as holidays and home improvements/maintenance. The importance of having a clear idea of expenditure, both now and in the future, will vary from person to person depending on the financial resources they have available. My advice is to be realistic about what you will spend throughout your lifetime as it is better to overestimate than to underestimate. There is no need to spend lots of time doing detailed budgets, just as long as you are totally confident that you have a true idea of how much you really are spending (or would like to spend).

Don't mention the 'R' word

If you are thinking about retirement as a goal, I suggest you ask yourself the following questions to see whether that really is the goal for which you are aiming.

- What does retirement mean to you?
- How will you live your life differently when you are retired?

- Do you have a role model of someone who is retired and, if so, what is it about their lifestyle that you admire?
- Do you have concerns about retirement and, if so, what are they?
- How would you feel about working less but for longer?

> 'For many, a conventional retirement may not be welcome. More than ever before, we are enjoying good health to an older age and many of us are not only capable of working well beyond retirement age, we also often have the desire to do so. Today's older generation can often be found using their retirement years to start a new career, set up a business or to consult in their specialist field. As a result, the notion that an individual should cease working at a pre-defined age is more of an illusion than a reality.'[4]

People who have never created any meaningful wealth are often amazed when they learn that many wealthy people are still motivated to continue working, often until they die. The thought process goes something like: 'They have all the money they could possibly need, why are they still working?' This displays a lack of understanding of both the role of work and the meaning of wealth for successful people. It also goes to the heart of one's life goals.

Frederick Herzberg was a US psychologist who carried out a study on human motivation in the workplace.[5] His main conclusion was that the most powerful motivator in our lives isn't money; it's the opportunity to learn, grow in responsibilities, contribute to others and be recognised for achievements. True happiness and fulfilment therefore are unlikely to be determined by your level of wealth or financial success, although life goals will, obviously, have a financial implication.

When I start working with a new client and I explore the motivations that drive them, it often becomes clear that work is actually a creative and defining part of their life. While building wealth may well have been an early motivation, more often than not the actual processes of leading people, innovating, building a business and making a difference are more important, particularly as the financial success becomes more tangible.

> 'They don't stop being an entrepreneur when they sell the company. Typically, an entrepreneur's business is what defined them.'[6]

---

[4] *Barclays Wealth Insights* (2010) 'How the wealthy are redefining their retirement', Vol. 12, p. 4.

[5] Herzberg, F., Mausner, B. and Bloch Snyderman, B. (1959) *The Motivation to Work*, Wiley.

[6] *Barclays Wealth Insights White Paper* (2007) 'UK landscape of wealth', March, p. 8.

If being involved in business is something that makes you happy or enables you to pursue other meaningful life goals, then why not include that in your wealth plan, rather than aiming for a 'retirement' that may take away a lot of your purpose and meaning? It's OK to still be working in your seventies or even eighties if it is in proportion to your other priorities and it makes you happy. As long as your life goals, which have a financial implication, are not dependent on you continuing to work, then why not work until you drop? Sometimes we need to look at wealth planning in a different way.

In Chapter 3 I'll explain how you can use this knowledge with other key planning assumptions to help develop a robust framework for making key financial decisions, but first we've got to examine the role of financial personality and behaviour.

CHAPTER 2
FINANCIAL PERSONALITY AND BEHAVIOUR

'Information is not knowledge. Knowledge is not wisdom.'

Frank Zappa

With the internet, information is widely available at the click of a button and you could be forgiven for thinking that making good financial decisions should be easy. It is possible to go online and compare financial products, buy investment funds or insurance and apply for a mortgage or a loan. What is rarely considered is both the context in which those decisions are made and the psychology of the person making them.

Understanding your financial personality and how this influences your decision making is the key to living the life you really want and to developing and sticking with a financial plan that will help to ensure that money enables you to be true to that ideal. Your financial personality is your unique combination of natural 'hard-wired' and learned behaviours. Your behavioural characteristics will have a big impact on how you see the world, process information and react to messages from your family, friends and colleagues. If you are employing a professional financial adviser, it can mean the difference between a successful long-term relationship or not.

Your financial personality is made up of a number of interrelated elements, which include:

- your life goals, aspirations and motivations (which we discussed in Chapter 1)
- your financial risk profile
- your natural 'hardwired' behaviour, which is instinctive
- your learned behaviour – education, upbringing, environment, career and life experiences

- your 'money style'
- your need for information and facts – how you like to receive this
- your planning propensity
- your level of emotional intelligence.

Financial risk profile

Knowing your personal financial risk profile is probably one of the most important aspects of making committed life and financial decisions. We all have a unique
risk profile which is determined by our core and learned personality traits and our
financial need to take, financial capacity to withstand and emotional tolerance to
accept financial risks, as set out in Figure 2.1. By 'risk' I mean that there is a degree
of uncertainty about what the actual outcome will be and, in the case of investments, their value will vary, sometimes extremely so. However, the payoff for that
uncertainty is the probability that the overall long-term return will be higher than
that provided by the no-risk investment and thereby enable you to achieve and
maintain financial independence and other life goals which have a financial implication. The key principle is that higher risk is the source of higher returns.

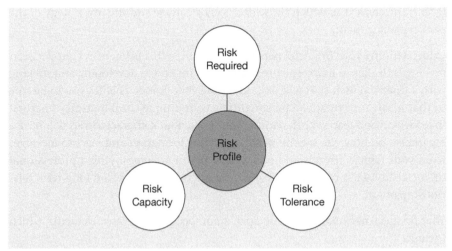

Figure 2.1 The three pillars of risk
Source: Finametrica.

In Chapter 1, I explained that the starting point with your financial plan is to
identify and quantify clear life goals and objectives. Once you know what you

are trying to achieve you need to determine whether your goals are achievable by investing only in no-risk assets such as cash and equivalents. If the plan requires a higher return than that available from risk-free assets and you can't find more resources or spend less, then you will need to invest some of your wealth into risky assets. Thus you have established your financial need to take risk (see Figure 2.2). A required return of just inflation could be achieved through investment in new-issue index-linked gilts and some cash, whereas a required return of 3% per annum over inflation would require a significant exposure to real assets such as equities and property.

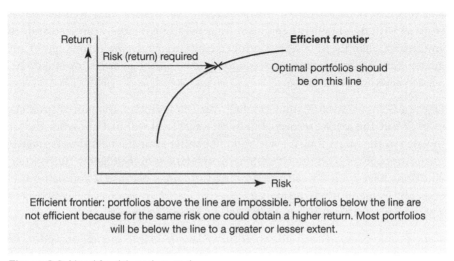

Efficient frontier: portfolios above the line are impossible. Portfolios below the line are not efficient because for the same risk one could obtain a higher return. Most portfolios will be below the line to a greater or lesser extent.

Figure 2.2 Need for risk and reward

Your ability to withstand, financially, the effect of a permanent loss of capital and/or future returns being less favourable than anticipated is called risk capacity. This represents your ability to live with the consequences of an adverse outcome (whether permanent loss of capital or lower investment returns) and the impact that this would have on your lifestyle and other goals, given your financial resources and human capital. If you have significant income-earning potential from employment/self-employment and/or you have most of your post-working lifestyle expenditure covered by a government-backed defined-benefit pension scheme, then you can withstand significant loss of capital and/or volatility in your investment portfolio.

A different, but very important, measure of risk is risk tolerance. Unlike required risk (to meet the required return) and risk capacity, which are both financial parameters, risk tolerance is a psychological parameter, which represents your emotional ability to cope with investment uncertainty or loss. In other words, risk tolerance identifies how you feel emotionally about investment risk, and is based on a combination of your 'core' personality traits (inherent) and those learned (evolved) from life experience, education and environment. Some academics believe that risk tolerance profiles are largely settled by early adulthood, although they concede that risk tolerance decreases slowly over time and, as with other aspects of personality, may be changed by life events, but is otherwise stable.[1] Having used psychometric assessments in my own firm for more than a decade, our experience is that with a majority of our clients we have seen their risk tolerance actually increase over the years. Clearly, there will be an upper limit to such increases, but the fact remains that for some reason their tolerance has increased and this is at odds with some of the academic analysis. It may well be that in working with us, our clients approach their wealth in a more structured and less emotive way, and together with continued education and appropriate support and guidance, they develop more understanding of why they are investing and do not react to news and other 'noise'.

Figure 2.3 shows the UK stock market over the period of the global financial crisis. While the market recovered to its pre-crisis level within a few years, the fall in value in the interval was severe and happening against a relentless barrage of media messages of 'This time it's different' or 'Markets in meltdown'. This is where emotions have such a wealth-destroying influence, because if you bail out of equity investments when the market has experienced a temporary fall, you make it a permanent loss, from which you'll almost certainly never recover.

Some people compartmentalise their financial affairs into mental accounts and think differently about each account. For example, imagine you have three portfolios: one for an emergencies fund, one for children's education and one for retirement. If you have a mental accounting mindset, you are likely to place different levels of importance on these three portfolios and the (emotional) value to you of a £1 loss (or gain) may differ from one portfolio to the others.

The time horizon of each goal might be a key influencing factor as to whether or not you wish to view each goal in a different way in terms of risk tolerance, perhaps having a much lower risk portfolio for goals with a shorter time horizon than those that might be a few decades away. The question then arises as to whether you combine the weighted risk exposure of each portfolio to determine the overall risk exposure.

---

[1] Roszkowski, M.J. and Davey, G. (2010) 'Risk perception and risk tolerance changes attributable to the 2008 economic crisis: a subtle but critical difference', *Journal of Financial Service Professionals*, July. www.riskprofiling.com/Downloads/Risk_Perception_and_Risk_Tolerance_JFSP.pdf

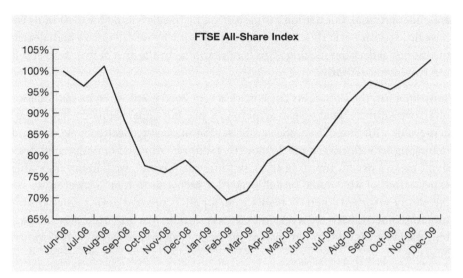

Figure 2.3 UK stock market during the global financial crisis
Source: Data from DFA Returns.

For example, imagine that you have a risk tolerance consistent with a 50% equities portfolio and you have two portfolios – a £100,000 medium-term portfolio for education expenses that is invested 30% in equities and a £200,000 portfolio for retirement expenses. If you are prepared to think of the two portfolios as a whole then the total allocated to equities would need to be £150,000 (50% of £300,000). As there is £30,000 in equities in the medium-term portfolio, £120,000 in equities in the retirement portfolio would bring the overall equities allocation to 50%, but the retirement portfolio would be 60% equities.

Risk perception can and does change depending on current experiences and events. You will usually have a higher investment risk perception when the stock market or property values are rising strongly and the world seems full of optimism and you feel wealthy. It can also vary depending on the type of investment or whether you are under pressure or stress.

When investment and property markets and the economy were booming, and before the global credit crunch hit, it was highly likely that your inherent risk tolerance traits were hidden. As we know, when the tide comes in, all boats rise! But what happened when the stock market dived or some other big negative event happened (the Iraqi invasion of Kuwait, 9/11, the global credit crisis, etc.) and your portfolio showed a large loss? The decision-making patterns for many of us can change radically when the good times turn to bad. This happens because when we are under pressure, our natural instincts instantly take over and for most of us we have little control over this: it just happens. This is why we often see a high degree of emotional decision making. This is not rational in the area of investing and it can cost investors dearly.

Tony Robbins, the US success guru, made a very good point when he said that we often overestimate what we can achieve in a year but underestimate what we can achieve in a lifetime. The same can be said of managing wealth in general and managing investments in particular. We get upset, annoyed or concerned if we don't make a decent return in three or four years because we had unreasonable expectations of what could be delivered over such a short term. However, we are pleasantly surprised when we realise that, for all its ups and downs, our pension fund has quietly delivered a return of 3% per annum over inflation over the past ten years at a time when our cash at the bank is yielding a negative real return after tax.

Understanding your risk profile will therefore help you to understand what portfolio you need and can cope with, both financially and emotionally. Where there is a mismatch between any or all of the three risk elements (as illustrated in Figure 2.4), you will need to reconcile these before deciding on the most suitable investment strategy. For example, you might have to lower your desired lifestyle annual spending in later life, defer the date at which you will become financially independent, work for longer to earn and save more, or accept that you are going to feel uncomfortable at certain times in the future when markets tumble.

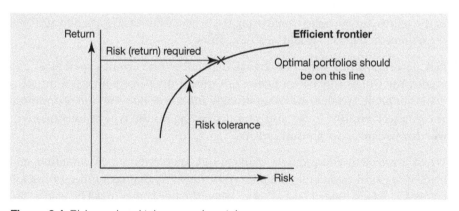

Figure 2.4 Risk need and tolerance mismatch

Natural behaviour is instinctive, very stable and highly predictable over time and is the ingrained response that shapes how you respond to external factors and scenarios. At the most basic and extreme level, these responses are triggered by the amygdala in the back of your brain, which could be described as your 'fight or flight' decision box. Natural behaviour usually surfaces when a person is under pressure – whether positive or negative. This natural behaviour is often masked by learned behaviour and as such it can become 'buried' and less obvious over time.

Learned behaviours are those that are shaped by your life experiences, education, environment and previous financial successes and failures, and these create your attitudes, beliefs and values. Overall your personality is dynamic, but it is driven by 'hardwired' natural behaviour and then shaped by these learned behaviours. Understanding your behaviour factors and how these surface in a stress or striving scenario is key to sticking with a unique life plan and avoiding 'noise' and other bad decisions that can blow you off course from leading a full life.

Emotions and money

The world is made up of lots of different types of people, all with their own idiosyncrasies and traits, experiences and preferences. The thing common to all human beings, however, is that, to a greater or lesser extent, most decisions, including those involving money, are made at an emotional level (see Figure 2.5). In his excellent book on investor psychology, Jason Zweig makes two important points: 'Emotions overwhelm reason' and 'Financial losses are processed in the same area of the brain that responds to mortal danger.'[2]

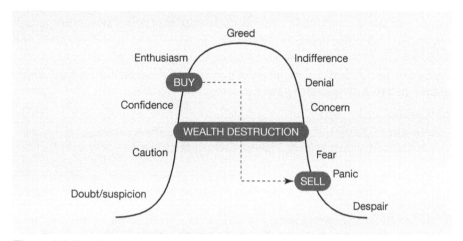

Figure 2.5 Emotions and investing

---

[2]   Zweig, J. (2007) *Your Money or Your Brain*, Simon & Schuster.

When emotions lead to bad financial decisions, this can result in complete loss of capital at one extreme (speculative investments) or lower investment returns than would otherwise have been available – known as the behaviour or performance gap. One analysis of UK investors showed that the performance gap was as much as 2.43% p.a. for UK smaller companies funds and 2.06% p.a. for growth funds.[3] A more recent UK study[4] found that:

> 'On average the investment timing decisions of retail investors with regard to equity mutual funds has cost them performance of just under 1.2% per year over the eighteen year period of our study. Although 1.2% may not sound very high, compounded over 18 years it represents a cumulated under performance of 20%, compared with a simple buy and hold strategy.'

It has been estimated[5] that the true cost to the average investor in forgone long-term returns, due to their inability to make rational decisions in the short term, is 2–3% per year, with the cost for many being even higher. This contention seems to be supported by recent analysis carried out by Morningstar, the investment fund information provider. In its 2014 review of US investors, it found that the behaviour gap to the end of 2013 was 2.49% p.a., up from 0.95% ten years ago.[6] Table 2.1 shows the performance gap for major fund sectors.

However, even using an annualised return gap of 'just' 1.2% p.a., a £1 million portfolio invested over 20 years would have translated into £940,000 in lost returns (see Figure 2.6) for the average investor, purely as a result of bad decision making.

Because emotions play such a large part in our financial decision making, having a great education or a high intellect is no guarantee of financial success or happiness. Sure, all other things being equal it is preferable to be well educated and to have a good intellect, but it isn't enough for financial happiness and success. That's why history is full of examples of people with high intellect, natural ability or inherited wealth, who died lonely, unhappy and penniless.

---

[3] Schneider, L. (2007) 'Are UK fund investors achieving fund rates of return? An examination of the differences between UK fund returns and UK investors' returns', PhD Thesis, July.

[4] Clare, A. and Motson, N. (2010) 'Do UK retail investors buy at the top and sell at the bottom?', Working paper, Centre for Asset Management Research, Cass Business School, September, p. 4.

[5] Barclays (2013) 'Overcoming the cost of being human (or, the pursuit of anxiety-adjusted returns)', March, **www.investmentphilosophy.com/uploads/cms/51f002473490d.pdf**

[6] Kinnel, R. (2014) 'Mind the gap 2014' Morningstar. **http://news.morningstar.com/articlenet/article.aspx?id=637022**

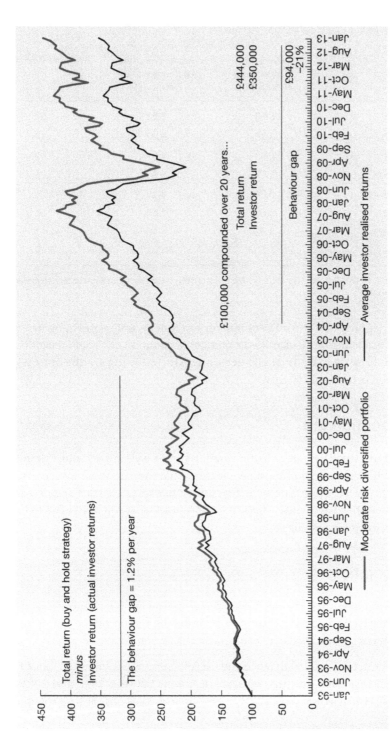

Figure 2.6 The long-term impact of the behaviour gap

Source: Barclays Wealth, 'Overcoming the cost of being human (or, the pursuit of anxiety-adjusted returns)', March 2013.

Table 2.1 Morningstar behaviour gap results

	Average 10 Year Total Return (%)	Asset-weighted 10 Year Investor Return (%)	Returns Gap (%)
US Equity	8.18	6.52	−1.66
Sector Equity	9.46	6.32	−3.14
Balanced	6.93	4.81	−2.12
International Equity	8.77	5.76	−3.01
Taxable Bond	5.39	3.15	−2.24
Municipal	3.53	1.65	−1.88
Alternative	0.96	-1.15	−2.11
All funds	7.30	4.81	−2.49

Source: Kinnel, R. (2014) 'Mind the gap 2014,' Morningstar. **http://news.morningstar.com/arti-clenet/article.aspx?id=637022**

Behavourial finance is the study of human psychology as it relates to money. Over the years academics have identified a number of common behavioural factors that influence how we make financial decisions. The following are the most widely understood behavioural factors.

Over-confidence

People think that they make better financial and investing decisions than they really do. It's similar to how most people think that they are above-average drivers. We tend to be over-optimistic when investment markets have risen and over-pessimistic when they have fallen. This is the opposite of what you need to do to have a good investment experience.

Extrapolation

People often base their financial decisions too heavily on recent events, or they give more weight to facts that support their beliefs and opinions, assuming that recent returns (good or bad) will continue in the future.

A good example of over-confidence and extrapolation was a survey of about 1,000 individual investors, on three separate occasions between 1998 and 2001 (see Figure 2.7). Participants were asked to give their predictions for how much they thought the stock market and their own investment portfolio would rise over the next 12 months. On two of the occasions, when the stock market had experienced a strong rise, investors' predictions for the rise in the stock market were bullish and for their own portfolios were even higher. On the occasion when the stock market had experienced a significant fall, investors' expectations for the stock market performance in the next year and for their own portfolios were about half of what they had been on the two previous occasions.

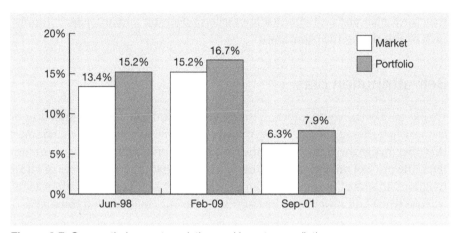

Figure 2.7 Over optimism, extrapolation and investor predictions

Source: Data from Fisher, K.L. and Statman, M. (2002) 'Bubble expectations', *Journal of Wealth Management*, 5(2), 17–22.

Hindsight bias

As the saying goes, hindsight is a wonderful thing. After the event, things seem obvious and we wonder why we didn't see them coming. 'How could I have been so stupid?' Hindsight bias therefore lulls us into thinking that it is easy to predict the future.

Familiarity bias

Investing in what you know gives a false sense of control and lower risk perception, compared with investing in things that are less familiar. This bias typically arises when an investor has a legacy shareholding arising from an inheritance or previous employment, and leads to an overconcentration of risk which is not compensated by way of higher returns. Someone once told me that the stock market does not reward investors with risk premiums for 'loyalty' or 'familiarity'.

Regret avoidance

This trait relates to the concept of 'once bitten, twice shy', in that when we have experienced the pain of losing money, we try to avoid the behaviour that caused it. We kid ourselves that we have learned from our mistakes, which leads us to avoid, for example, technology after the tech wreck in 2001, or the stock market as a whole after the heavy falls during the global financial crisis of 2008, even though we know that big market falls are followed by rapid market recoveries. Having a structured plan and a disciplined approach to decision making helps minimise such wealth-destroying behaviour.

Self-attribution bias

We like to take the credit for when things go right and blame other influences or factors when they go wrong. There is always a pundit who was so clever and smart that they made the right call on the direction of investment markets, interest rates, the price of oil, etc. because they could see what others didn't see or chose to ignore. Investors in Apple or even Facebook now say, 'Look how smart I am', whereas when Enron went bust investors said, 'No one could see that coming!'

Money styles

Money means different things to different people, although the core meaning and emotional connections relate to self-worth, love, security, power and attractiveness. If you have a greater understanding of the link between your emotions, financial habits and practices, as well as of the role that money plays in your family, you can become emotionally healthier. This should lead you to make better financial decisions and feel much happier and more content.

Money styles represent the core emotional motivations in relation to money (see Figure 2.8). These broad descriptions should help you to work out which is your primary style and what this means to your financial happiness. In my case I most associate with the 'Jock' money style because I relate to the attributes of that style of being hardworking, disciplined and responsible and using money to enable me to have fun and variety in my life. However, I am less inclined to the attribute of seeing money as a scorecard, because I realised many years ago that no amount of wealth would ever make me feel wealthy, so I don't define my happiness or success in terms of my net worth. I have to admit, however, that I feel much happier having accumulated wealth than when I had nothing.

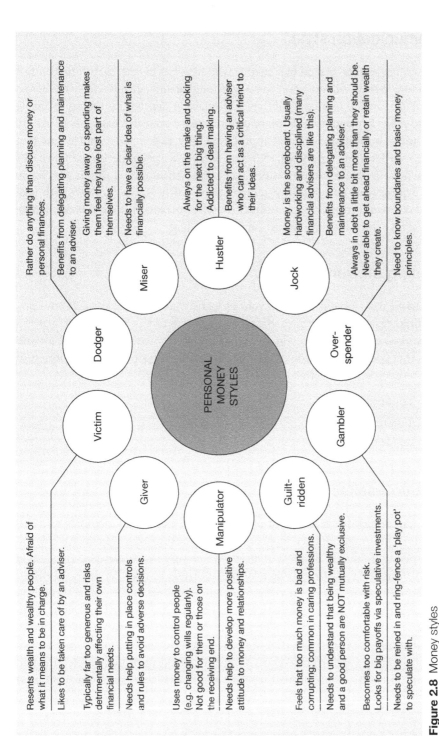

Figure 2.8 Money styles

Source: Data from Hallowell, E. and Grace, W. (1989) *What Are You Worth?: Coming to terms with your feelings about money,* Weidenfeld and Nicolson.

Communication style

Are you a 'big picture' person or someone who likes lots of detailed information? A 'big picture' person will not want to wade through a long, detailed report, whereas a 'detail' person will be anxious if they don't have in-depth information to enable them to make key decisions. Someone who is fast-paced and likes lots of variety and minimal information will not appreciate a long, slow and detailed lecture that labours over facts. Yet a reserved, reflective and slower-paced person will love this approach. Your core communication style also extends to the form in which you like to express yourself and how you prefer to have others communicate with you. To find out your preferred communication style you can visit **www.financialdna. com** and take the free Communication DNA Profile.

Planning propensity

Your financial personality includes your propensity and need to manage your personal finances and wealth or to engage the services of a professional. Once you have worked out which one you are, you can determine the type of advice and service that you need and from which you would derive good value for money. In simple terms you will be either a

- 'do-it-yourselfer' or a
- 'collaborator' or a
- 'delegator'.

Do-it-yourselfer

As the name suggests, this type of person has a strong need for control and will seek lots of information; they typically have an above-average intellect. They will enjoy spending time on financial matters and be very well organised. They rarely benefit from collaborating or delegating to others as they do not value their time more than the cost of the collaboration/delegation. If you are in this group then the only time you are likely to want, need or value professional advice is to help with a specific situation or a one-off, more complicated situation. Examples include complex property transactions; selling a business; setting up a family trust; structuring a sophisticated tax wrapper for a large portfolio; or selecting and arranging a tax-driven investment solution that is available only from authorised financial advisers.

Collaborator

This type of person is similar to a DIYer but usually lacks the confidence to make financial decisions on their own and will usually seek advice and assistance from professional advisers, salespeople and organisations like the Citizens' Advice Bureau, the Pensions Advisory Service or the Money Advice Service. They will also usually seek access to information from magazines, newspapers, websites, books (like this one) and friends and other contacts.

If you a collaborator then you may value and benefit from some form of periodic advice and services, but it will be important that this is not more extensive and expensive than you want or need. It is common for a collaborator to engage a 'full-service' advisory service, which is aimed more at those clients who are looking to delegate rather than collaborate. If you are willing and able to take more responsibility for your wealth and carry out some of the day-to-day aspects yourself, then you will probably save yourself money and become more confident about your financial decisions if you choose products and services that are less extensive and as a result less expensive than a full-service offering.

Delegator

This type of person is keen to 'outsource' most day-to-day aspects of managing their wealth, although they will want to have close involvement in formulating strategy. Typically, but not in all cases, a delegator will have more complex financial affairs and higher levels of wealth. Looking at the big picture is usually enough for delegators, as they have better uses for their time. Delegators are usually the most financially successful people precisely because they have learned when and to whom to delegate for best effect. They rarely do something themselves that they could delegate to someone else.

If you are a delegator, who has complex and significant wealth and/or a high surplus income, then a full-service advisory firm will probably be the best choice, as you will be able to derive the maximum value for the fees. When the value of your time is very high, you have little inclination to learn about financial matters in detail and/or your needs are complex, the price of a good, fee-only wealth management service will often pay for itself many times over. We'll discuss the role of guidance and advice in Chapter 4.

Emotional intelligence

Recent research into the human mind has found that the secret to success in any long-term endeavour, whether it is in business, relationships or investing, is an attribute called emotional intelligence (otherwise known as EQ). EQ is a type of intelligence that is significantly different from the standard IQ-based definition of 'clever' we're all used to. The topic of EQ has received significant coverage in the business world in the past few years, fuelled in particular by Daniel Goleman's books[7] aimed at helping business people to use the skill to further their careers and effectiveness.

With Goleman's model for EQ, the emotionally intelligent investor would, for instance, calmly make investment decisions based on a higher consciousness of who they are and with a positive personal relationship to money (the first facet, 'self-awareness'). This is instead of making decisions based on an emotional impulse that sabotages their financial position. They also handle stress, disappointment and uncertainty more rationally and don't allow those feelings or circumstances to control or initiate their decisions (the second facet, 'self-management').

Going further, the emotionally intelligent investor would also understand the emotions of others such as their partner, spouse or family members, recognising them and responding with empathy (the third facet, 'social awareness'). Finally, a person with high investment EQ would have the ability to maintain quality relationships with others around them when making investment decisions, knowing how to motivate them effectively and appropriately and manage their money energy using subtlety, delicacy and tact (the fourth facet, 'managing others').

The role of EQ in investment has been little publicised, even though its application can be invaluable for investors. Whether this is because the investment process is seen as an objective, numbers-based, non-emotional process or the investment industry has simply not been made sufficiently aware of the existence of EQ is unclear. My experience is that a high level of EQ *combined* with sound financial knowledge, strategy and support can make the difference between a successful and a bad investment experience.

So why is understanding investment EQ so powerful? It is the ability to give a person enough confidence, focus and rationality to remain committed to their strategies even when the market value of their portfolio is declining, not living up to expectations or being superseded by other events.

---

[7]   Goleman, D. (2005) *Emotional Intelligence: Why it can matter more than IQ*, Bantam Books.

Charles Ellis is one of the leading thinkers in investment management, the author of 6 books and 70 articles on investment and finance, and has taught the graduate school investment courses at both Yale and Harvard. He is a member of the Board of Directors of the Harvard Business School and a Trustee of Yale University where he also serves on the investment committee. Here's what he had to say about emotions and investing and the key to a successful investment experience:

'Principles that every investor should be thinking about. . . [that] investing is all about you, not about the market, about you and how you would feel most comfortable through thick and thin because there will be thick and there will be thin. There will be good times, there will be bad times and that's part of life's experience. And, you must be comfortable and candid about who you really are and what your investment capabilities are and what your emotional capabilities are so that you can set a pathway you can really stay with. Staying with it is the most important single principle.

'Don't be afraid of being candid about what your emotions are. Go ahead and accept who you are as a human being and if you can't handle turbulence, don't invest in turbulent securities. If you are more able to handle turbulence, take that chance because you can take it in your stride and invest that way. But, if you will aim at the right kind of investment mission and then stay with that mission you can have a winning experience and everybody in your family, everybody in your neighbourhood, everybody in the world can have a simultaneously winning experience if they each do what's really right for them.'[8]

You are more likely to make rational decisions if you have a high level of self-awareness, financial education and experience, a secure relationship with money and a high level of 'emotional intelligence'. Even then the instinctive aspects of your core personality will still have an impact on your financial decisions. With turbulent financial markets it is far more likely that your inherent risk tolerance will emerge and strongly influence your financial decisions.

At the end of the day you need to accept that there are some things you can control and some things you can't and you need to have the wisdom to know the difference. In that context, knowing your life purpose and financial personality is likely to give you the best chance of making good financial decisions.

---

[8]   Transcript of video interview with respected investment expert and author Charles Ellis on investment fundamentals: www.vanguard.co.uk/uk/portal/Library/interviews--video-ellis.jsp

Avoiding getting blown off course by the 'noise' from the media is difficult, but once you realise that their interests are not aligned with your own, you'll start to focus on what really matters – staying disciplined in the face of adversity and extreme events.

CHAPTER 3
THE POWER OF A PLAN

'Good fortune is what happens when opportunity meets with planning.'

Thomas Edison

I have already explained the importance of setting clear goals, developing financial planning policies and understanding your financial personality and risk profile. To develop a successful wealth plan, you need to put these goals into a wider context and review your overall financial position both as it is today and how it might be under various scenarios throughout the rest of your lifetime.

A good wealth plan should include the following elements:

- where you want to go – detailing your financial planning policies, goals, preferences, values and timescales
- where you are today – your current financial resources
- where you might end up – including analysis of your cashflow and family balance sheet, inheritance tax liabilities and insurance needs over the short, medium and long terms
- investment strategy – how you will allocate your current and any future resources across different asset classes
- other relevant planning issues such as tax, pension, gifting and charitable giving.

Where you want to go

In Chapter 1 we looked in detail at the importance of defining and quantifying clear goals, determining what is really important about money to you, and understanding your personal preferences. These should form the guiding principles on which your plan is based.

Where you are today

Knowing what you have and where documents can be located is a simple but important element of getting and staying well organised. How you choose to do this is up to you and it could just be a handwritten summary of your assets, liabilities, financial documents, insurance policies and trusts, or it could be a more formal spreadsheet. The important thing is to list what you've got and what you've done as this will help you to make more informed decisions. In addition, if you are incapacitated or die, it will avoid a drama for your family in trying to get to the bottom of your financial world.

Another common problem is not documenting or recording when gifts have been made. The type of gift, for example, whether to an individual or to a trust, whether it is exempt from inheritance tax or not, and when it was made, are all essential facts that need to be shared with your professional advisers, because this can have a dramatic impact on the eventual inheritance tax bill.

Where you might end up

Creating both a short-term and lifetime cashflow statement is, arguably, a very important measure for individuals when formulating a wealth plan. Although it will invariably turn out to be wrong in reality, it will provide a useful sanity check to the overall sustainability of your plan, from which you can draw some conclusions and assess progress. When you formulate your planning projections/analysis you will need to use some key assumptions. The following are the key ones that you (or your professional adviser) should include in your plan analysis.

Life expectancy

Clearly, your health will determine how long you expect to live, but with medical advances it may be longer than you think. The evidence suggests that most people underestimate their life expectancy by quite a big margin. As illustrated in Figure 3.1, a 65-year-old male has a one in three chance of living until age 90, and on average, a man and woman aged 65 can expect to live another 21.2 and 23.9 years respectively. Life expectancy at age 65 is projected to increase for men and women to 27 and 29.5 years respectively by 2062, but for the healthiest element of the population this is projected to be 35.7 for males and 37.9 for females, i.e. well in excess of 100. This is illustrated in Figure 3.2.

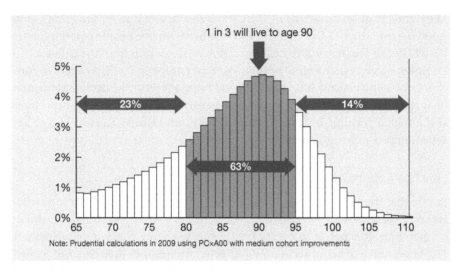

Figure 3.1 Distribution of age of death for males aged 65

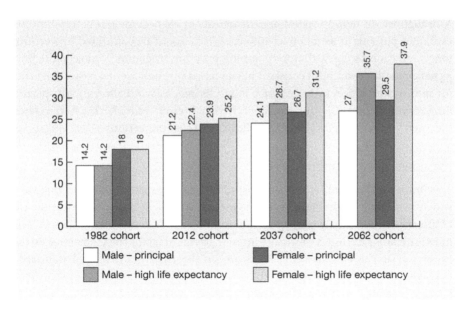

Figure 3.2 Projected life expectancy at age 65, 1982–2062

Source: Office for National Statistics (2013) 'Historic and projected mortality data from the period and cohort life tables, 2012-based, UK', December.

The numbers of centenarians in the UK has nearly quadrupled since 1981, from 2,600 to more than 12,000 in 2010, and nearly one in five people currently in the UK will live to see their 100th birthday.[1] However, research from the University of Denmark suggests that a child born in Western Europe in 2007 has a one in three chance of living beyond 100.[2] I recommend using age 99 as the default lifespan for financial planning purposes as this is well in excess of the average life expectancy at the time of writing, but you might wish to extend this to an even greater age, depending on your view on longevity.

Lifestyle expenditure

Ensure that the lifestyle expenditure assumption in your projection is reasonable and reflects what you do (or expect) to spend, not what you think you should be spending. It is better to overestimate your spending than underestimate it. The importance of being accurate about your current or desired expenditure will depend very much on the ratio of your regular spending shortfall (i.e. that not met by pension or other non-investment income) to your capital base and the investment strategy you adopt.

Although we do tend to spend less in later life as we become less active (various estimates put this at as much as 40% less), this might be countered by needing long-term care. I suggest that for planning purposes, therefore, you keep the projected expenditure amount constant in real terms throughout life, rather than aim for spurious precision by assuming a fall in living costs and allowing for specific long-term care costs. If your projected financial resources look a bit thin in later life, then you can drill into more specific expenditure projections.

Expenditure escalation

The Office for National Statistics publishes various measures of inflation that vary widely as a result of the different items included in the indices. The two that are of interest to individuals managing their wealth are the Retail Prices Index (RPI or RPIX; the latter excludes mortgage interest payments) and the Consumer Prices Index (CPI). The CPI measures inflation on internationally agreed standards throughout Europe and is now the basis on which allowances and most state benefits are escalated each year. The main difference between RPI and CPI is that RPI includes council tax and some other housing costs not included in CPI; it excludes certain financial services costs; and it is based on a smaller sample of the population. RPI also includes mortgage interest costs whereas CPI and RPIX don't.

---

[1] *Age UK* (2014) 'Later life in the United Kingdom' February, pp. 3, 6.

[2] Christensen, K., Doblhammer, G., Rau, R. and Vaupel, J.W. (2009) 'Ageing populations: the challenges ahead', *The Lancet*, 374 (9696): 1196–1208.

The CPI rate has tended to be lower than RPI/RPIX. The RPI/RPIX rate excludes items of expenditure incurred by the very poorest and very wealthiest members of society, on the basis that they are unrepresentative of wider society. In any case, it is highly likely that your 'personal inflation rate' will be higher than any of the official rates, particularly if you employ domestic help, pay childcare and/ or school fees, own a second home or pay for comprehensive private health insurance/care. I suggest that you visit the ONS website (**www.ons.gov.uk**) to use its inflation rate calculator to work out your own inflation rate. Failing that I suggest you escalate your expenditure by CPI + 1%.

Convert pension funds to a simple level annuity

If you have substantial money purchase pension benefits, then it is unlikely that you will buy an annuity with all of them at the same time, if ever. For tax and investment reasons, it is more likely that you will take benefits from the pensions in stages and possibly some or all as income or capital withdrawn from the fund or possibly an investment-linked, rather than gilt-linked, annuity, as this is likely to provide maximum investment flexibility and the option to minimise tax.

However, for the purposes of your financial planning analysis, I recommend that you assume the lowest-risk, highest-tax position first, as this is the most prudent approach. Therefore, assume in your projection that any pension funds are used fully to purchase a guaranteed annuity at one point (between ages 60 and 70), inflation protected (you can always use a level annuity if the plan doesn't work) and the maximum dependants' income protection (this is usually 100% of your own pension, so it does not reduce on your death). If your plan works with this cautious assumption then you know that you have a fair amount of 'wriggle room' if things turn out differently. You can then consider how and when you take benefits to minimise risk and tax.

Use reasonable investment return assumptions

For many years the actuarial profession consistently underestimated the present-day value of the future liabilities of many final-salary pension schemes. This arose because the discount rate (i.e. the rate of expected future investment returns) used to calculate the present-day value of the scheme's liabilities (the pensions due in the future) usually assumed a higher-risk investment strategy than many of the schemes were actually pursuing. So if you have half your capital in cash and half in bonds (fixed income), your expected return for long-term financial planning purposes needs to be lower than if you held, say, half in bonds and half in equities.

There has been much written about actual and expected returns from different asset classes but, as we will consider in Part 2, risk and return are related, and higher risks have a higher expected return. However, returns are rarely delivered in a straight line and there can be a range of outcomes (which is what makes them risky), as well as sometimes prolonged periods when actual returns are well below the long-term average. For this reason the forward-looking expected return in any wealth projection or analysis ideally needs to be below any historic returns.

In Figure 3.3 I've listed what I believe to be reasonable return assumptions for the main asset classes in nominal terms (i.e. inclusive of inflation) and before costs, which you'll need to also take off the nominal return to arrive at the true projected return. Those costs will be influenced by the investment approach that you adopt, which we discuss in Chapter 10.

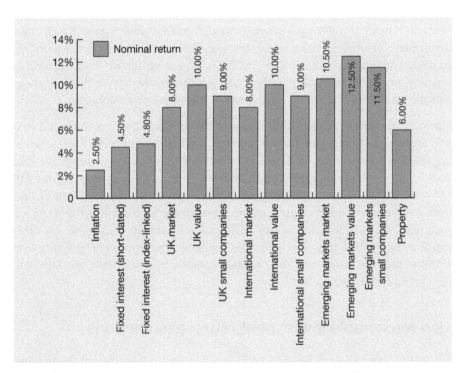

Figure 3.3 Asset class long-term annual investment return assumptions

Tax rates

If you (or your adviser) are using professional planning software, it will most probably calculate taxes reasonably accurately. However, it is not necessary to be spuriously precise about taxes as this is a moving target and tax rates will invariably rise and fall over your lifetime. It is perfectly reasonable to assume a simplified tax rate on investments of, say, 25% as reflective of the true rate of tax likely to be paid on income and gains, after allowing for allowances and other reliefs. Another key factor that will affect the amount of tax you pay will be where and how you locate your wealth – we'll discuss this issue in Chapters 11, 14, 15 and 16.

All businesses have three key elements to their accounting: a cashflow statement, a profit and loss statement and a balance sheet. Individuals and families should be no different, although it is rare for them to apply the same structured approach to their personal wealth planning.

Short- and long-term cashflow projections

For the short-term cashflow projection, I suggest using a three-year time period, because experience suggests that this is the longest that most people can envisage with any degree of accuracy. The short-term cashflow can be extremely useful to identify any shortfall in income to meet lifestyle costs and/or anticipated capital expenditure. In either case, you can then ensure that you have an adequate (but not excessive) cash reserve, to meet such outflows, so that you are not a forced seller of risky assets such as equities and property-based assets. It's a good idea to project the short-term cashflow with a 10% variance above and below the expected spending rate, as illustrated in Figure 3.4.

Although a lifetime net worth projection is almost certainly going to be wrong, as it is impossible to accurately predict all the factors that will impact on your wealth, it will give you a very useful idea of whether or not you have sufficient resources to meet your lifestyle and other long-term goals under a number of different, but plausible, scenarios. Professional wealth planners create cashflow projections as a starting point to help ascertain the client's most likely financial position over various timeframes. Some online tools do the same thing, although they often adopt a simplified approach. Whether you use a planner with sophisticated financial planning software, a simple online planning tool or your own spreadsheet, the most important thing is to create a reasonable baseline financial scenario, from which you can draw some broad conclusions.

I counsel clients to assume three levels of lifestyle spending for lifetime financial planning projections: required, desired and aspired. In Figure 3.5 I've set out three different scenarios for the same individual, with differing levels of spending leading to different potential terminal values. The lower projection shows the capital being exhausted during lifetime, the higher projection leaving a substantial value on death and the mid-range scenario neatly showing a zero value on death. In the real world, investment returns, lifestyle spending, taxes and inflation all vary

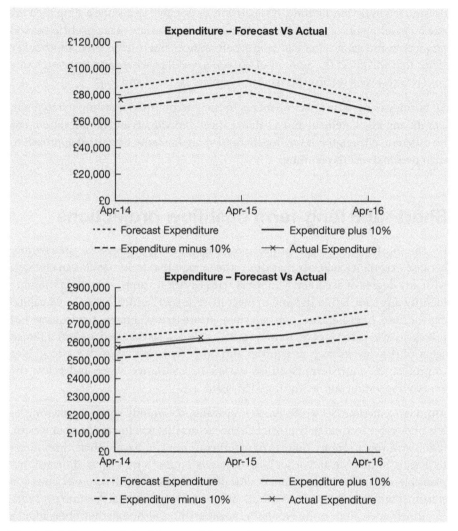

Figure 3.4 Example of short-term cashflow projection
Source: KMD Private Wealth Management.

from year to year, so the outcomes can be substantially different to straight-line projections like these. They do, however, give a useful context as the basis of your planning, investment and tax-planning decisions. The planning projection scenarios can be varied based on different levels of spending, investment returns, taxes, downsizing property or gifting, depending on your circumstances and preferences. The key is to regularly review your lifetime projection in the light of reality, so that you can take any necessary action well before your financial security is adversely affected, not when it is too late.

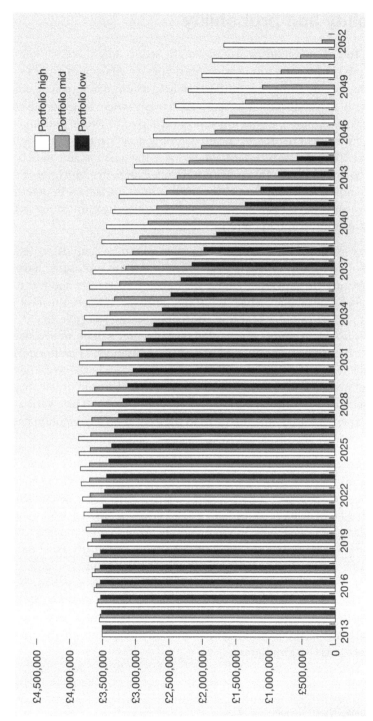

Figure 3.5 Example of lifetime financial viability analysis

Possibility and probability

In a world full of uncertainties it is easy to be seduced by those who profess to be able to predict how the future might turn out. We all want to avoid loss, pain and hardship, so anything that purports to help us do so is very appealing. The problem with any financial projection, particularly where it is over a long time period (20 years or more), is that it is almost certain to be wrong in reality. In the real world, investment returns, taxes and spending don't happen in a straight, predictable line. That said, it is better to understand the possible outcomes before it becomes too late to do anything about it. In my experience, the level of annual lifestyle spending is usually one of the most important factors in determining whether a wealth plan is sustainable, although of course investment returns, inflation and taxes are also important factors.

There are various ways to 'stress test' a financial planning analysis, to determine the degree of probability of it being viable or not. All the approaches have shortcomings because they invariably suggest a degree of certainty about the future outcome of a financial plan, which is just not possible. However, the most widely used technique is called a Monte Carlo[3] simulation. The investment return assumption used in a simple financial plan projection will be an average figure based on either historic returns achieved or (more usefully, as past performance is not a reliable guide to the future) that which the investor expects in the future. The 'flaw of averages' is that they mask the fact that there are usually big variations in the range of returns actually achieved, both above and below the average. Investors experience investment returns as they occur on a compound basis, i.e. they will vary from one year to the next.

In investment and financial planning, a Monte Carlo simulation program can be used to examine a random sample of historic or expected returns from an asset or portfolio of assets to determine a range of potential outcomes based on three key variables: the *mean return* (average from each period), standard deviation (a measure of risk) and *correlation* (how different assets perform when combined with each other). The software runs a year-by-year simulation of returns using a random sample of these three main variables to work out the probability of failure. Other factors such as inflation, expenditure and life expectancy are not changed, so no account is taken of the possibility that one or more of these might be affected by the investment return achieved. Most experts agree that it is necessary to carry out this simulation at least 100 times to be statistically robust, although some think that 300 iterations is the minimum.

---

[3]   An excellent in depth explanation of Monte Carlo analysis can be found in *The Kitces Report* (January 2012), which you can download from **www.wealthpartner.co.uk/downloads/Kitces_Report_January_2012.pdf**

The outcome of running the Monte Carlo simulations is a % probability of success, in the sense of how many of the simulations resulted in a surplus at the end of the investor's time horizon. Thus, if 55 of the 100 simulations resulted in the portfolio not running out, the success rate would be described as 55%. I prefer to look at the results the other way round, in terms of the % probability of failure, and set a target failure rate of under, say, 25% to provide an adequate safety margin.

The probability of failure suggested by the simulation is not, in itself, sufficient to say that a planning and investment strategy is or is not appropriate; rather, it can provide an additional sanity check or early warning signal that the chance of failure might mean more frequent reviews of the plan are necessary to avoid failure or perhaps that more vigilance as to the level of annual spending is required. In any event, knowing a probability based on assumptions that are all highly likely to be incorrect is not generally considered a robust basis for decision making.

A Monte Carlo simulator (like any tool where the user's understanding of it is flawed) in the wrong hands can be highly dangerous, but when used as one of a range of stress tests it can help avoid the false sense of security that a straight-line forecast might imply. Whether you work with a professional adviser or do your own planning, there is no substitute for regularly reviewing the sustainability of your financial planning and investment strategy.

The role of liquidity

Your wealth will almost certainly comprise short- and long-term liquid assets as well as used and unused illiquid assets. Liquid assets include cash deposits, most National Savings & Investments (NS&I) products, and quoted equities and bonds, both directly held and via daily priced investment funds. Used illiquid assets include your home, cars, boat or holiday home. Unused illiquid assets would include investment properties, business holdings, land/woodland, many structured investment products or alternative investments, such as hedge funds, that have long 'lock-in' periods.

Low-risk liquid investments such as cash or most NS&I products are easy to value as they comprise the capital and any accumulated interest. Such funds will also be accessible, depending on the terms of the account. They are also the best place to keep capital on which you expect to call within the next few years or just want to keep to hand for unforeseen emergencies. The only issue to watch is the financial security of the financial institution if you place more than £85,000 (£170,000 if you hold a joint account) in a UK-based account. Financial protection offshore is often less than that in the UK and, in any case, is only as good as the ability of the authorities in the jurisdiction to step up to the plate if an institution fails.

It is usually the case that most illiquid investments, like property, are valued less frequently than liquid ones and even then this is usually merely a matter of one person's opinion rather than the price at which the asset actually changes hands. Securities listed on quoted investment exchanges, meanwhile, are valued in real time and reflect the best collective assessment that buyers and sellers place on the present value of the current and future dividends and profits growth of companies (in the case of equities) and interest yield relative to the inflation and general interest rate outlook (in the case of fixed interest bonds). Obviously the same applies to funds that invest in these securities, although they are often valued and priced daily rather than by the minute.

Figure 3.6 illustrates the impact of daily versus annual valuation points for UK equities using the same index. The daily version looks more volatile than the annual version but this is purely a function of the different price points.

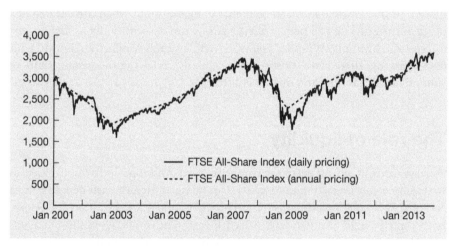

Figure 3.6 Valuation frequencies for FTSE All-Share Index 2001–2013
Source: Data from Bloomsbury Wealth Management, FTSE.

While it is true that some unused illiquid investments can produce very high returns, this usually comes with additional and sometimes unanticipated risks (always remember that risk and return are related). In addition, some illiquid investments such as property or unquoted trading businesses require more oversight and input from the investor and may have ongoing maintenance costs, which must be paid from any income arising from the investment or from your other (liquid) capital or income.

Illiquid investments are not necessarily a bad thing as long as you have access to sufficient cash inflows and reserves to meet current needs. The famous Yale

Endowment fund in the United States has achieved long-term returns well above a traditional liquid investment portfolio over the past 25 years, precisely because it invests much of its capital in illiquid holdings. Over the longer term the fund intends to invest half of its portfolio to the illiquid asset classes of private equity, real estate and natural resources.[4] We'll discuss investment fundamentals and options in Chapters 5–9.

Don't forget that your main home may well represent a large part of your wealth and as such may mean that you already have a high exposure to property. Just because you can see and touch something doesn't make it a sure bet. Investment property can form an asset base from which to build your wealth plan, but it is not a one-way street and to maximise your returns you either have to be prepared to spend time managing the asset or outsource this task to someone else (which has a further cost implication). Either way my advice is that you shouldn't kid yourself that property is the answer to your investment problems, nor that it provides superior long-term returns at lower risk than a liquid, highly diversified investment portfolio. Property is affected by the reality of the economic conditions prevailing. If people and businesses cannot afford the rent you want to charge or the purchase price then these will simply adjust to reflect the reality of supply and demand.

The perceived lower risk of property compared with equities is just that – a perception. Where property is represented by an index fund that is valued and traded daily on an investment exchange, it exhibits similar (but not exactly the same) fluctuations in price and sentiment as quoted equities. Listed global commercial property (known as securitised) has a correlation of about 0.50 against UK equities and 0.60 against global equities.[5]

Investment in an unquoted business (which can include the business of developing and/or renting property), whether your own or someone else's, usually offers the highest reward but also comes with a different, and sometimes much higher, set of risks. If you have owned your own business and have now sold it for cash, then you need to think very carefully about whether reinvesting your money, or at least the vast bulk of it, into another unquoted business is really in line with your future lifestyle and other life goals. If freeing up time is important to you and/or reducing the risk of losing money matters, then perhaps it would be better to invest your non-cash reserve capital into a fully diversified, liquid investment portfolio. However, there are always exceptions to the rule and the case study of Nigel and Mary (see below) is an example.

---

[4] The Yale Endowment 2013 investment report.

[5] Philips, C.B. (2007) 'Commercial equity real estate: A framework for analysis', Vanguard Investment Counseling & Research, **www.vanguard.com/pdf/s553.pdf?2210022068**

Some people who have been successful in business are interested in mentoring young and growing businesses. Sometimes this also involves investing some cash in the business, referred to as 'angel investing', and it can be extremely rewarding, both personally and financially. Allocating a small proportion of your capital to angel investing might make sense if you have the interest and necessary time to help nurture new and growing businesses. However, it is rarely good advice to put all your hard-earned capital into such a concentrated risk, particularly if preserving what you have is your key concern and you would not be able to recover from any loss. My advice is to view such investments as 'fun', like indulging a hobby, and to disregard them from your overall financial resources unless they become cash again.

Case study

The caravan couple – when business investment is best

Some years ago I met a couple, let's call them Nigel and Mary (not their real names), who had sold a successful caravan park business for several million pounds after 20 years' hard work. During the wealth-planning process it became apparent that neither of them wanted to stop being involved in a business (they were in their early sixties). They also felt that reinvesting the bulk of their liquid wealth into another caravan park business might be the best solution for their wealth plan, provided that they could delegate the day-to-day management of the business to staff. The couple looked at a number of suitable businesses and, drawing on their considerable experience of owning and running such a business, they decided that those on offer were not good investments.

After a few months a more suitable business came on the market and after hard negotiating the couple bought it. The business would comfortably generate an income of £100,000 per annum for each of them, which more than funded their lifestyle after tax. In addition, Nigel and Mary could employ their daughter on a part-time basis for £40,000 per annum, which, as well as being taxed at no more than 20%, allowed her to indulge her passion for regular travelling. The business was asset-backed in the form of the land on which it was sited and it would also qualify for exemption from inheritance tax after two years and capital gains tax at 10%, should they ever decide to sell it in later life.

This still left them with about £500,000 of surplus cash, which we decided should be spread between instant and notice deposit accounts and NS&I products so as to provide them with an adequate cash reserve while they settled into the new business. Nigel and Mary are very happy with their 'investment' and so is their daughter.

If you have attained financial independence or are almost there and have life plans that do not include spending your precious time overseeing business investments, properties or picking the next 'hot' investment, and you are looking for 'elegant simplicity', the best investment solution is likely to be to invest your long-term capital into a well-diversified, fully liquid investment portfolio allocated in line with your risk profile.

'We ignore the real diamonds of simplicity, seeking instead the illusory rhinestones of complexity.'

Jack Bogle[6]

Identifying and understanding financial planning risks

Even if you are clear on your money values, goals, personal preferences and have a robust wealth-planning analysis, before you think about how you might deploy your wealth, you need to also be clear on a number of risks. Risk means different things to different people, but as a financial planner I see it as the failure to achieve those life goals that have financial implications, however you define and quantify them. From a financial planning perspective, risks can be grouped into three areas: personal, behavioural and deep, as illustrated in Figure 3.7.

Personal risks

Examples of personal risks include long-term illness and the impact this might have on your lifestyle and human capital (earning ability/potential) – dying too soon or living too long relative to your financial commitments and resources. Illness and death can usually be dealt with by buying insurance (although not always for those with existing medical problems). Living too long, otherwise known as longevity risk, can be dealt with through a combination of insurance (in the form of annuities), accumulating sufficient wealth to sustain lifestyle spending and investing in a range of asset classes.

Another form of personal risk is where an investor overdraws from their portfolio to meet spending, thereby greatly increasing the possibility of plan failure. We'll look at the impact of regular portfolio withdrawals, and how this can affect plan viability, in Chapter 12.

---

[6] Bogle, J. (2009) *Enough!*, Wiley, p. 23. John Bogle is founder and former CEO of the Vanguard Mutual Fund Group.

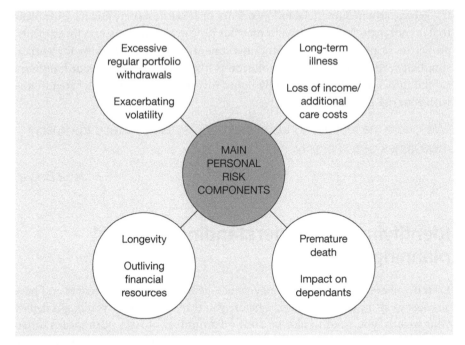

Figure 3.7 Main personal risk components

Source: Data from Bernstein, W. (2013) *Deep Risk: How history informs portfolio design*, Efficient Frontier Publications.

Behavioural risks

As we explored in Chapter 2, investors' wealth-destroying behaviour includes being either over-optimistic or over-pessimistic in the light of news and investment sentiment. This often leads investors to sell out when investment markets have fallen sharply (in March 2009 developed investment markets were almost 50% below their previous peak) and miss the inevitable strong rebound, or pile into the latest fad investment.

Deep risks

Financial theorist William Bernstein suggests that investors think of risk as either 'shallow' or 'deep', with shallow risks relating to personal and behavioural factors.[7]

---

[7]   Bernstein, W. (2013) *Deep Risk: How history informs portfolio design*, Efficient Frontier Publications.

Deep risk is the permanent loss of capital – defined as a real (that is, after inflation) negative return over a 30-year period. By analysing historic data to determine the causes for a permanent loss of capital, Bernstein has identified four main sources of deep risk: inflation, deflation, confiscation and devastation.

Inflation – the rate of increase in the price of goods and services each year.

Deflation – the rate of decrease in the price of goods and services each year.

Confiscation – when property or other assets are either seized by the state or subject to penal tax charges.

Devastation – mainly relates to environmental factors, such as earthquake, hurricane, fire, which leads to the permanent loss of assets.

Because these economic and political factors may permanently destroy part or all of your wealth, Bernstein suggests using a three-point scale for analysing and defending against these risks using four factors: probability, consequence severity, and both method and cost of insuring, as set out in Table 3.1.

Table 3.1 Deep risks

	Probability	Consequence severity	Method of insuring	Cost of insuring
Inflation	▲▲▲	▲▲	Global equities Commodities Gold Index-linked government bonds	▲
Deflation	▲	▲▲	Global equities Long-dated bonds Treasury bills Gold	▲▲▲
Confiscation	▲	▲▲	Foreign-held assets and property	▲▲
Devastation	▲	▲▲▲	Foreign-held assets (for local devastation only)	▲▲ or ▲▲▲*

*Depends on country of residence.
Source: Data from Bernstein, W. (2013) *Deep Risk: How history informs portfolio design*, Efficient Frontier Publications.

Bernstein concludes the following:

- Shallow risk is the main risk for investors in later life with little or no earned income.

- Shallow risk and inflation are the main risks for investors who have enough money to live on for the rest of their lives and inflation-linked government securities are most likely to be the favoured route. Although long bonds offer the best protection in a deflation environment, Bernstein thinks the probability of deflation is low and in any event, capital doesn't fall in real value and taxes would be lower.

- Shallow risk is a good thing for younger people who are still accumulating wealth, as long as they can stay the course and they or their adviser rebalances the portfolio when equities are over or under the target allocation. Bernstein suggests they invest in a geographically diversified equity portfolio, with 30–40% in international equities, possibly with an overweighting to precious metals and mining stocks as well as energy, which has also provided some protection against inflation, historically. Some fixed income is still needed, however, if only to allow for rebalancing.

- Investors who have a significant portfolio but haven't completely met their financial goals have a trickier decision to make. A more balanced portfolio, with high-quality bonds, such as inflation-linked gilts, and the equity allocation set out above is favoured, as long as the portfolio is rebalanced when shallow risk occurs.

- Bernstein concedes that there's not much most people can do to protect against confiscation and devastation risks 'beyond [having] an interstellar spacecraft'. He suggests owning a few gold coins and giving a bit more consideration to foreign real estate. 'If the client was already considering buying a flat in London,' he says, 'the potential for confiscation and devastation could be additional reasons to pull the trigger.'*

*Clearly UK-based investors would need to buy property outside the UK.

Investment strategy

An integral element of your wealth plan will be the design and implementation of your personalised investment strategy in the form of an investment policy statement (IPS). This sets out how you will allocate and maintain your long-term, liquid investment portfolio. This document should detail the following information:

- your financial goals for the investment portfolio
- the rate of return required, as identified in the lifetime cashflow analysis
- the monetary amount that you intend to withdraw from (or add to) the portfolio each year
- the asset allocation strategy and specific allocation to different asset classes
- the investment philosophy
- the rebalancing policy, including when and how this will be done
- a statement of the action that you will take in response to adverse life or investment events by reference to your financial planning policy statements
- your tax management approach or policy such as it relates to the portfolio.

The IPS should act as the key reference point for your investment strategy and provide you with the discipline to stick to the plan, particularly when things don't turn out as you expected. If you decide to delegate some or all of the management of your wealth to a professional investment manager, then the IPS can also be used as the basis of the manager's brief for managing the portfolio.

Writing down your financial position and key goals, getting financially organised, carrying out a viability analysis of your resources and articulating and documenting your investment approach will force you to think about the way that you manage your wealth. It will also serve as a useful reference point from which you will be able to measure your progress and also stay disciplined in the face of adversity.

The future is always uncertain

Working out what is financially possible, the probability of different financial outcomes, how best to structure your wealth and how you should respond and adapt to the inevitable changes that will arise in the future are key to maximising the likelihood of financial success. For this reason you may well benefit from the advice, assistance and counsel provided by a financial planning professional. In the next chapter we'll look at the role of guidance and advice and how to choose the right service and/or adviser.

CHAPTER 4
THE ROLE OF GUIDANCE AND ADVICE

'The investor's chief problem, and even his worst enemy, is likely to be himself.'

Benjamin Graham, legendary US investor

You probably derive much of your financial knowledge from what you read, hear or see in newspapers, magazines, websites, television and books. The internet gives us fast access to vast amounts of material, whether that is video on demand, discussion forums, social networks or knowledge archives. However, just because there is a lot of information available out there does not mean that it is necessarily accurate, objective or relevant to your situation.

The media is not your friend

The sheer amount of information, vested interests and speed of news, coupled with the huge amount of competition, means that journalists are fighting a losing battle when trying to be helpful, objective and independent in what they communicate to their readers on personal finance issues. Sometimes stories are inspired by real news events and other times by 'expert' comment from companies with some form of vested interest. The problem is that in the face of such a continual barrage of often conflicting and sensationalist news and information, the average person finds it hard not to be seduced into taking actions that they may turn out to regret. Even if you've decided on your overall planning and investment approach, it is hard not to be knocked off track by the relentless media messages that bombard us on a daily basis.

We often overreact to news and ignore the reality of long-term, steady norms. This is normal and totally expected. We place far too much weight on what happened yesterday rather than on what has happened over the past 50 years. The media focuses our attention on the daily movements in the capital value of the stock market. In a sense this fixation on capital values is the investment sizzle, when in fact the investment steak is compound returns. The magic of compounding works away in the background, with dividend/interest and capital gains generated by the portfolio reinvested to create more income and more capital gains. Compounding has been described as the eighth wonder of the world and it is rarely understood what a powerful impact it has on investment returns (see Figure 4.1).

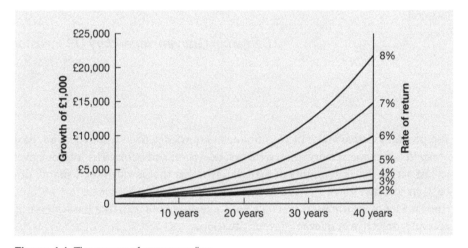

Figure 4.1 The power of compounding

The financial services marketing machine

There is a massive marketing machine deployed by the financial services industry, sometimes subtly and sometimes less so, that is seeking your attention for financial products and services. Jack Bogle, the founder of index fund group Vanguard, estimated that in 2000 the amount spent on financial media advertising was at least $1 billion,[1] so today it is likely to be much more than that.

Financial services companies make claims, promises and statements that often don't bear up to scrutiny. The chief problem is that financial companies are seeking to sell their products regardless of whether they are suitable, competitive or

---

[1]   Bogle, J. (2007) *The Little Book of Common Sense Investing*, Wiley.

value for money. In some cases these products offer a solution to problems that investors never knew they had. I'll talk about the cost of investment funds in Chapters 10 and 11, but remember that the amount spent on marketing is often in direct inverse relationship to the value being provided. In other words, the more spent on marketing, the higher is likely to be the real cost of the product. Oddly enough, the most profitable products for the provider may not be the best value for money for the investor.

Fund managers have a lot of form when it comes to launching new funds on the back of strong optimism about an asset class, usually following a period of strong performance. For example, at the height of the technology boom in 2000 fund managers were falling over themselves to launch technology funds on the back of tremendous past performance. I remember very well in early 2000 a taxi driver telling me that he was making more money on his investments in technology funds than he was from driving his cab. When taxi drivers start offering investment advice, you really do need to start worrying.

Aberdeen Global Technology was one of the largest technology funds around at the time and it attracted a lot of new money from private investors keen to join the party. Unfortunately the next ten years were not very kind to those investors, with the fund producing –4.49% p.a. compared with the FTSE All-Share index return of 2.93% p.a.[2] Although the fund return has since improved, it still managed only 7.67% p.a. compared with the FTSE All-Share Index return of 8.67% p.a.[3]

Another great example of active manager hype is that of Jayesh Manek, who was the winner of the Sunday Times Fantasy Fund Manager competition in 1994 and 1995, beating thousands of other entrants and winning £100,000 on each occasion. After initially managing £10 million for well-known investor Sir John Templeton, Manek established the Manek Growth Fund, a unit trust open to public investment. By 2000 he had attracted more than £100 million into the fund, which was up by 160% and worth nearly £300 million. After the tech wreck in 2000 the fund value crashed and since that time the performance of Manek Growth has been truly terrible, as shown in Figure 4.2.

When it comes to promoting their funds, fund managers are usually highly selective about what they show. They typically show those funds that have outperformed the particular measure they select while saying nothing about their underperforming funds. Often they quote a very short-term track record (three years is common) of one of their 'star' managers or their five-year, top-quartile-performing flagship fund. The media also gets sucked into quoting this highly

[2] Data source: Morningstar, FTSE, ONS ten-year performance to 31.12.2010.
[3] Data source: Morningstar, FTSE, ONS ten-year performance to 31.12.2013.

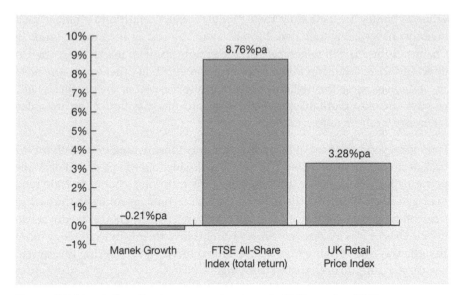

Figure 4.2 Manek Growth – ten-year performance to 31 December 2013
Source: Data sourced from Morningstar, Office for National Statistics.

selective past performance data as part of a story or feature on investing trends, often based on press releases originated by smart people in public relations firms. I know from experience that many journalists want to write about 'noise' rather than the boring reality that investing and financial decision making should be dull to be successful. 'Buy and hold' doesn't have the same ring about it as 'The next big thing is ...'.

Average investors and markets

As I explained in Chapter 2, the academic research tells us that investors rarely obtain anything like the returns the funds in which they are invested achieve. This is because the average investor flits from fund to fund based on the prevailing messages they pick up from the media and the financial services industry – 'this time it's different'. There is a powerful and very natural human tendency to want to do something in the face of adversity or if others are apparently doing better (investment wise) than you. A long-running US-based study carries out an analysis each year into the impact of investor behaviour on the returns that they achieve.[4] As you can see from Figure 4.3 the average investor doesn't get much of the returns that are there for the taking if only they could stay the course.

---

[4]   Dalbar Inc., *Quantitative Analysis in Investor Behaviour 2014*.

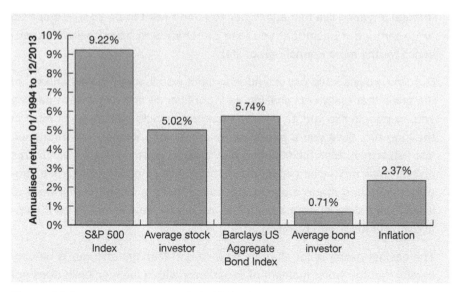

Figure 4.3 Investor returns compared with fund returns
Source: Data from DALBAR (2014) Quantitative Analysis of Investor Behavior (QAIB).

Over the 20-year period to the end of 2013 it seems that the average US equity investor achieved a return of 4.2% p.a. less than the main US stock market index and the average US bond investor achieved a return of 5% p.a. less than the main US bond index. Although the average equity investor did beat inflation, the average bond investor actually lost money in relation to inflation. This is nothing to do with fund manager competence or costs but poor discipline on the part of investors.

'Investors should remember that excitement and expenses are their enemies.'

Warren Buffett, Chairman, Berkshire Hathaway Corporation

Responding to changing economic conditions

In his lecture on what investors could learn from the stock market crash of 2008–2009, Charles Ellis put it like this:

'People often like to say, well, there's a great powerful experience in this terrible financial crisis, are there lessons to be learned? The answer of course is "yes", but be careful you don't learn too much because it's a very unusual experience that we went through and most people will never go through anything like that again. So, you don't want to be so well prepared to go through it again that you lose the chance to have positive experiences for the more normal part of life.

But, you really should pay attention to what was it about the experience of the crisis that really was shaking your confidence and might have caused you, or people like you, to do something that would have been horrible in the long run. Give you a good example: anybody who got so frightened last February or March [2009] that they cleared out their stock investments and put their money into either bonds or cash is someone who took a temporary loss and made a permanent loss. That's a lesson we all want to learn: don't allow current experience, no matter how acute, to be disruptive of your long-term planning.

The easiest example for all of us who've had teenage children is be very careful that the worst moment of experience with a teenage child does not dominate your behaviour towards that child. Be steady, be calm and in the long run your child will grow up to be a wonderful adult, just like you.'[5]

Media noise is just that, noise. Don't confuse the needs of media to sell copy and advertising with what is in your best interests. You wouldn't measure the distance between your home and place of work with a small ruler, so avoid reacting to short-term, random news. The best antidote to being blown off course might be to work with a decent adviser to develop and stick with a structured financial plan that enables you to make decisions in context with your values and key life goals.

Decide what help you need and would derive value from

There are several factors to consider when working out whether you need assistance with planning, implementing and managing your personal wealth. In no particular order these include:

- your financial personality (propensity, inclination, time, behaviour)
- your confidence in making financial decisions
- the financial impact on your desired lifestyle and other life goals
- the time you have available
- the complexity of your financial and family situation.

---

[5]   Transcript of video interview with respected investment expert and author Charles Ellis on investment fundamentals: **www.vanguard.co.uk/uk/portal/Library/interviews--video-ellis.jsp**

Advice

Providing financial advice on investments, pensions, certain insurance contracts and mortgages is highly regulated in the UK and most private individuals are classed as 'retail' investors. This means that any firm that provides advice has to follow strict rules in relation to suitability, appropriateness and fair dealing. Because some areas of advice relate to complex and difficult financial issues which can have a big impact on people's lives, there are various protections in place, including professional indemnity insurance (held by the advice firm), a financial ombudsman service (to adjudicate on complaints) and a compensation scheme funded by a levy of the financial services sector. It is a criminal offence for anyone to offer regulated financial advice without being authorised and regulated to do so.

Financial advice is based on a thorough assessment of your personal situation and is tailored to meet your specific needs. This results in written recommendations which should enable you to achieve your objectives. Such advice can be focused on one specific area, such as protecting your family against your death, but the advice firm is still responsible for pointing out if they think other matters need to be considered. You are perfectly in your rights to reject any suggestions to widen the scope of advice. Alternatively, firms will offer a general advice service which covers your entire situation, whether or not this relates to your specific objectives, and this is often referred to as full-service, comprehensive or holistic advice.

Passporting firms

Some European financial advice firms are regulated and established in one country but provide regulated services to residents in another, under a system known as 'passporting'. This means that the firm is approved and regulated by the host country's regulator and is permitted to operate, for example, in the UK as long as they agree to follow the UK's rules.

My understanding, from speaking to compliance experts, is that no other European financial services regulator is as strict and tough as the UK's Financial Conduct Authority. There is some evidence of previously UK-regulated advisers moving their business and regulatory authorisation to another European county with a more 'relaxed' regulatory approach and then passporting their services back to the UK. Apart from the obvious potential for regulatory arbitrage to arise (where firms seek the easiest regulatory regime), trying to get redress if things go wrong might turn out to be less than easy, particularly if you don't speak the language. You have been warned!

Guidance

Guidance is where a financial services company provides you with information to enable you to make your own decision, including arranging any financial products. The information is usually based on people like you, but is not specific to your situation. Although there is still protection in relation to financial products being fit for purpose, this does not extend to the suitability of such products for you, so if you have a bad outcome, you will have no protection or redress available to you. Over the past ten years or so, with the proliferation of online DIY investment platforms, new providers of low-cost investment and pension products, and consumer finance websites, some people have confused guidance with advice. For example, an online portfolio service that provides information on investment matters, including which portfolios might be suitable, appears as if it is providing specific and tailored advice.

What help do you need?

If you have relatively simple needs, modest wealth/income, high confidence, the outcome would have a low impact on your wealth and/or have a high interest level and time available, then guidance may well be the best solution for you.

If, however, your needs are complex, you have low confidence, the outcome would have a high impact on your wealth and/or you have little time or interest in personal finances, then you'll probably need advice that is tailored to your situation.

Frequency of advice

Assuming that advice is the service you need, you also need to decide whether you need an ongoing advice service or not, and if so, the frequency of that service, i.e. yearly, three yearly or a longer interval. If you wish to focus on one particular issue, for example reviewing your pension arrangements, protecting your family in the event of your death, or setting up a tax-favoured investment such as an Enterprise Investment Scheme, you might need one-off advice rather than an ongoing service. However, with more complicated circumstances and substantial wealth, where the financial impact is high (for example, where portfolio and/or pension regular withdrawals need ongoing monitoring), you will probably need and want a more comprehensive and ongoing advice service. Figure 4.4 sets out these choices graphically.

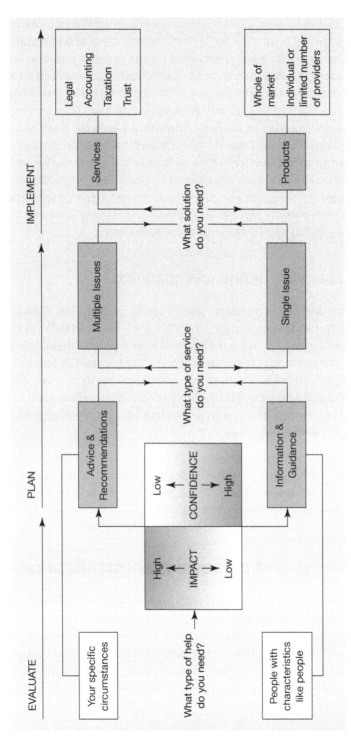

Figure 4.4 What financial service do you need?

My view is that there are a substantial number of people who are being over-served and overcharged by financial services firms because the firm is providing an ongoing annual service which is not necessary for the person's situation or not good value for money in relation to the financial outcomes achieved. This has become more apparent since the introduction of the ban on product-based commission incentives to UK advisers in January 2013. These new rules have seen many financial services firms trying to replace commission payments from products with 'adviser remuneration' facilitated by deductions from financial products, in return for an ongoing advice 'service'. I have spoken to many individuals over the past few years who are questioning the value of this ongoing 'service' and the amount of fee charged. Sending out periodic valuations and having a one-hour annual meeting is not an advice service, and unless value is being delivered in excess of the advice costs, it doesn't make sense to use such firms.

Financial advice or financial planning?

The term 'advice' has a specific regulatory meaning in the UK. Over the past 25 years or so the regulatory regime has defined advice in relation to the arranging of financial products but not the actual advice process itself. This is starting to change, but most regulations and rules are still couched in terms of someone needing a financial product. As a consequence there are some areas of advice that are not regulated and/or not subject to the commission ban, such as financial planning, tax planning, trusts, wills and certain life and disability products which do not acquire a surrender value.

About 40 years ago financial advisers in the United States developed a six-step process for personal financial planning, which provided a comprehensive, structured and consistent framework that professionals could use with their clients to help them achieve their life objectives (see Figure 4.5).

Experience and professional qualifications

Since January 2013 all individuals who provide UK-regulated investment and financial advice to individuals must have attained a level of professional qualification equivalent to that of the first year of a degree course. In reality, a number of areas of advice, such as pension transfers, have always required higher levels of qualification, but the new standard will apply across the board to insurance salespeople, bank advisers, financial advisers, stockbrokers and private bankers.

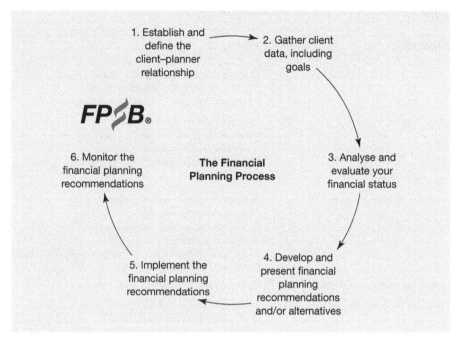

Figure 4.5 The six-step financial planning process

Source: Financial Planning Standards Board ltd. Copyright © 2014, Financial Planning Standards Board Ltd. All rights reserved.

Table 4.1 illustrates the levels of different types of designations and where they sit on the educational ladder, to give you an idea of the quality and difficulty required in attaining different levels of qualification. The Certified Financial Planner (CFP) accreditation is awarded to individuals who pass a rigorous financial planning case study assessment, in addition to possessing the necessary technical examination standards required by the regulator. This ability to apply technical knowledge to a given client situation makes the CFP a good standard by which to determine whether a professional adviser has the relevant skills and knowledge to provide high-quality advice. Today there are over 153,000 practitioners around the world who hold the CFP accreditation.[6]

In 2011, the Institute of Financial Planning (IFP), which administers the CFP accreditation in the UK, launched an Accredited Financial Planning Firm™ designation and register. To be awarded Accredited status firms have to:

---

[6] Source: **www.fpsb.org/** as at April 2014.

Table 4.1 Summary of financial services qualifications

Academic	Level	Vocational
PhD/CFA	7	Diploma in Wealth Management (CISI) Diploma for Chartered Banker (CCN) Chartered Financial Analyst (CFA Institute)
MSc/MA/MBA	6	Chartered Financial Planner (CII) Advanced Diploma in Financial Planning (CII) Chartered Wealth Manager (CISI) Certified Financial Planner (IFP)
BSc/BA	5	
1st year foundation degree	4	Diploma in Accounting & Business (ACCA) Diploma in Accounting (AAT) Diploma in Regulated Financial Planning (CII) Diploma in Investment Advice (CISI) Investment Management Certificate (new, CFA Institute) Certificate in Paraplanning (IFP)
International Baccalaureate	3–4	Certificate in Investment Management
A Level/City & Guilds	3	Certificate for Finanical Advisers (IFS) Certificate in Financial Planning (CII) Diploma in Financial Services (Chartered Banker) (CCN)
AS Level	2–3	NVQ in Retail Financial Services
GCSE	1–2	Foundation Certificate in Personal Finance Award in Personal Financial Planning

* meet the IFP's strict criteria for the delivery of a comprehensive financial planning service

* have easy-to-understand propositions, transparent charges and a clear investment philosophy

* have demonstrated their commitment to a professional code of ethics and practice standards

* ensure that their financial planning service is delivered by highly qualified practitioners

* have the ability to help you develop an effective plan to achieve your goals in life.

The Institute assesses all firms on an annual basis to ensure that they continue to meet the highest standards of professional practice. Accredited firms can be found in most regions of the UK, and I strongly recommend that you include at least one Accredited Financial Planning Firm on your advice firm shortlist.

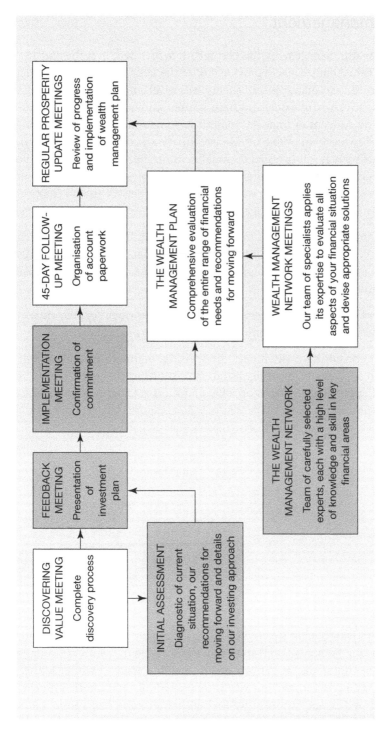

Figure 4.6 A typical wealth management consulting process

Source: Bloomsbury Wealth Management.

Wealth management

The term 'wealth management' has become more prevalent over the past 15 years, but not all firms that profess to provide it offer the same service. A lot of stockbrokers and investment managers call themselves wealth managers when they focus only on the investment assets and have limited understanding of tax and legal issues and no concept of financial planning. Some restricted financial advisers, with limited investment or tax knowledge, focus more on advising and arranging tax wrappers such as self-invested personal pensions (SIPPs) and insurance bonds. Some financial planners focus purely on the overall plan and do not provide investment services. A comprehensive wealth management service should comprise the various different disciplines and areas that go to make up a proper wealth plan.

A typical comprehensive wealth management consulting process is illustrated in Figure 4.6. While every firm will have its own approach and processes, this will give you an idea of the type of approach to look for. A firm that cannot explain its process is unlikely to deliver a slick and professional service.

As illustrated in Figure 4.7, this service should comprise three key elements: investment consulting, advanced planning and relationship management.

Investment consulting is the process of devising, maintaining and periodically updating an appropriate investment strategy or strategies that reflect your risk profile and other preferences, based on what empirical evidence suggests is the most effective approach.

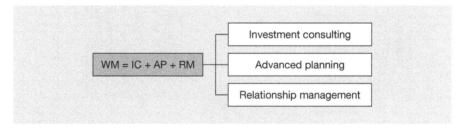

Figure 4.7 Key elements of a comprehensive wealth management service
Source: CEG Worldwide.

Relationship management (see Figure 4.8) is the ongoing process of ensuring that all advice is complementary and appropriate and action in one area of your wealth planning does not impact negatively on another. If you have existing advisers, for example a tax adviser, then your wealth manager must have both a process and the inclination to engage those other advisers in the wealth management process.

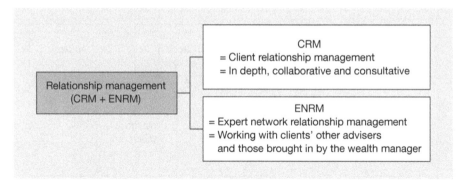

Figure 4.8 Components of relationship management
Source: CEG Worldwide.

The advanced planning component comprises four strategic areas of wealth enhancement, transfer and protection as well as charitable planning (see Figure 4.9). Each of these strategies usually involves several tactics that enable sophisticated wealth planning to be carried out and will usually be set out in a wealth management plan.

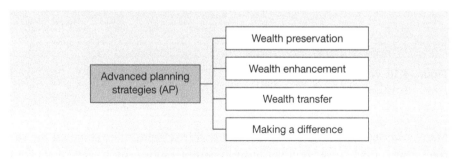

Figure 4.9 Key elements of a wealth management plan
Source: CEG Worldwide.

The expert network

A good wealth manager will have knowledge of you and your family and a broad understanding of strategies and tactics that you may need to adopt to achieve your goals. However, due to the sheer complexity of the financial and tax environment in which we live, it is unlikely that any wealth manager can be expert in all areas. Sometimes larger firms have different departments and seek to offer a 'one-stop shop', while others have a panel of outside experts in different disciplines on which they can call to provide focused advice and service as necessary (see Figure 4.10).

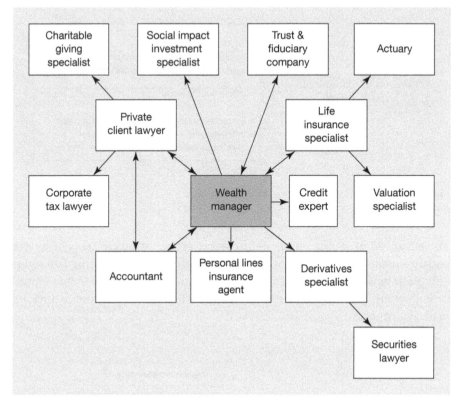

Figure 4.10 Wealth manager expert network
Source: CEG Worldwide.

Many years ago I saw a presentation in the United States that explained the key roles a good financial adviser performs as part of a long-term professional client relationship and these are shown in Figure 4.11.

The financial navigator

As we saw in Chapter 1, knowing what's important to you, where you are going and why are the keys to successful planning. A good adviser will make sure that you are clear about your goals and that such goals are true to your values. They will also help you to resolve any mismatches between what you want to achieve and what is possible, as well as determining alternative strategies and associated tactics.

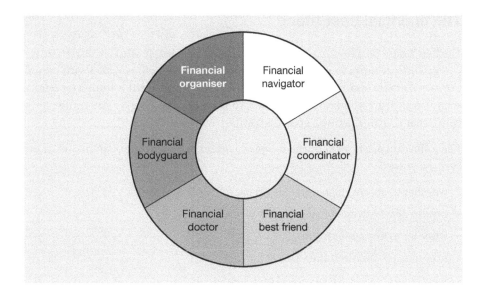

Figure 4.11 Key roles of a financial adviser

The financial coordinator

A good wealth plan for most people will include a number of different elements, such as investment, tax, legal aspects and insurance. Particularly if you have more complex needs and larger amounts of wealth, you will need to use the services of a number of professionals, each with specialist knowledge and skills in different disciplines. The danger is that the overall advice can be fragmented, more expensive than it need be and quite often not as effective as it could be.

A good wealth manager will help to coordinate the advice of these professionals to ensure that the constituent parts 'fit' together to form a bespoke and comprehensive solution. Often there needs to be a series of discussions and communication between, say, a trust specialist, a lawyer and a tax adviser, to ensure that any solutions 'fit' together. The wealth manager will understand the context of the family's overall financial position and objectives and ask the necessary questions so that, when a solution or shortlist of solutions is presented to you, all the technical analysis and evaluation has been completed.

The financial best friend

The best financial advisers and wealth managers are people who are also there for you in difficult times to provide moral support and can help you deal with opportunities, threats and life events. Sometimes you might want a sounding board, even if you think you know the answer to the question, to give you more confidence that you are making a good decision.

The following are typical of the range of issues that clients have shared with me over the years:

- whether to accept the remuneration package in a new job
- how to deal with aged parents' care needs
- whether to buy a new home
- how to teach children the value of money
- whether to make a gift of capital or to lend it
- whether to invest in a friend's or relative's business venture
- whether to retrain for a completely different career
- how best to determine a fair value for selling the family home to a close friend.

More often than not I didn't offer a solution as the clients came up with the answers themselves, but they found it helpful to share the issues with someone outside the family whom they trusted. As they say, a problem shared is a problem halved. A good adviser will also play devil's advocate when you have suggested a goal, value, preference or tactic, to ensure that you've really thought things through. They will also hold you to account in relation to the financial planning policies that you have created in your plan.

The financial doctor

Just like the medical doctor who knows your family well and can be trusted to keep confidences, a good adviser develops a deep understanding of you and your family over many years. Sometimes relationships are not always what they seem and it can take time to uncover subtle but important information. For example, some adult children might be reckless spendthrifts with a trail of broken relationships, while others might be hard workers who value wealth and are in a stable relationship. There might be stepchildren to whom the individual is closer than birth children who don't keep in touch.

A life partner who has never made important financial decisions will usually welcome the support and guidance of an adviser who is familiar with the family's wealth plan and the various components, in the event of their partner dying or becoming seriously ill. It can take several years to get to know a family and its dynamics and to uncover the various issues, and this takes investment in time and emotional energy on the part of the adviser. The more your wealth adviser gets to know you as a person, the more that trust and empathy will develop.

The financial bodyguard

Poor products and services, the constant barrage of media 'noise' and human emotions can conspire to mean sometimes you will need protecting from people, products and services that are not good for your wealth. The role of financial body-guard is not always one that you might associate with a good financial adviser, particularly if you have used transaction-based firms such as private banks, insurance salespeople or brokers who are reliant on commission from product sales. 'Bodyguard' is, however, a key role provided by advisers who do not represent or are not in any way tied to a product provider and whose remuneration is paid directly by you through pre-agreed fees.

The financial organiser

Being well organised means knowing what financial assets you own and why you own them. Knowing the location of important paperwork like legal papers and ownership certificates is also essential. A good adviser can help you to make sense of what you have and, where possible, simplify and rationalise things so that you have as few moving parts as possible. Minimising paperwork, information and other administrative tasks is the key to being well organised. The more organised you feel, the more confidence you will have about your wealth. The more confidence you have, the better your decision making will be and the more you'll enjoy life.

Keeping a good audit trail to substantiate certain financial planning strategies and solutions is another key discipline with which the better advisory firms will help you. For example, a useful but under-used inheritance tax planning technique is to make regular gifts out of surplus income. As long as various conditions are met, the amount gifted falls out of the inheritance tax planning net immediately. A key element necessary to prove to the tax authorities that you have met the conditions for the tax exemption is to have copies of an exchange of letters recording gifts made, including dates and names. A decent firm will help you to maintain the necessary records.

Planning and advice fees and value

There are numerous ways that financial planners and wealth managers charge for their services:

- fixed initial and service fees
- hourly charge
- percentage of assets invested
- proportion of tax saved
- product commissions received on non-regulated tax shelters, and insurance products.

Sometimes these charging methods are combined. The key point is to know what you are paying and why. Regardless of what the rules say and no matter how convenient it might be, I think you should agree the fees for the advice and services you use and pay them yourself, and ideally avoid paying them by way of deductions from financial products. An adviser who agrees and charges explicit fees rather than relying on payments from transactions or from product deductions has less of a conflict of interests in the advice that they give. It is also easier for you to determine whether or not those fees have been good value for money.

Many private banks and certain restricted financial advisers use their organisation's own products and funds, which are often more expensive than would be the case if you used an independent adviser, whether they agree an explicit fee for planning services or not. The more complicated the product or solution, the more likely it is to be expensive and to have high fees and costs. Some 'advisers', who do not charge stand-alone advice fees, insist on being paid by way of adviser charge deducted from investment products. This is a bit like your doctor earning a commission every time he prescribes you drugs; in such a situation you can expect most diagnoses to need medication.

If you use a good wealth manager then you should expect to pay a fixed planning fee for the initial work and this will vary depending on the complexity and value of your wealth, as well as the breadth and depth of the firm's professional staff. Ongoing management fees should relate to the ongoing value being delivered, as well as the degree of responsibility assumed and services provided by the wealth manager, so make sure you know what you are paying, what you are getting for those fees and that you have a means of assessing value for money.

Management fees are high and still rising

By Emma Dunkley

Despite mounting pressure on the financial services industry for greater transparency over fees and lower costs for investing, the charging structures of many wealth managers are still far from clear. Yet, although more investors are starting to pay more attention to charges, few wealth managers are taking decisive action to clarify or reduce them.

Most firms still apply *ad valorem* charges, levying a fee based on a percentage of assets under management, which means that costs increase as the value of assets under management grows. Some offset the impact with tiered fee structures, whereby the level of the *ad valorem* charge reduces as assets rise, but few firms apply a flat, fixed fee, which investors argue is a more transparent charging structure.

Gina Miller, founding partner of SCM Private, who spearheads the True and Fair Campaign on fees, says about 70 per cent of an investor's real return can be eaten by charges. The average wealth management charge, including the cost of the investments, amounts to 3.24 per cent a year.

But transaction costs incurred by the wealth firm and fund managers, which are often undisclosed, come to an average of 0.41 per cent a year, Ms Miller adds. That takes the total to an average 3.65 per cent a year – compared to an average real annual return on equities of 5.2 per cent. Transaction charges vary widely; some groups include them in the overall cost of management, others charge them at a flat-rate cost, such as £25 or £35, others charge a percentage transaction fee (which can be as high as 1.65 per cent) and there are often "settlement" or "compliance" charges on top.

Upfront charges can inflate that still further in the early years. Research by Numis Securities reveals that wealth managers charge as much as 7.5 per cent a year in some cases. An investor with £120,000 invested across funds, shares, investment trusts and exchange traded funds, split across a pension, investment account and individual savings account, could pay up to £8,970 in fees to St James's Place in the first year, according to Numis. The same portfolio at Barclays Wealth Advisory would cost £5,475 a year on a portfolio of £120,000. The Hargreaves Lansdown Portfolio Management Service charges £1,462 a year.

St James's Place pointed out that the charge includes the initial and ongoing cost of advice, which is not typically included in figures from other wealth managers. The figure also accounts for the charge for exiting the investment in the first year, which few investors would do.

Nonetheless, the research by Numis and others reveals the wide discrepancy in fees and how difficult they are to ascertain. Ms Miller says investors often believe the "annual management charge" represents the total cost. "Unless there's a standard method with all the explicit and implicit charges updated on an annual basis, there's no chance of understanding it," she says.

➡

Wealth managers say they are working towards a model of greater transparency. Last year, Rathbones and Quilter Cheviot joined forces to create a standard methodology for calculating total account costs, expressed as an annual percentage. And European regulation coming into force in the next few years should drive wealth managers towards improving their overall charging structures.

Aside from the lack of transparency over fees, investors are also concerned that charges are rising, rather than coming down. "We've noticed that a number of people are paying very high annual fees via discretionary investment services," says Justin Modray, founder of financial advice site Candid Money. Investors typically pay more than 1 per cent for the wealth manager's service plus fees for the underlying funds of about 2 per cent a year – often on hundreds of thousands of pounds.

Source: Dunkley, E. (2014) Management fees are high and still rising, *Financial Times*, 21 June
© The Financial Times Limited 2014. All Rights Reserved.

Vanguard, the mutual low-cost investment fund company, sets out how it sees good financial advisers delivering value, which it describes as 'adviser alpha', and it isn't related to beating investment markets:

'A more pragmatic answer for both parties might be "better than investors would likely do if they didn't work with a professional adviser". In this frame-work, an adviser as alpha (i.e. added value) is more aptly demonstrated by his or her ability to effectively act as a wealth manager, financial planner and behavioural coach – providing discipline and reason to clients who are often undisciplined and emotional – than by efforts to beat the market. ... On their own, investors often lack both understanding and discipline, allow-ing themselves to be swayed by headlines and advertisements surrounding the "investment du jour" – and thus often achieving wealth destruction rather than creation. In the adviser as alpha framework we've described, the adviser becomes an even more important factor in the client–adviser rela-tionship, because the greatest obstacle to clients' long-term investment success is likely to be themselves.'[7]

Until now gamma has been the term that academics used to describe the degree to which an investor is risk averse. Recently two academics redefined gamma as a measure of the additional expected retirement income achieved by an investor from making more intelligent financial planning decisions.[8]

---

[7]   Bennyhoff, D.G. and Kinniry, F.M. (2010) 'The adviser as Alpha: Insights from the US market', Vanguard White paper, December.

[8]   Blanchett, D. and Kaplan, P. (2012) 'Alpha, beta, and now ... gamma', Morningstar White paper.

In summary, these financial decisions relate to five main areas:

1 A total wealth framework (or plan) to determine the optimal asset allocation strategy.

2 A dynamic regular portfolio withdrawal strategy.

3 Incorporating guaranteed-income products (i.e. annuities) as necessary.

4 Tax-efficient investment allocation and withdrawal decisions.

5 Optimising the portfolio to take into account risks such as those from inflation and currency movements which would impact on achieving different goals.

A significant proportion of investors will want and/or need to take ongoing advice from a professional financial adviser to make these good decisions. Financial advice is not free and it's natural to wish to avoid incurring costs for something where the value is not clear. The academics have, however, calculated the value of getting these decisions right in terms of additional retirement income, which they calculate to be 22% more income, equivalent to 1.59% p.a. average additional return.

The majority of UK-regulated financial advisers are highly qualified, knowledgeable and professional. While advice fees are a cost, the value that you and your family should receive, in the form of a better financial outcome, should make the cost pale into insignificance in the long run.

Adviser checklist

The checklist below lists questions to ask a prospective adviser. Sources of good advice can be found in the useful websites and further reading section at the end of the book.

Checklist

Full-service advice firm – due diligence

- Do you provide structured financial planning as the core service before offering investments or other services?

- Do you offer a transparent 'fee for service' charging structure that is not linked to the arrangement of products or investments?

- Do you offer products, funds and financial solutions from the whole marketplace or do you offer only a restricted range from a few companies?

▶

- Do you have experience of dealing with people like me in terms of personality, family situation, level of wealth and wealth issues?
- Do you and your colleagues hold advanced-level professional financial advice qualifications and, if so, what are these?
- What arrangements do you have to bring in expertise from outside your firm if needed, such as legal or tax planning, and how is this integrated into your own service?
- Do you ever receive sales commissions from any source (e.g. insurance products or introducer fees from other professionals) and, if so, will you rebate this either back into the product or directly to me?
- What is your investment philosophy and do you have a comprehensive document that sets out your approach and rationale?
- How are the professional staff in your firm remunerated?
- Would you be able to allow me to speak to one of your clients in a similar situation to myself before committing to using you?
- Could you show me example outputs of your written work, including the financial plan, so I can have an idea of what to expect?
- How many meetings and discussions can I expect to formulate the initial strategy and how long is this likely to take?
- What is the minimum commitment required from me in terms of time and fees?
- What level of resources does your firm have in terms of financial planning, investment and tax expertise?
- Who are the actual people with whom I and my family will be dealing on a day-to-day basis?
- If something goes wrong with the service or your advice, to whom do I complain?
- What are the key financial results for your company in terms of balance sheet strength, revenue and profits?
- Do you think I am the type of customer you are looking for and could service well?

PART 2
WEALTH
PRESERVATION

CHAPTER 5
INVESTMENT PRINCIPLES

'An investment in knowledge always pays the best interest.'

Author unknown, commonly attributed to Benjamin Franklin

Cash has historically been a poor store of value, particularly over the medium to long term. It is, however, the best home for capital that may be needed within the next three years to meet any planned and unplanned expenditure. We refer to such capital as 'savings' because it is earmarked for short-term needs and as such we are less worried about inflation and more concerned that the value won't fall in nominal terms (i.e. excluding the effects of price inflation). There is no point in committing capital to a diversified investment portfolio, only to find that you need to sell some of it at the same time as the portfolio has suffered a temporary fall in value – as it invariably will from time to time – because you need to spend the money on something in the short term or your nerves are fraying.

Your savings capital will be secure if you are a UK resident and invest no more than £85,000 with a UK-registered financial institution (this is the current limit for the Financial Services Compensation Scheme), otherwise you will be dependent on the financial strength of the deposit taker to ensure that it can repay your capital.

Cash savings interest rates have fallen substantially around the world since the onset of the global financial crisis in January 2008. Figure 5.1 illustrates savings rates in the UK from January 2005 to January 2014. Further recent research shows the top-paying UK instant access account in March 2009 was paying 3.35% p.a. compared with the rate of the top-paying equivalent account in March 2014, which was just 1.50% p.a.[1] The loss in return is almost £19 a year for every £1,000 saved, and that's before tax and inflation.

---

[1]   www.Moneyfacts.co.uk: 'Five years of historically low BoE rate', 3.03.14.

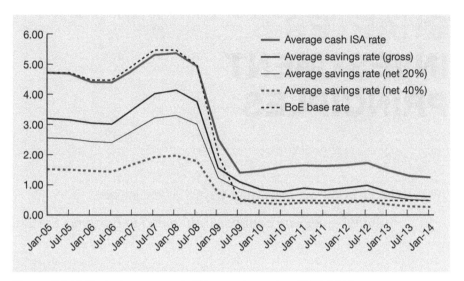

Figure 5.1 UK Instant access cash ISA vs savings rates 2005–2014

Source: Which? (2014) 'From hero to zero', April. Moneyfacts Group.

Just to ensure that your savings maintain their value relative to inflation of 3% you would need to earn 3.75% if you are a basic-rate taxpayer, 5% if you are a higher-rate taxpayer and 5.45% if you are an additional-rate taxpayer. While before tax it should be possible to at least match inflation by holding cash over the long term, most individuals are unlikely either to be non-taxpayers or to obtain the most competitive interest rates on a consistent basis. Although savings interest rates will almost certainly rise at some stage, as the global economy recovers, the timing and rate of any increase are not clear, as evidenced by comments from a member of the Bank of England's Monetary Policy Committee:

'The equilibrium [i.e. the normal interest rate] is a bit lower than the level we used to think of as normal – five per cent. We will not get back to the old normal. ... The long-term "normal" rate for interest rates will be around 2.5 per cent.'

David Miles, Member of Monetary Policy Committee, Bank of England[2]

The term 'investing' means the process of allocating your capital in such a way as to protect against inflation and fund your desired lifestyle, however long that might last, as well as any other objectives. This involves exchanging capital

---

[2] As quoted in *The Telegraph*: 'Interest rates could rise threefold in three years', 11 March 2014.

security, to a greater or lesser extent, in return for higher returns than are likely to be produced from savings. To be successful at investing, all you need is a sound intellectual philosophy, a functional and practical process for implementing and managing the investment portfolio, and a framework to provide context and discipline to stay the course. The benefits of this approach are:

- it has a high probability of meeting your defined lifetime required rate of return
- it is robust and able to withstand a range of economic and investment conditions
- it delivers you, the investor, a fair share of the market returns that are due to you for the risks that you take
- it helps take much of the wealth-destroying emotion out of investing
- it will help you to stay focused on your long-term strategy.

In formulating your investment strategy, whether you work on your own or with professional advisers, you need to:

- review the available evidence and decide what works
- decide on a route that offers the highest probability of a successful investment experience
- build a functionally robust portfolio
- implement the portfolio in the most efficient manner possible
- monitor the progress of the portfolio on an ongoing basis against your lifestyle goals
- maintain the balance of risk and reward.

Speculating is not investing

It is easy to confuse speculating with investing. Speculating is trying to second-guess what investment markets will do with the intention of exploiting those expected movements for financial gain. Speculating is win–lose in that if you make the right choice you win and if you make the wrong one you lose. Investing is not win–lose because capitalism will provide a return on your capital over the long term. You lose only if your belief in capitalism fails or capitalism itself collapses. Most retail investment advice is actually speculating advice. While speculating might be exciting, the available evidence suggests that it is like all gambling and is seriously bad for your wealth. History is full of examples of wealth destroyed by those two powerful human emotions of greed and fear.

Speculation is what fuels an investment 'bubble', whether that is equities, property, gold or tulips bulbs. As more and more people see the easy money that others are making, they start speculating until eventually the whole thing collapses, as is well illustrated by Figure 5.2. The sad thing about bubbles is that in seeking abnormal investment returns, speculators miss out on the meaningful and worthwhile reasonable investment returns there for the taking.

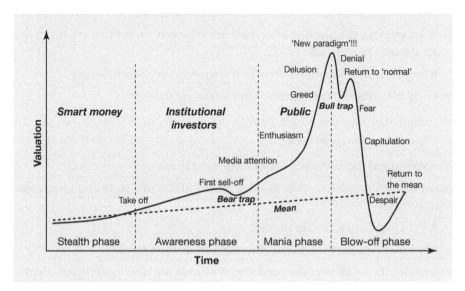

Figure 5.2 Main stages in a bubble

Source: Reproduced by kind permission of Dr Jean-Paul Rodrigue, Department of Global Studies and Geography, Hofstra University.

Capitalism and markets do work

For all its faults and shortcomings, the capitalist system is the only economic system that has actually stood the test of time. Capital and resources (both human and physical) are the two essential ingredients for economic activity, which arise directly from the human race's desire to maintain and improve its standard of living (see Figure 5.3). In a perfect world all capital and resources would be used in the most efficient manner and the maximum return would be achieved for the minimum effort. However, we don't live in a perfect world and, as such, capital and resources are not always allocated efficiently. This does not mean that the capitalist model is wrong, just that it is imperfect.

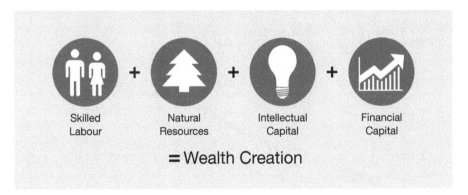

Figure 5.3 Capitalism creates wealth

Over the past few decades we have seen major changes in the world economic order and this came to a head with the recent global financial crisis. There is no doubt that many things went seriously wrong with regulation, product innovation and world economic policy, but that is not to say that capital markets failed. In proper open capital and labour markets, with no political interference and rigorous and credible pricing and clearing/settlement mechanisms, returns would be properly allocated in the most efficient way.

The accumulated empirical evidence, research and theory suggest we should trust in capitalism as this is the only system that creates wealth and allocates capital effectively enough over the long term, as illustrated in Figure 5.4. In addition, capital markets are generally efficient and provide an effective equilibrium (self-levelling) system in terms of setting the price of securities. The aggregate current market view is the best gauge of the value of an investment and represents the value of expected future dividends and earnings for companies and interest payments for fixed-income investments.

Risk and return are linked

Risk and return go hand in hand and if you want higher returns you have to take higher risks. There are no shortcuts and if an investment offers more than the risk-free rate (generally defined as very short-term government deposits) then it comes with higher risks, in terms of capital loss and the possibility that the investment return will turn out to be lower than anticipated. Diversification means allocating your capital across different asset classes (not having all your eggs in one basket) and it can help reduce the various risks associated with investing. In this regard

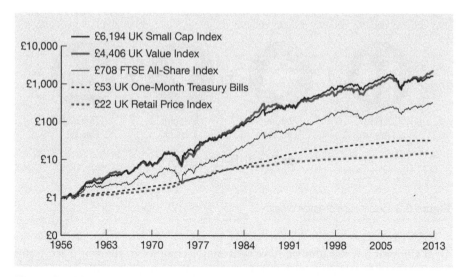

Figure 5.4 Monthly growth of wealth (£) 1956–2013

Source: Data from Dimensional Fund Advisors, FTSE, Office for National Statistics, London Business School; Bloomberg securities, StyleResearch, London Share Price Database.

diversification can be viewed as just about the only 'free lunch' available in investing, in that no one else has to lose to enable you to benefit.

The next step is to identify the various investment risks and how they are compensated, then decide whether (or not) to take them. Once you have decided on how much exposure you will have to the various risk factors, you (or your adviser) need to manage that exposure closely to ensure that it doesn't increase over time.

Equity risk

William Sharpe shared the Nobel Prize in Economics in 1990 for his pioneering contribution to asset pricing theory. He developed the Capital Asset Pricing Model (CAPM) to try to explain, using simplifying assumptions, that an equity's expected return is a function of its volatility (price movements) relative to the volatility of the universe of risky assets. The expected higher returns from equities come with associated risks. These risks are a combination of 'systematic' and 'unsystematic' risk.

- Systematic risk includes macroeconomic conditions affecting all companies in the stock market. Systematic risk cannot be diversified away.

- Unsystematic risk includes company risk (the specific risk of owning shares in, for example, Barclays, GlaxoSmithKline or Rolls-Royce) and industry risk (such as pharmaceutical, banking or telecom shares) specific to individual securities. The effect of these can be reduced through sufficient diversification (i.e. allocating capital across a number of different securities, sectors and markets).

Sharpe's conclusion was that the most efficient portfolio, from a risk–return perspective, is one containing the entire universe of risky assets. The CAPM model is the intellectual foundation of the total stock market index fund. The lesson for investors is that they should not expect markets to reward them for risks that can be diversified away. Rather, they should expect compensation only for bearing systematic risks. Figure 5.5 illustrates this concept visually.

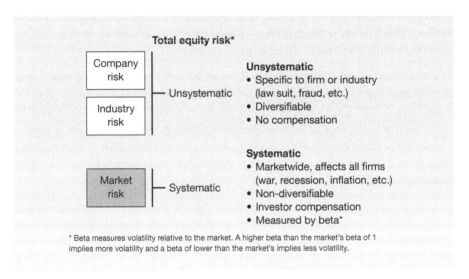

* Beta measures volatility relative to the market. A higher beta than the market's beta of 1 implies more volatility and a beta of lower than the market's implies less volatility.

Figure 5.5 Total equity risk

The multi-factor model

Sharpe's CAPM model was developed further in the early 1990s by two eminent US finance academics, Professors Eugene Fama and Kenneth French. They developed a framework, known as the multi-factor model, for explaining two more systematic risk factors relating to equity investment.[3] Fama and French found that 96% of the variation in returns among equity portfolios can be explained by the portfolios' relative exposure to three compensated risk factors:

---

3   Fama, E.F. and French, K.R. (1993) 'Common risk factors in the returns on stocks and bonds', *Journal of Financial Economics*, 33(1): 3–56.

1   Market factor – equities have higher expected returns than fixed-income securities.

2   Size factor – small capitalisation (i.e. smaller companies') equities have higher expected returns than large capitalisation (i.e. larger companies') equities.

3   Value factor[4] – lower-priced (relative to their accounting value) 'value' equities have higher expected returns than higher-priced 'growth' equities.

The market factor

The first factor in the model relates to how much of a portfolio is allocated to the stock market, i.e. equities, which is defined as the complete universe of companies on a market value-weighted basis. Because equities have a higher risk than fixed interest investments and cash deposits, they have to have a higher expected return, otherwise no rational investor would be willing to own them. This higher expected return is known as the equity risk premium (ERP).

The ERP is not a static figure and will rise and fall with changes in economic conditions and the supply of and demand for capital by companies. Intuitively we know that an ERP must exist, otherwise investors would invest solely in less risky investments like cash and bonds. There is no definitive or universally accepted way of measuring the equity risk premium, but it is reasonable to say that the long-term ERP has a floor of around 0.50–1% p.a., this being the real yield on index-linked gilts.

Historical analysis of the UK, US and global (in US$ terms) equity markets' ERPs to the end of 2013 was 3.9%, 4.5% and 3.3% respectively.[5] Some academics expect the ERP for global developed equity markets in the next ten years or so to be lower, about 3–3.5%, whereas others think that it will be about 4%, which is in line with its long-term historic average.[6] Figure 5.6 shows the historic and forward-looking estimates for the ERP. While the historic ERP is almost certainly unlikely to be repeated, no one has devised a reliable method of forecasting what it might be in the future. It is precisely because there is so much uncertainty about the ERP that investors need to regularly review their investment strategy and spending levels in the light of actual returns achieved.

---

[4]   The proper term for this risk factor is 'book-to-market' (BtM) factor or ratio.

[5]   Dimson, E., Marsh, P. and Staunton, M. (2014) *Credit Suisse Global Investment Returns Yearbook 2014*, Credit Suisse.

[6]   Hammond, P.B. Jr and Leibowitz, M.L. (2011) 'Rethinking the equity risk premium: An overview and some new ideas,' Research Foundation of CFA Institute, December, 1–17, available at **www.cfainstitute.org/learning/products/publications/rf/Pages/rf.v2011. n4.7.aspx**

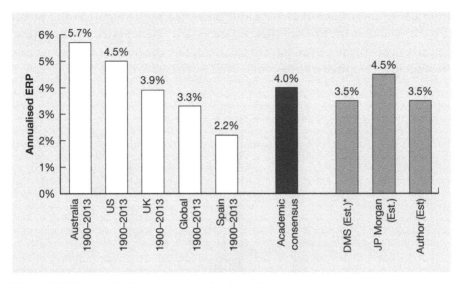

Figure 5.6 The equity risk premium in developed markets

Sources: Data from Dimson, E., Marsh, P. and Staunton, M. (2014) *Credit Suisse Global Investment Returns Yearbook 2014*; Hammond, P.B. Jr and Leibowitz, M.L. (2011) Rethinking the equity risk premium: An overview and some new ideas', *Research Foundation of CFA Institute*, December, pp. 1–17; Dimson, E., Marsh, P. and Staunton, M. (2006) 'The worldwide equity premium: A smaller puzzle', 7 April, EFA 2006 Zurich Meetings Paper; JP Morgan Asset Management (2013) 'Long-term capital market assumptions 2014', 30 September.

Source: Historical ERP – footnote 5 (above); Academic consensus ERP – footnote 6; DMS estimate – footnote 9; JP Morgan estimate – footnote.[7] Note* – top end of 3.0% to 3.5% estimate.

Jack Bogle, the founder of index fund provider Vanguard, suggests a simple way to determine the future return from equities.[8] If the dividend yield is 2–3% and long-term real growth in earnings is 2–3%, the real return from equities would need to be in the region of 5%, which is a 4% premium over T-bills (a cash-like government security), assuming no change in the price/earnings ratio. This seems a reasonable assumption for the basis of financial planning decisions, providing that regular reviews of the financial plan and investment strategy are carried out.

'The main message is that the unconditional expected [i.e. future] equity premium … is probably far below the realised [historical] premium.'[9]

There are periods when investors in equities experience extreme negative real returns. As illustrated in Figure 5.7, over 20 years or more even the worst returns

---

[7] JP Morgan Asset Management Long-term Capital Market Return Assumptions 2014 – 30 September 2013.

[8] Bogle, J.C. (1999) *Common Sense on Mutual funds: New imperatives for the intelligent investor*, Wiley, p. 37.

[9] Dimson, E., Marsh, P. and Staunton, M. (2006) 'The worldwide equity premium: A smaller puzzle', EFA 2006 Zurich meetings paper, April 7.

from UK equities since 1899 have still generated positive purchasing power growth, but that isn't to say this will necessarily be repeated in the future. Uncertainty is the price you have to pay to capture the higher expected returns from equities compared with cash and bonds (see Figure 5.8).

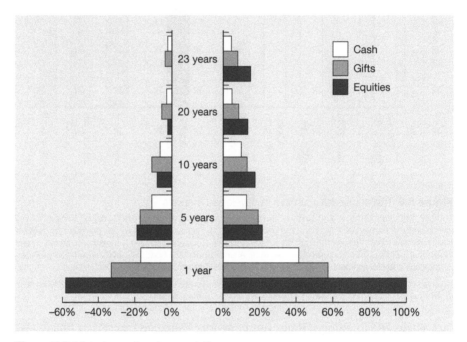

Figure 5.7 Historic equity return variations
Source: Barclays Equity Gilt Study 2014.

The size factor

The second risk factor that Fama and French identified as impacting on returns is the size of the company. Smaller companies have lower capitalisation than larger ones and tend to be more vulnerable to adverse trading conditions. As such, even if such companies have high growth prospects, they are more risky than big companies and therefore have to pay more for their capital. This higher cost of capital for the company translates into additional potential return for the investor. The smaller companies' premium (the additional return) fluctuates all the time and sometimes larger companies outperform (see Figure 5.9). However, Fama and French's multi-factor research indicates that there is a greater probability of higher long-term returns from smaller companies to compensate investors for these additional risks. While some experts reject the notion of the size factor, and it is certainly less compelling than other factors, it does stand up to academic scrutiny.

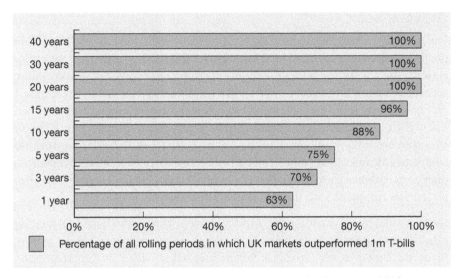

Figure 5.8 Equities versus cash over the past 57 years to 31 December 2012

Source: Data on UK one-month T-bills provided by Datastream; prior to January 1975, UK three-month T-bills.
UK market is the FTSE All-Share Index. FTSE data published with the permission of FTSE.

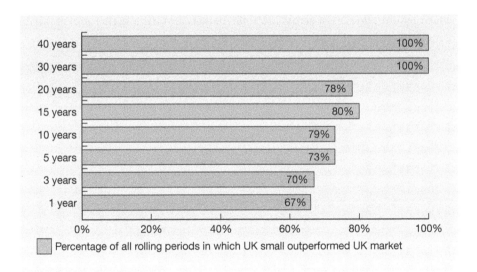

Figure 5.9 Smaller companies premium – UK small versus UK market to 31 December
2012

Source: UK small data simulated from StyleResearch securities data; prior to July 1981, Hoare Govett Smaller
Companies Index, provided by the London School of Business. UK market is the FTSE All-Share Index. FTSE
data published with the permission of FTSE.

The value factor

The third factor that Fama and French identified was the value factor. Some companies are viewed by the market as 'unhealthy' and this can arise for a number of reasons, such as having poor growth prospects, being involved in a risky trading activity or having suffered continued falls in profitability. As a result, these companies have to pay more for their capital to compensate investors for the additional risk to their capital, which translates into the investor's additional potential return over that available from the main equity market. These financially unhealthy companies are known as 'value' companies because they have what is known as a high book (balance sheet) to market (share price) ratio. Put another way, the share price is low compared with the net assets of the company.

Some of the few successful active fund managers, those who have achieved significant outperformance of the stock market, have actually been value company investors. However, once the risk factors associated with value companies are stripped out, we can determine that in most cases the investment manager's skill actually had little influence on the outperformance. Just as the equity risk premium fluctuates all the time, so does the value premium. There have been periods when growth companies (those that the market views as healthy and less risky) have outperformed value companies. However, the research suggests that the value premium does exist across multiple markets and has a higher probability of being delivered over long time periods (see Figure 5.10).

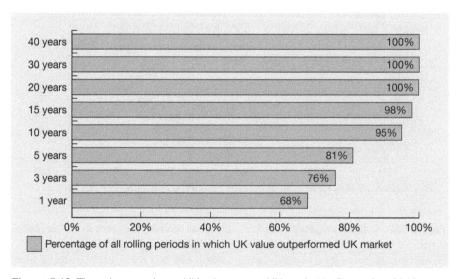

Figure 5.10 The value premium – UK value versus UK market to December 2012

Source: Data from UK market is the FTSE All-Share Index. FTSE data published with the permission of FTSE. UK value simulated Bloomberg securities data; prior to 1994, data provided by London Business School.

Various research papers have confirmed that the small companies' and value companies' risk premia exist in both overseas developed and emerging markets and are of the same quantum as for UK markets (see Figure 5.11).

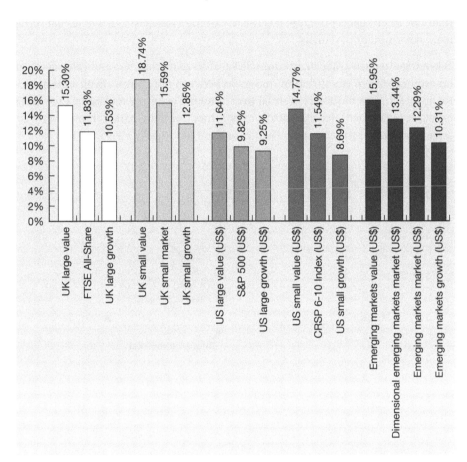

Figure 5.11 Size and value effects across global equity markets to December 2012

Source: US value and growth index data (ex utilities) provided by Fama/French. FTSE data published with the permission of FTSE. The S&P data are provided by Standard & Poor's Index Services Group. CRSP data provided by the Center for Research in Security Prices, University of Chicago. MSCI Europe Index is gross of foreign withholding taxes on dividends; copyright MSCI 2013, all rights reserved. Emerging markets index data simulated by Fama/French from countries in the IFC Investable Universe. Value stocks are above the 30th percentile in book-to-market ratio. Growth stocks are below the 70th percentile in book-to-market ratio. Simulations are free-float weighted both within each country and across all countries. UK and Europe data provided by London Business School/StyleResearch.

The multi-factor model therefore helps us to decide how to allocate a portfolio to the different asset classes based on risk and expected returns. It also supports the contention that making further distinctions between different sectors such as industrials and mining is unlikely to add much value because they are merely components of equities as an asset class and don't have sufficiently different risk and return attributes from equities as a whole. In the same way, geographical distinctions in overseas developed or emerging markets are probably less important than one might expect because it is the risk of the asset class as a whole that is the main determinant of returns.

Taken together, the three main equity risk factors of market, size and value account for around 96% of the variation in returns between portfolios. Using a multi-factor approach, you have the potential to earn higher expected returns by increasing exposure to compensated risk factors rather than trying to market time either your asset allocation or the underlying equity or bond holdings (see Figure 5.12).

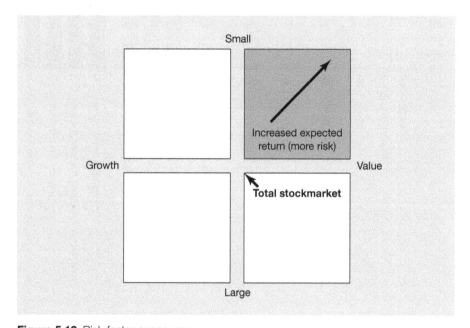

Figure 5.12 Risk factor exposures

Expected profitability

A relatively new investment factor – expected profitability – has emerged over the past decade.[10] Researchers have observed that certain highly profitable companies,

---

[10] Expected direct profitability is a measure of a company's current profits. Profits are defined as operating income before depreciation and amortisation, minus interest expense, and then scaled by book equity.

which have a statistically higher probability of maintaining those profits, tend to have higher returns than the stock market as a whole.[11] All other things being equal, if two companies have the same expected profitability ratio then it makes sense to buy the cheaper of the two. Similarly, if two companies have the same share price, it makes sense to buy the one with the highest expected profitability ratio. Some experts are of the opinion that expected profitability is not a new factor but merely another way of assessing value-type companies that under-invest and achieve higher profitability for a period of time. Whether or not they are correct, some innovative investment managers are starting to incorporate expected profitability into their trading strategies, as a means of enhancing returns from this factor.

'It has always been about the price, and it still is. If two firms have the same number of shares outstanding, we buy the one with the lower price. If two firms have the same book value, we buy the one with the lower price. If two firms have the same profitability, we buy the one with the lower price. It just makes sense.'

David Booth, Co-CEO Dimensional Fund Advisors[12]

Bond maturity and default premium

The real return from government bonds (fixed interest securities issued to fund government debt) has averaged about 2.5% p.a. compounded over the past 50 years.[13] Bonds with a longer time until they mature usually pay a higher return than cash or bonds with a shorter time until maturity. Although not identified by them, Fama and French's multi-factor research also referred to two other factors that related to bonds: maturity date and credit quality (the credit rating of the organisation issuing the bond). (See Figure 5.13.)

Bonds issued by companies and governments that are perceived to be more risky, as they may not meet some or all of the bond interest payments or repay the capital on maturity, pay a higher return than those from less risky issuers. However, if the role of fixed income is to lower the risk of a portfolio, then if you invest in

---

[11] Fama, E.F. and French, K.R. (2013) 'Average returns, B/M, profitability, and growth', Dimensional Fund Advisors' *Quarterly Institutional Review*, 8(1): 2–3.

[12] David made this statement at a US investment conference I attended in May 2013 and I think it nicely sums up how a multi-factor approach is applied in practice.

[13] Barclays Capital, 'Equity Gilt Study 2014', p. 97.

longer-term bonds and/or those with a lower credit quality you are unlikely to be sufficiently compensated for the risks taken. We'll go into more detail about bonds in Chapter 6.

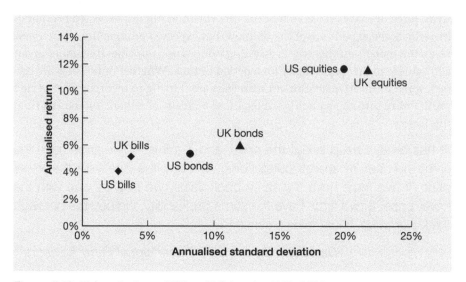

Figure 5.13 Risk and return of UK and US bonds, 1900–2000

Source: Data from Dimson, E., Marsh, P. and Staunton, M. (2001) *Millennium Book II: 101 years of invest-ment returns*, ABN AMRO and London Business School. This publication defines the data used for the above chart and matrix as follows: UK bills are UK one-month Treasury bills (FTSE). UK bonds are the ABN AMRO Bond Index. UK equities are the ABN AMRO/LBS Equity Index. US bills are commercial bills 1900–1918 and one-month US Treasury bills (Ibbotson) 1919–2000. US bonds are government bonds 1900–1918, the Federal Reserve Bond Index 10–15 Years 1919–1925, Long-Term Government Bonds (Ibbotson) 1926–1998, and the JP Morgan US Government Bond Index 1999–2000. US equities are Schwert's Index Series 1900–1925, CRSP 1–10 Deciles Index 1926–1970, and the Dow Jones Wilshire 5000 Index 1971–2000.

Focus on the mix of assets

'Let every man divide his money into three parts, and invest a third in land, a third in business, and a third let him keep in reserve.'

Talmud, c. 1200 BC–AD 500

Asset allocation is the process of dividing up your capital and allocating it to one or more different types of asset classes. An asset class is the term given to a group of investments that share similar risk and return characteristics – examples include cash, equities, fixed interest, property and commodities. In addition, there are a number of investment types known as 'alternative' asset classes, because they fall outside the mainstream asset classes (although, confusingly, some regard property and commodities as 'alternatives'). Table 5.1 shows the main investment characteristics of the three key asset classes – cash, fixed interest and equities – that are the main building blocks used in most portfolios.

Table 5.1 Characteristics of the main asset classes

Asset class	Cash	Bonds	Equities
Returns	Low but volatile	Medium and more stable	High but more volatile
Inflation	Real risk of devaluation over long term	Some risk of devaluation over long term if not short dated or inflation linked	High inflation protection over the long term
Return mechanism	Purely through interest	Primarily through interest/yield	Dividends and growth
Key role in portfolio	Liquidity	Stable but low returns over long term or to reduce risk of volatile assets	Core real return generator

Because asset allocation is the principal determinant in the variation in returns in a broadly diversified portfolio,[14] it is critical to get the right strategic asset mix in place at the outset and to maintain that mix. At the high level you need to determine the overall split between growth (equity-type) and defensive (bond-type) assets. Think of growth as whisky and defensive as water. If you like a strong drink you may not add any water, but be prepared for a big kick. If you don't like alcohol or can't hold your drink then water will probably be all you need. The same goes for investing, in that you need to determine the right blend of assets, taking into account the return that you need and the risks with which you can cope. Equities are expected to generate higher returns than cash or bonds over the long term. This makes sense as equity owners are taking the highest level of risk of these three asset classes.

---

[14] There have been numerous academic studies on this subject, the most respected and well known of which include: Brinson, G.P., Hood, L.R. and Beebower, G.L. (1986) 'Determinants of portfolio performance', *The Financial Analysts Journal*, July/August; Brinson, G.P., Singer, B.D. and Beebower, G.L. (1991) 'Determinants of portfolio performance II: An update', *The Financial Analysts Journal*, 47(3); Ibbotson, R.G. and Kaplan, P.D. (2000) 'Does asset allocation policy explain 40%, 90%, or 100% of performance?', *The Financial Analysts Journal*, January/February; Statman, M. (2000) 'The 93.6% question of financial advisors', *The Journal of Investing*, 9(1): 16–20.

Income-type assets provide most if not all the return in the form of income. Income investments include cash, bonds and certain equities. Returns tend to be more stable but lower over the long term and are more vulnerable to the effects of inflation. Growth-type investments provide most of the return in the form of capital growth over time. Examples of growth investments include most types of global and emerging market equities. Growth investments have the potential to produce higher real returns than defensive asset classes over the long term, but usually pay low or no dividends. However, this usually translates into them having much more volatile returns, due to more frequent trading and changes in investor sentiment. Figure 5.14 sets out a graphical asset allocation decision framework to help you to understand the three stages and the components of each stage.

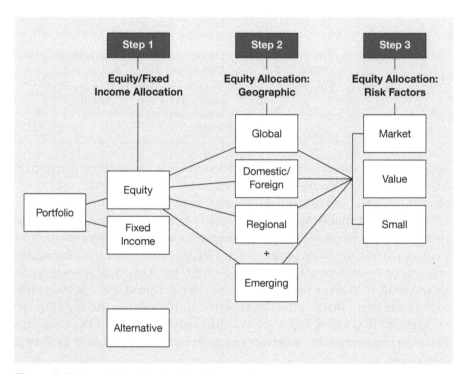

Figure 5.14 Asset allocation decision framework

Measuring investment risk

Investment risk can take various forms, including currency risk, inflation risk, interest rate risk and credit risk. However, a widely used measure of risk relates to how investment returns vary from the long-term average, otherwise referred to as the volatility of investment returns; therefore, the term *volatility* may be used interchangeably with risk.

Standard deviation is a means of measuring volatility over a series of time periods.[15] As illustrated in Figure 5.15, the higher the standard deviation figure, the more the returns have varied from the average. As a general rule, higher average returns usually come with a higher standard deviation (as risk and return are related); such investments can and do experience big swings in returns above and below the average.

The magnitude and likelihood of the return varying from the average is expressed as a multiple of the standard deviation number. Assuming that the data set is large enough to be representative, a particular period's return will fall within one standard deviation either side of the average about 65% of the time, while it will fall within two standard deviations about 95% of the time and within three standard deviations about 99% of the time.

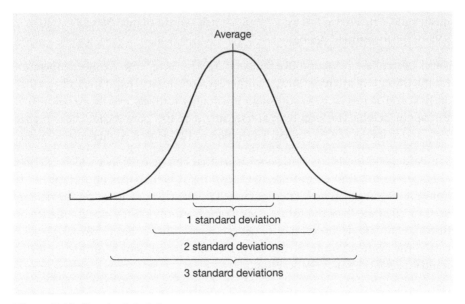

Figure 5.15 Standard deviation

To help you to understand standard deviation, consider the following two investments set out in Table 5.2. Investment X has a lower average annual return (3%) than investment Y (8%), but it also has a much lower range of higher and lower annual returns. So, 65% of the time (one standard deviation) we can see that

[15] The 'average' referred to here is the arithmetic mean.

investment X delivered a return as low as 2% (3% – 1%) and as high as 4% (3% + 1%). By comparison, investment Y delivered a return as low as –7% (8% – 15%) and as high as 23% (8% + 15%).

Table 5.2 Investment returns and risk

Investment	Average annual return	Standard deviation	65% probability	95% probability
X	3%	1%	2% and 4%	1% and 5%
Y	8%	15%	–7% and 23%	–22% and 38%

However, if we want to include a wider range of outcomes, we need to look at the range of returns that falls within 95% of the investment period (two standard deviations). In this instance, we can see that investment X delivered as low as 1% (3% – 2%) and as high as 5% (3% + 2%) in 95% of the investment period. Investment Y, meanwhile, delivered as low as –22% (8% – 30%) and as high as 38% (8% + 30%) in 95% of the investment period.

Think of standard deviation like temperature. The long-term average temperature for the UK in July might be 20°C, but there is a possibility that it might be as high as 30°C and as low as 10°C, although it is highly unlikely ever to go below 0°C. Perhaps in October the long-term average might be 10°C, but it could be as high as 22°C and as low as –2°C (a standard deviation of 12°), thus it could go below zero.

Standard deviation is a statistical measure that can be used in a wide variety of applications not limited to financial planning. It is therefore important not to imbue it with magical predictive value as it is entirely dependent on the data set used to calculate it. If the future is different from the past, placing reliance on historic standard deviation to forecast future volatility could prove dangerously costly. The evidence from the historical record of investment performance is that standard deviations do vary over time.

Slow and steady wins the race

Focusing on average investment returns is a bit like focusing on how many buses left the bus station in the morning and returned in the evening. Due to unforeseen factors (traffic delays, breakdowns or delays boarding passengers), passengers might wait ages for a bus only to have three turn up at once. The fact that ten buses left the bus station in the morning and then returned in the evening is of little consolation to the passenger who waited an hour for his bus along the route.

If two portfolios have the same expected return but one suffers higher volatility than the other, then over the medium to long term, the portfolio with the lower volatility will produce a higher return than the more volatile portfolio. This is because the long-term average investment return masks the fact that investment returns are not delivered in a straight line but vary from one year to the next. The return achieved each year contributes to the overall long-term return, an effect known as compounding. The value of your wealth will be determined by the compound average return achieved, not the arithmetic average return.

The greater the portfolio loss in any given year, the higher the level of future growth required to recover from that loss. For example, a 50% fall in portfolio value requires 100% growth to recover, whereas a 10% fall in portfolio value requires only 11.11% growth to recover. Minimising portfolio volatility, therefore, should be one of your key objectives, and will prove its worth *when* we experience the next market downturn.

Figure 5.16 shows a simplified example of how this concept applies in practice. Two portfolios start with a value of £100,000 and have the same average annualised return of 10% over a five-year period. However, the volatile portfolio has a much higher level of volatility in annual returns achieved compared with the consistent portfolio and as a consequence the compound annualised returns are 5.45% and 10% respectively. This translates into an end value of £130,410 for the volatile portfolio and £161,051 for the consistent portfolio, a difference of more than £30,000.

Year	CONSISTENT INVESTMENT		VOLATILE INVESTMENT	
	Rate of return	Ending value	Rate of return	Ending value
Start value		£100,000		£100,000
1	10%	£110,000	35%	£135,000
2	10%	£121,000	–20%	£100,000
3	10%	£133,100	15%	£108,000
4	10%	£146,410	–30%	£86,940
5	10%	£161,051	50%	£130,410
Arithmetic annual return	10%		10%	
Compound annual return	10%		5.45%	

Figure 5.16 Impact of volatility on hypothetical £100,000 portfolio

We can calculate the probability of losing money from equity investment, in real terms (i.e. after inflation), in the future over different time periods by making an estimate of future expected investment returns and standard deviations. In Figure 5.17 you can see the results of a Monte Carlo simulation,[16] which shows that, based on the data and assumptions used, the probability of losing money from equities over the long term is very low, but it's likely that the investment experience to get there won't be plain sailing. These risks need to be weighed up against the potential upside and the consequences of not receiving that upside had you never invested in equities in the first place.

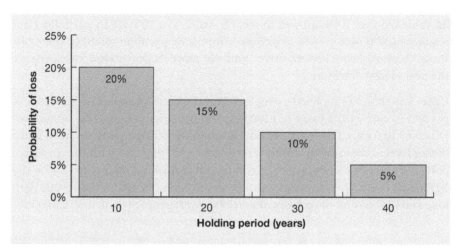

Figure 5.17 Probability of losing money from equities
Source: Albion Strategic.

What's right for me?

There is no 'perfect' portfolio and you need to take into account your life goals, income need, life expectancy and risk profile in helping to determine your asset

---

[16] Any mathematical analysis of probability is only as good as the data and assumptions used. If the assumptions turn out to be wrong, then so will the conclusions. For this reason a Monte Carlo simulation should be viewed as providing a useful insight as to what might happen in the future, not a prediction.

allocation strategy. A prudent approach for most investors will be to diversify capital across the major asset classes. Figure 5.18 shows a range of possible portfolio allocations, along the risk–return spectrum, which might provide you with a reasonable starting place. If you are looking for your portfolio to provide a regular and rising income throughout your lifetime, your asset allocation decision will also need to take that into account.

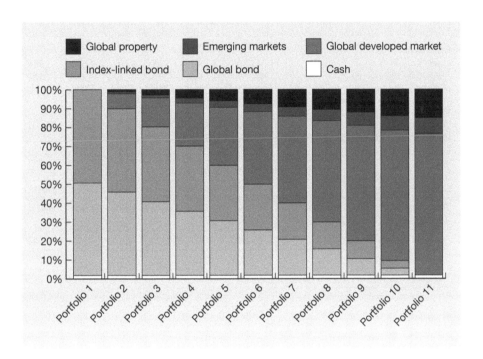

Figure 5.18 Range of asset allocations

Table 5.3 shows historic risk–return simulations for a range of asset allocations, which allocate the equity across global markets for the period 1956–2013, to give you an idea of how they performed. However, do remember that the past is unlikely to be repeated and I suggest that in your plan assumptions you assume much lower investment returns (see Chapter 3 for my suggested investment assumptions).

Table 5.3 Historic risk-return simulations 1956–2013

		Portfolio					
		0	20	40	60	80	100
	Defensive:	100%	80%	60%	40%	20%	1.5%
	Growth:	0%	20%	40%	60%	80%	98.5%
Defensive							
Cash		1.50%	1.5%	1.50%	1.50%	1.50%	1.50%
Short-dated global bonds		49.25%	39.25%	29.25%	19.25%	9.25%	0.0%
Index-linked bonds		49.25%	39.25%	29.25%	19.25%	9.25%	0.0%
Growth							
Global core		0.00%	15.19%	30.38%	45.56%	60.75%	74.80%
Emerging markets core		0.00%	1.69%	3.38%	5.06%	6.75%	8.31%
Global property		0.00%	3.13%	6.25%	9.38%	12.50%	15.39%
Returns (simulated, net of all costs)							
One-year ending 31/12/2013		−2.49%	1.22%	5.01%	8.89%	12.86%	16.61%
Three-year annualised ending 31/12/2013		1.63%	2.37%	3.03%	3.60%	4.08%	4.43%
Five-year ending 31/12/2013		2.41%	4.26%	6.01%	7.66%	9.21%	10.54%
10-year annualised ending 31/12/2013		3.20%	3.98%	4.66%	5.25%	5.73%	6.07%
15-year annualised ending 31/12/2013		5.99%	7.11%	8.11%	8.98%	9.73%	10.27%
20-year annualised ending 31/12/2013		3.68%	4.14%	4.49%	4.72%	4.84%	4.84%
Annualised 01/1956 to 12/2013		5.98%	7.12%	8.13%	9.02%	9.78%	10.34%
Annualised standard deviation 01/1956 to 12/2013		2.14%	3.67%	6.44%	9.42%	12.46%	15.17%
Lowest one-year return		−2.49%	−5.96%	−15.28%	−26.37%	−36.38%	−44.30%
Lowest annualised three-year return		1.63%	−0.58%	−4.57%	−8.58%	−12.61%	−16.14%
Highest one-year return		15.23%	23.79%	39.40%	55.96%	73.48%	89.62%
Highest annualised three-year return		13.52%	15.36%	21.60%	27.94%	34.31%	39.92%
Growth of £1 01/1956 to 12/2013		£29.04	£53.87	£93.07	£149.76	£224.31	£300.78

Due to the effect of rounding, some allocations may not total 100%

Source: Bloomsbury – calculated using Dimensional Returns 2.3. Asset class data have been used that represent close proxies for the asset classes included in the portfolio strategies. 1956 marks the starting point of this asset class data providing a reasonably informative proxy. As later asset class data become available, they are added into the calculation. Includes allowance for typical fund, custody and advice fees.

CHAPTER 6
THE INVESTMENT BUILDING BLOCKS

'The only thing we know for certain about investing is that diversification is your buddy.'

Merton Miller

As we identified in the last chapter, fixed income and equities are the key asset classes used in most personal investment portfolios. In this chapter we'll take a more detailed look at these two asset classes so that you can gain a better understanding of the risks and rewards and how you might deploy your capital.

Fixed interest investments

Fixed interest investments (which from here on we'll refer to as 'bonds') are loans by investors to governments and companies that will be repaid at a pre-agreed date in the future (although a small number of bonds are undated). In return for lending their capital, bondholders are paid a fixed amount of interest, referred to as the 'coupon'. Holders of corporate bonds (those issued by companies) usually rank ahead of normal shareholders in the event of the wind-up or failure of the company, but behind other creditors such as the tax authorities and banks.

The principal use of fixed interest investments in most long-term portfolios is to provide a reliable source of cashflow and to lower risk by dampening the volatility (the degree to which the value of an asset moves up and down) of risky assets such as equities. This is partly because the price of bonds changes at different times and to a different degree (direction and/or magnitude) than that of equities (known as lower correlation[1]). See Figure 6.1 for a range of simulated risk and return outcomes for different bond allocations.

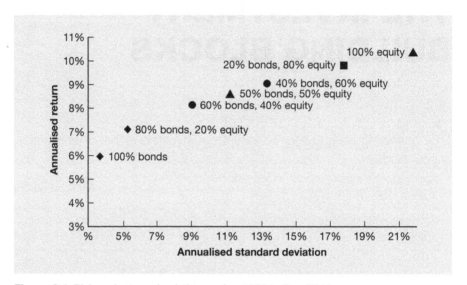

Figure 6.1 Risk and return simulations – Jan 1956 to Dec 2013
Source: Bloomsbury Wealth Management: Simulated returns using Dimensional Returns 2.3 after all costs.

Future returns

The total return assumption for bonds should logically be linked to current bond redemption yields (the return that will arise between now and when the bond is redeemed). Yield represents the primary driver of returns, as capital losses and gains occurring due to interim movement in yields tend to even out over time. A simple but effective forecasting guide for bonds is:

Real return = [Current yield] – [Inflation] [2]

Given current yields, return assumptions for gilts and corporate bonds are currently low. After inflation, returns from gilts are expected to be in the region of 0–1% and those from high-quality-rated bonds higher at around 2%, over the longer term.

---

[1]   A correlation of 1 means that two assets are perfectly positively correlated so they should move in line with each other, so any number less than 1 means that asset class are less likely (but it is still possible) to move in tandem.

[2]   Bogle, J.C. (1999) *Common Sense on Mutual Funds: New imperatives for the intelligent investor*, Wiley, pp. 48–49.

The impact of duration

Duration measures the sensitivity of a bond's price to yield movements on a straight-line (linear) basis. A rise in bond yields results in a fall in bond prices and vice versa. Duration represents the weighted average time until receipt of all cash flows paid on the bond, including regular interest (i.e. coupons), and the return of capital at the bond's maturity, calculated on a discounted basis. The rule of thumb to calculate this is as follows:

Duration × 1% rise (fall) in yield = Capital loss (gain)

So, a 2% rise in yield will broadly result in a 30% capital loss on a bond with a 15-year time until maturity. This is one of the most important numbers for bond investors. The impact of duration on return volatility is illustrated in Figure 6.2.

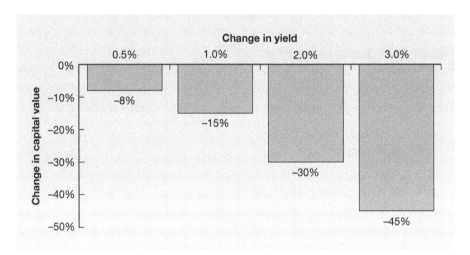

Figure 6.2 Impact on 15-year bond capital value arising from changes in interest rates

No surprises

Fama and French's multi-factor model referred to the two key risk factors associated with fixed interest as being the default (credit quality) premium, being the additional return provided to investors lending money to companies with lower credit ratings, and the maturity premium, being the additional return for holding bonds that have a long time period until they mature. See Figure 6.3. Many investment experts have concluded that the return premia for these two risk factors, when bonds are being used to reduce equity risk, are not sufficient compensation for the risks involved.

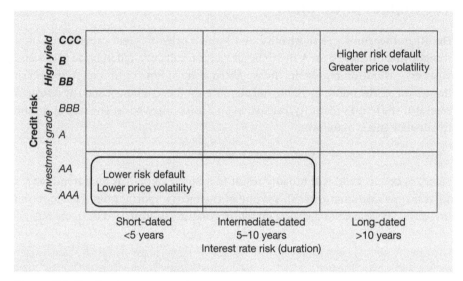

Figure 6.3 The fixed income spectrum
Source: Albion Strategic.

There are several ways to avoid these unnecessary fixed income risks such as:

- reducing maturity risk by holding shorter-term bonds, i.e. those with less than five years to maturity
- reducing default (credit) risk by holding only high-quality bonds, i.e. those with AAA/AA investment grades, and/or
- eliminating currency risk through hedging a basket of global bonds back to the currency in which you expect to spend any portfolio withdrawals.

Replacing long-term fixed income with short-term bonds of higher quality reduces volatility of that part of the portfolio and thus enables an investor to pursue higher expected returns in the equity component. Where the role of fixed income is to lower risk and provide cashflow, it doesn't make sense to take any more risk with this asset class than is absolutely necessary.

Figure 6.4 shows four ways in which one might allocate the fixed income element of a portfolio with 60% equities and 40% bonds. Portfolio 2 reflects a move from long-term to short-term fixed interest. A reallocation to short-dated bonds improved annualised compound returns with a modest increase in annualised standard deviation during this time period.

If the small expected additional reward does not justify the higher risk of longer maturity and lower credit quality, an investor may be better served by holding shorter-term bonds and then 'spending' the risk budget on greater exposure to equity risk factors (small cap or value), where the expected return premiums are potentially increased. Even the riskiest bond returns only 100p in the £1 at maturity, whereas returns from equities are theoretically infinite.

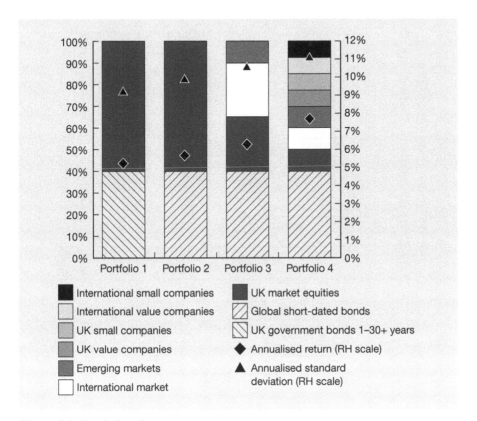

Figure 6.4 Bond allocations

Global short-dated bonds (currency hedged)

Recommended for between 50% and 100% of bond exposure.

High-quality, short-term bonds (or a fund that invests in them), i.e. those with less than five years to maturity, have lower volatility and lower correlation to equities than long-term bonds, i.e. those with ten or more years to maturity (see Figure 6.5). In addition, short-term bonds have a much lower probability of suffering a large loss than long-dated bonds. If your equity allocation is less than 70%, then the additional risks associated with long bonds don't seem worth it. Even if you

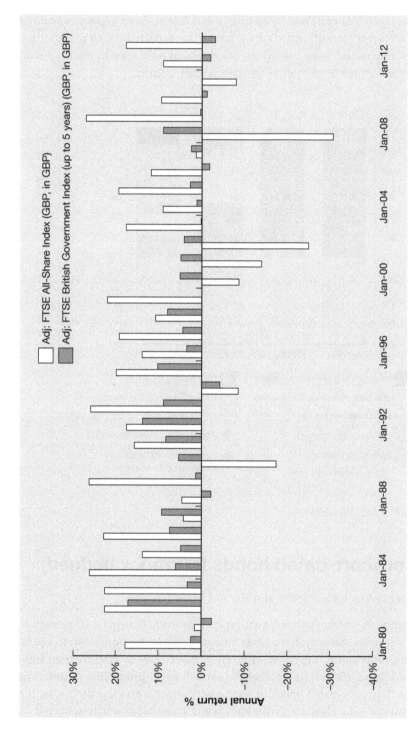

Figure 6.5 Diversification benefits of high-quality short-dated bonds

Source: FTSE Group.

have a high equity allocation, the evidence suggests that the possible additional return of long bonds probably isn't worth pursuing given the disproportionate associated risk. The evidence also supports adopting a global fixed income exposure rather than only or mainly using domestic fixed income, as noted in a recent research paper:

'A hedged global investment would have produced a better outcome than an investor's local bond market in the majority of rising-rate periods across many markets since 1985. This is a direct effect of the imperfect correlation of global interest rates.'[3]

Table 6.1 is extracted from a 2013 presentation by Vanguard,[4] which demonstrates why owning shorter-dated bonds is generally also a sensible strategy at times of rising short-term interest rates (e.g. the Fed funds rate in the US or the Bank of England base rate in the UK). With global interest rates at historic lows, there is little scope for further falls, so when rates eventually rise, short-dated bonds should avoid the largest falls in value.

Table 6.1 Returns on US bonds by maturity during periods of rising Fed funds rates

	Average annualised return of US Treasury investment		
Maturity	1 to 5 year	5 to 10 year	10+ years
Oct 1993 – Dec 1994	–0.5%	–5.0%	–8.4%
Oct 88 – Jan 00	1.4%	–3.8%	–5.6%
May 03 – May 06	1.1%	0.4%	0.9%

Source: The Vanguard Group

Removing the risk of different currencies in a bond fund (known as currency hedging) makes more sense with bonds that are being used to dampen portfolio volatility, because short-term currency fluctuations can have a negative as well as a positive impact on the value of the bond holding. The cost of a fund manager hedging currency risk for short-dated bonds is relatively low (unlike equities where it is expensive) and although it will reduce the returns achieved on the bonds, it will also reduce risk.

---

[3] Westaway, P. and Thomas, C.J. (2013) 'Fearful of rising interest rates? Consider a more global bond portfolio,' Vanguard Research, November.

[4] Vanguard (2013) 'Down but not out: The role of fixed income in a low yield environment', Investment presentation given by Vanguard at UK financial advisers' investment symposium, June.

Intermediate dated index-linked gilts

Recommended for between 50% and 100% of bond exposure or for risk-averse investors who require only inflation protection.

Index-linked gilts have been in existence since 1982, as a direct result of the hyper-inflation of the 1970s, and are government-backed, fixed interest investments that pay a guaranteed and fixed return plus inflation. The actual yield to maturity will depend on the actual inflation rate arising over the period between issue and maturity, although the real return (the amount over inflation) will be locked in at the outset as long as the gilt is held to maturity. The historic real return on index-linked gilts, as set out in Figure 6.6, has typically been in the range of 1–2% p.a. (with a standard deviation of about 12%). However, in the mid-1990s the real return was as high as 4% and at the time of writing it was actually negative for all maturities. The most recent new-issue index-linked gilts have been issued with a real yield of below 0.50%, and the longest-dated ever index-linked gilt was recently issued with a coupon of just 0.125%.[5]

If the real yield on new index-linked gilts rises to reflect a reduction in demand, i.e. more competition for capital from other asset classes, then the value of existing index-linked gilts will fall to reflect these new investment conditions. Although this will not adversely affect the investor who holds their existing gilts to maturity, it does mean that they can't easily switch from the lower real return to the higher one without suffering a loss before maturity, if they sell for less than they paid. Index-linked gilts are, therefore, not risk-free and are highly sensitive to demand from investors (most commonly pension funds) and the inflationary outlook. Intermediate index-linked gilts, i.e. those with a time to maturity of between five and ten years, have about half the standard deviation of longer-duration issues but have a similar expected return. Therefore, it makes a lot of sense to invest in intermediate-dated issues or a fund that does so.

In the absence of NS&I index-linked certificates (more of which later), index-linked gilts (and other inflation-linked bonds, such as those issued by a few large companies) provide a structural link to inflation through an indexing mechanism based on common inflation indices such as the Retail Prices Index. They provide a strong level of protection against inflation, which is critical to investors whose portfolios contain moderate to high levels of fixed income exposures and who have medium- to longer-term investment horizons. Inflation is one of the biggest risks that this type of investor faces.

---

[5]   The 0 1/8% Index-linked Treasury Gilt 2068 was issued in September 2013.

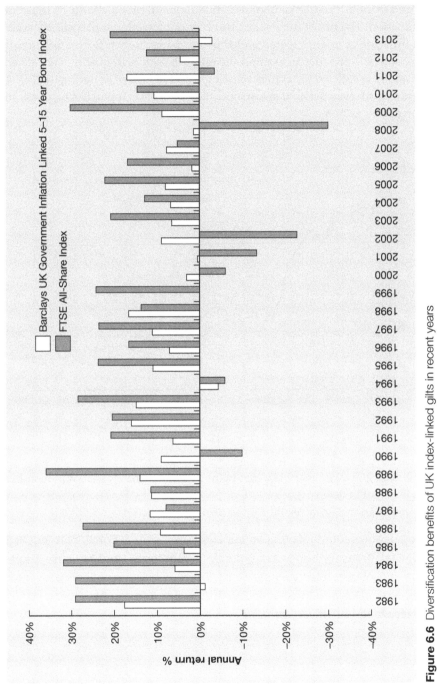

Figure 6.6 Diversification benefits of UK index-linked gilts in recent years

Source: Barclays Capital and FTSE Group

Cash and non-indexed-linked bonds can be poor stores of wealth in times of high inflation. The risk of not owning this type of protection is particularly acute when inflation is unanticipated and thus not adequately reflected in current yields. Figure 6.7 provides an example. Investors in both high-quality, short-dated bonds and cash suffered losses to purchasing power of 25% or so during the 1970s. Holders of cash, even before tax, lost more than 10% of their purchasing power in the three years to 2014.

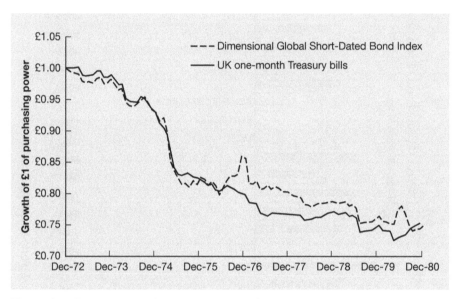

Figure 6.7 The dangers of high, unanticipated inflation

Index-linked gilts is an asset class that helps to manage the erosion of purchasing power inherent in defensive assets. As such it makes a very important contribution to any multi-asset class, diversified investment portfolio.

> 'Because expected inflation varies over time, conventional, non-indexed (nominal) Treasury bonds are not safe in real terms; and because short-term real interest rates vary over time, Treasury bills are not safe assets for long-term investors. Inflation-indexed bonds fill this gap by offering a truly riskless long-term investment.'[6]

6   Campbell, J.Y., Shiller, R.J. and Viceira, L.M. (2009) 'Understanding inflation-indexed bond markets,' *Brookings Papers on Economic Activity*.

Conventional long-dated gilts

Not recommended for risk-averse investors with long-term horizons or moderate equity allocations, but could be useful for those with significant equity exposure who feel that deflation is more likely in the future.

As I've already explained, and particularly at the more aggressive, equity-orientated end of the risk spectrum, fixed interest's role is primarily that of a diversifier against times of equity market trauma and financial crisis. In this role, and despite normally positive correlations to equities, at times of equity market trauma high-quality bonds (such as UK gilts) have the potential, although not the certainty, of acting as havens of safety and liquidity, with commensurate positive consequences for yields (downwards) and prices (upwards). Gilts with a long time to maturity (known as long duration) magnify this positive effect.

When the market anticipates mild positive inflation in the future, the yield on gilts usually is higher for gilts maturing later than those maturing sooner. Thus gilts with six months to maturity should normally yield less than those with five years to maturity. This makes sense as investors require a higher return on longer maturities to compensate for the potential risk of higher inflation. Thus if we plotted on a graph the redemption yields (the total return from holding the gilt until maturity) on all gilts, starting with the shortest duration to the longest duration, and joined up the plots, we would see a line that slopes upwards over time. This is referred to as a normal yield curve (see Figure 6.8).

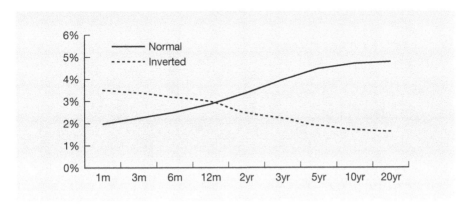

Figure 6.8 The bond yield curve

However, if the market anticipates a fall in inflation in the future, perhaps because a recession is expected, the yield on longer-dated gilts will fall, possibly below that of the shorter-dated ones, which will rise. This is known as an inverted yield curve and is characterised by interest rates on accessible deposit accounts yielding much more than long-term gilts, as happened in 2007–2008. Investing in conventional long-term gilts when the yield curve is inverted would be a very unwise thing for an investor to do if they had other alternatives.

Sometimes technical factors can cause the yield curve to move in a way that is not in line with the inflation outlook. For example, several years ago, due to changes in the rules on how certain big pension funds calculated their liabilities, such schemes were forced to invest a lot more in long-term gilts to match their long-term liabilities, thus causing a fall in the yield on long-term gilts, even though long-term inflation was still a threat.

Long-term bonds experience higher volatility than short-dated bonds (since the range of possible inflation outcomes over the next 30 years is greater than that over the next five), as illustrated in Figure 6.9, and the distribution of annual returns on the downside means there is also a higher likelihood of suffering a large loss. Over this period, the standard deviation was 2% for short-dated gilts and 9% for long-dated gilts. The maturity risk premium relates to the difference in returns between owning UK Treasury bills and long-term gilts in compensation for the additional uncertainty that comes with owning longer-dated issues.

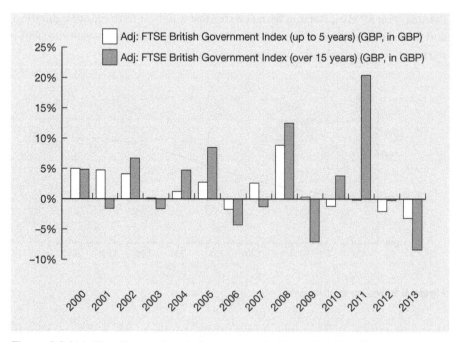

Figure 6.9 Volatility of longer dated gilts compared with short-dated gilts
Source: FTSE Group.

These factors, together with the poor inflation protection provided, mean that long-dated conventional gilts are not recommended for risk-averse investors with limited human capital (the ability to earn income or generate wealth through their own efforts), low allocation to equities and who are looking to preserve their investment capital in real terms. They are, however, potentially useful for those with high equity allocations and who wish to hedge against future deflation (falling prices).

National Savings Certificates

Recommended as proxy for cash or short-dated fixed income.

National Savings products are 100% backed by the UK Treasury and as such offer the highest level of capital protection available. The range and competitiveness of products changes from time to time based on market conditions and the level of funds required by the UK government. Over the past five years National Savings has withdrawn most of its most attractive savings products as they had been too successful in attracting funds for the government. Existing maturing products are permitted to be reinvested and new products can be expected to be launched early in each financial year as the government resets its borrowing targets. However, given the negative real yields on existing index-linked gilts and the very low yield on recent new issues, raising money through new Savings Certificates would be very expensive for the UK government, so it is unlikely for the foreseeable future.

Index/LIBOR-linked high-quality corporate bonds

Not recommended for risk-averse investors due to equity-type risks.

In recent years big companies like Royal Bank of Scotland, Barclays and Tesco have issued a type of corporate bond that pays the higher of a minimum yield (typically 3–4% p.a.) or the increase in either the Retail Prices Index (RPI) or the London InterBank Offered Rate (LIBOR – basically the variable interest rate that banks charge for lending each other funds).

While on the face of it these issues appear to offer the best of both worlds, a minimum fixed rate of interest and protection against rising inflation or interest rates, you are effectively taking on the risk that your capital could be wiped out if the issuing company goes bust or seeks to reorganise its balance sheet as a result of financial difficulties. Remember that risk and return are related. If something pays a higher return – in this case higher than index-linked gilts – then it comes with higher risk.

While the risk of a large quoted company going bust or suffering financial pressures might seem to be low, it is much higher than for UK gilts – one only needs to reflect on what happened to RBS a few years ago. In addition, the bondholder will receive only the original capital back as and when the bond matures, which is likely to be between 10 and 15 years from issue. If the holding is sold in the market before maturity, the price will be determined by the yield on the bond, which is influenced by both the economic conditions at the time and the financial strength of the company behind the bonds.

Permanent interest-bearing shares (PIBS)

Not recommended due to capital risks.

These are securities issued by building societies, usually at relatively high fixed rates of interest (although a small number of issues pay variable interest), which are quoted on the stock market. PIBS have no maturity date, although with some issues the society can redeem the PIBS early on a certain specified date. The two principal risks of PIBS are that the investor may not get all or any of their capital back if the building society gets into financial difficulty or goes bust, and the capital value of the PIBS will fluctuate in line with supply and demand for the holding based on prevailing economic and investment conditions. Gains and losses arising on disposal are not chargeable or allowable for capital gains tax purposes. If a building society demutualises with PIBS in issue, these become perpetual subordinated bonds (PSBs).

We've seen that there is insufficient return premium to compensate for the additional risk of holding one company's bonds. This point was starkly illustrated by the emergency nationalisation of Bradford & Bingley plc in September 2008. Under the terms of the nationalisation, interest payments to bondholders, i.e. those holding PSBs, were cancelled and no repayments of capital will be made until the bank has fully repaid the £14 billion owed to the Financial Services Compensation Scheme and the £4 billion owed to the government, with interest. It is likely to be many years before bondholders will know how much, if any, payment they will receive.

High-yield bonds, lower credit quality bonds, convertible preference shares, convertible bonds, emerging market bonds

Not recommended due to uncompensated equity-type risks.

Figure 6.10 indicates that owning longer-dated lower credit quality bonds appears to hold little appeal, unless you are an active investment manager with great timing skills. Figure 6.11 shows how the default rates on bonds by US corporations go up in times of extreme market trauma, illustrating how long-term investors have to weigh up the reward of a slightly higher yield against a much higher probability of loss of capital arising from default by the company issuing the bond.

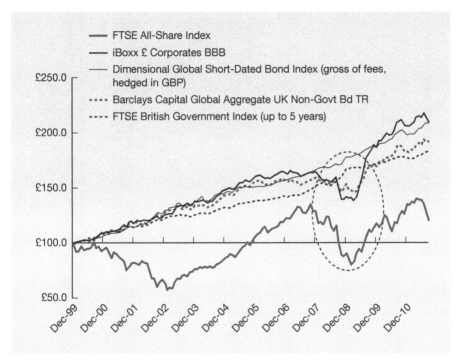

Figure 6.10 Intermediate investment-grade bond performance
Source: Albion Strategic.

Because risk-averse investors in a diversified, multi-asset portfolio allocate capital to bonds to reduce risk, it doesn't make sense to include in the portfolio any of the above bond-type investments, because they represent a similar risk to equities but without the same level of upside. Any available risk 'budget' would be better allocated to equities for a higher expected return. For this reason these bond investments are not recommended.

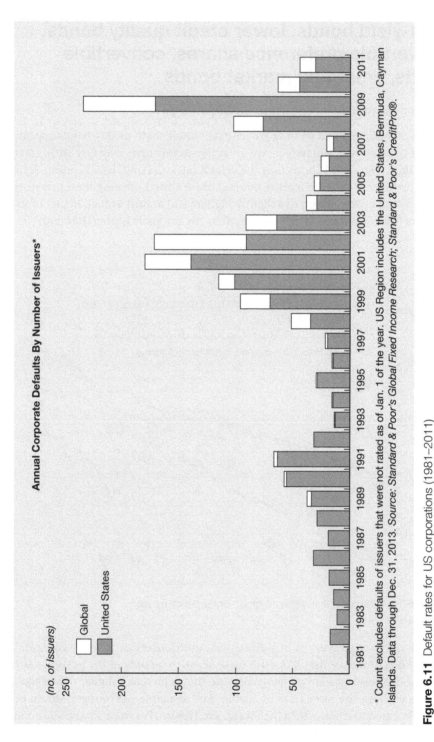

Figure 6.11 Default rates for US corporations (1981–2011)

Source: Vazza, D., Kraemer, N., Gunter, E., *Default, Transition and Recovery: 2011 Annual US Corporate Default Study and Rating Transitions,* 23 March 2012. Published by Standard & Poor's Ratings Services, a division of The McGraw-Hill companies, Inc.

Equities

'If inflation continues to soar, you're going to have to work like a dog just to live like one.'

George Gobel, American comedian

The role of equities in your portfolio is as a core return generator, which manifests itself through dividends and earnings growth. As illustrated in Figure 6.12, equities have historically offered the highest long-term return and inflation protection of all the asset classes. However, this higher return comes with high volatility and uncertainty, which has a greater variation over shorter time periods, i.e. less than 20 years.

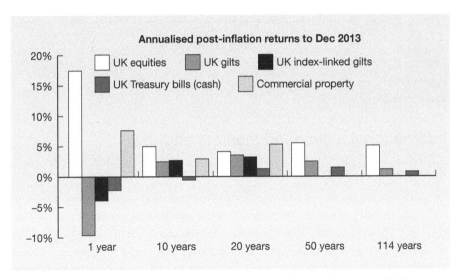

Figure 6.12 Post-inflation investment returns by asset class to December 2013
Source: Barclays Equity Gilt Study 2014.

Equities represent ownership in businesses and as such offer the opportunity for investors to participate in current and future profits generated by those businesses. Profits are either paid out by way of dividends or retained by the company to reinvest with a view to grow profits further. Either way, over the long term, investors expect to earn a significant premium over and above the return that they could earn from risk-free assets, such as cash. As I explained in Chapter 5, this extra return is known as the equity risk premium (ERP). Figure 6.13 sets out the historic probability of equities outperforming cash and bonds over various time periods, with 18 years being the shortest time period for almost certain probability of outperformance.

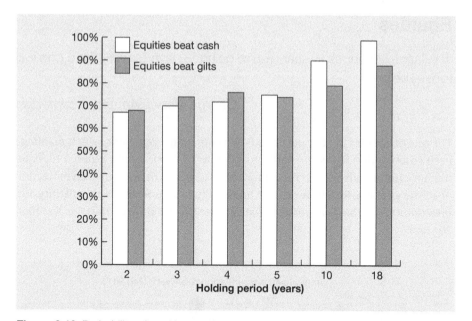

Figure 6.13 Probability of equities producing higher returns than cash or gilts
Source: Barclays Equity Gilt Study 2014.

International developed markets equities

Recommended as a core return provider and diversifier.

There should be no excess return available from international developed markets over the UK stock market as there is no additional systematic risk. Those overseas countries should experience similar rates of economic growth to the UK and that should lead to similar rates of earnings growth by overseas companies in developed markets. In addition, international companies have a similar cost of capital to UK companies. The primary reason to allocate some of the equity exposure to overseas developed markets is to provide additional diversification. Table 6.2 shows the historical returns from developed markets over various periods.

'In the long run, stock markets in Germany, Japan and the United Kingdom ought to generate returns similar to those of the United States, while exposing investors to similar risk levels.'[7]

David F. Swensen, Chief Investment Officer, Yale University

---

[7] Swensen, D.F. (2000) *Pioneering Portfolio Management: An unconventional approach to institutional investment*, The Free Press, p. 113.

Table 6.2 Developed market annualised real returns

Market	Since 1900	Since 1964	Since 2000
UK equities	5.3%	6.0%	1.2%
US equities	6.5%	5.8%	1.8%
Global equities	5.2%	5.4%	1.7%

Source: Dimson, E., Marsh, P. and Staunton, M., Credit Suisse, pp. 59–61 *Global Investment Returns Yearbook 2014*, Credit Suisse, 59–61. Returns are quoted in GBP for UK equities and USD for US and global equities.

Emerging markets equities

Recommended as a return enhancer and diversifier.

Emerging market companies are those located in parts of the world that are still rapidly developing and are characterised by young and growing populations, rising living standards, increasing access to education and development of infrastructure. While some emerging countries have established democracies, many have less stable regimes or controlled economies. Emerging countries include big states such as Brazil, Russia, India and China (the so-called 'BRICS') and small states like Vietnam, Malaysia and South Africa (see Figure 6.14). Although the growth rates of these countries has been, and is expected to be, higher than developed countries like the US and the UK, they are also much riskier. Sometimes governments impose restrictions on investors accessing their investments, seize ownership of industrial assets or impose unexpected tariffs or taxes.

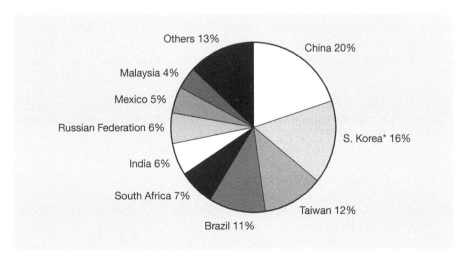

Figure 6.14 Emerging markets by capitalisation
Source: Data from MSCI January 2014. *Excluded in FTSE EM indices.

Emerging market equities offer two key benefits. First, investors expect higher long-term returns from these markets to reflect both the higher levels of growth generated by countries that are developing from agricultural to industrial and service-based economies, and as compensation for the higher level of risks involved (i.e. political, currency, legal, liquidity and higher costs). The second benefit is that emerging markets provide additional diversification because the economies of many emerging countries, and as a result their stock markets, often move out of sync with developed markets. Although this lower level of correlation (the degree to which an asset class acts more or less like another asset class) has been narrowing, recent research confirms that the benefits of diversification remain.[8]

The return history of emerging markets is considerably shorter than that of developed markets, making any firm inferences difficult. Figure 6.15 shows that emerging markets are significantly more volatile than global equities. Over the period 1988 to 2013 emerging markets returned an annualised 12.68% p.a. compared with developed world markets' return of 8.48%. The outcome is, however, sensitive to start and end dates. For example, for the 34 years to the end of 2009, emerging markets, as measured by the S&P IFCG Composite Index (S&P Emerging plus BMI index from 2008), delivered an annualised return of 9.5% versus global equities (MSCI World Index) of 10.6%.[9] Respected academics suggest that the return from emerging and developed/world markets over the 114 years to the end of 2013 was 7.4% and 8.3% respectively.[10]

While some academics think that emerging markets will offer a risk premium (i.e. a higher return for the additional volatility) over world markets of about 1.5% p.a.,[11] estimates made by Yale University Endowment Fund, one of the leading institutional investors,[12] and JP Morgan Asset Management[13] suggest that it will be more like 2.5% p.a. with an estimated volatility of around 30%, a full 10% above their developed market equity risk assumption. By comparison, the historic volatility of emerging markets over the period shown in Figure 6.15 was 25%. As

---

[8]   Christofferson, P., Errunza, V.R., Jacobs, K. and Jin, X. (2010) 'Is the potential for international diversification disappearing?', available at **http://papers.ssrn.com/sol3/papers.cfm?abstract_id=1573345**

[9]   Dimson, E., Marsh, P. and Staunton, M. (2010) *Credit Suisse Global Investment Returns Yearbook 2010*, p. 8.

[10] Dimson, E., Marsh, P. and Staunton, M. (2014) *Credit Suisse Global Investment Returns Yearbook 2014*, p. 7.

[11] Dimson, E., Marsh, P. and Staunton, M. (2014) *Credit Suisse Global Investment Returns Yearbook 2014*, p. 15.

[12] Swenson, D.F. (2000) *Pioneering Portfolio Management*, The Free Press, p. 112.

[13] JP Morgan Asset Management Long-term Capital Market Assumptions 2013, available at **www.jpmorganinstitutional.com**

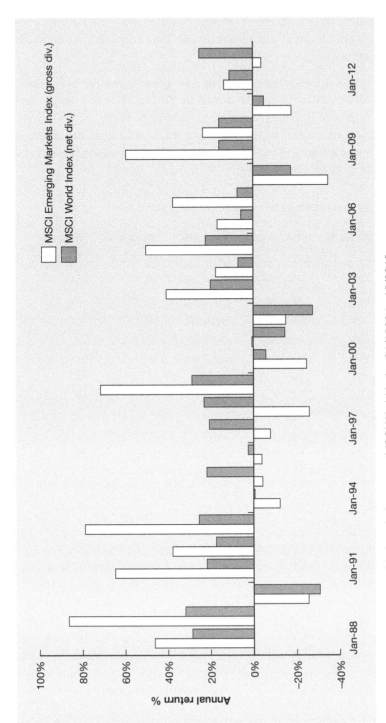

Figure 6.15 MSCI Emerging Markets Index versus MSCI World Index 01/1988 to 12/2013

Source: Data from MSCI Barra.

we'll see in Chapters 10 and 11, many emerging market investment funds have very high charges, which can eat up any return premium that might be delivered through this asset class.

Because we know that risk and return are related, we need to consider the elevated risks that come with investing in emerging markets. Table 6.3 provides insight into the short-term falls seen in emerging market stocks since 1988. Such falls have been severe and frequent and as an investor you need to be aware of this, particularly at times when emerging markets have experienced very strong returns and look like a tempting investment prospect.

Table 6.3 Emerging market equity falls >10% from 1988 to 2014

Peak date	Decline %	Trough date	Recovery date	Decline (m)	Recovery (m)
Aug 1994	−58%	Aug 1993	Feb 2005	48	78
Oct 2007	−45%	Nov 1988	Dec 2009	13	13
Jul 1990	−32%	Nov 1990	Mar 1991	4	4
Mar 1992	−25%	Aug 1992	Oct 1992	5	2
Oct 2010	−21%	Sep 2011	Feb 2013	9	6
Jan 1994	−15%	Jun 1994	Aug 1994	5	2
Feb 2013	−15%	Jan 2014	N/A	11	–
Apr 2006	−13%	May 2006	Dec 2006	1	7
Feb 1990	−12%	Mar 1990	May 1990	1	2
May 1989	−12%	Jul 1989	Sep 1989	2	2

Source: Data from MSCI Emerging Markets Gross Return in GBP. Morningstar, Inc. All rights reserved. Reproduced with permission.

Notwithstanding the historical risk and reward argument, with western countries' economic growth lagging and populations ageing, some commentators have suggested that investors should allocate a lot more of their capital to emerging countries with faster growth prospects and reduce their weighting to the US and other main developed markets. The investment industry has certainly been busy launching new funds based on this premise and the story certainly sounds compelling. However, the investment opportunity is not the same as the economic opportunity. Take a look at Figure 6.16, which ranks the top 20 countries by gross domestic product (GDP). The US is currently ranked number 1, with China ranked 2, India 3, Russia 6 and Brazil 9. The UK is currently clinging on to 8th place

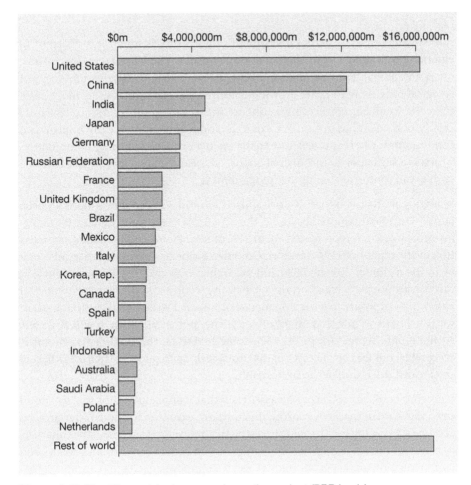

Figure 6.16 Top 20 countries by gross domestic product (PPP basis)
Source: World Bank 2012

(narrowly beaten by France), but predictions[14] are for this to slip to 15th place by 2020 while the BRIC countries will all be within the top 7 positions, behind the US in first place. By contrast, emerging markets economies represented around 38% of global GDP at the end of 2010 and are estimated to overtake the output of developed markets before 2020.[15] More than 65% of the world's population lives in the emerging economies.

Let's now look at the country weights of the world market capitalisation (free float) data in Figure 6.17. This illustrates the true investment opportunities for global investors, taking into account any restrictions imposed locally on foreign

---

[14] Centre for Economics and Business Research (2010) 'Global prospects report'.
[15] The Economist (2011) 'Emerging vs. developed economies,' 4 August.

share ownership. The actual investment opportunity is somewhat different for emerging economies from their economic output. The UK market, by contrast, offers a much larger investment market than the BRIC countries combined. This is logical because with faster growing countries the economies grow much faster than the financial markets that support them. Emerging economies are not a clearly homogeneous group. For example, India and China are big importers of commodities, whereas Brazil and Russia are big exporters of those commodities. China is a big exporter of finished goods, whereas India mainly exports services such as call centres and computer programming.

Emerging markets capitalisation stands at around 30% on a non-float-adjusted basis.[16] On a float-adjusted basis, i.e. the actual stocks that are available for foreign investors to own, it represented about 11% of total global equity market capitalisation at the end of 2013.[17] However, Goldman Sachs has estimated that this could be in the region of 20% by 2020 and more than 30% by 2030. If you weight your investment portfolio based on the GDP of the world economy, you'll end up with a very high exposure to emerging markets compared with a market capitalisation-weighted basis. While that might offer a higher potential return, it will also come with a much higher risk profile. For some investors, that higher risk might be acceptable, but for the majority of investors, seeking to preserve their wealth, such an elevated risk is unlikely to be desirable.

Emerging markets are a separate asset class that complement, not replace, developed investment market exposure. In addition, exposure to these faster-growing economies is achieved through investment in developed market stock markets, to the extent that some of the companies within them derive revenue from activity in emerging market economies. A recent estimate suggests that around 16% of earnings in FTSE 100 companies comes from emerging markets.[18] For example, BHP Billiton, which is a member of the UK FTSE 100 Index, is the world's largest mining company and a significant proportion of its global revenue comes from China. Imperial Tobacco, another FTSE 100 listed company, now derives a large amount of its revenue from China and the Far East.

Although in times of extreme market turbulence, as happened in 2007–2009, emerging markets experience similar falls, over longer time periods they can be much more volatile than developed markets. For this reason your allocation to emerging markets should be moderate in the expectation, but not the guarantee, that there may be additional returns and a lowering of overall risk to the portfolio.

---

[16] Ernst & Young (2013) 'Moving toward the mainstream' found at **www.ey.com**

[17] Source: Market cap data is free-float adjusted from Bloomberg Securities Data, 31 December 2013.

[18] Credit Suisse (2013) *Global Equity Strategy 2014*, December, p. 65.

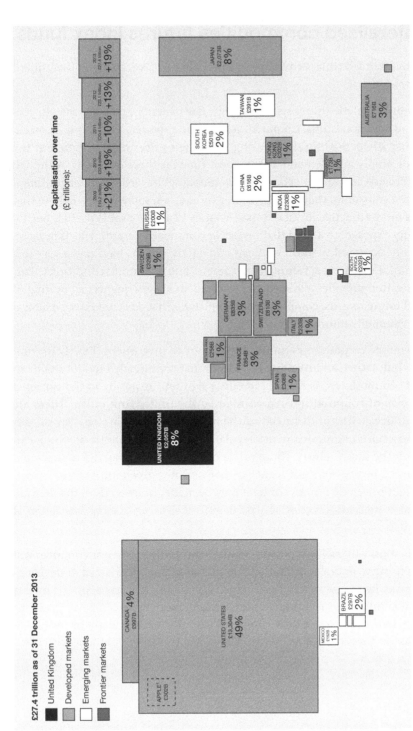

Figure 6.17 World market capitalisation

Source: Dimensional Fund Advisors. In British pounds. Market cap data is free-float adjusted from Bloomberg securities data. Many nations not displayed. Totals may not equal 100% due to rounding.

Collateralised commodities futures index funds

Not recommended unless investors are prepared to give up some investment return for lower risk.

Commodities include things such as energy, raw materials, precious metals, gem stones and basic foodstuffs. Commodities have no expected return and no mechanism (like dividends) for distributing one. Their prices merely represent the impact of supply and demand at any given time for these materials. Although equities provide an implicit exposure to commodities by virtue of their consumption by the companies that are represented by equities, some experts believe that it can be more attractive for risk-averse investors to allocate some of their portfolio's equity exposure to a fund that invests in commodity futures. This is because, historically, commodity futures returns and equity returns have had a very low correlation, i.e. they react differently to news and economic conditions. This low correlation provides a lowering of risk and, as a consequence, a lowering of expected future returns, compared with a portfolio that does not have an allocation to commodity futures.

A collateralised commodities futures fund is not an investment directly in commodities but, rather, an investment in a fund that continually buys futures in an index of commodities. As such it presents a synthetic exposure to the expected future price of commodities represented by the underlying index. There are several indices with funds linked to them and they can have significant differences in both composition and rebalancing frequency, both of which can impact on the index return. Those prices can and do react rapidly to news and there can be periods of significant positive and negative returns to investors. The current price of a futures contract may be higher or lower than the delivery price and as such futures contracts are described as being in either contango or backwardation.

Backwardation will lead to a positive return contribution, whereas contango will lead to a negative return contribution. There is additional risk related to the counterparty, usually an investment bank, which is providing the return on the futures index, and, unlike a conventional index-tracking fund, there can be a significant difference in the return of a fund compared with that of its underlying index. For these reasons, these are not recommended, unless you are comfortable with these additional risks.

Global commercial property – real estate investment trusts (REITs)

Recommended as a core return provider and diversifier.

As pointed out in the Talmud a few thousand years ago, property has always been an integral part of a sensible investment strategy. As an asset class, property has a low correlation with equities and bonds. This is primarily because property performance is usually linked to rental value growth, which is in turn linked to economic growth, unlike the earnings of non-property companies that are less correlated to economic growth.[19]

REITs are property investment companies that pass their income directly to shareholders and thus avoid corporation tax. They have been around in one form or another for about 25 years, but have seen most growth in the last ten years. REIT details vary across global markets but broadly follow the same principles. A UK REIT is exempt from tax on profits arising from property rental, subject to 90% of the income of the tax-exempt business being distributed to shareholders within 12 months of the end of the accounting period. A further condition is that 75% or more of its assets must be investment property and 75% or more of its income must be rental income.[20] Figure 6.18 shows how REITs are distributed globally.

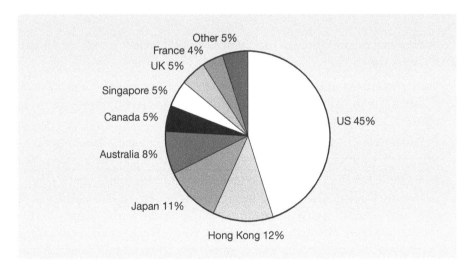

Figure 6.18 Global REIT exposure by geography
Source: Data from FTSE EPRA/NAREIT Developed Real Estate Index 31/12/2012.

---

[19]   UBS (2006) Pension Fund Indicators 2006.

[20]   HMRC, found at: **www.hmrc.gov.uk/pbr2006/pbrn3.htm**

Figure 6.19 illustrates the correlation between global REITs and global equities using three-year rolling periods. Exposure to commercial property was highly beneficial to investors in 2000–2002, but the benefits were less evident in 2007–2009 as the correlation, like most risky assets during the credit crisis, rose significantly. Diversification benefits are not consistent.

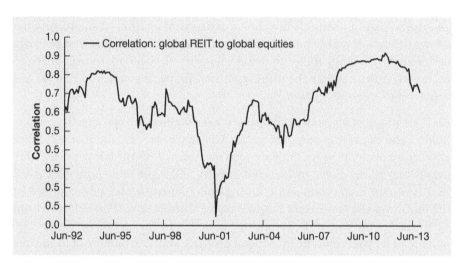

Figure 6.19 Rolling three-year correlation 1989–2013
Source: Albion Strategic.

Recent research supports the diversification benefits of including REITs in a multi-asset class portfolio:

- 'Since real estate indices are not found to be co-integrated with the US stock market, REITs are likely to bring equivalent long-term diversification benefits to a stock portfolio as direct real estate.'[21]

- 'In the short term, REITs tend to move in line with equities. But over longer periods, REIT returns tend to be positively correlated with real estate returns and lowly-correlated, even negatively correlated at points, with equity returns.'[22]

- 'As investors look to diversify risk in their multi-asset portfolio, allocations to listed real estate allow a balance of property exposure across country, sector and markets in an efficient and cost-effective way. The liquid nature of listed real estate also enables the investor to spread risk across property management teams, tenant profile and industry.'[23]

[21] Oikarinen, E., Hoesli, M. and Serrano, C. (2009) 'Linkages between direct and securitized real estate,', Swiss Finance Institute Research, available at **ssrn.com/abstract=1427794**

[22] JP Morgan Asset Management (2012) 'The role of REITs in a portfolio: A "core" plus real estate allocation'.

[23] EPRA Research (2009) 'Real estate equities – real estate or equities?'

The expected return from property is somewhere between bonds and equities. This is because rental income provides regular cashflow like bonds and, as that rent rises, so should the capital value, similar to equities. However, this generalisation masks the fact that there is a range of different types of property, with differing risk–return profiles. Property that is let to a very high-quality tenant on a long, upward-only lease will act more like a bond. Property that is let on very short tenancies, such as hotels, will act more like equities in that the capital value fluctuates in line with rental income based on the demand for rooms. That demand in turn is affected by economic conditions.

If commercial property as a whole has a risk–return profile that is between a bond (with a 2% p.a. real return) and an equity (with a 5% p.a. real return), the midpoint is half the difference between them, i.e. 1.5%. Adding 1.5% to the 2% real return from bonds gives a reasonably conservative estimate of future expected returns from unleveraged commercial property of circa 3.5% p.a. over inflation. Thus commercial property provides an effective hedge against unexpected inflation. It is also easier to borrow to fund property investment, which can increase (and decrease) overall returns.

Although REIT data series covering US property, e.g. NAREIT (National Association of Real Estate Investment Trusts®), are longer, the return history for global REITs starts in July 1989. The correlation of global REITs to UK equities over this period has been about 0.5. As illustrated in Figure 6.20, during the period December 1990 to December 2013 the global REIT index delivered a nominal return of 8.5%, which was just above the UK equity markets return. In addition, over the same time period, the return pattern of global commercial property had no relationship to that of UK residential property, as illustrated in Figure 6.21.

Recent academic research[24] supports the contention that how commercial property is held, whether directly, by a fund or owned by a REIT, has little effect on return and volatility in the long term on an unleveraged basis. After all, the underlying properties are unchanged by their ownership structure:

- 'The result is clear – listed real estate performance is significantly influenced by the direct real estate market over the medium to long-term . . . This conclusion suggests that an investment in listed property delivers the accepted security, appreciation and inflation hedge characteristics of bricks and mortar.'[25]

- 'Over most five-year periods, changes in real estate prices have played a huge role in determining what happened to REIT prices.'[26]

---

[24] Hoesli, M. and Oikarinen, E. (2012) 'Are REITs real estate? Evidence from international sector level data,' Swiss Finance Institute Research Paper Series No. 12–15.

[25] EPRA Research (2009) 'Real estate equities – real estate or equities?'.

[26] Green Street Advisors (2011) 'The wrapper doesn't matter', July.

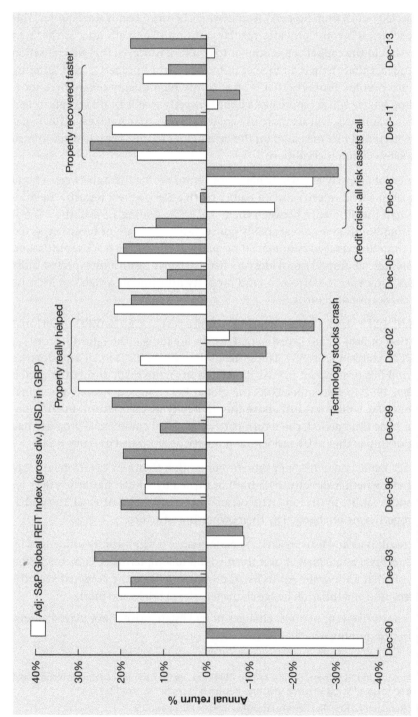

Figure 6.20 Global REITs versus UK equity returns (after inflation) 1990 to 2013

Source: Data from FTSE All-Share, S&P Global REIT Index.

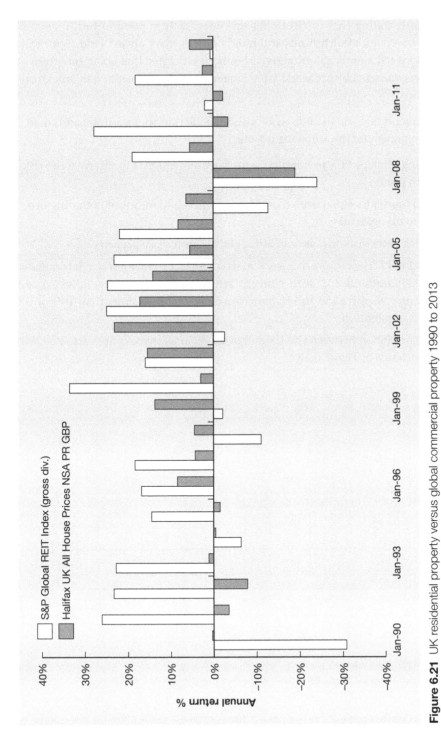

Figure 6.21 UK residential property versus global commercial property 1990 to 2013

Source: Data from Halifax UK All House Price Index from Morningstar Encorr. All rights reserved.

It is worth stating that institutional investors, such as pension funds, endowments, sovereign wealth funds and family offices, have always held significant allocations to commercial property. It has been estimated that about one-third of the assets managed by the world's 100 largest asset management companies focus on property.[27]

I recommend that you include an allocation to REITs in your portfolio and adopt a global approach for the following reasons:

- Adding global REITs to a multi-factor portfolio appears to improve the risk–return profile.

- A REIT provides a practical, cost-effective and liquid means of obtaining exposure to this asset class.

- The UK represents only around 5% of global commercial property.

- Limiting REITs exposure to the UK market restricts an investor to a low number of REITs (around 20), with concentration risks in a few large ones – Land Securities, British Land and Hammerson alone represent more than 40% of UK REIT capitalisation.

- The correlation between the UK and other regional markets appears to be low, as illustrated by Figure 6.22.

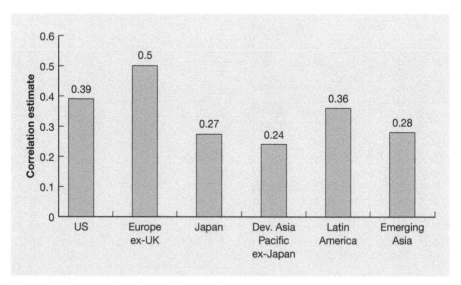

Figure 6.22 Low regional correlation to UK property

Source: Data from Morgan Stanley (2011) 'The rationale for investing in global real estate'.

---

[27] Towers Watson as quoted in 'Real estate: Investors build on the diversity of the property market', 7 July 2013, **www.ft.com**

CHAPTER 7
SOCIALLY RESPONSIBLE AND IMPACT INVESTING

'Not everything that can be counted, counts; and not everything that counts can be counted.'

Albert Einstein

Ethical and moral principles have always influenced and guided a proportion of investors and businesses. The Quakers are a good example of a religious group whose principles included opposition to slavery, alcohol and war, and support for prison reform and social justice. Quaker-founded businesses include Barclays, Cadbury, Clarks, Friends Provident, Lloyds and Rowntree, all of which had a long tradition of ethical and fair treatment of their employees and the communities in which they operated.

Increasingly, investors, both private and institutions, are questioning the impact that some businesses and their activities are having on the environment and on society. These investors do not want to support companies that are contributing to environmental degradation, or whose activities are unethical, unjust or unsustainable. More recently, the global financial crisis, increasing global inequality and clever tax planning by multinational companies have created further momentum for a reform of the way capitalism operates. Socially responsible investing (SRI), which is also known as sustainable and responsible investing, broadly refers to any investment strategy that seeks to consider both financial return and social good. There are many different types of SRI but unfortunately no clear consensus of what the myriad different terms mean (see Figure 7.1).

There is, however, consensus that there are three main advocacy issues within SRI: social, environmental and ethical (SEE risks) or environmental, social and corporate governance (ESG risks), as set out in Figure 7.2. According to the European

Figure 7.1 Socially responsible investing descriptions

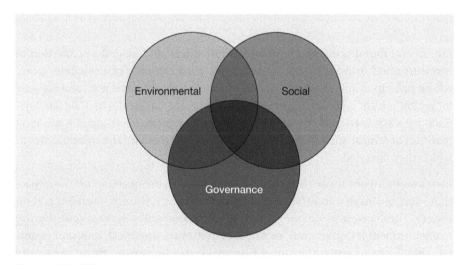

Figure 7.2 ESG framework

Sustainable Investment Forum (Eurosif), SRI is implemented mainly through investment analysis, portfolio construction, shareholder advocacy and community investing. Sustainable investing is generally regarded as covering environmental, social and governance categories; ethical and impact investing fall within the social category; and shareholder advocacy falls within the governance category.

Although the SRI sector has been around in one form or another for about 100 years, it is in the past 30 years or so that it has seen the strongest growth and most innovation. An entire industry of advisers, fund managers, research groups and experts has emerged to provide appropriate investment solutions incorporating these environmental, social and ethical concerns. While SRI has been established in the US for longer, the capital invested via SRI funds is actually higher in Europe and has been growing at a much higher rate than the entire fund universe, as illustrated in Figure 7.3.

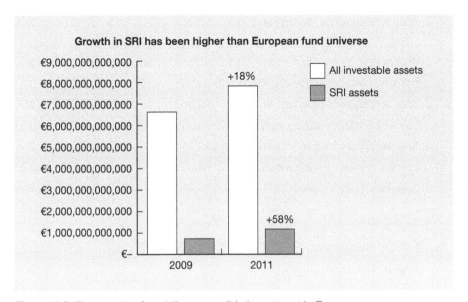

Figure 7.3 The growth of socially responsible investment in Europe

Source: Data from RBC Wealth Management and Capgemini (2012) 2012 World Wealth Report; EUROSIF (2012) 'High net worth individuals and sustainable investment 2012', p. 9.

In the early days of SRI, most investment solutions were solely focused on applying strict ethical criteria as an initial screen to the quoted equity market. Negative criteria means the company is engaged in an activity that does not meet the ethical screen, for example arms manufacturing, tobacco or gambling, and is therefore excluded from the fund manager's range of permitted investments. A positive screen, meanwhile, identifies those companies that score highly on a range of desired criteria, such as combating climate change, excellent corporate governance, or providing new technology or services that have a positive impact on society. An example of positive and negative ethical screening criteria is shown in the box.

Positive criteria

Supplying the basic necessities of life, for example healthy food, housing, clothing, water, energy, communication, healthcare, public transport, safety, personal finance, education

Offering product choices for ethical and sustainable lifestyles, for example fair trade, organic

Improving quality of life through the responsible use of new technologies

Good environmental management

Actively addressing climate change, for example, renewable energy, energy efficiency

Promotion and protection of human rights

Good employment practices

Positive impact on local communities

Good relations with customers and suppliers

Effective anti-corruption controls

Transparent communication

Negative criteria

Tobacco production

Alcohol production

Gambling

Pornography or violent material

Manufacture and sale of weapons

Unnecessary exploitation of animals

Nuclear power generation

Poor environmental practices

Human rights abuses

Poor relations with employees, customers or suppliers

By its very nature, ethical (social) screening involves a high degree of subjectivity, as evidenced by this caveat in the ethical guidelines of one leading ethical fund: 'We recognise that Stewardship's core aim of investing only in those companies which, in what they do and the way they do it, on balance make a positive contribution to society cannot be fully captured in the policies described here.

Accordingly, we may on rare occasions exclude companies which we judge conflict with that aim even when they do not fall foul of any of the negative criteria set out in this document. We may also on rare occasions where a company is considered, on balance, to make a positive contribution to society, include a company that breaches a negative investment selection criterion in a minor, inconsequential or non-material way.'[1]

It is essential, therefore, to carefully review the ethical filtering criteria of any ethical fund, to ensure that it does, in fact, reflect your own ethical views, because what is acceptable to one person might not be to someone else.

Thematic or trend investing

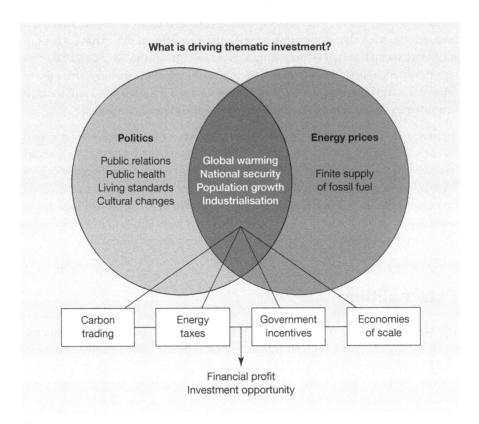

Figure 7.4 Thematic factors and concepts
Source: Blue & Green Investor.

---

[1] Friends Life, 'Stewardship criteria & policies' p. 2.

The SRI industry has evolved over the past decade with more of a focus on thematic investing to which an ethical screen may or may not be applied. Thematic funds typically invest in companies that are meeting a specific human need, such as clean energy/water, or positioning the fund to benefit from global trends such as rising population or climate change (see Figure 7.4). The main thematic funds are water, clean energy, environment, carbon, agriculture and forestry. Some funds invest in more than one of these themes and are known as multi-thematic funds.

Figure 7.5 is an informative and visual representation of the various global risks to human prosperity and how they are interconnected. It is against this backdrop that thematic managers try to spot the trends, opportunities, challenges, emerging thinking and future innovations, which could avoid or reduce these risks, while also generating good financial returns for investors. The majority of thematic and multi-thematic funds focus on environmental factors and criteria when deciding how to choose investments, and this makes it easier to define, screen and measure the underlying selection criteria than an ethical fund that focuses on subjective social issues. It is interesting to note that since 2013 all UK-listed companies have had an obligation to report their greenhouse gas emissions. There are no universal standards for assessing SRI investments for a thematic fund and much of this involves labour-intensive, time-consuming and expensive research.

By their very nature, thematic funds generally have a much higher exposure to smaller companies and/or companies based or operating in emerging markets. In addition, they typically have a much smaller number of underlying securities, leading to less diversification and increased risk compared with most conventional investment funds. Unlike a traditional investment fund, where we can look at past returns and risk characteristics, it is difficult, if not impossible, to determine what the risk–return characteristics of, say, a water or clean energy fund will be.

Externalities

The body of literature on externalities is huge and even efficient markets proponents like Eugene Fama and Ken French embrace the existence of them and accept that capital markets don't price the environmental cost of their activities such as greenhouse gas emissions, water use, land use, air pollution, land and water pollution and waste. As a result, world stock market values may well be overstated relative to what they should be, if such environmental costs were included.

A good example of an unpriced externality is carbon. Many experts believe that the cost of releasing carbon is not correctly factored into energy companies' costs. Research suggests that we need to hold the increase in global temperature to

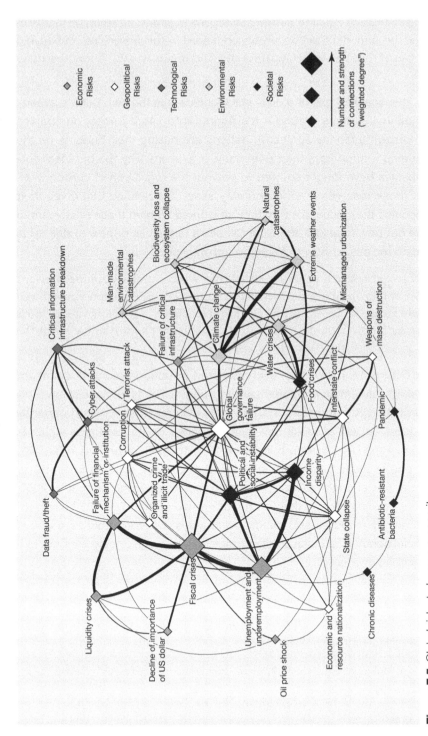

Figure 7.5 Global risks to human prosperity

Source: World Economic Forum.

2°C. This increase is equal to burning about 565 gigatons of carbon until 2050.[2] However, the amount of carbon already contained in the proven coal and oil and gas reserves of the fossil-fuel companies and countries is actually almost five times as much – 2,795.[3]

> 'Yes, this coal and gas and oil is still technically in the soil. But it's already economically above ground – it's figured into share prices, companies are borrowing money against it, nations are basing their budgets on the presumed returns from their patrimony. It explains why the big fossil-fuel companies have fought so hard to prevent the regulation of carbon dioxide – those reserves are their primary asset, the holding that gives their companies their value. It's why they've worked so hard these past years to figure out how to unlock the oil in Canada's tar sands, or how to drill miles beneath the sea, or how to frack the Appalachians.'[4]

Another recent research paper suggested that 'a precautionary approach means only 20% of total fossil fuel reserves can be burnt to 2050'.[5] This concept is shown visually in Figure 7.6, based on 50% and 80% probability of reaching various levels of warming for given levels of carbon. The researcher had this to say about the impact of carbon on the UK stock market:

> 'The CO2 potential of the reserves listed in London alone account for 18.7% of the remaining global carbon budget. The financial carbon footprint of the UK is therefore 100 times its own reserves. London currently has 105.5 GtCO2 of fossil fuel reserves listed on its exchange which is ten times the UK's carbon budget for 2011 to 2050, of around 10 GtCO2. Just one of the largest companies listed in London, such as Shell, BP or Xstrata, has enough reserves to use up the UK's carbon budget to 2050. With approximately one third of the total value of the FTSE 100 being represented by resource and mining companies, London's role as a global financial centre is at stake if these assets become unburnable en route to a low carbon economy.'

---

[2]   Meinshausen, M., Meinshausen, N., Hare, W., Raper, S. C. B., Frieler, K., Knutti, R., Frame, D. J. & Allen, M. Greenhouse gas emission targets for limiting global warming to2°C. Nature, doi: 10.1038/nature08017 (2009).

[3]   Leaton, J, 'Unburnable Carbon 2013: Wasted capital and stranded assets' – Carbon Tracker (2013).

[4]   *Rolling Stone* – 'Global Warming's Terrifying New Math' Bill McKibben 12.08.12.

[5]   Ibid footnote 3.

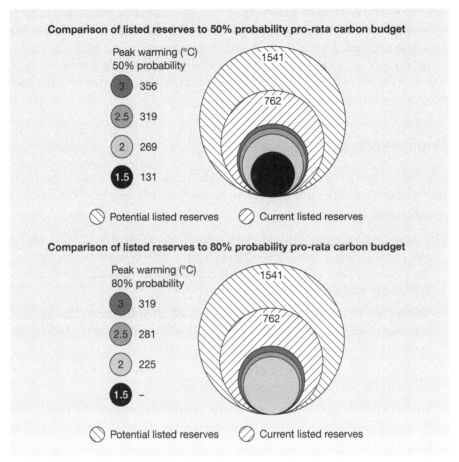

Figure 7.6 Unburnable carbon – listed carbon reserved compared with climate change maximum useable

Source: Carbon Tracker.

The majority of institutional investors and a minority (but growing) proportion of individual investors invest significant amounts in passive funds that track the UK and international stock markets. An even larger proportion invests in actively managed investment funds that are benchmarked against market indices. So, one way or another, most investors have significant exposure to companies that are valued on the basis of huge fossil fuel reserves, which may never be possible to use.

As we explored in Chapters 5 and 6, finance theory suggests that capital markets do a good enough (although not perfect) job of pricing risk and as such current prices should reflect all known information. If this is the case, how can it be that the world's brightest and cleverest people working in investment banks and fund management companies are not pricing the externalities associated with energy companies' assets which, based on the science, they can never use? Experts in this field have suggested various theories, but perhaps the main one, which intuitively might make sense, is the fact that the investment world is using flawed valuation metrics based on outdated business and economic models, and that have not been adapted to the new environmental reality.

Implications for investors

In my view there seem to be five possible approaches you could adopt to deal with the various externalities that investment markets don't or can't factor into current securities prices:

1   Maintain a traditional unfettered passive investment strategy and allocation, rebalancing as necessary in the light of market movements, on the basis that any repricing of risk will happen gradually over time and eventually be reflected in world stock market values.

2   Overweight the portfolio to thematic and multi-thematic funds that focus on alternative energy, forestry, clean water and other trends connected with the environment.

3   Allocate capital to private equity that invests in renewable energy and other innovations such as carbon capture and storage.

4   Invest in a passive portfolio that applies a sustainable investment screen.

5   Do a mixture of 1–4.

Before you decide on your approach we need to consider the potential role of a more recent innovation in the world of investing, that of sustainable investing.

Sustainability

While 'sustainability' may have different meanings to different people, the term is often associated with general concern for the environment. The United Nations describes sustainable development as 'development that meets the needs of the present without compromising the ability of future generations to meet their own needs'.[6] With this framework in mind, business practices that exhaust resources or cause irreversible changes to the earth's climate are considered unsustainable.

---

[6]   United Nations (1987) 'Report of the World Commission on Environment and Development', General Assembly Resolution 42/187, 11 December.

Sustainable investing is different from other types of SRI because it uses much more objective screening criteria, based on measuring, rating and ranking the things that scientific consensus identifies as being important to sustainability. Examples[7] of business practices that relate to sustainability include the following:

- Reducing resource consumption: sustainable companies are efficient in their use of natural resources – particularly non-renewable resources and energy that contribute to global climate change.

- Reducing emissions of toxics and pollutants: companies that emit harmful chemicals, break environmental laws or show wanton disregard for local environments are not performing sustainably.

- Implementing proactive environmental management systems and initiatives: embedding environmental thinking into the business structure maximises sustainability thinking at every point, rather than only after the fact.

- Helping customers achieve sustainability: thinking beyond the walls of the company to design products that reduce the environmental impacts during product use is key to sustainability.

With these business practices in mind, it is then possible to develop a screening process and apply this to the universe of equities and/or bonds to determine which holdings are sustainable. There are various ways that the sustainability screening can be done but the approach of one leading investment manager is shown in the box.

Rank companies within industries on these factors:

- Climate change variables – 30% weighting
  - Sector-normalised CO_2 emissions intensity
  - Climate change solutions users
  - Climate change reporting
- Environmental vulnerability variables – 35% weighting
  - Hazardous waste
  - Environmental regulatory problems
  - Toxic emissions
  - Environmental controversy
  - Environmental negative economic impact

▶

---

[7] Sustainable Holdings & Esty Environmental Partners, Environmental Sustainability Ratings.

- Environmental strength variables – 35% weighting
  - Environmental management systems
  - Pollution prevention
  - Recycling
  - Environmental initiatives
  - Beneficial products and services
- Overweights: those that score above average
- Underweights: those that score below average
- Excludes the worst 10% in each industry

Source: Dimensional Fund Advisors Inc.

Expected returns – market versus sustainable portfolio

Having applied a sophisticated sustainability filter to the universe of securities, we then need to ask ourselves what impact, if any, this will have on expected returns compared with investing without the filter. Factors that suggest higher expected returns from a sustainable portfolio include the fact that such firms are better prepared for the future, will profit as more consumers make green choices, and have lower risk exposures to disaster, regulations and negative PR. Factors that suggest lower expected returns from a sustainable portfolio include the fact that this type of investing is more costly to research and implement, many companies might package themselves as green but are far from being truly sustainable in reality, and, if sustainable firms are lower risk, they must by definition deliver lower returns.

On balance it would seem that the return enhancing and reducing factors balance themselves out and the expected returns from a traditional and a sustainable portfolio should be broadly similar. However, there are explicit and implicit costs involved in SRI in general, not just sustainable investing. Explicit costs relate to the research and screen process so the total ongoing cost of SRI funds might be higher than that of non-SRI funds. Implicit costs relate to the opportunity costs arising from the screening process excluding companies that might have higher realised returns. In addition, because the universe of companies that the fund holds is smaller, there is some reduction in diversification, leading to a slight elevation of risk. These elevated costs suggest that if the expected return of a traditional portfolio is broadly the same as a sustainable portfolio before costs, then after costs the sustainable portfolio must, by definition, deliver a slightly lower return. The differential is unlikely to be large in relation to achieving one's financial goals, but seems to be the price one needs to pay to invest on a sustainable basis.

Research into SRI has been going on for many years. An analysis of 68 SRI academic studies published between 2000 and 2012 suggests that the empirical evidence presents a rather mixed bag.[8] About 44% were positive, 18% were negative, 32% were neutral and the remaining 6% were mixed between neutral to negative and neutral to positive.

A 2012 study of high net worth individuals suggests that people invest sustainably for varied reasons beyond simple fear and greed and their motivations are not just economical but also involve deeper values that are important to them.[9] These are set out in Figure 7.7. If you share any of these views, it may well be appropriate for you to invest your portfolio partly or wholly on a sustainable basis.

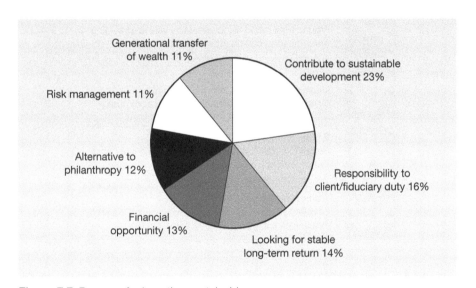

Figure 7.7 Reasons for investing sustainably

Source: EUROSIF (2012) 'High net worth individuals and sustainable investment'.

---

8   Source: Dimensional Fund Advisors Inc. 2013.

9   EUROSIF (2012) 'High net worth individuals and sustainable investment'.

Social impact investment

'Social investment enables social goals to be achieved via engagement with projects which feature recognisably commercial elements. Unlike charitable donations, the funds are potentially recyclable.'

Gavin Francis, founder, Worthstone Limited

Social investment, or impact investing as it is more widely known in the United States, is the provision of finance to charities and other social organisations to generate both defined and measurable social and financial returns. Unlike traditional charitable giving, however, the capital is an investment, *not* a donation, and as such social impact investors expect at least a return of their capital, as well as good social outcomes. Figure 7.8 summarises the key elements of social impact investments.

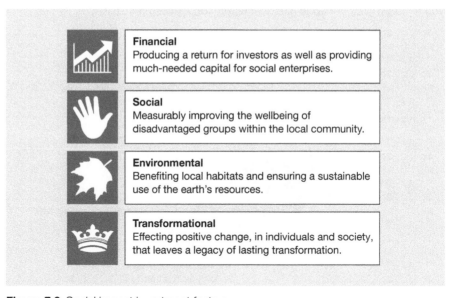

Financial
Producing a return for investors as well as providing much-needed capital for social enterprises.

Social
Measurably improving the wellbeing of disadvantaged groups within the local community.

Environmental
Benefiting local habitats and ensuring a sustainable use of the earth's resources.

Transformational
Effecting positive change, in individuals and society, that leaves a legacy of lasting transformation.

Figure 7.8 Social impact investment factors
Source: Worthstone Limited.

The range of possible social outcomes is wide and these outcomes are summarised in Table 7.1. It is essential, therefore, to ensure that you invest in an activity with a social outcome that matches your own values and concerns.

Table 7.1

Outcome area	Individuals	Community, Sector & Society
Employment, training and education The person is in suitable employment, education, training or caring work Jobs, education and training opportunities are available for everyone	1. Is in suitable employment, education or training and has the ongoing support to maintain it if necessary 2. Has developed the necessary soft skills and attitude through employment, education or training (including social skills, attitude and motivation) 3. Has developed the necessary technical (hard) skills through employment, education or training (including literacy and numeracy, job search skills and job-specific qualifications) 4. Has found a way to address barriers to employment, education or training (including childcare, disability or benefits issues)	5. High quality employment, training and education within a healthy local economy 6. Strong corporate and institutional governance 7. Strong public awareness and participation in matters relating to education and employment, and good sectoral understanding of how to address them 8. Public policy and expenditure that supports good quality employment, training and education
Housing and local facilities The person has a suitable and secure place to live, affordable utilities and access to local facilities and transport Investment and availability of different forms of tenure ensure that all housing needs can be met now and in the future	1. Has a secure and suitable place to live in fit condition 2. Has the skills needed to manage and keep a place to live 3. Is motivated and able to live as independently as possible, and has the ongoing support to maintain that if necessary 4. Has access to local shops, transport, facilities and recreation	1. Provision of adequate, affordable accommodation 2. Sufficient accessible and affordable transport, utilities and local facilities 3. Strong public awareness and participation in matters relating to housing, and good sectoral understanding of how to address them 4. Public and corporate policy and expenditure that supports good quality housing and local facilities
Income and financial inclusion The person has sufficient income to meet their essential needs and access to suitable financial products and services Everyone reaches an optimum level of income for health and wellbeing, and income differentials support social cohesion	1. Has sufficient sustainable income, including benefits if appropriate 2. Has access to appropriate financial advice, products or services 3. Is managing finances well	1. Ethical responsible and suitable financial services and products are available to all 2. Strong public financial capability, literacy and management, and understanding of legal matters 3. Income equality 4. Strong public awareness and participation in matters relating to financial inclusion, and good sectoral understanding of how to achieve it 5. Public and corporate policy and expenditure that supports fair income and financial inclusion

Table 7.1 (cont.)

Outcome area	Individuals	Community, Sector & Society
Physical health The person looks after their health as well as possible. The person recovers as quickly as possible, or, if recovery is not possible, their health and quality of life are maximised Good general physical health across the population	1. Looks after physical health, maintains a healthy lifestyle and keeps safe 2. Enjoys good support and quality of life in relation to any long-term conditions 3. Makes use of the health services to recover from episodes of ill-health or following injury 4. Has a positive experience of healthcare and attitude toward own physical health	5. Healthy and physically active people and communities 6. Equal access to good quality, safe health and social care services 7. Strong public awareness and participation in matters relating to physical health, and advanced sectoral understanding of what makes for good health 8. Public and corporate policy and expenditure that supports good physical health
Mental health and wellbeing The person has a sense of wellbeing. Those who experience mental illness recover where possible and lead a positive and fulfilling life even if symptoms remain Good mental wellbeing and life satisfaction across the population	1. Has confidence, emotional balance and is resilient in the face of difficulties 2. Has a sense of purpose, engages in meaningful and fulfilling activity, and has aspirations for the future 3. Enjoys good support in relation to any mental health problems 4. Has a positive experience of care and a good understanding of own mental health and emotional wellbeing	5. Good mental health and well-being 6. Equal access to good quality mental health services 7. Strong public awareness and participation in matters relating to mental health and wellbeing, and good sectoral understanding of how to optimise it 8. Public and corporate policy and expenditure that supports good mental health and wellbeing
Family, friends and relationships The person has a positive social network that provides love, belonging and emotional practical support A society that supports and encourages families and/or good personal relationships	1. Feels and is socially connected 2. Enjoys positive and constructive relationships with others 3. Has the skills, strategy and support to maintain and manage relationships 4. Family, partners, friends and carers of those with specific needs are supported	5. A resilient society with meaningful connections 6. Good quality services for family, friends and relationships 7. Strong public awareness of the value of families, friends and relationships, and good sectoral understanding of how to build them 8. Public and corporate policy and expenditure that supports families, friends and relationships
Citizenship and community The person lives in confidence and safety, and free from crime and disorder. The person acts as a responsible and active citizen and feels part of a community Stronger, active, more engaged communities	1. Stays within the law and has addressed any offending behaviour 2. Does not discriminate against others, and is not discriminated against, on grounds of ethnicity, religion, gender, sexual orientation or disability 3. Understands their rights and responsibilities as a citizen 4. Feels they have a stake in their community and society at large, and makes a conscious contribution 5. Has a positive perception of local community and area	6. Strong and safe communities 7. Strong public participation in citizenship and communities, and good social cohesion 8. Public and corporate policy and expenditure that supports citizenship and communities

Table 7.1 (cont.)

Outcome area	Individuals	Community, Sector & Society
Arts, heritage, sport and faith The person finds meaning, enjoyment, self-expression and affiliation through informed participation in the arts, sport and/or faith A thriving cultural landscape with high levels of participation and engagement	1. Finds meaning and fulfillment from engaging with arts, heritage, sport and faith 2. Develops cultural skills and confidence in areas that interest them	3. High quality, affordable, accessible and inclusive cultural services available to all 4. Strong public awareness of and participation in the arts, heritage, sports and faith 5. Public and corporate policy and expenditure that supports the arts, heritage, sport and faith
Conservation of the natural environment The person has an appreciation of the natural environment and plays their part in protecting it, including reducing their carbon footprint The natural environment is protected for the benefit of people, plants and animals and habitats, today and in the future	1. Accesses and enjoys the natural environment and heritage 2. Understands the importance of and reduces personal impact on the natural environment	3. Conservation of Natural Spaces 4. Sustainable Agriculture 5. Sustainable energy 6. Sustainable buildings and transport 7. Recycling, waste and sustainable water use 8. Strong public awareness of and engagement with the natural environment, and good sectoral understanding as to how to sustain it 9. Public and corporate policy and expenditure that supports the natural environment

Source: Big Society Capital Outcomes Matrix 2013, developed in partnership with New Philanthropy Capital, the SROI Network, Triangle Consulting and Investing for Good.

Social impact financing can take the form of short- or long-term loans, preference type share funding, or long-term committed equity such as capital. Such finance might be used to fund:

- asset purchase (i.e. property and plant)
- working capital (i.e. cashflow)
- growth capital.

Charities and social enterprises repay the loan capital with interest and the investor is then able to reinvest in other projects to multiply the social impact of the original investment. Clearly not all loans will be repaid, but, if you invest in a reputable social investment fund, the manager will carry out thorough due diligence so that loans are made only to well-managed organisations with sound business plans. Alternatively, you could research individual social impact investments yourself, but if you do this, avoid putting too much in any one holding. Figure 7.9 shows the range of social impact investments available at the time of writing.

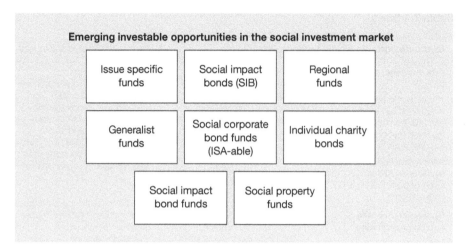

Figure 7.9 Types of social impact investments
Source: Big Society Capital.

CAF Venturesome was one of the first social investment funds set up to support UK social investment. The fund provides loan capital to charities, social enterprises and community groups so that they can deliver services that have a high social impact. However, an increasing number of social impact and micro-financing opportunities have started to emerge over the past few years. UK social investment was given a big boost in April 2012 when the UK government set up Big Society Capital, to make finance available to organisations tackling major social issues. Big Society Capital has £600 million to invest in a range of social investment intermediaries, which then lend on to charities and social enterprises.

Most social impact investors understand that the bulk (if not all) of the return is likely to be in the form of a positive and tangible gain for society. When the capital is eventually returned to the investor by the social enterprise (with or without any financial return), the investor is then free to recycle the capital into new social investments. However, because social impact investments now also qualify for generous tax benefits,[10] just obtaining a return of capital after three years would still represent an annualised return of in excess of 10% just from the initial tax relief. See Chapter 14 for a worked example of how combining income tax and capital gains tax deferral and staggered encashment of a social investment, merely with a return of capital, could generate a cash uplift of circa 100%, equivalent to an internal rate of return of 25%.

---

[10] Since the 2014/15 tax year social impact investments benefit from virtually the same tax benefits as for enterprise investment schemes (EIS).

Social impact investment can be done instead of or in addition to charitable giving, although I would encourage you to do both, because they meet different funding needs. My experience is that where someone was previously not keen to do any, or increase existing, charitable giving, they will often consider making social investments because they don't perceive that it is 'dead' money, never to be seen again. It seems that for some people, the act of choosing and following the progress of a social impact investment makes them feel more engaged with the social impact objective.

Making good and doing good

By Norma Cohen

Suzanne Biegel's story is probably typical of that of most active social investors. She started her career at IBM in the late 1980s and 1990s. The business she built and sold, IEC, was an e-learning business that she ultimately sold to a larger company. In 2000, she found herself living in California and wealthy, but looking for new challenges.

She devoted herself to organisations focusing on her passions: the environment, social and economic justice and the status of women and girls. She actively campaigned for 'change not charity' after selling her business.

But, like many who find themselves drawn to social investment, she grew dissatisfied. "Fundamentally, I'm a business person," she says.

In the US, what is known as "impact investing" has been around for 20 years and is modelled on what are known as Theatre Angels, wealthy private individuals who are prepared to take a risk on stage productions. As in the UK, it is most likely not to pay off, but when it does, the returns can be spectacular. But most importantly, the investors gain close engagement with the production and earn their rewards in part by promoting theatre to the world at large.

So it is for social impact "angels" who often are successful entrepreneurs themselves and offer their particular skills to fledgling businesses. Biegel said she is seeking returns "in double digit returns" but often finds that she does better than that.

Peter Wilson, a director of Omnia, a legal firm, had a background in diplomacy and international development and established himself as a post-conflict stabilisation specialist, overseeing projects in countries such as Iraq. After leaving public service, he set up his own consulting firm.

"It grew from a bunch of guys working out of my bedroom to a growing business," he says. When it was sold to a larger firm, Wilson had money to invest.

While most of his investments are "arm's length" – held purely to deliver returns – he has also made social investments. Currently, he holds stakes in five social enterprise companies. "I'd be looking for a rate of return similar to that on conventional companies," says Wilson.

➡

But for those companies he becomes engaged with, there is another form of payback: intellectual challenge. "I am not at the stage where I can just give away money. But when I set up my first company, we watched things that were intellectual things." Keeping that up, he says, is important to him.

Jonathan Adams, a fund manager at Investec, had been an investor in "angel" companies for years, although none had social objectives. But three years ago, his employer offered him a chance to mentor a company, JuJu films, supported by the Bromley-by-Bow Centre, a charity founded by renowned social entrepreneur Lord Mawson.

That opened his eyes to the possibility of social impact investment. "I do have a target rate of return," Adams says. "I just haven't quantified it. You're willing to bear a lower target return across the portfolio.

"If you're looking for zero return, you are right at the charitable end of things," he adds.

Source: Cohen, N. (2013) Making good and doing good, 23 March 2013. ©The Financial Times Ltd 2013. All Rights Reserved.

SRI in context

As we've seen, SRI covers a wide spectrum of investing styles, risk–return profiles, values/beliefs and solutions. Whether you want to invest some or all of your money in SRI, there is now a wide range of investment solutions which can enable you to reconcile any deeply held views, beliefs and values with the need to invest your wealth to achieve your financial goals (see Table 7.2). However, it's also important to be totally clear about where the different types of SRI sit in the context of your overall wealth plan in general and your investment strategy in particular. This is because they all deliver different things and there is a big difference between SRIs that seek to offer a return on your capital, a return of your capital or just a tax incentive. Figure 7.10 will help you to understand how the different SRIs fit across the 'money for purpose' spectrum. You'll notice that this includes philanthropy, so in Chapter 24 we'll look at the role of philanthropy and why and how this might fit within your overall plan.

Table 7.2 How to access SRI

Investment type	Bonds	Equity	Commodities	Passive management	Alternatives
Ethical Screen	✓	✓	✗	✓	✗
Engagement	✓	✓	✗	✗	✗
Sustainability	✓	✓	✗	✓	✓
Green themes	✗	✓	✓	✓	✓
Social impact	✗	✗	✗	✗	✓

Source: Blue & Green Investor.

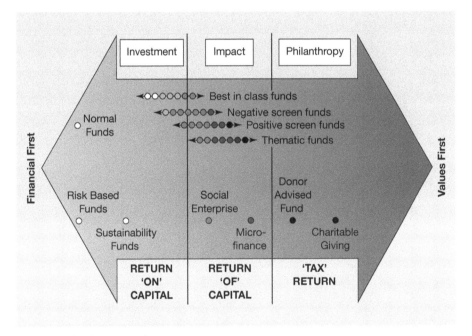

Figure 7.10 The money for purpose spectrum

CHAPTER 8
ALTERNATIVE INVESTMENTS

'Investors require unusual self-confidence to ignore the widely hyped non-core investments and to embrace the quietly effective core investments.'

David Swensen, CIO, Yale Endowment[1]

There are a number of asset classes other than cash, bonds and equities that you might consider as part of your wealth plan. In this chapter I'll explain the main types and whether or not I recommend their inclusion in your portfolio.

Gold

Not recommended, in a multi-asset portfolio held for the long term because its expected return does not cover its risk as a portfolio asset, but hold a small amount if it helps you to stay disciplined.

Gold has been a store of value for thousands of years and has as much emotional appeal as it does potential for investment. Some investors view gold as the ultimate protection against rampant inflation and corrupt or profligate governments, with its appeal and thus value rising as confidence in governments' economic policies declines. Gold is also seen as a means of hedging currency risk and as an attractive alternative to low real return asset classes.

In many Middle Eastern and Asian countries, particularly those with less developed banking infrastructures and less stable political institutions, gold is still a

---

[1] Swensen, 2005.

trusted form of exchange for goods and services. In addition, there are strong cultural traditions that perpetuate the allure of gold. For example, at Indian weddings it is usual for the bride and groom to be given gold as a wedding present.

The capital return from gold can come only from a rise in the price due to increasing demand. A large part of the demand for gold arises from its use in jewellery and other goods, known as the 'consumption dividend'.[2] This pushes up the price of gold and as such lowers its expected capital return. If you invest in gold bullion or a gold fund as part of your investment portfolio, all you will receive is the expected capital return as you are not receiving the consumption dividend.

Figure 8.1 shows the return from gold after adjusting for inflation over the past 40 years compared with the S&P 500 and FTSE 100. As is clear, gold has lagged well behind most equity indices, although it has performed in line with many fixed income benchmarks. Taking the data from 1990 to 2008 and dividing it into three types of environment – high inflation, high uncertainty and normal – gold delivered negative real returns in normal conditions, and positive real returns in high inflation and uncertainty.[3] Recent research appears to suggest that gold is a hedge (i.e. it is uncorrelated with stocks and bonds on average) and acts as a safe haven asset class, providing support in extreme stock market conditions, reducing investors' losses just when they need that protection most.[4] However, when buyers acquire gold on the day after a shock (i.e. after the price has already risen), they lose money, which suggests that any gold allocation should be at the strategic asset allocation level, not in response to news.

In another recently updated research paper,[5] the authors find little evidence that gold has been an effective hedge against unexpected inflation. They also question the assertion that gold really provides a true 'safe haven' in an environment of very low real yields. In terms of an inflation hedge, equities and index-linked gilts provide alternative asset classes to achieve this objective. Gold does, however, appear to act as a hedge against a weakening US dollar, which is attractive from a sterling-based investor's perspective. Although gold has diversification characteristics, because it has very low correlation with equities and bonds, its expected return should be low because of its role in reducing risk in the portfolio overall.

---

[2] The term 'consumption dividend' means the utility value that comes from actually using gold in products or owning gold for pleasure or status. Owning gold bullion or a gold fund does not provide this consumption dividend to the investor.

[3] Index Investor (2010) 'What is the proper role of gold?'

[4] Baur, D. and Lucey, B. (2009) 'Is gold a hedge or a safe haven?', available at **www.ssrn.com**

[5] Erb, C.B. and Harvey, C.R. (2012) 'The golden dilemma', **http://sssrn.com/abstract=2078535**

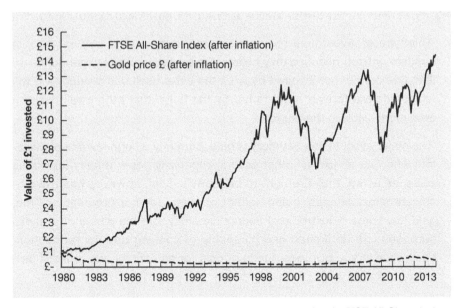

Figure 8.1 Historic after-inflation return from gold compared with FTSE All-Share Index
Source: Dimensional Fund Advisors, with data from the FTSE Group. Calculated using Returns 2.3.

'I am recommending gold as I have done for many years. I will continue to do so until the gold price hits the blow-off stage, which is nowhere in sight. ... The environment for gold couldn't be better ... Gold could go to $5,000 or even $10,000.'

Fred Hickey, High Tech Strategist[6]

Many gold enthusiasts believe that gold is 'under-owned' by investors and we are on the cusp of a major increase in the amount of investment capital allocated to gold. Even a small increase in demand for gold, we are told, will cause the price to soar. While acknowledging that such a strategic shift would lead to a significant increase in the price of gold, the same academics who questioned the inflation-hedging characteristics of gold had this to say about the price of gold: 'Given the most recent value for the CPI [Consumer Price] index, this version of the "gold as an inflation hedge" argument suggests that the price of gold should currently be around $780 an ounce.'[7] At the time of writing (May 2014) the spot price of gold was US$1,300, compared with a low of US$252 (June 1999) and a high of $1,913 (August 2011) over the past 30 years.

---

[6]   Barron's (2013) 'Stirring things up', 3 February.

[7]   Erb, C.B. and Harvey, C.R. (2012) 'The golden dilemma', http://sssrn.com/abstract=2078535

Warren Buffett[8] put the case succinctly against gold, positioned against equities:

'This type of investment requires an expanding pool of buyers, who, in turn, are enticed because they believe the buying pool will expand still further. Owners are not inspired by what the asset itself can produce – it will remain lifeless forever – but rather by the belief that others will desire it even more avidly in the future.

'The major asset in this category is gold, currently a huge favorite of investors who fear almost all other assets, especially paper money (of whose value, as noted, they are right to be fearful). Gold, however, has two significant shortcomings, being neither of much use nor procreative. True, gold has some industrial and decorative utility, but the demand for these purposes is both limited and incapable of soaking up new production. Meanwhile, if you own one ounce of gold for an eternity, you will still own one ounce at its end.

'What motivates most gold purchasers is their belief that the ranks of the fearful will grow. During the past decade that belief has proved correct. Beyond that, the rising price has on its own generated additional buying enthusiasm, attracting purchasers who see the rise as validating an investment thesis. As "bandwagon" investors join any party, they create their own truth – for a while.'

Owning gold as an investment seems to be driven as much by emotions and market-timing decisions in the face of news as it does for any rational, empirical reasons. If allocating a small strategic amount of, say, 5% of your portfolio to gold helps you to feel better about the future and to stay disciplined with the remaining 95% of your portfolio, then that might be the right approach to adopt. Otherwise I'd suggest you restrict your portfolio to comprising an appropriate amount of equities, short-dated and inflation-linked bonds and benefit from the dividends and interest arising. You can then restrict your investment in gold to objects of beauty.

Hedge funds/funds of hedge funds (FoHFs)

Not recommended due to their complexity, high costs and unsubstantiated risk/reward characteristics.

---

[8] Berkshire Hathaway Inc. (2011) *Annual Report*, chairman's letter, p. 18, available at **www.berkshirehathaway.com**

There is no definitive description of what a hedge fund is. They have been described as a variety of skill-based investment strategies with a broad range of risk and return objectives that takes a performance fee. As such hedge funds are not an asset class but a class of active investment management. On the face of it, hedge funds appear to provide attractive characteristics to investors, including low correlation to equities and bonds, high returns and low risk. Investment can be by either individual funds or funds that invest in a number of other hedge funds (known as funds of hedge funds). The hedge fund industry claims that, in aggregate, their funds generate returns over and above those of the market due to the skill of investment managers. However, because we know that there are no high-return low-risk investments, such claims should be treated with a significant degree of scepticism.

The most commonly available risk and return databases for hedge funds contain a number of biases that overstate returns and understate correlations (against other asset classes) and volatility. In addition, the data conceal the fact that there is usually an increased probability of very large losses.

Research suggests that returns from hedge funds may in fact be systematic exposure to alternative sources of market-based returns (beta) rather than manager skill.[9] During the period November 2007 to March 2009, when the UK equity market fell almost 40%, diversified FoHFs failed to live up to their diversification and skill-based returns sales pitch, losing more than 20% in dollar terms.[10] This suggests that such products are simply the result of taking directional market bets, for very high fees. Over the long term these high fees will have a detrimental impact on investor returns, even if a manager gets those directional bets right (and there is no evidence that those who do so can repeat their success in a way that can reliably be attributed to skill rather than luck).

Assessing hedge funds is an expensive, time-consuming and complex task, which involves trying to understand the underlying strategies, selecting truly skilful managers and performing the necessary due diligence. (Bernie Madoff fooled a number of wealthy professional investors and large private banks with his US-based fraud, so assessment is not as easy as it might appear.) The costs of a typical hedge fund are very high, with typically a 2% annual management charge and 20% of any gains, plus 1% and 10%, respectively, on top of that for a fund of funds. The costs incurred by the manager in buying and selling holdings are likely

9   Géhin, W. and Vaissié, M. (2005) 'The right place for alternative beta in hedge fund portfolios: An answer to the capacity effect fantasy', EDHEC and *Journal of Alternative Investments*, 9(1): 9–18; Jensen, G. (2005) 'Hedge funds selling beta as alpha', *Daily Observations*, Bridgewater Associates.

10   HFRI Fund of Funds Diversified Index in US$.

to add significant additional costs, which will be at least as much as traditionally managed funds, but most likely much higher, given the typically higher portfolio turnover within hedge funds.

Research released in a book[11] by an asset manager who formerly chose hedge funds for major US bank JP Morgan reveals some interesting and thought-provoking insights about hedge funds:

- Between 1998 and 2003 hedge fund returns were positive in aggregate in each year. The industry at that time was small, with around $200 billion in assets.
- Due to its strong performance during the 2000–2003 period (the technology sector crash), the industry attracted assets rapidly.
- By 2008 it is estimated that hedge fund assets amounted to $2 trillion, a tenfold increase.
- The average performance loss in 2008 was 23%.
- The author estimates that these money flows and the consequent asset-weighted returns, i.e. the returns received by investors based on the timing of their investments, cancelled out all of the profit made in the previous ten-year period. To the end of 2010 investors were still below water, yet hedge fund managers extracted more than $100 billion in fees between 2008 and 2010.
- The 18% return on hedge funds in the nine years to November 2011 was easily beaten by the total 29% gain from the US S&P 500 Index (in US$ terms). The gap was even starker for investment-grade corporate bonds, which in the same period gained 77%, as measured by the Dow Jones Corporate Bond Index. The underperformance of hedge funds over this period was *before* accounting for the typical 2% p.a. management fee and 20% performance fees.
- If individual hedge fund managers are generating additional returns above those of the market, then the benefits of that skill (if it is skill and not luck) tend to go to the managers themselves rather than to investors. Hedge fund managers extracted $379 billion for themselves between 1998 and 2008 out of the $449 billion returns generated in excess of cash, meaning that investors took all the risk but the hedge fund managers took virtually all the excess returns. On a risk-adjusted basis, investors would have been better off simply placing their funds in a cash deposit account.

While the hedge fund industry would no doubt contest the findings of Lack's book, one doesn't have to agree with his numbers still to harbour reasonable doubts about risking one's hard-earned savings by investing in hedge funds.

---

[11] Lack, S. (2012) *The Hedge Fund Mirage: The illusion of big money and why it's too good to be true*, John Wiley & Sons.

Hedge fund returns data tend to be packed with all sorts of biases (self-selection – many funds (often the poorer performers) never even make it to the databases; survivor bias – some fail and fall out; and back-fill bias – where managers back-fill prior performance, which is likely to happen only when it has been good). One piece of research[12] reveals that over the 15 years of the study to 2009, hedge fund net returns were around 14% p.a., which sounds good but when stripped of these biases they were more like 8%, not much different from the US equity market. In the dataset being used (TASS database), the authors found that 63% of funds were now dead and only 37% had survived. Interestingly, around two-thirds of returns came from simple market factors (owning bonds and equities) and one-third from manager skill. Costs were very high at an average of around 3.5% p.a. – which is a lot given that 60% of the return is simply delivered by the market.

The authors note an important point – that although market-beating returns appear to exist, there is no easy way for investors to secure this average and even if the funds could, the investors only ended up with a market return as the hedge fund managers took all the outperformance for themselves.

Another piece of research[13] from 2011 explains that, due to the lack of disclosure around returns, it is difficult to determine how much market-beating returns, if any, hedge funds generate. This is in addition to other drawbacks of hedge funds, such as illiquidity, relative lack of oversight, the additional costs of leverage and derivatives and, of course, the substantial fees charged by the managers themselves. The research concludes that the highly uncertain payoff from hedge funds, the high expense ratios and the lack of disclosure around them mean that investors should exercise caution before investing in them.

Investing is a zero-sum game before costs (for every winner there must be a loser) and over the medium to long term hedge funds have a very high hill to climb in achieving sufficient investment returns just to cover their increased costs. In order to do this, they need to take more risk (with your money). Synthetic hedge funds, which replicate underlying market risk factors at far lower cost and with greater liquidity, could be a possible option for investors in the future, but it is still too early to establish their efficacy in delivering the desired characteristics and there is still a lack of available funds of this type.

In concluding I'll leave you with some wise words from one of the investment world's most acclaimed users of hedge fund strategies:

[12] Cheng, P., Ibbotson, R. and Zhu, K. (2011) 'The ABCs of hedge funds: Alphas, betas and costs' – summarised in Chen, P. (2013) 'Are you getting your money's worth? Sources of hedge fund returns', **www.dfaeurope.com**

[13] Shah, R.R. (2011) 'Demystifying hedge funds: A review', Dimensional Fund Advisors, December.

'Casual approaches to hedge fund selection lead to almost certain disappointment. Hedge funds belong in the domain of sophisticated investors who commit significant resources to manager selection ... Investors who fail to identify truly superior active managers face a dismal reality.'

David Swensen, CIO, Yale Endowment[14]

Structured products

Not recommended for long-term investors due to high costs, additional provider risks and loss of return upside but may be suitable for very short-term investors who accept the downsides.

Structured products, created by investment banks and enthusiastically promoted by their private banking divisions, started gaining popularity with European retail investors in the 1990s and with US retail investors in the mid-2000s. Recent estimates put the amount of UK investors' money currently invested in structured products at £42 billion.[15] In simple terms, a structured investment pays a return based on the performance of an underlying asset, such as an index, commodity or equity, according to a pre-set formula, usually over a set time period of up to six years. In some issues it is possible to encash the investment early, but this may be subject to certain penalties and even then will depend on the market price of the underlying asset.

On the face of it these products can be useful to investors who desire a specific payoff structure linked to the performance of the underlying asset(s) at apparently lower risk than owning the assets directly. Certainly the promise of capital protection with market upside participation looks appealing to the average investor. However, behind the sales message is usually a complex payout mechanism that even the most mathematically minded would struggle to understand and risks that may be neither immediately obvious nor quantifiable.

'They are horrible investments for retail investors ... Simple portfolios of bonds, stocks or the S&P 500 [Index] will beat structured products 99.5% of the time because of the heavy profit built into the pricing.'

Craig McCann, former SEC economist

---

[14] Swensen, 2005.

[15] UK Structured Products Association (2012), **www.ukstructuredproductsassociation.co.uk**

The combination of a simple investment proposition supported by extremely complex financial engineering means that most retail investors buy structured products on the advice of 'experts' such as private banking and other financial advisers. As I've stated previously, there are no high-return, low-risk investments. Therefore, as an investor you know intuitively that a fixed income product that pays a high yield and offers additional upside potential must carry some form of downside risk. A financial institution will not offer more benefit without getting something in return.

In fact, a few years ago the UK's financial regulator reviewed the practices of several institutions that account for 50% or so of all structured products sold in the UK. The regulator's Head of Conduct Supervision commented: 'Many of the problems we found with the product design process were rooted in the fact that the firms are focusing too much on their own commercial interests rather than the outcomes they are delivering to consumers.'[16]

It is worth noting, too, that the popularity of these types of products with banks, building societies and insurance companies is driven not only by the direct pricing benefits to the issuer of the product but also because they represent a cheap source of funding for the institution.

The usual price of capital protection is giving up part of the return from the underlying index, security or commodity on which the structured product is based. Dividends are the regular cash payment made to shareholders, as part of the compensation for taking on the risk of equity ownership, the other component being a rise in the price of the shares of the company. An important insight into equity investing is that share price rises alone have historically delivered a return only just higher than inflation. It is the reinvestment of cash dividends into the portfolio that accounts for the bulk of the attractive returns that equities delivered, and are expected to deliver, over time. This is illustrated in Figure 8.2.

Typically, structured products sold by banks usually promise to deliver only the 'price return' of the index, such as the FTSE 100, rather than a 'total return' index where reinvested dividends are included. With dividend yields around 3% p.a., over the lifespan of a five-year product an investor would give up more than 15% due to compounding compared with the underlying asset from which dividends are included. Looking at this another way, this is a 15% cushion for an investor taking on the full risk of equities, by simply buying an equity index tracker fund. Rolling from one structured product to the next gives up this important long-term driver of returns. Promising to give you your capital back

---

[16] Financial Services Authority (2011) Guidance consultation, 'Retail product development and governance – structured products review', November.

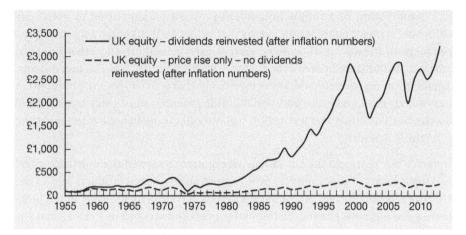

Figure 8.2 Reinvesting dividends is a major contributor to long-term equity returns
Source: Barclays Capital Equity Gilt Study 2014.

sounds like a reasonable deal if Plan A does not come off (for example, the FTSE 100 ends lower over five years than its start point). Where the product guarantees a return of principal, this is only in nominal terms (invest £100, get back £100) and a period of high inflation could seriously erode purchasing power.

By placing your money onto the balance sheet of a bank or other financial institution, you are opening yourself up to the risk that it goes bust. That is not a trivial decision to make, particularly as some products sit outside UK investor-protection schemes. The owners of the $18 billion invested globally in structured products issued by Lehman Brothers lost most of their money despite such promises.[17] In fact, the bank backed $900 million of structured products in 2009 alone, before filing for bankruptcy in September of that year.[18] UK investors who bought structured products from Keydata have been told that the whereabouts of their money, which was invested by a further counterparty, SLS Capital, is unknown. It's still unclear whether they will be able to make claims from the UK's compensation scheme.

A common feature of these products is high, but rarely quantifiable, costs. It is in the issuer's interests to make the product as complex as possible so that it is hard for investors and advisers to quantify the costs and the profits accruing to the issuing bank. Many investors wrongly equate complexity with high returns, to their

---

[17] Securities Litigation & Consulting Group (2009) 'Structured products in the aftermath of Lehman Brothers'.

[18] Light, L. (2009) 'Twice shy on structured products?', Wall Street Journal, 28 May.

detriment. While the return payout may appear to be passive in nature, being linked to an index or other asset class measure means that many structured products are simply gambles on the direction and magnitude of the movement of a market or a basket of markets.

'Some of the more exotic structured products offered by firms ... have often been mind-bogglingly complicated financial gambles – almost like spread bets on steroids.'

Martin Wheatley, Chief Executive of the Financial Conduct Authority[19]

Private equity

Not recommended due to high costs and poor return characteristics.

Private equity, i.e. leveraged buyouts and venture capital, appear to provide exciting opportunities for higher returns than the public market and additional diversification benefits. In reality, capturing these higher returns comes at the price of illiquidity, higher risk and higher costs. A study by former banker Peter Morris found that private equity managers often charge excessive fees (typically a 2% annual fee and 20% performance fee) and overstate potential returns. 'Calculating returns on private equity is not a trivial issue', Morris says. 'The most widely used measure, the internal rate of return, is misleading and often overstates realised returns. This creates room for uncertainty, at best, and, at worst, manipulation.'[20]

Morris questioned the extent to which the returns that the managers do deliver relate to their skill and the extent to which they come from what the market would have provided anyway and from the leverage involved. For instance, his study analysed the returns on 110 deals in the UK and Europe over a decade from 1995 to 2005. The average internal rate of return in those deals was 39%, of which debt accounted for 22% and a rising stock market 9%. The other 8% was the contribution of the private equity managers. Given that the average annual fee in private equity was at least 8%, this meant the investors who provided the bulk of the money would have done just as well investing in the market directly and borrowing from the bank. See Figure 8.3.

---

[19] Speech at the London School of Economics, 10 April 2013.

[20] Morris, P. (2010) 'Private equity, public loss?', Centre for the Study of Financial Innovation, July.

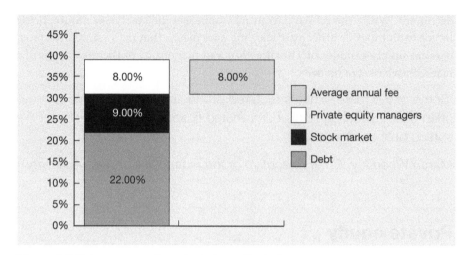

Figure 8.3 Return composition of private equity deals

Source: Data from Morris, P. (2010) 'Private equity, public loss?', Centre for the Study of Financial Innovation, July.

Another European study[21] looked at cashflows from more than 4,000 liquidated private equity investments and found that the market-beating return (alpha), or return unexplained by risk factors to which investors could have obtained low cost exposure anyway, was zero. This study inferred an historical risk premium from private equity of around 18%, of which about 10% was the market premium, 5% was the value (or book-to-market) premium and the remaining 3% was the premium from liquidity risk – the risk of not being able to sell out of the asset sufficiently quickly to avoid a loss.

'Private equity is simply public equity with additional layers of leverage; it is therefore likely to be a good deal more risky than quoted equity markets, while several orders of magnitude more expensive in management fee structures ... From an accounting perspective, private equity might appear to be a lower risk investment than quoted equities, while delivering historical returns that display low correlations with equities. In the real world, nothing could be further from the truth.'

Barclays Capital, 'Equity Gilt Study 2007'

---

[21] Franzoni, F., Nowak, E. and Phallippou, L. (2010) 'Private equity performance and liquidity risk', Swiss Finance Institute, 17 June.

Leading finance academics Fama and French expressed their view that, to the extent that private equity managers add value through the application of their skills, the evidence indicates this additional return tends to go to the managers themselves.[22] Fama and French also dispute that private equity is a diversification tool, because the types of targets chosen by private equity – small companies and start-ups – tend to be highly sensitive to the market.

There is a wide range of possible outcomes for the returns from private equity when compared with those from the quoted stock market. However, these returns are driven by chance, which makes it hard for investors to discern whether the returns they are paying for are due to skill or luck, so, while private equity can generate good returns, once these returns are adjusted for market risk, value and size risk and liquidity risk, there is little sign of the managers adding any further value through their own skill. In any case, the size of the fees involved suggests that what additional spoils are on offer tend to go to the managers, not the investors.

Life settlement funds

Not recommended due to poor upside, lack of transparency and significant counterparty risk.

Life settlement funds purchase life insurance plans from individuals with impaired life expectations at a discount and then receive the proceeds on the death of the original policyholder. Given that returns are uncorrelated to financial markets and some existing funds have delivered returns in the region of 8% per annum with low volatility, they are, at least superficially, attractive.

There are four main points to consider when weighing up whether or not to use life settlement funds. First, returns are based on someone else's misfortune, which may not be acceptable to some people. Second, the risk exists of a misselling scandal, not only of life policies but the fact that there may well be alternatives to the original policyholder selling a policy, which may not have been properly explained to the policyholder and would be financially more attractive to them. Third, you need to remember that high returns may be arbitraged away as more players enter the life settlements marketplace. Finally, you need to understand the various risks associated with this type of investment.

---

[22] Fama, E.F. and French, K.R. (2010) 'Q&A: Public vs private equity', Fama/French Forum, Dimensional Fund Advisors, 7 July.

You are relying on the skill of the manager to make the correct assumptions about the life expectancy of the policyholders from whom policies are purchased. If they underestimate how long policyholders will live, the overall return from the fund will be much less than anticipated as they will need to find cash to pay ongoing premiums and this may require the forced sale of other policies at a discounted price. In addition, like structured products, life settlement funds have a rather opaque product structure that combines relatively high costs with multiple counterparties, including the manager, life policy adviser, policy administrator and custodian.

While there have been several high-profile disasters involving life settlement funds, the most high-profile one to date remains the $1 billion Ponzi[23] scheme involving the Mutual Benefits Corporation in the US. The UK's main financial regulator has also made it clear that it sees a very limited audience for life settlements and, in recent guidance,[24] it outlined six key risks presented by these funds:

- Longevity – inaccurate estimation of life expectancy of the lives insured by the policies could negatively impact on the investment return and liquidity of the investment scheme.

- Liquidity – traded life settlement policies are illiquid and have a limited secondary market, which means that value could be significantly discounted if funds are required by the manager at short notice.

- Structure – yields are promised to previous investors which can be sustained only by using new investors' money, which appears to share some of the characteristics of a Ponzi scheme.

- Location of the underlying asset – investors face exchange rate risk on the ongoing policy premiums and the final payout on maturity if denominated in a currency (e.g. US$) different to that of the investor.

- Offshore distributors – investors will have limited or no recourse to the Financial Ombudsman Service or Financial Services Compensation Scheme.

- Counterparties – the failure of the insurance company underwriting the policy would mean that claims would not be paid on the death of the original policy holder.

---

[23] Ponzi schemes are named after a 1920s' fraudster who promised high returns to attract investors, using new investors' money to repay outgoing investors. This continued until eventually the entire scheme collapsed when investors all wanted their money back. A case of robbing Peter to pay Paul.

[24] Financial Services Authority (2012) 'Finalised guidance, traded life policy investments (TLPIs),' April.

Zeros

Not recommended due to equity-type risks.

Investment trusts companies are quoted companies that exist solely to invest in other companies and they have been in existence for well over 150 years. Zero dividend preference shares, known as 'zeros', are a class of investment trust share issued by split capital investment trusts that provide a predetermined return on the maturity of the zero, similar to a zero coupon bond (a fixed income investment that pays all its return at maturity rather than regular interest payments throughout its term). The zero is assured of being repaid as long as the company's assets grow by a fixed amount, which is defined at its launch date.

In the early 1990s some investment companies invested in each other and also took on debt to boost returns further, thus increasing risk beyond that which would have applied in a fully diversified market portfolio. In the early 2000s, with equity markets in free fall, the impact of those market falls was amplified by the cross-holdings and debt, and banks started calling in their loans. Like the proverbial deck of cards, this led to a number of companies becoming insolvent and defaulting on payouts to their shareholders at maturity. In the mid-2000s the investment trust industry agreed a compensation package to provide limited compensation to those who lost out in this situation. Today there are relatively few zeros, most of which relate to specialist fund sectors, with redemption dates falling within the next three or four years.

Convertible bonds

Not recommended due to equity-type risks.

These are fixed income securities issued by companies that also offer the holder the option to convert to ordinary share capital of the issuing company at a predetermined price in the future. The concept is that the investor receives a known return through the interest paid and capital security, with the potential to share in the upside of the company. As a result convertible bonds act more like bonds when they are issued and gradually take on more and more equity risk characteristics as they near maturity. While investing in convertibles via a convertibles fund deals with the diversification issue, it doesn't deal with the fact that mixing bond and equity risks in the same asset class means it's hard to know in which bit of the portfolio it should be held (and it drifts from one to the other). Therefore, the equity-like nature of convertibles is incompatible with the principal role of fixed income in most portfolios – that of reducing the risk of risky assets.

Art and wine

Art and wine are certainly things that have a value and in some cases can appreciate significantly, if you buy correctly, store properly and sell at the right time. I have met many people who have amassed a small fortune from collecting wine and/or art over many years. However, despite the items apparently appreciating in value significantly, people often fail to take into account storage and insurance costs, nor how the return compares with a diversified multi-factor investment portfolio.

If you have an interest in this area and enjoy wine and/or art, by all means allocate some of your wealth to it. However, if your main priority is to use your accumulated wealth to sustain your lifestyle over several decades, and you don't see yourself as a wine or art expert (and don't want to spend the time necessary to become one), I suggest you limit the amount you spend to an amount that won't impact on your overall financial security. Enjoying wine and/or art for the pleasure they bring is probably the most prudent approach.

Wise words with which to leave you

While there will be some people who can see merit in using the various alternative investments discussed in this chapter, I am not one of them. I advocate keeping investing as simple, transparent, liquid and low cost as possible, and on that basis, none of these alternatives passes the test. David Swensen, CIO of the Yale University Endowment, and one of the most respected institutional investors (including alternatives), seems to agree:

> 'You should invest only in things that you understand. That should be the starting point and the finishing point. For most investors the practical application of this axiom is to invest in index funds (low-fee investments that aim to mirror the performance of a particular stock market index). The overwhelming number of investors, individual and institutional, should be completely in low-cost index funds because that's easy to understand.'
>
> David Swensen[25]

---

[25] *Financial Times*, 8 October 2009.

CHAPTER 9
PROPERTY AND LAND

'It's tangible, it's solid, it's beautiful. It's artistic, from my standpoint, and I just love real estate.'

Donald Trump

Many people love property, perhaps because, unlike an investment portfolio, it is tangible and they feel that they understand it. Everyone's got to have somewhere to live and businesses need premises from which to trade. In this chapter we'll examine residential investment property, agricultural property and land/woodlands, so you can consider what role, if any, they play in your overall wealth strategy.

Residential rental property

In the UK we have an obsession with residential property and for various reasons we seem to think that it represents a type of investment 'get out of jail' option. There's no doubt that many have made good money from buy-to-let investments which have, as a consequence, attracted many followers into an investment strategy that seems to be a sure thing – buy a property, get a mortgage, pay the mortgage with the rent, take some extra income each month and sell the property for a big capital gain. If only it were so straightforward. Much of this success has been down to timing and luck in many cases.

Savings interest is at an historic low, with variable rates below 2% p.a. In fact, over the three years to the end of June 2014, the value of a saver's assets has decreased in purchasing power terms by more than 10%. Against this backdrop a gross average annual yield of 5.6% (the consensus[1] at the time of writing) would appear to

---

[1] Source: this is the average of the UK average rental property yield quoted by Countrywide (6.1%) and LSL Property Services plc (5.2%) in their annual rental property index reports in January 2014.

make residential property an attractive alternative. However, as I'll demonstrate, when you take into account maintenance costs, arrears from bad tenants and void rent (where no rent is received due to the property being empty), you'd be lucky to get 3.5% net and that's before tax, inflation and any borrowing costs.

Some believe that the equity market has been disappointing over the past decade or so. Only a few years ago the headlines were of 'the lost decade' in terms of stock market investment. In fact, from the start of 2000, which was the height of the market before the dot com crash – so a pretty tough place from which to measure – to the end of April 2014 the UK equity market, with dividends reinvested, was actually up 72% and even stripping out inflation its purchasing power rose by around 14%. Emerging market equities would have more than doubled your purchasing power during this period. A well-structured portfolio, as we will see later, did a remarkable job during an emotionally tough period for investors.

While there are clearly a number of people who have made money out of residential buy-to-let property, as the market has grown over the past 15 years, most of this arose from unsustainable growth in capital values fuelled by cheap money and lax lending activity by financial institutions. There are a number of factors that will affect whether residential buy-to-let makes sense as a viable long-term investment. Tenant demand has risen steadily over the past five years or so, in the face of increasing prices and reduced mortgage finance. Estate agents would have us believe that tenant demand will continue to grow in the future.

Recent reforms to housing benefit are also likely to have a negative impact on overall rent levels. It is undoubtedly the case that high rents paid for some social tenants, particularly in London, had been pushing up rents across the board. Therefore, cutting state funding of the most expensive social housing must have a negative impact on overall yields. The average yield masks regional variations. For example, in January 2014 the yield in Scotland was 6.6% compared with London where it was 4.8%.[2] Single properties let to multiple tenants, like students, can offer yields as high as 10%.

> 'Beyond the nationwide figures lies an even more complicated picture. Local trends can be highly detailed, while dozens of different factors can affect the rent for any given property. Ultimately the ever-changing patterns of demand and the availability of local property at any given time will keep very local patterns in a constant state of flux. Some good deals are

---

[2] Source: Countrywide: 'Annual lettings index,' January 2014 shows Scotland has the highest average yield of 6.6% and Central London has the lowest yield of 4.8%. Clearly within these averages there will be further variations.

always there to be had, for tenants and landlords alike, if they have the right information.'

David Newnes, LSL Property Services plc[3]

Even if rents can be maintained at current levels, it still looks challenging to make a decent return once the true costs of repairs and maintenance are accounted for. Add in the strong probability of loan interest costs rising in the near term, the potential for rent voids and having a bad tenant and the chances of experiencing negative cashflow look likely.

When individuals enter the buy-to-let market with borrowed money, they are in fact starting a highly geared business with all the costs, tax and reporting issues and material risks that go with the territory. Successful buy-to-let enterprises have to be run in a disciplined and professional way if they are to avoid, or at least mitigate, the very material financial risks that they entail. Investors who go into the buy-to-let market without anything more than a naïve set of gross yield numbers, basic cost estimates and the hope of a rising market may not get the sort of outcome for which they are hoping.

The impact of borrowing on returns

If a good friend advised you that they were going to borrow up to three times the value of their investment portfolio to 'gear up' their investments, you'd rightly be concerned. Yet for many buy-to-let property investors this seems a perfectly sensible and clever way to make their money work harder. Property investing provides an easy opportunity to leverage or gear up their capital. Most buy-to-let mortgages demand around one third of the value of the property to be put down as a deposit – if you buy a £150,000 house you can put down £50,000 and borrow £100,000. Obviously, you could put down all £150,000 if you have it and not borrow anything. That choice will depend on your individual circumstances and risk preferences. Using debt to help fund investment property acquisitions might well not feel that risky, given that you may have experience of managing a mortgage on your home.

For those who go down the borrowing route, the reward on their capital – and risk on the flip side of the equation – increases in line with the multiple of their capital that they borrow. For example, disregarding borrowing costs, if the property increases in price by 20% over a period of time, the geared investor in the example

---

[3] Source: LSL Property Services plc press release February 2014, **www.lslps.co.uk/documents/buy_to_let_index_jan14.pdf**

above will make £30,000, which on their capital invested is a return of 60%. If, however, the market declines by 20%, they will lose £30,000 of their £50,000 capital invested (a 60% loss). Borrowing to leverage assets cuts both ways. It is possible to lose more than the value of your equity capital – for example, a fall of 35% in the property value would wipe it out. This is the curse of negative equity.

There have been two big falls since the mid-1980s, starting in 1989 and 2007 respectively. Property values around the country fell by between 20% and 35% on both occasions, as you can see in Table 9.1, which provides some insight into these two big falls and is a reminder of the magnitude of the capital losses that investors would have suffered in these periods.

Table 9.1 Gearing magnifies losses – effect on £50,000 equity capital

Period	Inflation	Price fall	Ungeared	1 x geared	2 x geared	3 x geared	4 x geared
1989–1993	Unadjusted	–15%	£42,500	£35,000	£27,500	£20,000	£12,500
	Adjusted	–34%	£33,000	£16,000	–£1,000	–£18,000	–£35,000
2007–2008	Unadjusted	–22%	£39,000	£28,000	£17,000	£6,000	–£5,000
	Adjusted	–32%	£34,000	£18,000	£2,000	**–£14,000**	**–£30,000**

Source: Albion Strategic using data from Halifax UK All House Price Index. Morningstar Encorr. All rights reserved 2014. Bold = negative equity.

On the upside, an investor investing in 1983 would have doubled the purchasing power (after inflation) of their capital with no gearing, based on the house price appreciation alone and before any positive yield on the property (February 1983 to December 2012).

Working out the net yield

If the average gross buy-to-let yield in the UK is currently around 5.6% and the average rent is £800 per month,[4] this implies an average property value of around just £171,500. We must also include the costs of a buy-to-let investment, which come in three stages: initial purchase and set-up ready for tenants, ongoing costs and, eventually, sale costs. Investors need to keep a tight record

---

[4] This is the average of the UK average rental property yield/monthly rent quoted by Countrywide (6.1%/£854) and LSL Property Services plc (5.2%/£742) in their annual rental property index reports in January 2014.

of all of these items for tax reporting. A cashflow model is essential to begin to understand the rewards and undoubted risks of running a geared (or even an ungeared) buy-to-let business.

Initial costs: initial purchase and setup include the costs of purchase that all homeowners know only too well, including stamp duty (1–7%) and professional fees. The property may well need to be repaired and redecorated, white goods installed, new furnishings purchased if it is to be let furnished, as well as gas and electrical equipment checked and certified.

Ongoing costs: these break down into annual costs and longer-term amortised costs to cover longer-term maintenance items. Property is a naturally depreciating asset – it falls to pieces, over time, if not looked after properly – and you need to invest hard cash into it to maintain or grow its value. Annual costs include insurance costs for buildings, landlord cover and utility and white goods maintenance, perhaps. You also need a general maintenance budget of, say, 1% of the property value for smaller items. If you buy a leasehold building then you may well have an annual service charge/sinking fund contribution to pay as well as the ground rent on the property. Many buy-to-let investors also use agents to manage the property to take some of the hassle out of it – a charge of 10–15% of the monthly rent is quite normal for this. There may well be void periods when no suitable tenants can be found and no rental income is being received. Finally, mortgage payments need to be deducted from the gross yield. Current mortgage rates with a 30% deposit are in the region of 4.5%, often with a hefty up-front arrangement fee.

The longer-term costs that are often either overlooked or grossly underestimated include repairs to boilers, central heating and appliances or worn-out showers, cookers, carpets, etc. – it is surprising how quickly rented accommodation begins to look shabby. The property will probably need to be redecorated every 3–5 years. Kitchens and bathrooms may need replacing every 5–10 years and don't forget guttering, gardens, drains, roofs, wiring, drives, etc. that need some long-term care and attention. Tired-looking properties are hard to rent in an increasingly competitive and discerning rental market.

Scouring the internet[5] you can begin to get a feel for what these costs are in aggregate from those who have been doing this for some time. The best rule of thumb appears to be to expect to budget for around 30–35% of the gross income for all general ongoing costs, before mortgage repayments. Any income remaining after costs – most of which are allowable against tax, including mortgage interest – will be taxed at the investor's marginal rate.

---

[5] For example, UKpropertyexpert.com: '£250 per month per property. The real cost of buy-to-let?'

Sale costs: finally, if you sell the property you will have to pay agent's fees and capital gains tax at the prevailing rate (currently 18–28%), although if the investor lives in it for a certain period of time they may be able to deem it to be their primary residence and thereby reduce the amount of tax payable. However, that may not suit some investors, either practically or morally.

So, when some basic numbers are calculated, the true net yield is far less compelling than the news headlines. These basic calculations are set out in Tables 9.2 and 9.3.[6]

Table 9.2 Assumptions used in the example

Basic assumptions	£	%
Annual rent	£9,600	
Gross rential yield		5.6%
Occupancy %		95%
Property value	£171,429	
Investor's capital	£50,000	
Interest only mortgage	£121,429	
Mortgage interest rate		4.5%

Table 9.3 Net yields aren't great

Monthly budget	In	Out
Monthly rent	£800	
Vacant periods		£40
Monthly maintenance/management		£250
Mortgage interest		£455
Net income	£55	
Net rental yield before tax (on property value)	0.38%	
Tax @ 40%		£22
Monthly income net of tax	£33	
Net rental yield after tax (on property value)	0.23%	
Yield on investor's captial (£50,000) after tax	0.79%	
Annual income net of tax	£396	

[6] Ideally, investors should calculate the internal rate of return that any buy-to-let property opportunity could deliver from *all* of the cashflows involved to see where the risks and return truly lie.

Some buy-to-let investors may dispute the numbers and it is acknowledged that rental yields can vary quite widely across the UK, but it is a reasonable insight that provides a framework for making better informed decisions. On these numbers, an investor with no mortgage would have received a net yield after tax of just over 2% on their capital[7] – still below current inflation (Retail Prices Index).

What is interesting about the numbers in this example is that if the mortgage interest rate is raised by only 0.5% p.a., then the net yield after tax is near enough zero, before inflation. It is worth remembering that rents do not necessarily go up just because interest rates do. Those who lived through the property market slump of the early 1990s and interest rates of 15% (which I did) still remember the pain of having to find cash from their own earnings to cover mortgage payments on rented properties and of a prolonged period of negative equity. It took more than five years from the bottom of the market in 1993 to recover to the former peak, before inflation is taken into account. The geared buy-to-let investor in our example would have had to find £1,000 per month in 1991 to cover the rental shortfall to meet the costs and mortgage interest payments. Many were forced to sell, creating a downward spiral on prices.

Thinking like an investor

In many case, because the true net yield is so low, buy-to-let property is in effect a big punt which depends on price appreciation for its long-term success. A sensible investor will look at an asset class dispassionately and consistently, looking solely at neither yield nor capital gain, but on a total return basis being the combination of the two. To make a better informed comparison and to try to level out the playing field, if we generously assume a net post-tax yield of 2% on an ungeared buy-to-let investment and add this to the price return of the UK house price series, we can get a rough picture of how it has performed against other more traditional investment portfolios. Costs of 1% per annum have been deducted from the traditional portfolios for fairer comparison. No initial setup costs for the buy-to-let strategy have been deducted, even though these can be material. The outcome is illustrated in Figure 9.1.

As you can see, the ungeared buy-to-let simulation delivered strong returns during the equity market crash of 2000–2003 but suffered badly during the credit crisis. It was outperformed marginally by a typical equity/bond portfolio and materially

---

[7] Tax rates may be lower than 40%, e.g. achieved by owning the property in a partner's name whose total income falls within a lower tax band. Net yields after tax would thus be a little higher.

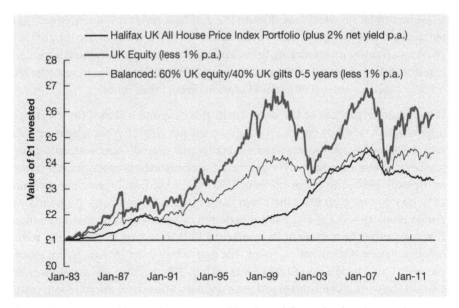

Figure 9.1 Ungeared buy-to-let versus traditional portfolios – simulated strategies
Source: Albion Strategic.

by equities over the period. Looking at the worst case downsides of each portfolio, one can see that ungeared property is similar in risk to the 'balanced' portfolio (see Table 9.4). That is what one would expect from a hybrid asset class that derives regular income by way of rent, similar to a bond, but with the capital appreciation potential of equities. Borrowing 100% of the capital invested would double the downside risk to capital, making this approach comparable to equity investments.

Table 9.4 Downside risk – worst case returns over different horizons (after inflation)

Period	1 year	3 years	5 years	10 years
UK equity portfolio	–38%	–18%	–10%	–4%
Balance portfolio	–22%	–9%	–4%	–1%
Buy-to-let	–18%	–7%	–6%	–1%

Source: Data from Albion Strategic. Simulated returns as described in the note to Figure 9.1.

The role of residential property

One of the key problems with property, and one usually glossed over by investors when comparing it with a fully diversified investment portfolio, is that property is an illiquid asset class. If you want to realise your investment (and any accrued capital gains that will arise in a single tax year) you need to find someone else willing to buy it from you. Property, other than your home, has a place to play in your wider wealth plans, perhaps through an allocation to global commercial property as part of a well-balanced and diversified traditional investment fund, by way of some sort of collective investment scheme or even held directly as part of a self-invested pension plan. Currently residential property cannot be held in a pension plan.

Perhaps the biggest risk of the buy-to-let market is the concentration of risk in not just one narrow asset class – residential property – but in one house or flat, on one street in one town. This lack of diversification is an unattractive attribute for a plan to deliver wealth and happiness in retirement. It is difficult (indeed usually impossible) to rebalance a portfolio by selling part of the property should you wish to reduce your exposure to that asset without outright disposal.

Perhaps if you could build a large diversified portfolio of, say, 30 properties, or several large houses with multiple occupants (HMOs) like students, possibly with a dedicated property manager, you might be able to withstand the occasional negative cashflow on a small proportion of rental properties and derive economies of scale on running costs. But the reality is that most buy-to-let investors are on a small scale and have relied on capital gains to provide the bulk of their returns. Once those capital gains evaporate and negative cashflow kicks in, property equity can quickly be wiped out.

If you want to run a business and you have an interest in property then by all means invest in residential rental property, but make sure that you understand the significant risks you will be exposed to compared with the potential returns, that you can handle the lack of liquidity and the demands on your time, and that you do it on a big scale.

Residential development

One way to make high returns from residential property which is not to be used as your primary residence, and that is potentially much lower risk and more liquid, is to engage in either developing or redeveloping residential properties for immediate sale. Make no mistake, developing and/or redeveloping property of any type is a business first and an investment second, and it requires discipline, organisation and know-how to do well. Why developing/redeveloping has more appeal is because the tail-end risk inherent in rental properties (rent voids, interest rates rises, maintenance costs and stagnant rent) does not exist. The main risk is being able to sell the property, bank a profit and receive the cash proceeds to reinvest in another project.

An uplift of 18% on purchase price plus development costs seems a prudent basis on which to assess a project, but assuming this holds good, and the property market is stable (neither increasing nor decreasing in value), a pre-tax return of more than 10% seems entirely reasonable. If you become good at this, and manage to buy better-value properties with more upside and/or lower refurbishment costs, and the property is located in an up-and-coming area, you could do even better than this. But – and it's a big but – there are many moving parts to a property development or redevelopment and it will need your constant attention.

Running a property development business also benefits from certain tax benefits, which might make it more appealing than a residential rental business (see Chapter 14). If you have the time and inclination, and don't put all your capital into this activity, it could be a legitimate element of your wealth plan. But do remember that risk and return are related and you don't generate returns in excess of 10% per annum without taking on a fair degree of risk, not all of which will be apparent at the outset.

At the time of writing, much of the UK residential property market has seen strong increases in values. I have no idea how this will turn out, but I do know that value is a product of affordability. With prices stretched, mortgage finance becoming harder to obtain (due to a mixture of new eligibility rules and tougher bank capital rules), house builders increasing supply and interest rates set to rise from the current historic low level, it doesn't feel like the beginning of a gold rush to me.

Example property development transaction

Purchase price of property	£300,000 (A)	
Stamp duty@ 3%	£9,000	
Legal fees	£2,000	
Refurbishment costs	£60,000 (B)	
Total costs	£371,000 (C)	
Selling price ((A + B) + 18%)	£424,800 (D)	
Selling costs@ 1.5%	(£6,400)	
Legal fees	(£2,000)	
Interest lost on capital @ 1.75%	(£6,500)	Assume £371,000 for 12 months
Total costs	£14,900 (E)	
Net proceeds (D−(C+E))	£38,900 (F)	
Annual return F/C = 10.50%		

Agricultural property, farmland and woodlands

'Buy land, they're not making it anymore.'

Mark Twain

Farming is one of the world's oldest businesses. The industry ranges from huge multinationals farming millions of acres down to smallholdings of a few acres. Activities include arable farming, livestock production, growing and harvesting timber, and conservation activity. Although the vast majority of owners of farms and agricultural property in the UK are farmers (50%), a significant proportion are owned by people who are not farmers (40%), with a much smaller proportion owned by institutions and companies (10%).[8] The increase in ownership of farms and agricultural land by non-farmers has occurred mainly over the past ten years caused by a combination of factors, including:

- the perception of farms as a tangible 'safe haven' against the backdrop of the global credit crisis and volatile investment markets
- tax-efficient means of transferring wealth to the next generation
- a subsidy regime that provides attractive government-backed cashflows
- meets desired lifestyle and/or aspirational needs (trophy asset) of the individual
- conservation and environmental motivation.

Figure 9.2 shows the price of land globally and how this has changed over the past few years, while Figure 9.3 illustrates the significant after-inflation increase in value of high- and low-grade UK farmland over the past 20 years. Farmland has certainly proven to be a very good investment over the past ten years or so, in the region of 20% p.a. for the world since 2002 and 13% p.a. for the UK. Over the ten years to 2013 the cumulative gains from UK farmland has been 273%, compared with 135% for prime residential property in central London.[9]

Property experts predict continued growth in asset values, in the region of 5–8% p.a. However, it's important to bear in mind the risks associated with investment in this sector. These risks include:

- unpredictable maintenance costs
- illiquid asset
- agricultural subsidies may be reduced or stopped in the future

---

[8] Source: Savills World Research, Market Survey – UK Agricultural Land 2014.

[9] Ibid.

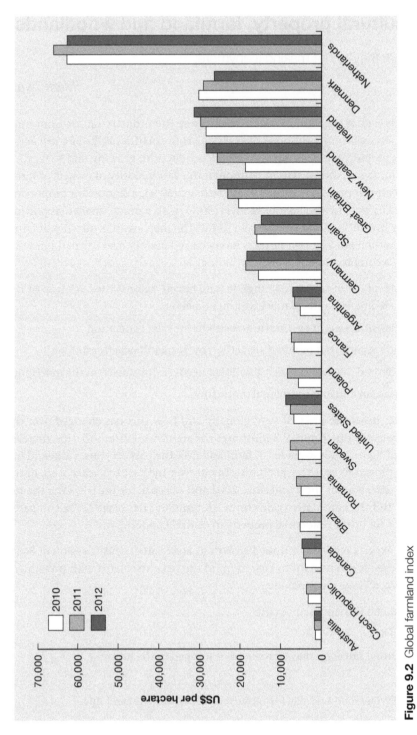

Figure 9.2 Global farmland index

Source: Savills Research.

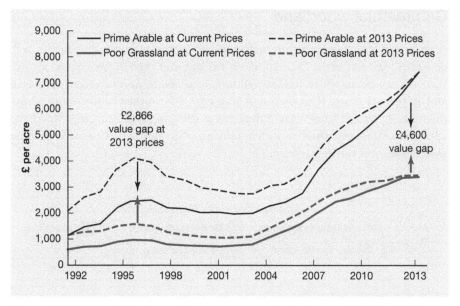

Figure 9.3 Average GB prime arable and poor grassland values adjusted for inflation
Source: Savills Research.

- if the land is not actively farmed this may lead to loss of tax benefits
- possible reduction in demand from non-farmer owners, as the world economy improves and competition for capital increases
- any borrowing used to fund the purchase needs to be serviced from rental income or farming profits and a rise in interest rates will alter the return profile and cashflow position
- rental income may depend on finding a successful farm tenant to farm the land
- if not to be let out, the land will need to be farmed by the owner as a farming business and all that that entails.

Unlike residential property, it is possible for a pension plan to invest in agricultural land and associated commercial properties, as long as this is done on full commercial terms.

Farms and agricultural land also benefit from attractive tax treatment, including in relation to inheritance tax, which makes them particularly attractive to wealthy families as a means of passing on family wealth to the next generation (see Chapter 14 on tax planning for an overview of these tax benefits). Unless you are very wealthy, buying agricultural land is likely to make sense only if this is part of your desired lifestyle (you want to run a smallholding) or wider business aspirations.

Commercial woodland

Commercial woodland is an alternative, tangible asset class, which benefits from generous tax treatment. Depending on the age and type of trees being grown, the trees can be harvested or sold standing, to generate cashflow from between 3 and 30 years or more. The benchmark index for UK commercial woodland performance is shown in Figure 9.4. On the basis of these figures commercial woodland appears to offer attractive investment returns, which are broadly similar to other asset classes over the longer term.

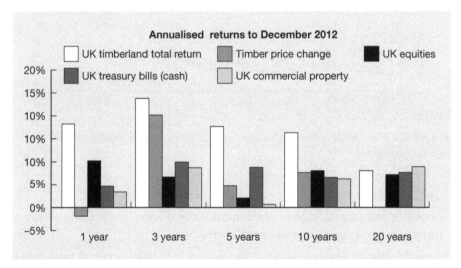

Figure 9.4 UK timberland performance 1993–2012

Source: Data from Forestry Commission Nominal Price Index of Coniferous Standing Sales (for Great Britain), FTSE All-Share Index, FTSE UK Gilts Index 5–15 yrs, IPD UK Annual Property Index.

Woodland covers about 3.1 million hectares or about 13% of the UK, with 60% being privately owned and the balance owned by the Forestry Commission. Interestingly, the Domesday Book in 1086 noted that 15% of England was covered by woodland, but this fell to a low of 5% for the UK just after the Second World War. The trend is that UK woodland cover is increasing year on year and 13,000 hectares of new woodland were planted in 2012.[10]

However, it should be noted that this index is calculated from a small sample of about 150 private-sector coniferous plantations of predominantly Sitka spruce in mainland Britain, with a value of £220 million. It is not, therefore, a statistically

---

[10] Source: Forestry Commission website, accessed April 2014.

robust basis on which to determine the investment characteristics of woodland. There appears to be a significant regional variation in the value of woodlands. The split between the value of the land and timber is typically about 20% and 80% respectively.

The economic rationale for investment in commercial woodland (environmental, sustainable fuel, rising demand for timber products and lack of supply) certainly seems compelling, but the following commentary on the history of UK commercial woodland values over the past 15 years reminds us that values can fall substantially as well as rise:

> 'Between the late 1990s and mid-2000s, forestry property values fell in response to timber price falls and strengthening of sterling against the US dollar and Swedish kroner. UK-grown timber products experienced high levels of competition from unsustainable levels of timber imports from the Baltic States. Timber prices fell by over 70%. From 2004, forestry returns recovered. Inward capital investment in timber processing and infrastructure impacted on efficiencies; sterling weakened; timber prices increased; whilst global demand from the Far East impacted commodity supplies generally. From the late 2000s the incentives to use wood as an energy source have helped move timber prices to new levels. At the same time, land-based assets have provided an alternative home for cash deposits in times of low interest rates and for investors in general seeking less volatile markets.'[11]

Notwithstanding the return potential, commercial woodland also benefits from the availability of subsidies and generous tax treatment. Each year there are usually a number of grants available to help landowners fund the cost of creating a woodland plan and establishing new woodlands and/or improving existing ones, which meet certain government environmental objectives. These grants vary from £10 to £20 per hectare for planning work, and 50% to 80% of establishment and maintenance costs. In addition, the income from harvesting woodland is exempt from personal or corporation tax, as is any capital gains arising on the sale of the trees (but not the land). After two years of ownership, the value of the timber (but not the land it sits on) is exempt from inheritance tax.

However, there are numerous risks and ongoing maintenance costs associated with woodlands, which should not be underestimated. Storm damage, diseases (such as the recent Ash Dieback) and government regulations can wipe out much of the financial returns on offer, although insurance can help mitigate these to a degree. If you are not thinking of engaging in commercial forestry as part of a new

---

[11] IPD UK Annual Forestry Index factsheet 2012.

or existing farming business, and don't want to spend lots of time managing the investment, but you still wish to invest in it for the tax and return benefits, there are two main options open to you:

- Management service – where you have at least £1 million to invest directly into commercial woodland, you could use the services of a specialist investment adviser, who will help with investment selection, management supervision, financial control, valuations, annual report and accounts, VAT administration, insurance, timber marketing, property realisation, and research and performance measurement. Clearly, the professional fees will reduce your overall return, but at least it removes much of the hassle involved with direct investment.

- Woodland fund – where you wish to invest more modest amounts into commercial woodland, you can invest in an unregulated fund that provides all the benefits of direct ownership, including the various tax breaks, together with the economies of scale and geographic diversification associated with larger investments. Additionally, once investment is made into the fund, investors are not liable for further capital calls.

My own view is that commercial woodland does offer a highly tax-efficient, established and non-aggressive means of passing on wealth to future generations. Where inheritance tax and/or capital gains tax deferment is a concern and investment in a tangible asset is preferred to a trading business and/or other simpler IHT planning has already been done, commercial woodland, either direct or via a fund, offers a useful means to achieve this. As long as you choose wisely, don't put too much of your wealth in it, and understand the risks and rewards, it might form part of your overall wealth-planning strategy.

CHAPTER 10
ACTIVE OR PASSIVE?

'I don't try to be clever at all. The idea that I could see what no one else can is an illusion.'[1]

Daniel H. Kahneman, Nobel Laureate 2002

Once you have a good idea of your overall wealth plan and asset allocation policy you will need to make a third key decision: should you pursue an active or a passive investment approach or a combination of the two? Figure 10.1 sets out the key characteristics of each approach.

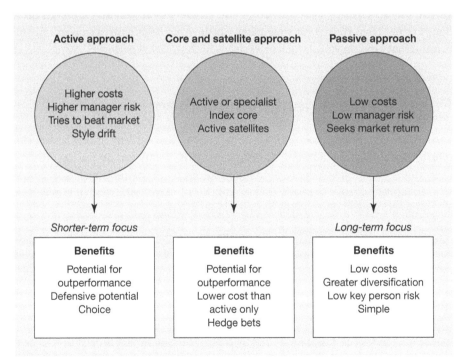

Figure 10.1 The three investment management approaches
Source: The Vanguard Group.

---

[1] Bogle, J. (2007) *The Little Book of Common Sense Investing*, John Wiley & Sons, pp. 98–99.

Active investment management

Active investment management is where a manager (or investor) aims to beat, rather than simply match, the return of an investment market or agreed benchmark. Active investment management can be at the asset allocation or stock selection level or a mixture of the two.

Market timing is where an investor makes bets about whether to place more or less in a particular asset class at any given time. For example, the manager might believe that UK equities are likely to provide a higher return over the next year than, say, UK gilts and as a result might increase their allocation to UK equities and reduce the allocation to UK gilts. A few years ago many investors were attracted to gold and increased exposure to this asset class because they thought it offered better return prospects than other asset classes such as equities and property.

Active stock selection is where the investor makes bets on whether to invest in certain sectors or individual holdings within an asset class, for example banking shares versus drug companies or Merck versus GlaxoSmithKline. In the past few years a lot of investors were attracted to companies that were paying high dividends rather than those that were paying little or no dividends, as a result of the turmoil that arose in world stock markets in the 2007–2009 period.

Passive investment management

Passive investment management is where the manager aims to closely match the returns of a market, benchmark or risk factor. This is achieved by buying either a representative sample of the underlying holdings or all the holdings in an index so as to replicate, as far as possible, the market. This approach is called indexation and is the most common form of passive management.

A smaller proportion of the passive management sector follows a slightly different approach, which is known as evidence-based investing. Managers of such funds do not attempt to replicate or follow traditional indices but instead seek to hold shares that reflect a particular risk characteristic. For example, a fund investing in smaller companies may use a different definition of what is a smaller company compared with the established indices and also may adopt a more flexible approach to trading than an index fund that has to rigidly follow the benchmark index.

Core and satellite investing

This approach aims to deliver the benefits of passive and active management. The portfolio comprises a core of long-term investments and a periphery of specialist or shorter-term holdings (see Figure 10.2). Core investments are usually represented by long-term, low-cost index funds that closely track an index such as the FTSE All-Share. Satellite investments usually include specialist investments that are not highly correlated with core investments. Examples of satellite funds include hedge funds, commodities, thematic and emerging market equities.

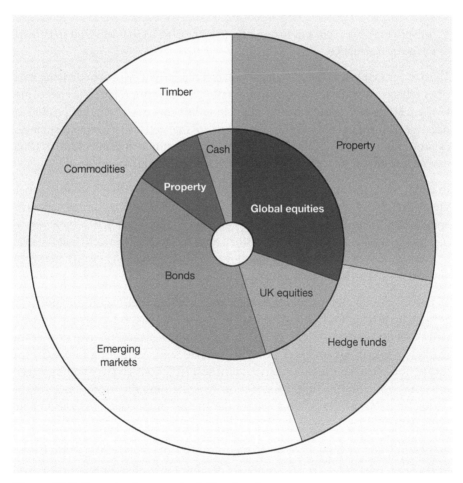

Figure 10.2 Example of core and satellite allocation
Source: The Vanguard Group.

The efficient market hypothesis

A key concept to understand is what is known as the efficient market hypothesis. This is a model that was developed back in the 1960s to understand how investment markets behave.

Basically, the efficient market hypothesis[2] states that:

- current prices incorporate all available information and expectations
- current prices are the best approximation to intrinsic value
- price changes are due to unforeseen events
- 'mispricings' do occur but not in predictable patterns that can lead to consistent outperformance.

The basic principle is that in an efficient market the current price of underlying securities reflects all publicly available information. As new information (news) comes to the market, prices immediately adjust to reflect that news, whether positive or negative. The implications of this hypothesis are that active management strategies cannot consistently add value through security selection and market timing, while passive investment strategies reward investors with capital market returns.

In 2008, when Lehman Brothers went bust, investors immediately changed their view of risks and returns, fearing an immediate collapse of the entire financial system, and prices adjusted to reflect this new scenario. By March 2009 investors had become even more negative and stock markets around the world had fallen to all-time lows. When the financial meltdown didn't turn out as expected, investors' appetite for risk returned and prices adjusted upwards.

So unless investors can predict the future or have (illegal) inside information, it is extremely difficult for them to do better than the market, certainly not consistently over any period of time. Traditional investment managers strive to beat the market by taking advantage of pricing 'mistakes' and attempting to predict the future. Too often, this proves costly and futile. Predictions go awry and managers miss the strong returns that markets provide by holding the wrong stocks at the wrong time. Meanwhile, capital economies thrive – not because markets fail but because they succeed.

As we discussed in Chapter 5, investment markets throughout the world have a history of rewarding long-term investors for the capital they supply. Companies

---

2   Fama, E.F. (1970) 'Efficient capital markets: A review of theory and empirical work', *Journal of Finance*, 25(2): 383–417; Fama, E.F. (1977) 'Foundations of finance', *Journal of Finance*, 32(3): 961–964.

compete with each other for investment capital and millions of investors compete with each other to find the most attractive returns. This competition tends to drive prices to fair value, making it difficult for investors to achieve greater returns without bearing greater risk. The futility of speculation is good news for the investor. It means that prices for public securities are generally fair and persistent differences in average portfolio returns are largely explained by differences in average risk. It is certainly possible to outperform markets, but not, in general, without accepting increased risk.

Testing times for the efficient market hypothesis

Behavioural scientists have been critical of the efficient market hypothesis, contending that investors' irrational behaviour causes greed to lead to asset price bubbles and fear to lead to price crashes. However, the behavioural school seems to now agree that the most practical solution for most investors is to hold a diversified portfolio based on one's lifestyle goals and tolerance for risk. Professor Richard Thaler is a leading member of the behavioural school and now thinks that the recent financial crisis has strengthened the efficient market hypothesis. In an article in the *Financial Times*, Professor Thaler explained his view:

> 'While markets could make mistakes, it was still impossible to profit from how they were wrong . . . Lunches are not free. Shorting internet stocks or Las Vegas real estate two years before the peak was a good recipe for bankruptcy, and no one had yet found a way to predict the end of a bubble.'[3]

Concentrated risks can and do have big payoffs and so if you do want the highest returns possible, and can live with the highly probable consequences of failure, put all your eggs in the same basket, but watch that basket! The problem is that most concentrated risks are unlikely to be compensated. In other words, you are unlikely to be adequately rewarded for the risks that you take with such investments.

'The four most dangerous words in investing are, It's different this time.'

Sir John Templeton, legendary investor

Some commentators suggested that diversification failed during the financial crisis and 'this time it is different' and active asset allocation and stock selection are now key to investment success. All that the global credit crisis of 2008–2009 has proved is that markets can and do experience extreme price fluctuations

---

[3] Professor Thaler (2009) 'The price is not always right', *Financial Times*, 5 August.

in response to the rapid changes in economic conditions. The problem is that a large body of investors started to believe an outcome that was, statistically, likely to happen once in a lifetime, would happen in someone else's lifetime, not their own. For example, in the 12 months ended 31 December 2008 American Express returned −63.67% while Wal-Mart returned +19.95%. So even in a market melt-down some companies will do much better than others. The problem is correctly, and consistently, picking the winners in advance.

In the summer of 2009, just a few months after world stock markets hit their historic lows, Professor Eugene Fama – the man widely considered to be the father of the efficient market hypothesis – had this to say:

> 'The market can only know what is knowable. It can't resolve uncertainties that are unresolveable. So there is a large amount of economic uncertainty out there, there's going to be a large amount of volatility in prices. And that's what we've been through. As far as I'm concerned, that's exactly what you'd expect an efficient market to look like.'[4]

Harry Markowitz, an academic and Noble Laureate who is considered the father of modern financial economics with his theory of the efficient portfolio in the 1950s, had this to say about portfolio theory during the recent financial crisis:

> 'During a crisis almost all securities and asset classes will move in the same direction. This does not mean that individual securities are no longer subject to idiosyncratic risks. Rather it means that the systematic risk swamps the unsystematic risk during this period.'[5]

Even large and apparently prosperous firms can fail. Take Enron, for example, which was, for many years, a star performer of the stock market and appeared to have a bright future. Within a matter of months the company imploded and filed for bankruptcy. Shareholders in Enron suffered a total loss of their capital. BP is another example of a massive company that got into difficulty when it suffered a major accident at one of its oil wells in the Gulf of Mexico in 2010. As a consequence of suspending dividends and uncertainty about the eventual compensation costs arising, the share price fell from around £6.50 before the accident to just over £3 within six weeks of the accident, as investors reassessed the risks associated with holding BP shares. One year later the shares stood at £4.50 as more information became available and BP resumed paying dividends, albeit at a lower level.

---

[4] Fama, E.F. (2009) 'Fama on market efficiency in a volatile market', Fama/French Forum, Dimensional Fund Advisors, 11 August, **www.dimensional.com**

[5] Markowitz, H.M., Hebner, M.T. and Brunson, M.E. (2009) 'Does portfolio theory work during financial crises?' **www.ifa.com/pdf/Does%20Portfolio%20Theory%20Work%20 HMM%20mbedits%205-19-09.pdf**

The folly of market timing

If it were possible to avoid the worst-performing investment days and capture returns from the best-performing days, then it would be possible to produce both positive returns all the time and significant outperformance of the market as a whole. It is the allure of these potential high returns that causes many investors, both professional and non-professional, to ignore the reality of market efficiency and to speculate on the future direction of markets. The evidence shows that markets experience gains often in short, unpredictable bursts. This means that it is easy for an investment trader to enter and leave the investment market at the wrong time. Sometimes missing just a few – usually the best – days in the stock market can result in significant long-term underperformance. For example, over a 27-year period (1986–2013), we can see in Figure 10.3 that missing the best 25 trading days would have cut the FTSE All-Share Index annualised compound return from 10.10% to 5.24%. Trying to forecast which days or weeks will yield good or bad returns is a guessing game that can prove costly for investors.

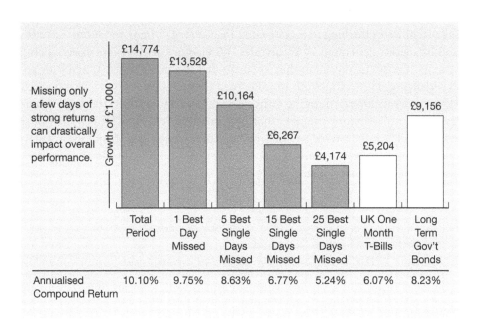

	Total Period	1 Best Day Missed	5 Best Single Days Missed	15 Best Single Days Missed	25 Best Single Days Missed	UK One Month T-Bills	Long Term Gov't Bonds
Annualised Compound Return	10.10%	9.75%	8.63%	6.77%	5.24%	6.07%	8.23%

Figure 10.3 Missing the best days in the UK stock market
Source: Dimensional Fund Advisors.

Market timing is challenging, as identified by a research study that looked at the US and UK stock markets from 1871 to 2004 and 1899 to 2004 respectively. The researchers compared a range of market-timing approaches to a simple buy-and-hold strategy. While market-timing techniques were found to work in identifying cheap and expensive markets, resulting in a return differential over a buy-and-hold strategy, investors are still better off with a buy-and-hold approach. This is what the authors had to say:

> 'Our findings are not encouraging for proponents of active management using very long-run mean reversion: we find investors are inevitably better off with a simple buy-and-hold equity strategy rather than trying to time the market using moving average rules.

> 'The returns from equities, even during the sub-optimal periods when they are expensive, have been markedly better than cash.'[6]

Bulls and bears

Investment markets have been described as voting machines in the short term, reflecting current sentiment based on news and other economic data, but weighing machines in the long term, reflecting the value of current and future earnings and dividends generated by companies. When stock markets are experiencing strong increases in valuation they are described as a bull market. When they are experiencing severe reductions in value then they are described as a bear market. When markets are not moving either up or down much they are described as 'range bound'. History suggests that bull market cycles last longer than bear market cycles and produce cumulative gains that more than offset losses experienced in bear markets. Figure 10.4 shows the time and magnitude of those rises and falls for the UK stock market since 1955.[7]

---

[6]   Gwilym, O., Secton, J. and Thomas, S. (2008) 'Very long-term equity investment strategies', *The Journal of Investing*, 17(2): 15–23.

[7]   The graph in Figure 10.4 documents bull and bear market periods in the FTSE All-Share Index from February 1955 to December 2012. The market cycles are identified in hindsight using historical cumulative monthly returns. Monthly index returns are total returns, which include reinvestment of dividends. All monthly observations are performed after the fact. A bear market is identified in hindsight when the market experiences a negative monthly return followed by a cumulative loss of at least 10%. The bear market ends at its low point, which is defined as the month of the greatest negative cumulative return before the reversal. A bull market is defined by data points not considered part of a bear market. The rising trend lines designate the bull markets occurring since 1955, while the falling trend lines document the bear markets. The bars that frame the trend lines help to describe the length and intensity of the gains and losses. The numbers above or below the bars indicate the duration (in months) and cumulative return percentage of the bull or bear market.

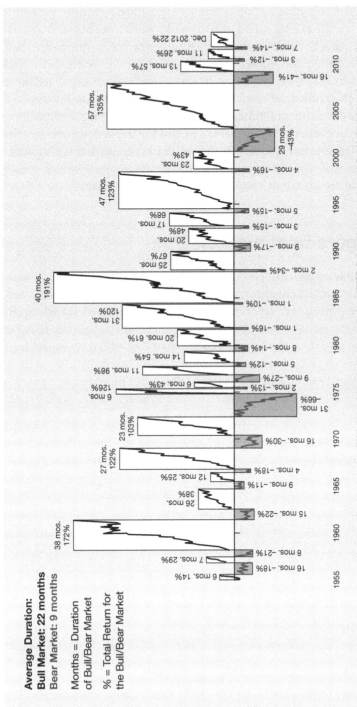

Figure 10.4 The past 57 years of bull and bear markets

Source: Dimensional Fund Advisors, the FTSE Group.

The chart in Figure 10.4 does not show total compounded returns or growth of wealth. Once the cycle is established in retrospect, the first month of that cycle resets the performance baseline to zero. Fluctuating performance within each trend illustrates that volatility and uncertainty occur even within established market cycles: bull markets may have short-term dips and bear markets may have short-term advances. The immediate trend is not readily apparent to market observers and may become clear only in hindsight. This analysis highlights the difficulty of accurately predicting and timing market cycles and the importance of maintaining a disciplined investment approach that views market events and trends from a long-term perspective. If you react emotionally to short-term movements, you are likely to make bad decisions that compromise long-term performance.

Do managers beat markets?

There is no credible evidence of persistence of success of active investment management and that success outperformance cannot, in the vast majority of cases, be explained by exposure to risk factors. One study examined 115 US equity mutual funds between 1945 and 1964 and found 'very little evidence that any mutual fund was able to do significantly better than that which we expect from mere random chance'.[8] Another study examined 4,686 US equity mutual funds between 1965 and 1998 and found 'none of the styles included in the study are able to generate positive abnormal returns, compared to the Fama/French (1993) benchmark'.[9]

'All the time and effort that people devote to picking the right fund, the hot hand, the great manager, have in most cases led to no advantage.'[10]

Peter Lynch, legendary US fund manager

A report prepared for the Norwegian government found that: 'The average active return from January 1998 to September 2009 generated by Norges Bank Investment Management has been statistically indistinguishable from zero.'[11] Another paper examined the empirical evidence and logic for investing using a

---

[8] Jensen, M. (1968) 'The performance of mutual funds in the period 1945–1964', *Journal of Finance*, 23(2): 414.

[9] Davis, J.L. (2001) 'Mutual fund performance and manager style', *Financial Analysts' Journal*, 57(1): 19–27.

[10] Lynch, P. (1993) *Beating the Street*, Simon & Schuster, p. 60.

[11] Ang, A., Goetzmann, W.N. and Schaefer, S.M. (2009) 'Evaluation of active management of the Norwegian Government Pension Fund – global', Ministry of Finance, Norway, p. 65.

passive approach in the UK by reviewing UK-based equity and bond funds over the 15-year period through to 31 December 2012. After deducting the results of all the funds that were closed in that period, only about 26% of UK equity funds beat the market and virtually no funds beat the market for UK-government bonds over ten years. The authors came to the following conclusion:

'Actively managed funds have in the past tended on average to underperform their benchmarks and to underperform relative to low-cost passive funds targeting the same benchmark. For any period, there will inevitably be some fund managers within the total distribution that are nevertheless able to outperform, but the challenge for investors is to pick those fund managers in advance. Our results suggest that a lack of persistence of performance by specific funds makes it difficult to use past performance as a guide to future outperformance. This paper has shown that there is a compelling case for investors to invest in passive funds on the grounds that they provide higher returns on average and at lower volatility.'[12]

Time after time, analysis of past performance shows that the majority of active investment managers deliver returns below that of the market as a whole. Figure 10.5 shows the returns from more than 130 UK equity funds that existed over the 20 years to 31 December 2012. We can see that the majority of managers (and don't forget that this excludes all the funds that failed to survive 20 years) underperformed the market as represented by the FTSE All-Share Index, which is consistent with the principles of efficient markets.

'There are two kinds of investors, be they large or small: those who don't know where the market is headed, and those who don't know that they don't know. Then again, there is a third type of investor – the investment professional, who indeed knows that he or she doesn't know, but whose livelihood depends upon appearing to know.'

William Bernstein, US financial theorist and author

Due to the lower expected returns from fixed income, actively managed funds have to work particularly hard to generate market-beating returns, net of the additional ongoing and turnover costs. A recent analysis concluded that most of the historical outperformance of active global bond funds has been the result of risk which managers assumed beyond that of the bond benchmark. Once this excess risk exposure is taken into account, the relative performance of global bond funds

---

[12] Westaway, P., Thomas, C.J., Philips, C. and Schlanger, T. (2013) 'The case for index fund investors for UK investors', Vanguard Research, April.

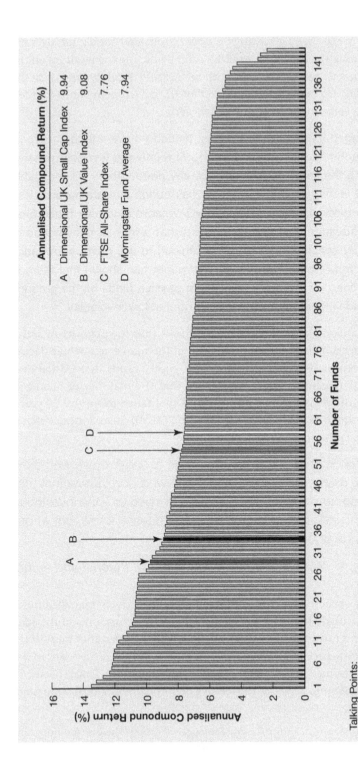

Figure 10.5 UK equity unit trust returns: 1993–2012

Source: Dimensional Fund Advisors, Morningstar.

Talking Points:

Active managers put the Efficient Markets Hypothesis to the test every day as they strive to identify "mispricing opportunities" – or securities that do not accurately reflect all available information. Most managers fail to consistently deliver returns above the market average.

is less favourable. The researchers showed that global bond index funds – and in particular, *hedged* global bond index funds – provide an attractive alternative to achieve the exposure of the asset class.[13]

What about less efficient markets?

Emerging markets are generally agreed to be less efficient than more liquid developed markets. The active management industry suggests that this should allow them to identify mispriced stocks and to manage the country- and stock-specific risks that investors are exposed to, such as the high state ownership of companies and resultant earnings highlighted above. This contention seems reasonable, but the empirical evidence suggests that a large percentage of managers – 80% over five years[14] – fail to beat the emerging market benchmark. In part this is likely due to the annual expenses and trading costs incurred by actively managed emerging market funds. Trading costs have been estimated to be in the region of almost 140 basis points for a round-trip trade, which compares with that in developed markets (ex-UK) of around 35 basis points.[15] It is possible to mitigate stock, country and active manager risk by owning a broad emerging markets fund, diversified across countries and stocks. For example, the MSCI Emerging Market Index covers around 2,700 companies across market capitalisation.

It's not just bonds and equities for which a passive approach makes sense. A recent study[16] revealed that of 80 active US real estate mutual funds (REITs), none of the managers, over a long sample period (1995–2008), exhibited stock-selection skill. The authors concluded: 'The empirical findings show that even apparently successful funds ex-post display "poor" skill in that they perform significantly worse than they would be expected to simply due to luck.'

A passive approach seems the most reasonable one to adopt to capture the returns from global commercial property. Although there are relatively few products that provide the opportunity for gaining exposure to global commercial property on a passive basis, there are few OEICs and ETFs with costs in the region of 0.50% p.a. and below.

---

[13] Philips, C., Schlanger, T. and Wimmer, B, (2013) 'The active/passive decision in global bond funds', Vanguard Research, November.

[14] SPIVA® US Year-end Report 2013, available at **http://us.spindices.com/resource-center/ thought-leadership/spiva/**

[15] Miller, A. and Miller, G. (2012) 'Promoting trust and transparency in the UK investment industry', SCM Private, **www.scmprivate.com**

[16] Layfield, L. and Stevenson, S. (2011) 'Separating skill from luck in REIT mutual funds', Working paper in Real Estate & Planning, 06/11, University of Reading, **www.reading. ac.uk/REP/fulltxt/0611.pdf**

Luck versus skill

Random chance dictates that at any one time we would expect a small number of money managers to outperform the market average. The problem is they are rarely the same managers each time and picking the winning managers in advance is virtually impossible to do consistently. A large group of chimpanzees throwing darts at the share pages of the *Financial Times* has more chance of picking winning shares than a group of experienced equities analysts!

The issue of luck versus skill is rarely addressed in academic studies. A working paper from the respected finance professors Fama and French, however, looked at whether or not individual fund performance was distinguishable from luck.[17] The key findings were that active managers show no statistical evidence they can enhance returns and they do not have enough skill to produce risk-adjusted returns that cover their costs. Only the top 3% of funds perform as well as might be expected if their true alpha (excess return) was not down to luck. A key conclusion of the authors was that 'some [funds] do extraordinarily well and some do extraordinarily poorly just by chance'.

In his book *The Wisdom of Crowds*, James Surowiecki gives a good example of why the aggregate view is generally right more often than not.[18] He cites an ox weight-judging contest held at the 1906 West of England Fat Stock and Poultry Exhibition. The average weight guessed by the 797 contestants was 1,197lb compared with the actual weight of 1,198lb. In another example, a Professor Treynor asked his finance class students to guess how many beans were in a jar. There were in fact 850 beans in the jar compared with the group estimate of 871. Only one of 56 students made a more accurate guess.

Winning the loser's game

Active investment management is a zero-sum game before costs and a loser's game after costs – for every winner there has to be a loser and costs reduce returns. In aggregate the maths does not support the proposition that there is a credible, reliable and replicable way of consistently outwitting the investment marketplace. None of us is smarter than all of us. Every penny that you save in costs is either more returns for you or you can take less risk to obtain the same level of return. See Figure 10.6.

---

[17] Fama, E.F. and French, K.R. (2009) 'Luck versus skill in the cross-section of mutual fund returns', Tuck School of Business Working Paper No. 2009–56, Chicago Booth School of Business Research Paper and *Journal of Finance*, LXV(5): 1915–1947.

[18] Surowiecki, J. (2005) *The Wisdom of Crowds*, Anchor.

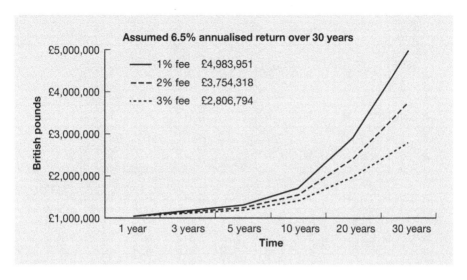

Figure 10.6 Impact of different annual fund costs on investment values over 30 years

There are two main costs associated with investment funds: ongoing costs and turnover. Ongoing costs include things such as trustee and custodian fees. Turnover costs include the hard costs to the fund of buying and selling investments as well as the impact that buying and selling have on the price of the investments. Recent analysis (Figure 10.7) into the average expense ratio for various categories of index and actively managed open-ended investment funds shows that investors in actively managed UK equity funds were paying an average of approximately 1.28% annually versus 0.45% for index funds, a differential of 0.83% annually. The annual cost differential for overseas equity funds versus their indexed equivalents was even higher at 1.40% for European funds, 1.0% for euro zone funds, 1.13% for US funds, 0.91% for global funds and a staggering 1.27% for emerging market funds. Remember, these are weighted averages, so many investors will be paying even more than these relatively high amounts.

'After costs, the return on the average actively managed dollar will be less than the return on the average passively managed dollar for any time period.'[19]

William F. Sharpe, 1990 Nobel Laureate

---

[19] Sharpe, W.F. (1991) 'The arithmetic of active management', *Financial Analysts' Journal*, 47(1): 7–9.

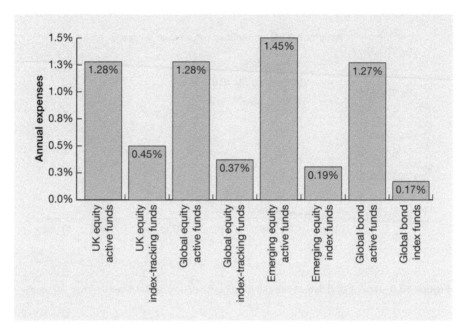

Figure 10.7 Value weighted annual expense ratios on open-ended investment funds
Source: Data from The Vanguard Group (2013) The case for index investing by UK investors.

The odds in terms of costs are so heavily stacked against active management it is no surprise that persistency of outperformance is so low. If you have to recoup an annual cost of c. 2.5% (comprising the annual charges and the effect of turnover within the fund) just to break even, then failure seems assured.

Charles Ellis, in his seminal book *Winning the Loser's Game*, explained how to be an investing winner:

> 'The objective of beating the market is in fact a loser's game and that most people striving to beat the market actually have very unhappy experiences. They do not succeed. And, when I say most I'm not talking about 52% or 55%, I'm talking about 85 or 90%. So, the first part is do not play the game, you will not win, which is I'm going to beat the market, here I go. There's an alternative where you can easily win and therefore I would call it a winning game. And, the winner's game is what is it you're really trying to accomplish, what would work really well for you? And, then go about that specific objective. And, each of us has different characteristics of what we're trying to do. Sometimes the characteristics have to do with how long you're going to stay invested. If you're investing for the very, very long time

. . . I have a three year old, a six year old and two three year old boys as my grandchildren. Any investments that they're making are investments for 80 years – that's a long time. And, they can invest differently than could someone who was saving to buy a home or saving for college or saving for some other specific purpose that's going to come up in a year or two. So, your time horizon's number one.'[20]

The passive detractors

A research paper that, on the face of it, gives some support for active management analysed 31,991 UK mutual funds (excluding index funds) in 73 categories over 30 years through to February 2010, representing $7 trillion of assets.[21] Returns before costs (which has the effect of flattering active management returns) were then compared with the appropriate indices (after removing obsolete funds) to identify whether or not active managers had delivered excess return over the market (known as alpha). The findings were that, of the 73 categories, active management was recommended in 23, passive in 22 and in 28 the case was neutral.

The author's main conclusion was as follows:

'Our studies have found that both types of investing have their strengths and weaknesses. It depends on the market segments and the economic climate. We believe investors should utilize a blend of both active and passive investing with the goal of optimizing their portfolio.'[22]

The first observation is the staggering fund selection choice faced by investors – nearly 20,000 funds, of which 12,000 failed to survive! Also, it is interesting to note that even on a gross performance basis (i.e. before deduction of costs), active management was not the preferred approach in many major categories: inflation-protected bonds, government bonds, world bonds, foreign equities, global real estate and commodities. If costs had been taken into account, the proportion of cases when active management would have been recommended would have been even lower. The conclusion that active and passive investing are not rivals but complementary is not justified by this paper and its somewhat biased approach.

[20] Ellis, C. (2009) *Winning the Loser's Game: Timeless strategies for successful investing,* McGraw-Hill.

[21] Li, J. (2010) 'When active management shines vs. passive: Examining real alpha in 5 full market cycles over the past 30 years', FundQuest White paper.

[22] Ibid, p. 2.

A more recent piece of analysis presents results showing that the IMA UK All Companies series beat the 'average' index fund over one, three, five, ten years to 9 January 2014.[23] The author makes some valid observations:

- The index performance is not the same as an index tracker fund's performance due to costs and other tracking error inefficiencies.
- There are some shockingly priced and poorly managed tracker funds that hold material amounts of investors' money.
- An example of such a fund is the Halifax UK FTSE All-Share Tracker that has returned a cumulative 89.6% over ten years (to 9 January 2014) compared with 129.6% for the FTSE All-Share Index.
- The FTSE All-Share beat the IMA UK All Companies series over ten years (not explicitly stated, but evidenced in the author's return table).
- There are some very low-cost index funds with exceptionally good tracking error, such as those offered by Vanguard.
- As passive supporters focus on the average active fund versus the market, it is only fair to focus on the average passive fund in any analysis.
- The funds representing the IMA UK All Companies return series tend to have a bias to lower capitalisation stocks than the index.

There are, however, a number of points to take issue with in the analyst's argument and conclusions:

- If an index fund could replicate the performance of the index, then it would have beaten the ten-year IMA UK All Companies return. Reality is not that far off.
- For example: Vanguard's ability to deliver near market returns is exemplified in the returns of its UK index tracker fund, which since inception – 23 June 2009 to 30 November 2013 – delivered an annualised return of 15.67% net of fees versus 15.78% for the index – a difference of only 11 basis points p.a. or a little over 1% implied over a ten-year period.
- In terms of what the future may hold, looking at Vanguard funds in the US,[24] the Admiral share class available to retail investors (which targets the return of the S&P 500 Index) delivered the market less 2 basis points per annum over the past ten years, which is a fantastic achievement. See Table 10.1.
- You cannot capture the returns of the IMA UK All Companies series unless you own all the funds in it – a practical nightmare.
- Picking winning active funds, ex-ante, is extremely difficult as performance rarely persists.

---

[23] Ausden, J. (2014) 'Active funds trounce passive funds over all time periods', **www.trustnet.com**, 13 January.

[24] **https://personal.vanguard.com/us/funds/snapshot?FundId=0540&FundIntExt=INT**

- But picking an excellent index fund, ex-ante, is relatively simple, as the Vanguard experience demonstrates.

Table 10.1 Vanguard delivers the bulk of the market return – US fund data

	1 year	3 year	5 year	10 year	Since Incept. 13/11/2000
Admiral share class	32.33%	16.14%	17.94%	7.39%	4.41%
S&P 500 Index	32.39%	16.18%	17.94%	7.41%	4.43%

Source: Data from The Vanguard Group.

To have any credibility and meet normal academic rigour it is necessary to carry out a regression of the performance against known risk factors in the IMA UK All Companies series. The author did not do this and makes this point: 'One potential flaw of using the UK All Companies sector as a means of comparison is the number of funds with a natural bias towards small and mid-caps. It could be argued that taking this view shows skill on behalf of the manager: active funds are also able to reduce their weighting to the mid-caps when they think that sector is due a fall, and our data shows that the mid-caps fall harder when markets correct.'

No further explanation or analysis was offered. Having an exposure to the size premium is not a function of active skill in market timing but of positioning the portfolio appropriately along the size continuum, as we have discussed earlier, so as to take advantage of this priced risk factor, using well-structured passive products. Lumping in FTSE 100 index funds with FTSE All-Share index funds and then comparing them with an unregressed index that has higher exposure to smaller and mid-sized companies is unsound. A regression analysis on the IMA UK All Companies series over the ten-year period gives an apples-to-apples comparison as to what returns would have been delivered by a passive alternative would have been more rigorous. The returns of different market cap indices during the ten-year period 2004 to 2013 are set out in Table 10.2.

Table 10.2 Annualised returns ten years to December 2013 of UK equity by market capitalisation

FTSE All-Share Index	FTSE 100 Index	FTSE 250 Index	DFA UK Small Cap Index
8.8%	8.0%	13.7%	12.5%

Source: The FTSE Group.

It is evident that any tilt to mid/smaller companies would have made a material impact on returns. Astute investors using passive funds can make strategic tilts to the size risk factor quite simply and effectively. In order to explore the impact of the suggested small cap bias, our investment research consultants regressed the monthly returns of the IMA UK All Companies series against the UK market, size and value risk factors. The result is graphically depicted in Figure 10.8. The IMA UK All Companies series had a statistically significant exposure to smaller size and a statistically insignificant exposure to the value risk factor. A simplistic proxy for the IMA UK All Companies series was created – which they named the IMA UK Passive Index Proxy – holding 71% exposure to the FTSE All-Share and 29% exposure to the DFA UK Small Cap Index. This places it in comparable market/size space to the actual IMA UK All Companies Index. They did not attempt to replicate the statistically insignificant weighting to growth stocks, which would have helped the active managers marginally, as value underperformed during this period.

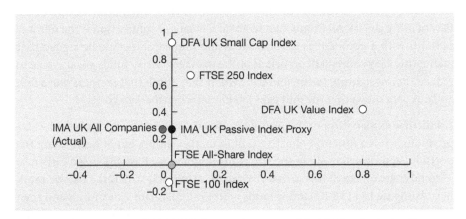

Figure 10.8 Regression: IMA UK All Companies versus IMA UK Passive Index Proxy 2004–2013
Source: Albion Strategic.

The return of the IMA UK Passive Index Proxy, over the ten years to the end of 2013, was 9.93% versus 8.82% for the IMA UK All Companies series. This reveals a 1.1% performance advantage for the passive index proxy over active managers, thus flipping the conclusion of the previously mentioned Trustnet study on its head. Deducting 0.3% for passive costs still leaves a performance advantage of 0.8%. This 1.1% differential provides enough margin to have executed the strategy using the appallingly highly priced index tracker funds (ongoing charges of 1% p.a.) that the report refers to, while still keeping up with the active managers, whose return aggregate return cannot, in practice, be captured.

Looking forward, with single-digit-basis-point ongoing charges coming, and firms capable of delivering market-returns-less-a-few-basis-points already in the UK market, a passive approach looks like a highly effective way to execute an asset allocation strategy.

Strategic valuation measures

The price earnings (P/E) ratio is a standard stock market valuation measure which is calculated by dividing a company's current share price by its per-share earnings. Earnings can be historic (last four quarters) or prospective (estimate of the next four quarters) or a mixture of the two (last two and next two quarters). The historical average P/E ratio depends on which stock market and time period are selected. The average P/E ratio for the S&P 500 index of leading US shares the past 100 years or so has been about 15, compared with 19 at the time of writing. However, it has been as low as 5.3 (December 1919) and as high as 123.79 (May 2009).[25]

The CAPE (cyclically adjusted price earnings) Index is an alternative stock market valuation measure devised by American economist and academic Robert Shiller, which calculates P/E ratios based on the past ten years of earnings to smooth out temporary fluctuations in profits caused by business cycles. Shiller's contention is that the current CAPE P/E gives a strong indication of the investment returns from equities over the next ten years. When an index is trading on a high P/E ratio – the multiple an investor is willing to pay for each £1 in earnings – this appears to lead to lower, subsequent ten-year returns and vice versa. Figure 10.9 illustrates the CAPE Index for the S&P 500 from 1900 to 2013.

Shiller believes that the stock market becomes increasingly overvalued when it exceeds it long-term average P/E ratio (about 15 for the S&P) and better value when below it. His view, that market valuation levels matter, is at odds with the basic contention that markets are broadly efficient and current prices reflect all known information. Shiller's critics suggest that higher P/E ratios merely reflect the market's rationale forecast of high rates of earnings growth.

Historic analysis of the CAPE shows that it appears to predict the 1929 crash, the buying opportunity and subsequent high returns predicted by the low P/Es of the early 1980s, the 2000 tech crash and the fact that in 2007 the market was still 'overvalued'. Although the CAPE Index stands at around 25 at the time of writing, suggesting that markets are overvalued, Shiller makes clear that CAPE is not a short-term market timing tool but a means of adjusting up or down the long-term

---

[25] Shiller, R. (2006) *Irrational Exuberance*, 2nd edition, Crown Business.

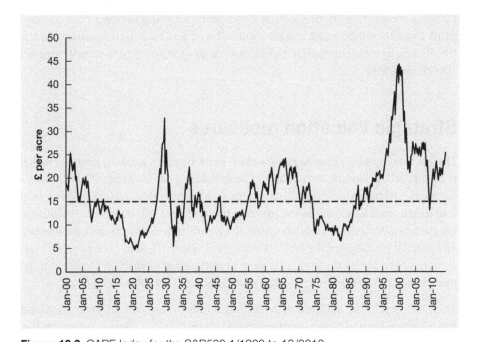

Figure 10.9 CAPE Index for the S&P500 1/1900 to 12/2013

Source: Data from Yale University, Department of Economics **www.econ.yale.edu/~shiller/data/ie_data.xls**

allocation to equities, as he states in a 2013 interview with *Business Insider*.[26] It's worth mentioning that Shiller did predict the tech crash in 2000 and the housing crisis leading up to the credit crisis, based on his valuation indices, and his book, *Irrational Exuberance*, is a best-seller.

Jeremy Siegel,[27] Professor of Finance at the Wharton School of the University of Pennsylvania, thinks the methodology for calculating the cyclically adjusted earnings may be overly pessimistic, where certain accounting practices introduced in the 1990s may understate true earnings, driving up the P/E ratio. Siegel gives the example of the requirement for companies to write down assets when they fall in value, but not to have to write back any growth in these assets until they are sold. In addition, as companies earn more from overseas subsidiaries and a higher proportion of earnings comes from technology in the US, which tends to have higher

[26] Blodget, H. (2013) 'SHILLER: Stocks are priced for (relatively) crappy returns', 25 January, **www.businessinsider.com/**

[27] Siegel, J. (2013) 'Don't put faith in Cape crusaders', *Financial Times*, 19 August.

margins, companies have become much more profitable. For these reasons Siegel believes markets are not as overvalued as CAPE might suggest.

Based on the available evidence, the Shiller CAPE Index certainly seems to be a valid valuation tool. The question is whether it can be used by investors to improve long-term performance. As we have seen earlier, there is little evidence that actively managed balanced funds deliver any long-run outperformance despite access to a range of valuation methodologies, including CAPE.[28]

Markets seem to be broadly efficient at setting prices, but sometimes historically high valuations can continue for a long time. For example, according to Siegel, in the 22 years since 1990 (to the time of the article referenced earlier) the CAPE Index had been above the long-run average for all but nine months and thus broadly pessimistic about the return on equities. During the period January 1990 to December 2013 the S&P 500 Index has delivered an annualised nominal, total return of 9.3%. Underweighting equities would have had a significant negative impact on portfolio returns.

Any valuation measure is only as good as the inputs used, and the outcomes can be highly sensitive to changes in assumptions. Who knows, in the future companies might see even higher profits, greater opportunities and bigger markets for their goods and services. The internet didn't exist 20 years ago, computer tablets didn't exist 10 years ago and social networks were just getting going 5 years ago. Several academic studies have reviewed the efficacy of various market-valuation methodologies, including other P/E-related measures, and suggest that there is no sure-fire way of valuing markets effectively and profiting from it consistently.[29]

Changing the long-term asset allocation mix of an existing portfolio on the basis of the CAPE seems to be a risky approach. However, for a new portfolio funded from cash, once you've established your asset allocation strategy, you might want to drip feed your money into the portfolio over, say, 24 or 36 months, if the CAPE indicates valuations are at extreme levels. At least that way you don't invest all your money at a market extreme but you still get invested and benefit from market returns in the long run. Periodic rebalancing of the portfolio provides some protection from market extremes and is a valuable part of a sensible, robust portfolio strategy, which we'll discuss in Chapter 12.

---

[28] Bogle, J.C. (2007) *The Little Book of Commonsense Investing*, John Wiley & Sons.

[29] One of the most extensive and highly regarded studies on this subject is by Welch, I. and Goyal, A.A. (2008) 'A Comprehensive Look at the Empirical Performance of Equity Premium Prediction', *The Review of Financial Studies*, 21(4), July, 1455–1508, available at SSRN: **http://ssrn.com/abstract=1211941**

Making a choice

Having looked at a range of the available evidence there are several key questions that you need to answer:

- Do you believe that an active manager can, after adjusting for risk factors such as the value and smaller companies premiums, beat the market after costs from skill?

- If a manager can show that they have demonstrated skill in the past that has caused outperformance of the market rather than exposure to risk factors, do you think they can do so consistently over time?

- How confident are you that you can predict which manager will have the skill to provide this outperformance?

- How will you manage the risk of style drift?

- How will you manage your emotions and make rational decisions if the manager is underperforming?

- What will you do if the manager leaves (and managers move around quite a lot)?

Just because a manager or economic forecaster has called things right in the past, it doesn't mean that they will repeat this in the future and stock markets can be irrational longer than you can stay solvent.

My view is that an evidence-based strategy, using low-cost funds, should be your default investment approach unless you have a strong conviction that an active investment approach will be successful, you disbelieve the evidence, or you need to believe active investment management works.

'Most investors, both institutional and individual, will find that the best way to own common stocks is through an index fund that charges minimal fees.'[30]

Warren Buffett, Chairman, Berkshire Hathaway Corporation

Diversification is the only free lunch (don't put all your eggs in one basket). Because we don't know which asset classes will produce the best return or the lowest risk at any given point in the future, by combining them in varying proportions we can avoid or reduce the probability of big losses and participate in the returns that markets do deliver.

---

[30] Chairman's letter, Berkshire Hathaway 1996 annual report, **www.berkshirehathaway.com**

CHAPTER 11
OPTIONS FOR INVESTING

'Simplicity is the ultimate sophistication.'

Leonardo da Vinci

Whatever investment approach you follow, you and/or your adviser will need to use investment funds to gain access to the various investment asset classes. Investment funds provide effective diversification as your capital is pooled with that of other investors to gain exposure to the underlying investment holdings. In the UK, investment funds are either regulated or unregulated.

Unregulated funds, now known as 'non-mainstream pooled investments' (NMPI), may not be promoted to the general public in the UK, but can be proposed to certain limited categories of investors, including:

- certified high net worth investors
- sophisticated investors
- self-certified sophisticated investors, and
- existing investors in unregulated collective investment schemes (UCIS).

In most cases, to qualify under one or more of these categories, an investor must be assessed by someone authorised under the Financial Services Act. Unregulated funds do not have to comply with any of the regulatory rules that apply to regulated funds, which cover things such as diversification, pricing, gearing and security. However, some unregulated funds do abide by listing or regulatory rules in the country in which they are based, but in my experience these are rarely equal to the standards required of regulated funds. Unregulated funds therefore have additional risks over and above pure investment risks, which are associated with how they are operated. You should ideally avoid unregulated funds because carrying out effective due diligence is difficult and in most situations there are plenty of suitable alternative regulated funds. There are some investments, however, such as commercial woodlands or socially responsible/thematic investment funds, which are available as unregulated funds only, due to the nature of their underlying holdings.

Only regulated funds may be promoted to members of the general public in the UK because they are subject to detailed rules on how the fund must be operated and administered. There are three main types of regulated investment fund:

- unit trusts, open-ended investment companies (OEICs) and Société d'Investissement à Capital Variable (SICAVs – open-ended collective investment schemes)
- exchange-traded funds (ETFs)
- investment trusts.

Unit trusts, OEICs and SICAVs

These are open-ended funds in that investors purchase units from the fund manager who then invests their capital in a range of investments according to the mandate of the fund (e.g. UK smaller companies). When investors want their money back they sell their units back to the fund manager. If more money is received from new investors than is being repaid to investors who are leaving the fund, the manager can just create more units, and vice versa. In most open-ended funds the manager usually holds some of the fund in cash to meet day-to-day redemptions from investors. This is shown graphically in Figure 11.1. Over the long term, holding any of the funds in cash will serve to reduce investment returns compared with a fund that is always fully invested. In addition, if large numbers of investors all require their money back at the same time, the investment manager can be forced to sell some of the fund's more liquid and favoured holdings to meet those redemptions, thus potentially having an adverse impact on long-term performance. Unlike closed-ended investment funds (more of which later), most open-ended investment funds are not permitted to borrow to increase their investment exposure.

Open-ended funds are usually traded once a day at 12 p.m. based on the underlying portfolio value the previous day. This is not usually a problem for long-term investors but it can be restrictive for investors who want to trade at other times in the day or when markets are moving very quickly. In terms of investor protection, most OEICs and unit trusts will be subject to supervision by the UK regulator and covered by the Financial Services Compensation Scheme in the event of financial failure of either the fund manager or the fund being unable to meet its obligations.

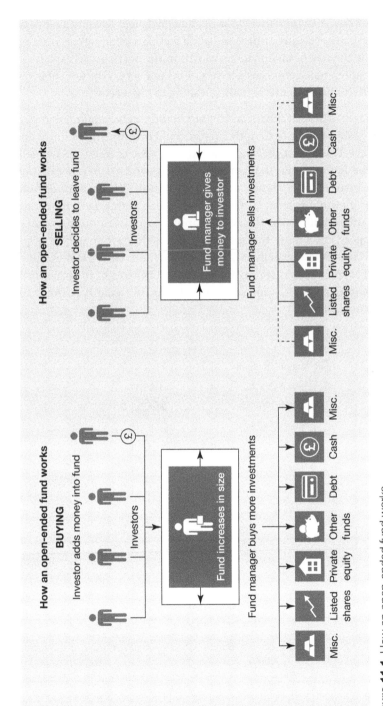

Figure 11.1 How an open-ended fund works

Source: Association of Investment Companies.

The ongoing costs of a fund include annual management fees and a range of other fixed costs, such as custody, trustee and audit fees. The ongoing costs do not, however, include the cost of trading incurred within the portfolio. As explained in the previous chapter, transaction costs have a direct impact on the level of investment returns, with higher amounts of trading leading to higher costs.

Prior to January 2013, UK financial advisers could receive commission payments from fund groups and prior to April 2014 so could investment platforms and fund supermarkets. This meant that the total expense ratio of most open-ended funds needed to be high enough to incorporate such payments. While existing holdings may continue to pay renewal commission until the account or holding is changed, all new funds must be arranged on 'clean' terms, i.e. with no commission entitlement built in for the adviser or platform. In addition to making the fund managers' costs more transparent, this should have the effect of pushing down fund costs. A recent analysis of open-ended funds costs has shown, however, that not all fund managers are passing on the full benefits of the ban on commission payment for post-2012 fund sales, as illustrated in Figure 11.2. The researchers made this conclusion:

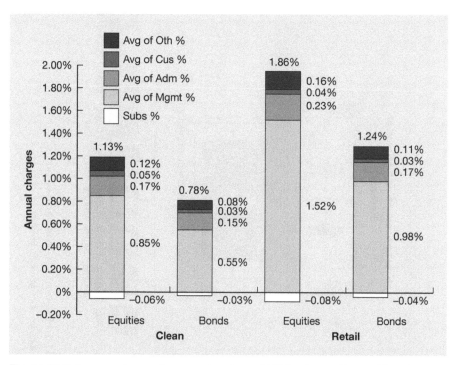

Figure 11.2 Average charges for cross-border and UK funds: equities and bonds
Source: Fitz Partners.

'Stripping distribution fees out of the fee structure as a result of RDR [the new rules which ban commission] has certainly pushed the overall fund expenses down but it is remarkable that the drop is not even across all asset classes. For some funds the reduction is more than enough to compensate for any external new [advice/platform] fees that will be paid directly by an investor, for others that gap will be much tighter.'[1]

Given that there is about £750 billion invested in UK authorised open-ended funds, and even more in foreign-domiciled funds, it's likely that a large proportion of investors will be paying a high price for investment exposure. In January 2014, the total net inflow to all open-ended funds amounted to £189 million. It is interesting to note, however, that this comprised inflows to retail open-ended funds of £1.1 billion, compared with outflows from institutional open-ended funds of £911 million.[2]

Exchange-traded funds (ETFs)

Exchange-traded funds are a relatively recent development, although they originate from the institutional investment world, where they have been used for many years to gain investment exposure to different asset classes. The global market for ETFs has grown from just over $450 billion in 2005 to $2,288 billion in 2013[3] and this is expected to continue to grow (see Figure 11.3). There are ETFs covering almost every type of asset class, from the largest and most liquid asset classes such as US equities to the smallest and most esoteric ones, for example Mexican smaller companies.

An ETF fund is represented by shares that are listed on the Stock Exchange, with the share price reflecting the value of the underlying investment portfolio. The manager of the fund acts as the market maker and ensures that there is a liquid market in the shares so that buyers and sellers can be matched. If there are more buyers than sellers in the market, the fund manager can create more shares, and if there are more sellers than buyers, they will buy those shares and cancel them to reflect the redemption of those funds.

---

[1] Source: Fitz Partners (2014) 'Cross-border & UK fund fees benchmarks', February.

[2] Source: Investment Management Association, www.investmentuk.org/fund-statistics/
Total funds under management as at January 2014 was £757 billion.

[3] ETFGI, Global ETF and ETP Industry Insights, February 2014.

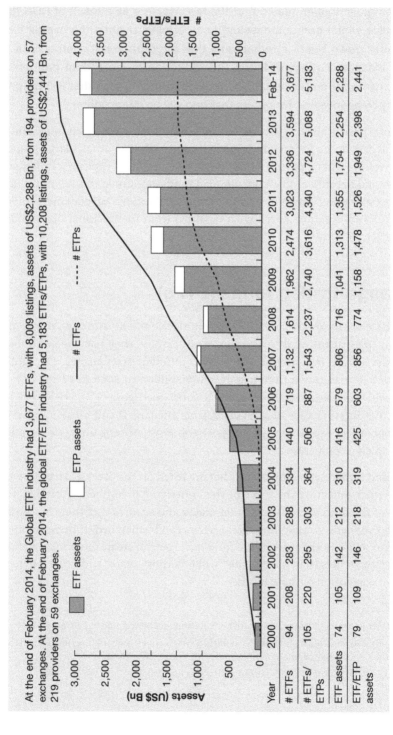

Figure 11.3 Growth of funds held within ETFs

Source: ETGI.

ETFs are used to provide access to a range of asset classes, the majority of which are passive, although some are actively managed. Some funds obtain investment exposure by buying all or some of the underlying holdings in proportion to the index it is seeking to track – known as 'physical replication'. Other funds use what are known as 'swaps' (where the fund manager pays another counterparty, such as an investment bank, to provide the return of the index or market to which exposure is desired) to obtain such exposure. This is also known as 'synthetic replication', more of which later.

ETFs don't attract stamp duty as normal equities do, and costs tend to be competitive but are often higher than other nil-commission collective funds. For most long-term investors, however, ETFs hold no particular benefit over low-cost passive, open-ended funds, other than where the desired asset class is available only via an ETF. A final point worth making about ETFs is the position of investor protection in the event of the failure of the fund manager causing a loss to investors. In many cases ETFs listed on the London Stock Exchange hold funds that are domiciled elsewhere in the EU, such as Luxembourg and Ireland, and as a result are neither supervised by the UK financial regulator nor covered by the UK Financial Services Protection Scheme. Non-UK-domiciled ETFs are supervised by their own regulator and covered by investor compensation protection that may be different from that provided to UK-domiciled funds.

Investment trust companies

Investment trust companies are listed companies that invest in other companies. The underlying portfolio is managed by a professional fund manager, usually on an active basis, but a small number of investment trusts are run on a passive basis. Investment trust companies are described as closed-ended because there is a set number of shares in issue and investors buy shares in the trust through the stock market (see Figure 11.4). The value of the underlying portfolio of the investment company is called the net asset value (NAV).

Unlike open-ended funds, investment companies can borrow to increase their investment capital, which they have been increasingly taking advantage of, as explained in the *Financial Times* article.

Investment trusts gear up before rate rise

By Emma Dunkley

Record low interest rates and rising markets are creating the opportunity for investment trusts to borrow money and target enhanced returns for investors.

A number of trusts have recently increased their long-term borrowing to "gear up" their investment in the stock markets, before the bank interest rate is raised.

The Perpetual Income and Growth trust, managed by Mark Barnett, is borrowing £60m over 15 years at a fixed rate of 4.37 per cent, which analysts at JPMorgan Cazenove believe are "attractive" terms. The Hicl Infrastructure trust has also boosted its borrowing facility from £100m to £150m, providing the flexibility to make further investments without having to issue more shares. At the start of this year, the City of London trust issued £35m of fixed-rate debt at 4.53 per cent over 15 years.

"Over the longer term, it's a good opportunity to borrow and reinvest in the market," said Job Curtis, manager of the City of London trust. "With a 15-year view, this feels like a great rate to be borrowing at. In a rising market, it's helpful to have that extra boost."

Analysts at Winterflood Securities believe it "makes sense" for trusts to borrow for the longer term at this stage before a rate rise, which economists forecast could happen as early as next spring. "The majority of investment trusts that gear use short-term credit facilities, mostly up to a year," said Innes Urquhart, analyst at Winterflood Securities. However, he said more trusts, especially the larger ones generating income, should consider longer-term debt on the right terms.

Like other companies, investment trusts are able to borrow money, whereas open-ended funds, such as unit trusts, cannot gear up. Although gearing can enhance returns when markets are rising, it can exacerbate losses when markets turn down.

"The ability to use gearing is a key advantage of investment trusts," said Alan Brierley, an investment trust analyst at Canaccord Genuity. "If it doesn't use the tools available, then why not just use an open-ended fund?"

Research by Winterflood shows the average level of gearing is equivalent to 8 per cent of a trust's net assets. Nearly 60 per cent of all trusts have no gearing, while 24 per cent have up to 10 per cent.

Source: Dunkley, E. (2014) Investment trusts gear up before rate rise, *Financial Times*, 12 April.
©The Financial Times Ltd 2013. All Rights Reserved.

There is a wide choice of investment styles and asset classes, whether you want to invest in one of the big globally diversified international general investment companies, or in a small, specialist sector such as European smaller companies. Some investment companies have a split capital structure (known as 'splits'), which means that they offer different classes of share. The simplest type of split is one that has two share classes: one that has the right to all the income generated by the holdings in the underlying portfolio (and minimal capital growth) and the other that has no right to any income but the right to all the capital growth arising from the increase in the value of the holdings in the underlying portfolio, at the date of wind-up of the investment company. This could be useful if, say, you want to avoid taxable income and instead have your return in the form of capital gains since you could, for example, realise the future gain within your capital gains tax exemption or offset against a future loss.

In more complicated split investment companies they offer other classes of share, including limited life, zero dividend preference and highly geared.

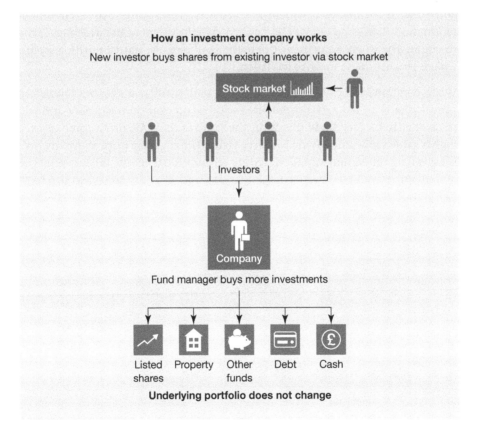

Figure 11.4 How an investment company works
Source: Association of Investment Companies.

Typical to most classes of shares in spilt capital investment companies is the fact that they have a predetermined wind-up date, when the company will be liquidated and each shareholder will receive their final entitlement to the investment companies' assets. Each split capital investment company has a different risk and reward profile and unless you have the time to research them, it is usually best to engage a specialist adviser or investment manager to help you choose the right shares.

With most investment companies the share price trades below the NAV to reflect (i.e. at a discount) the fact that there are usually more sellers than buyers (institutions are long-term sellers of investment trusts). The typical discount is about 5%, but some trusts trade at much higher discounts and others at much lower. This means that with, say, a 5% share price discount to the NAV, the investor obtains 100% of the investment returns for only 95% of the cost. If the discount doesn't change or it narrows (i.e. the share price increases more than the NAV), this is a good deal. If the discount widens but the NAV rises strongly, the shareholder return can still be good but will be dampened to the extent of the widening of the discount. The worse outcome is where the NAV remains static but the discount widens because the share price has fallen.

When demand for shares in a trust is strong and/or the manager buys back and cancels shares in issue, the share price will rise quicker than the NAV and will trade at either a very small discount, the same as the NAV, or, in some cases, a higher value to the underlying NAV (see Figure 11.5). A share price above the NAV is known as a premium and is effectively an additional charge for accessing the underlying portfolio. When a company trust trades at a very large discount to its

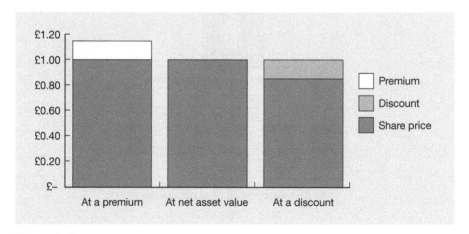

Figure 11.5 Investment company pricing

NAV it can be a sign that there is low confidence in the underlying investment manager or the trust's investment approach. For example, Alliance Trust plc is one of the oldest and largest international general investment trusts and it has traded at a significant discount for some years (10% at the time of writing). Over the past few years hedge fund investors have built up large stakes in the company and have been lobbying the manager to make changes to the way the trust is managed in the hope that this will cause a narrowing of the discount of the share price to NAV.

In recent years many investment companies have introduced discount control policies, such as share buybacks. As well as controlling the discount rate, this usually results in lower share price volatility, which gives investors greater confidence. As Figure 11.6 shows, investment trust discounts have narrowed over the past five years and the average is now less than 5%. Whether discounts will narrow further is anyone's guess.

Figure 11.6 Investment company discounts over the past ten years
Source: Association of Investment Companies.

Historically, investment companies have had lower costs than open-ended funds, but this is mainly because most do not pay sales commission to brokers and advisers. This advantage was removed by the growth of investment platforms and the introduction of nil-commission open-ended funds as a result of the banning of adviser commission in 2013. To the time of writing 15 investment companies, aimed at retail investors, had abolished or announced the abolishment of their performance fee since the start of 2013.[4]

Table 11.1 Historic performance of investment companies compared to open-ended funds

Price total returns to 31 December 2013 (unweighted, £ adjusted, basic = 100)	1 year		5 years		10 years	
Sectors	Invest-ment Trusts	OEIC/ Unit trusts	Invest-ment Trusts	OEIC/ Unit trusts	Invest-ment Trusts	OEIC/ Unit trusts
Global	121.5	121.7	206.5	172.2	273.4	208.6
Global Equity Income	125.3	119.8	246.7	174.4	304.3	207.7
UK Equity Income	128.6	125.2	257.6	195.8	315.8	225..6
UK Growth vs. UK All Companies	130.9	126.2	270.5	207.5	265.5	230.0
North American	119.1	130.5	187.3	190.8	212.3	192.6
Europe vs. Europe ex UK	133.4	126.1	223.1	165.0	346.5	238.2
Global Emerging	100.7	96.1	151.4	174.8	341.6	305.7
Asia Pacific ex Japan	102.8	101.7	242.0	186.5	365.4	289.6
Japan	156.4	125.9	233.1	132.4	210.0	151.2
Property	129.6	105.4	335.5	144.2	169.9	149.7
UK SmallCap	145.8	137.4	387.0	304.3	393.4	306.7
Japanese SmallCap	139.6	135.8	231.5	168.2	161.1	176.0
TMT	144.0	127.4	342.0	238.5	529.0	218.3
European SmallCap	147.5	130.6	245.8	223.1	340.3	339.3
North American Smallers	128.7	136.6	249.6	235.3	208.1	263.7
Asian Pacific Japan	109.8	110.0	204.9	160.3	284.7	225.5

Unshaded results indicates investment company outperformance v OEIC / unit trust performance over given time period
Shaded results indicates OEIC / unit trust outperformance v investment company performance over a given time period
Source: Association of Investment Companies.

Investment companies are not covered by the same investor protection as open-ended funds, although they do have to comply with the UK listing rules. In

---

[4]   Source: Association of Investment Companies. Examples of fee reductions include: Scottish Mortgage from 0.32% to 0.30% of gross assets; Edinburgh Investment Trust from 0.60% to 0.55% and abolished its performance fee; RCM Technology from 1% to 0.8% and lowered the maximum percentage of performance fee and capped it.

general, investment companies represent more cost-effective exposure to active management compared with open-ended funds. However, they do not represent the most efficient means of obtaining passive investment exposure compared with the lower-cost, open-ended funds. The closed-end structure of investment companies makes them particularly suitable for investment in less liquid assets classes such as property, private equity and infrastructure assets, because the investment manager is not forced to sell underlying assets or holdings on account of investors requiring their capital back.

However, due to the issues around discounts and premiums to the NAV potentially distorting returns, the potential for gearing to amplify losses (as well as gains), and the predominance of active management approaches, they should be viewed as slightly more risky than open-ended funds.

Passive management approaches

As explained in the previous chapter, I recommend that you use passive funds to obtain asset class exposure. The question then arises as to what type of passive funds you should use.

Most ETFs and tracker funds aim to replicate the performance of a basket of securities by reference to an 'official' index such as the MSCI World or FTSE UK All-Share Index. The problem with most of the official indices is that they include many securities that either dilute or skew the return of the required asset class. Take, for instance, the FTSE All-Share, which includes investment companies and foreign companies that have a listing in London. Investment companies invest in other companies and so represent a dilution of the asset class. A South African mining company, for example, isn't really representative of a UK equity but is, in fact, more an emerging market equity, which would be better held within an emerging market fund.

In the case of the FTSE 100 Index, each quarter the index is reconstituted based on the market prices and number of shares in issue and this inevitably leads to companies being added and removed from the index. Because such changes happen on pre-set dates, other market participants can take advantage of a traditional index managers' need to buy shares that have been added to the index or to sell those that have left it, because an index portfolio manager needs to maintain a portfolio that matches the index composition as closely as possible. The consequence is that prices rise prior to a company's inclusion in the index and then decay shortly afterwards (see Figure 11.7). Over the longer term this can have the effect of reducing (or dampening) returns from a traditional index fund.

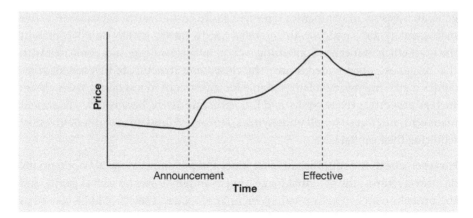

Figure 11.7 Price impact when an equity joins the index

When a company is first listed on a stock market, its initial listing value is determined by the sponsoring investment bank and broker based on what they think the market will pay for the shares. Several pieces of research[5] suggest that most initial public offerings (IPOs) go on to experience relatively poor performance over the next five years or so. Clearly some companies experience price rises after they are listed, but a significant majority does not. Traditional index funds and ETFs must buy into these new IPOs as they enter the index, causing them to buy shares that more often than not will experience a decline in value while investors determine the true market value.

A good example of an IPO that entered the FTSE 250 Index is Betfair plc. The company was listed on the London Stock Exchange in October 2010 with an opening price of £13 and by the end of its first day of trading it had risen 20% to close at £15.50. The sponsoring banks – Barclays Capital, Goldman Sachs and Morgan Stanley – all hailed the float a success and more than justified their £15 million of arranging and underwriting fees. Sadly, the share price drifted down and six months later was trading at just under £9, representing a fall of more than 30% from the offer price. The price (at the time of writing) has recovered slightly to around £11, but this is still a fall of 15% from the offer price for a company that is profitable and seems to be recession-proof.

5   Loughran, T. and Ritter J.R. (1995) 'The new issues puzzle', *Journal of Finance,* 50(1); Ritter, J.R. (2009) *Some Factoids About the 2009 IPO Market,* University of Florida; Gregory, A., Guermat, C. and Al-Shawawreh, F. (2010) 'UK IPOs: Long run returns, behavioural timing and pseudo timing (2009–11)', *Journal of Business Finance & Accounting,* 37(5–6): 612–647.

A more recent and high-profile example is that of Facebook, which came to the market in May 2012. After several upward revisions the company floated on the US Nasdaq stock exchange with an opening price of $38 per share. Within a week the price had fallen to $26.81 per share and by late August it had hit an all-time low of $20 per share. The price then rapidly recovered and at the time of writing was standing at just over $68 per share.

Some companies that make up the index can be in extreme financial distress and might be near to receivership. Until the shares are suspended an index manager is compelled to buy shares in that company in proportion to the index, even if it is evident that the company is in dire financial condition.

Is the index an appropriate representation of the market?

Stock market indices are not designed as an optimal investment proposition (the first index funds appeared only in the early 1970s, long after indices were introduced). Consequently, some indices are less useful than others when it comes to representing the market they measure. The levels of the US Dow Jones Industrial Average and the Japanese Nikkei 225 Index, for example, are determined solely by the prices of the constituents, so a movement in a single security can give rise to a large index movement; the market capitalisation of the constituents is not considered.

There are four main ways that passive funds obtain returns on the various asset classes, as follows.

1. Full replication

This is where the manager chooses an appropriate index, e.g. the FTSE All-Share Index, and then buys all the underlying holdings that make up that index in as near to the same proportions as the index as possible. Consequently this method is mostly used to track the largest and most liquid markets. As well as the price effect explained previously, full replication usually generates relatively high trading costs (dealing commissions and the spread between buying and selling prices) and market-impact costs (the tendency of prices to move against the investor when they place large trades). Almost all index managers who use this approach carry out stock lending – lending their investments to other investors in return for a fee.

2. Stratified sampling

This is where the manager uses a sophisticated computer program to buy a range of holdings that represents a reasonable proxy for the index being followed and that can be expected to display almost the same risk and reward characteristics. This approach usually gives the manager more flexibility on what is bought and sold (thus reducing market-impact costs) and should also have lower explicit costs than full replication. It does, however, also have a higher likelihood of exhibiting performance that is different from the index that it is seeking to track, as the portfolio itself will differ from the index. Such funds also engage in stock lending.

Securities lending – who benefits?

Institutional investors regularly lend each other securities in return for a fee. For an investment fund that is a long-term owner of such securities, this lending offers an attractive additional revenue stream, for little additional effort. For the borrowing institution, the fee it pays to borrow the securities means that it can carry out trading of a security without having to outlay the entire cost of the holding. Hedge funds often borrow securities so that they can sell them, in the hope that they can buy them back at a cheaper price in the near future. Securities lending gives rise to two important questions on which investors need to be clear.

First, what security is taken by the lending institution to protect its investors and what does it do with that security? Some funds accept bank guarantees or cash held on deposit, while others insist upon a third party holding liquid securities that are at least twice the value of the securities lent. Sometimes a fund manager will accept cash security but then use that cash to engage in speculative trading activities, thereby introducing additional risk to the fund.

Second, how much of the stock lending fee received from the borrowing institution is passed back to investors in the fund? BlackRock, for example, which owns the iShares range of ETFs, retains 40% of such income and passes 60% to investors in its funds. HSBC, another large passive provider, retains 15%. Dimensional Fund Advisors and Vanguard, both big fund managers, pass 100% of stock lending income back to investors in their funds. Figure 11.8 illustrates stock lending graphically.

Many ETFs declare low ongoing fund costs, but these are effectively subsidised by the income they retain from stock lending and/or because they obtain asset class exposure from what is known as synthetic replication (see next section).

▶

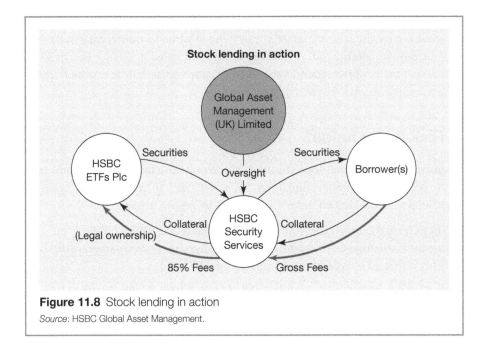

Figure 11.8 Stock lending in action
Source: HSBC Global Asset Management.

3. Synthetic or swap-based replication

This is where the fund manager uses 'swaps' or other derivatives to obtain exposure to the chosen asset class, rather than physically buying the underlying investments. The manager gives the ETF's capital to an institution that undertakes to deliver the index return on that capital. In exchange, the ETF manager takes security over or possession of other assets of at least equal value to the capital given to the institution, so as to provide protection in the event the institution goes bust. The contractual undertaking from the third party (such as an investment bank) to provide the return of the asset and security, in the form of other assets from the bank, introduces what is known as *counterparty* and *collateral* risk.

Sometimes, the assets pledged as security to the ETF manager can be illiquid and this can introduce additional problems if the counterparty providing the index goes bust and the ETF manager needs to liquidate the assets that were provided as security. Selling illiquid assets in a hurry invariably involves some compromise in terms of the price that the seller must accept. Funds that use 'synthetic replication' may, therefore, represent a higher risk than physical replication as they rely on the financial security of the various counterparties (the participating investment banks) and their ability to honour their obligations associated with the 'swaps' contract as well as the quality of the collateral held as security.[6] Lehman Brothers is a recent example of what can happen when a counterparty fails. It is estimated by its administrators that when the bank failed in 2008 it had nearly 1 million contracts worth around $45 billion of swaps outstanding, of which nearly 90% remained unsettled in March 2011.

4. Risk factor funds

These were originally developed in the 1980s to provide a low-cost and more effective exposure to US smaller companies. Such funds seek to avoid the key problems associated with tracking an index and have the following features:

- They create their own definition of the asset class and which holdings can and cannot be included, for example removing investment companies, utilities or other restricted securities and avoiding recent IPOs.

- In addition to having a more flexible approach over which holdings may be included in the asset class, the manager has a flexible trading policy that does not force them to buy or sell specific securities on set days.

- Because the manager has a flexible trading policy, they can take advantage of difficult trading conditions by being able to buy, at a discount to normal market price, securities that others need to turn into cash. Research suggests that this could add between 0.60% and 0.80% per annum to the asset class return alone.[7]

- The unit price is the same for buyers and sellers and there is no need for complex and costly trading activity to achieve this.

- All stock-lending income is passed back to investors in the fund.

- Some risk factor funds have a slight exposure (known as a tilt) towards smaller and financially depressed companies (known as value companies) and this provides an expected return premium over the main stock market due to the higher risk of these companies.[8]

- Ongoing charges on these types of funds are generally much lower and trading costs a fraction of those incurred by actively managed funds on average, but they tend to be slightly more expensive than the most competitive index funds, as illustrated in Figures 11.9 and 11.10.

---

[6] Financial Stability Board (2011) 'Potential financial stability issues arising from recent trends in exchange-traded funds (ETFs)', April.

[7] Wahal, S. (2010) 'Trading advantages of flexible portfolios', www.dfa.com, p. 1.

[8] Expected return premium on DFA UK Core Equity Index of 0.97% p.a. and risk of 2.25% compared with return drag on FTSE 100 of –0.41% p.a. and risk of 2.52%. This is based on simulated index data from January 1993 to December 2010. (*Source:* Dimensional Fund Advisors.)

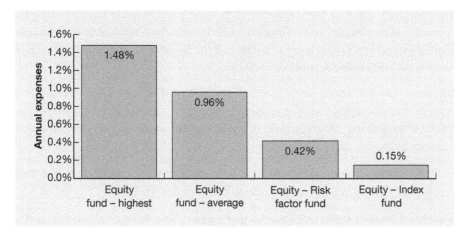

Figure 11.9 Comparison of fund ongoing costs

Source: Fitz Partners (2014), 'Cross-Boarder & UK Fund Fees Benchmarks' (February).

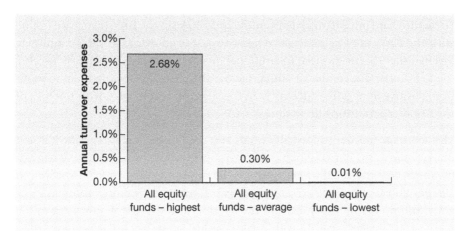

Figure 11.10 Comparison of fund turnover costs

Source: Fitz Partners, Fund Charges and Portfolio Turnover analysis April 2014.

What are the *full* costs?

Any portfolio, index fund or ETF that slavishly follows an index (as its mandate requires), whichever method of replication it uses, will have to carry out regular buying and selling of holdings and this generates *turnover* costs. Obviously, actively managed portfolios and funds also experience portfolio turnover, which is usually considerably higher than for passive portfolios. The higher the turnover, the higher the trading costs.

Trading costs come in two forms: hard trading costs include dealing charges, spreads between buying and selling prices and stamp duty, while soft costs such as market-impact costs (which are a function of the liquidity of a security) are largely hidden but still erode the investor's return.

Based on several independent studies over a period of ten years, Fitzrovia,[9] a respected financial research organisation, suggests it is reasonable to assume that a fund experiencing 100% turnover in a year leads to an annual performance drag of around 1%.

> 'We estimate trading costs for a large sample of equity funds and find that they are comparable in magnitude to the expense ratio.'[10]

Another difference between ETFs and open-ended index funds, such as unit trusts or OEICs, is how the share or unit price is calculated to represent the value of the underlying index. With an open-ended fund the manager sells and buys back units based on the value of the underlying securities, known as the net asset value. ETF shares are traded on a stock exchange and as a result supply and demand can cause the share price to deviate from the NAV. To keep the ETF share price in line with the NAV, the ETF manager relies on what is known as a 'spread arbitrage mechanism'. This means that institutional investors (usually the bank sponsoring the ETF) undertake complex trading that has the effect of allowing them to profit from positive or negative differences in the share price compared with the NAV of the ETF after accounting for trading costs.

This arbitrage mechanism usually works very well in the largest and most liquid markets such as US or UK large companies, as the costs incurred have a negligible impact on the accuracy with which the fund tracks the index. However, in smaller and less liquid markets, such as international smaller companies or emerging market companies, the transaction and execution costs are much higher and, as such, the ETF will usually produce a return quite a bit lower than the index (known as a negative tracking error). Over the long term this tracking error adds up to a loss of return to the investor and is one that many ETF enthusiasts rarely mention.

---

[9]   Moisson, E. (2011) 'Trading costs: research review', Lipper Fitzrovia, April.

[10] Edelen, R.M., Evans, R. and Kadlec, G.B. (2007) 'Scale effects in mutual fund performance: The role of trading costs', Working Paper, 17 March.

Other types of investment funds

Fund of funds (FoFs)

This is an investment fund that invests in other investment funds, the idea being that the investor obtains access to several managers who are all specialists in their respective areas, overseen by the main professional manager who does all the initial and ongoing due diligence. The manager of the main fund decides which funds/managers to invest in and when to move money to other managers based on their performance.

FoFs are often used to obtain alternative investment strategies such as hedge funds, where due diligence and fund costs can be prohibitive for most individual investors. They are, however, extensively used to provide standard investment exposure, particularly by financial services companies that do not offer their own, in-house investment management service. The manager of the FoFs levies an annual management charge on top of the annual charges levied by the underlying fund managers. The additional costs involved in most FoFs make them unattractive for most investors, although if you are keen to obtain exposure to alternative investments they might be useful.

Target/lifestyle funds

Target funds are a type of FoF managed with the intention of meeting a known objective or liability at a specific date in the future. Target funds have a range of dates, with the minimum being ten years. Initially the manager pursues capital growth through exposure to risky assets such as equities. As the target date approaches, the manager gradually reduces exposure to equities in favour of increased exposure to more defensive assets such as bonds and cash. The change in asset allocation takes place over several years so that by the time the fund meets the target date the fund holds no risky assets and, as such, it cannot fall in value. This is shown graphically in Figure 11.11.

While target funds do, on the face of it, appear to offer an attractive and hassle-free way of investing a lump sum for a specific need at a known date in the future, particularly for modest amounts or those investing in retirement funds, they suffer from a number of drawbacks that make them unattractive for most affluent and wealthy investors, including:

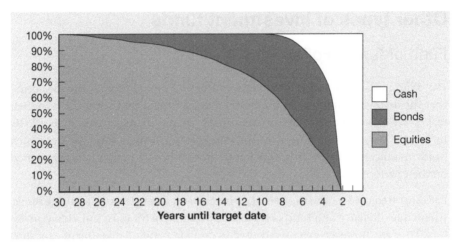

Figure 11.11 How target funds work

- higher costs due to active management charges and/or duplication of fund costs
- may not capture all available returns by reducing exposure to risky assets (which have a higher expected return) too soon
- accessing funds before the target date may be either not permitted or subject to penalty
- require the investor to commit to having their funds managed by the chosen target fund provider for the term until the chosen target date (great for the fund manager but not so good for the investor who is unhappy with performance and wants out).

Multi-factor funds

Multi-factor funds are open-ended investment funds that invest in a range of other risk factor funds with a choice of equity allocation from 30% to 70%. The equity component has a tilt towards smaller, value and emerging market companies to obtain risk exposures that have the potential to generate returns higher than the market as a whole. The manager carries out periodic rebalancing as necessary to maintain the risk exposure, and because this arises within the one fund, there is no capital gains tax liability until the units in the multi-factor fund are disposed of. Typical charges for these funds are in the range of 0.35% p.a.

Index of index funds

Typically this is an open-ended fund (although there are some ETFs) offered by the major traditional index fund managers, which is allocated to a range of their index fund in a proportion selected by the investor, e.g. 80% equity exposure and 20% bond. Like the multi-factor fund, the manager carries out periodic rebalancing as necessary to maintain the risk exposure, and because this arises within the one fund, there is no capital gains tax liability until the units in the index of multi-index funds are disposed of. Typical charges for these funds are in the range of 0.30% p.a.

Making a choice

In choosing which type of fund to use in your portfolio you need to weigh up cost, counterparty risk, asset class return method, liquidity, tax treatment and investor protection. If you are using the services of a portfolio manager or wealth manager, you need to make sure you are happy that they have considered these factors. You have a right to expect your adviser to have carefully researched the types of funds that they use and to have a detailed rationale they can share with you. There is no point having a great wealth plan and investment strategy if the funds you use are not up to the job or have hidden risks that go beyond those applying to the asset class in general.

CHAPTER 12
OTHER INVESTMENT CONSIDERATIONS

'By all means let's be open-minded, but not so open-minded that our brains drop out.'

Richard Dawkins, English ethologist, evolutionary biologist and writer

There are a number of other issues that you need to consider in relation to your investment strategy and these include:

- the impact of dividends on investment returns
- the impact of regular withdrawals from your portfolio
- the importance of rebalancing your portfolio
- the use of debt with investing.

Impact of dividends on overall investment returns

It is regularly stated that reinvested dividends make a big difference to overall equity investment returns over the medium to long term. This is well illustrated by Figure 12.1, which shows the FTSE All-Share Index with and without net dividends reinvested over the past 30 years.

I've heard some investment 'experts' suggest that high dividend-paying shares are better to own because they pay you for owning them and that in difficult investment conditions investors are somehow more likely to retain ownership of dividend-paying shares than those that pay no or a very low dividend. Research[1]

---

[1]   Miller, M. and Modigliani, F. (1961) 'Dividend policy, growth, and the valuation of shares', *Journal of Business*, 34(4): 411–433.

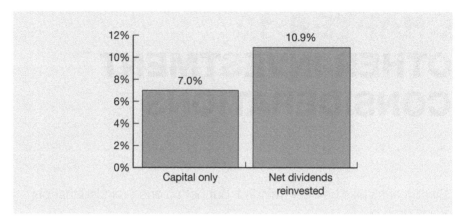

Figure 12.1 Returns of the FTSE All-Share Index with and without dividends reinvested (returns for 30 years to 31 December 2013)
Source: Barclays Capital Equity Gilt Study 2014.

suggests that high dividend-yielding stocks may be more risky and indeed the dividend may be high (when expressed as a percentage yield) because the price of the company has fallen. Dividends do not provide downside protection because current share prices reflect whether the earnings of a company have been paid out or retained. Dividends do not prevent encroaching on your capital because the distribution of dividends is reflected in companies' share prices. The notion that owners of dividend-paying shares are somehow more committed shareholders may have some merit, but it is unlikely to be of any material consequence for most long-term investors.

Another downside to focusing on companies that pay dividends, of whatever amount, is that you are highly likely to miss out on the significant investment returns arising from high-growth companies. Microsoft, Starbucks and Apple are just a few of the massive global companies that paid no dividends for many years. Highly profitable and fast-growing companies such as Amazon, eBay and Google still don't. In both cases these companies' share prices have grown much faster than those of many dividend-paying companies. The key point to appreciate is that whether companies pay dividends or not makes no difference to the total investment return, whereas the investment policy of the underlying investee companies will. Where dividends are paid, it makes sense to reinvest them to benefit from compounding, but specifically seeking out high-yielding shares is unlikely to give you the best investment outcome.

The impact of regular withdrawals from your portfolio

If you need your portfolio to fund your lifestyle over the long term, then you need to factor this into your investment strategy. The required amount of regular withdrawals, the portfolio's time horizon (which may be your life expectancy), your risk profile and asset allocation are closely interrelated. If the amount regularly withdrawn from the portfolio is too high, you might run out of money before you die or not be able to leave a legacy. If the portfolio is too risky and suffers high volatility, the regular withdrawals may exacerbate the negative returns experienced during market downturns. Figure 12.2 illustrates this point well with the risky portfolio volatility being compounded by the regular withdrawals.

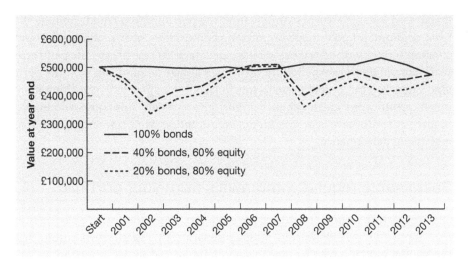

Figure 12.2 Effect of £15,000 p.a. withdrawals on portfolio value

There are a number of approaches that you could adopt when it comes to taking withdrawals from your investment portfolio and the right one will depend on your spending needs, investment strategy, risk profile and tax status.

● Natural yield. You take whatever interest or dividends are generated from the portfolio. Although the yield will vary from year to year, you could expect this to increase in real terms if you have made reasonable allocations to equities and property. Although initially this approach is likely to produce a relatively low level of income as a proportion of the portfolio, over the long term it should rise significantly.

- Fixed sum. You take a fixed monetary sum each year (e.g. £50,000) regardless of actual investment yield or overall returns. While this provides a constant level of 'income', it needs much closer monitoring, particularly if you have a reasonable allocation to risky assets and a high amount of withdrawal relative to the portfolio value. You may have to stop or reduce the amount withdrawn during market downturns.

- Percentage of portfolio. The withdrawal is expressed as a percentage of the portfolio, which may be higher or lower than the natural yield or overall return. The actual amount of withdrawals will vary up and down in line with fluctuations in the portfolio value, with higher allocations to risky assets leading to higher volatility in income withdrawals. However, the chances of running out of money with this approach are likely to be quite low, provided that the withdrawal percentage is not excessive.

If you need a stable level of cashflow from the portfolio, you could combine the fixed-amount and percentage-of-portfolio approaches. Such an approach could combine a fixed withdrawal based on a percentage average of, say, the past three years' annual lifestyle expenditure with a percentage amount based on the portfolio value. You can weight these factors to favour your preference for either more stable cashflow or a greater chance of portfolio survival. This allows you to customise your withdrawals to smooth out consumption while responding to actual investment performance.

Sustainable regular withdrawals from your portfolio

Over the years a number of studies have tried to determine sustainable levels of regular portfolio withdrawals for various scenarios. By sustainable we mean that the portfolio will not be exhausted in your lifetime or a given time horizon.

The earliest research into safe portfolio withdrawal rates was undertaken in 1994.[2] The analysis used historical data from the US market and established, using 50-year rolling periods, what the safe withdrawal rate would have been to avoid running out of money over any 30-year period. The author recommended that investors should hold between 50% and 75% equities in their portfolios – any less and the risks of running out of money were too great on account of the lower returns of bonds. On this basis he concluded that the sustainable annual withdrawal rate was 4% – which he called the SAFEMAX rate of withdrawal – with a caveat that the sustainable rate of withdrawal was dependent on the sequence of returns.

[2] Bengen, W.B. (1994) 'Determining withdrawal rates using historical data', *Journal of Financial Planning*, **www.retailinvestor.org/pdf/Bengen1.pdf**

'Therefore I counsel my clients to withdraw at no more than a four-percent rate during the early years of retirement, especially if they retire early (age 60 or younger).'[3]

Another academic study[4] found that, over a 30-year time horizon, a portfolio that was allocated 50% to equities and 50% to bonds and with 4% annual withdrawals increasing with inflation, historically, had a 95% success rate, i.e. the investor would not have run out of money in 19 out of 20 instances. This approach is commonly known as the 4% rule. Other researchers have made similar studies using backtested and simulated market data and other withdrawal systems and strategies and the general approach is widely endorsed, particularly in the United States.

The report's authors, however, made this qualification:

> 'The word planning is emphasized because of the great uncertainties in the stock and bond markets. Mid-course corrections likely will be required, with the actual dollar amounts withdrawn adjusted downward or upward relative to the plan. The investor needs to keep in mind that selection of a withdrawal rate is not a matter of contract but rather a matter of planning.'[5]

On the face of it this level of withdrawal seems sensible. If the real return from equities is 5% and the real return from bonds is 2%, a simplistic calculation for the expected returns on a 60/40 portfolio would be (60% × 5%) + (40% × 2%) = 3.8%. So, a 4% withdrawal rate would, if that return was achieved each year (and ignoring costs and tax), substantially maintain purchasing power. In the real world, investment returns don't arise in a straight line, and the sequence of returns can make this rule of thumb vulnerable, without regular reviews and flexibility to varying the amount of regular withdrawals.

More recent research[6] has highlighted the limitations of the 4% rule and put forward some alternative approaches. The researchers highlighted the obvious mismatch between financing a constant, non-volatile spending plan with a risky, volatile investment strategy and the investment inefficiencies arising from such an approach. The study found that the typical withdrawal rule 'wastes' 10–20% of the portfolio funding future investment surpluses the investor doesn't spend and a further 2–4% is used to fund overpayments in years when performance is lower

---

[3]   Ibid.

[4]   Cooley, P.L., Hubbard, C.M. and Walz, D.T. (1998) 'Retirement savings: Choosing a withdrawal rate that is sustainable', *AAII Journal*, 10(3): 16–21.

[5]   Ibid.

[6]   Scott, J.S., Sharpe, W.F. and Watson, J.G. (2008) 'The 4% rule – at what price?', April, **www.stanford.edu/~wfsharpe/retecon/4percent.pdf**

than the amount withdrawn. Thus, those adopting the 4% rule (and the associated risky asset exposure) pay a relatively high, but not always apparent, price for the income they receive. The study concludes that if investors can afford to take lower withdrawals than 4% p.a. of the portfolio and adopt a less risky portfolio strategy, they dramatically reduce the likelihood of exhausting the portfolio.

Example portfolios and withdrawal rates

A recent simplified analysis[7] of the 4% rule, carried out for my firm, provides some useful insights into safe withdrawal rates. The analysis was based on a portfolio allocated 60% to equities and 40% to bonds, based on a range of 30-year historic performance outcomes as set out in Table 12.1. Note the wide range of 30-year returns and how they compare to the 113-year average.

Table 12.1 Balanced 60/40 portfolios: 30-year horizons (1900–2013) – annualised real returns

Worst 30 years	2nd worst 30 years	Worst 15-year start	Median 30 years	Total period average
1945–1974	1947–1976	1960–1989	1939–1968	1900–2013
0.1% p.a.	0.8% p.a.	4.0% p.a.	4.0% p.a.	3.8% p.a.

Data source: Barclays Equity Gilt Study 2014.

These return periods are plotted in Figure 12.3. The two worst time periods, perhaps not surprisingly, incorporate the worst one-year fall in 1974, effectively giving back much of the gain made up to that point. It is also worth noting that the purchasing power of gilts was substantially eroded by high inflation in the 1970s. This is a pretty extreme and tough test for the 4% rule.

These data were used to model a scenario of a 4% initial withdrawal rate on a £1 million portfolio. As the returns are in real terms, a constant £40,000 was withdrawn at the start of every year and the remaining portfolio value was indexed up by the real return that year. The purchasing power balances, over a 30-year period for the five different scenarios above, are plotted in Figure 12.4. The average return is equivalent to a straight-line approach to modelling future performance in a lifetime cashflow projection (see Chapter 3).

---

[7] Albion Strategic Consulting (2014) 'SmarterInsight governance update 7', 31 January.

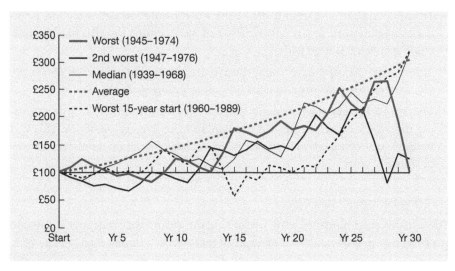

Figure 12.3 30-year return pathways in real terms
Source: Albion Strategic.

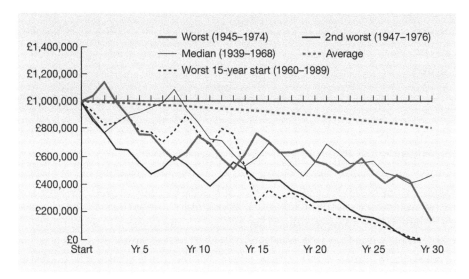

Figure 12.4 Impact on portfolio size withdrawing £40,000 p.a. (an initial 4% rate)
Source: Albion Strategic.

From this analysis we can make several observations:

- The two worst periods suffered badly, with the 2nd Worst scenario actually failing to survive through 30 years. The Worst portfolio did marginally better due to strong positive returns in the first two years of the sequence.

- The Median portfolio, despite delivering a comparable return of around 4% to the average return for the entire period of 3.8%, ended up with half the purchasing power it started with.

- The straight-line approach using the average return ended up with £800,000. The dangers surrounding a straight-line approach are evident.

- The Worst 15-year start scenario actually ran out of money despite returning more or less the same as the Median and the Average scenarios. This was because the portfolio had been eroded by withdrawals and poor market returns in the early years.

Fixed withdrawal strategy

The analysis then modelled a 4% initial balance withdrawal strategy (i.e. £40,000 p.a.).[8] A range of goals, and outcomes against these goals, is summarised in Table 12.2.

Table 12.2 Purchasing power outcomes of a 4% withdrawal strategy

Time from start	<Initial	<Half initial	Run out
10 years	53%	15%	0%
20 years	55%	32%	8%
30 years	57%	43%	25%
40 years	59%	49%	38%

Source: Albion Strategic.

It is evident that a 4% withdrawal rate is risky over a 30-year horizon, based on a portfolio with the parameters above, with a 25% chance of running out of money. The challenge is that for 75% of investors this strategy works. Simply reducing the withdrawal rate across the board to, say, 3% is a blunt tool as the majority of investors would be spending less than they need to. If the investor is working with a financial planning firm that reviews withdrawals at least annually, there is scope to adjust the withdrawal and plan, provided that the investor has the flexibility to do so. This illustrates the importance of having a range of annual lifestyle spending goals and an adequate cash reserve.

---

[8]   This was done using the risk and geometric real return of a 60/40 portfolio for the whole period 1900–2013 of 3.8% – which equates to an arithmetic return of around 5% – with an annualised standard deviation (risk) of 15.5%.

Dynamic withdrawal strategy

A similar analysis, but instead with a dynamic withdrawal rate (as per Tables 12.3 and 12.4), reduces the income withdrawal when the portfolio value falls below a certain target level.

Table 12.3 Dynamic withdrawal rate parameters

Rate of withdrawal	Upper limit	Lower level
4% of start value p.a.	No limit	80% of start value
3% of start value p.a.	<80%	>60%
2% of start value p.a.	<60%	No lower limit

Source: Analysis Albion Strategic.

Table 12.4 Purchasing power outcomes of a dynamic withdrawal strategy

Time from start	<Initial	Halve	Run out
10 years	51%	9%	0%
20 years	51%	18%	0%
30 years	50%	25%	3%
40 years	50%	30%	9%

Source: Analysis Albion Strategic.

As can be seen from Figure 12.5, it is evident that the dynamic withdrawal strategy dramatically improves outcomes compared with a static withdrawal strategy, without penalising theoretical investment outcomes that are favourable.

Running a similar dynamic withdrawal analysis on the historical data scenarios of 2nd Worst and Worst 15-year start scenarios, which both failed at a static 4% withdrawal rate, we can see the positive impact it has on outcomes. Recent research by JP Morgan supports the adoption of a dynamic withdrawal strategy: 'Based on this analysis, a dynamic withdrawal model may offer substantial advantages to help investors make the most of their assets throughout their retirement years.'[9]

---

[9] JP Morgan (2014) 'Breaking the 4% rule', February, available at **www.jpmorganfunds.com/ blobcontent/4/185/1323375351903_ES-DYNAMIC.pdf**

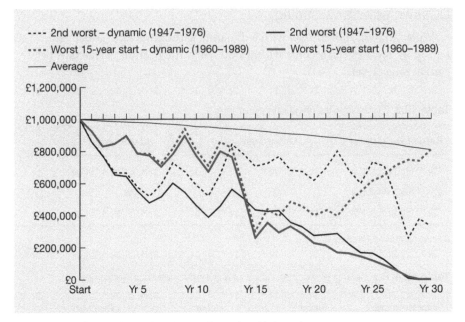

Figure 12.5 Comparison of static vs. dynamic withdrawal rates
Source: Albion Strategic.

Interesting thoughts on asset allocation – the upward sloping equity glide path

A 2013 research paper[10] suggests that investors should own the lowest allocation to equities at the time of retirement, as this is when they are most vulnerable to portfolio losses. Beyond that point, the allocation should rise to help to increase the chances of the pot surviving the investor. If equity markets do badly in the early years, the investor will not have suffered the full brunt of any fall and will, by averaging their way into the equity market over time, benefit from any market recovery. If equity markets have done well in the early years, there will be little concern. This strategy has been dubbed a 'rising equity glide path' by the authors and is counter to the perceived wisdom that the older one gets, the lower the allocation to equities should be.

---

10 Pfau, W.D. and Kitces, M.E. (2013) 'Reducing retirement risk with a rising equity glide-path', 12 September, available at **SSRN: http://ssrn.com/abstract=2324930**

Determining the right portfolio withdrawal strategy

While there is no single answer, there are some principles that you can use to help you determine and manage the right portfolio withdrawal strategy.

- Historic average investment returns disguise the fact that such returns are not delivered in a consistent manner and, depending on the investment strategy adopted, will vary from year to year. This means that any financial modelling done to determine a sustainable regular withdrawal strategy, on the basis of average annual investment return assumptions, may overstate the viability.

- Plan viability is greatly affected if regular withdrawals are high in the first five years or so and the portfolio suffers significant volatility and/or a fall in value.

- Risk analysis systems such as Monte Carlo modelling can provide useful insights into the probability of portfolio sustainability, but oversimplify the outcome as either success or failure. In reality, all of the assumptions together will almost certainly prove to be wrong, and the plan (such as annual withdrawals) can be modified well before the plan gets into danger territory.

- It is likely to be helpful to model lower rates of return and/or lower levels of annual withdrawals, to gain a better insight into plan viability.

- Some of the more sophisticated planning tools allow the portfolio withdrawals to be stress tested in the event of a major stock market crash at different stages of the plan.

- A dynamic portfolio withdrawal strategy, based on rules along the lines of those set out in this chapter, is likely to improve the probability of the portfolio surviving across a range of investment return outcomes.

- The highest chance of success and most efficient use of capital is likely to arise if regular withdrawals are and remain low (<2.5% p.a.) in proportion to the portfolio value and the investment strategy has a low-risk profile (i.e. with low volatility).

- Assuming that the portfolio will be investing entirely in index-linked gilts and a low withdrawal rate will be taken (broadly equivalent to the natural yield) seems to be a sensible base scenario to compare with other withdrawal strategies, as this represents a low-risk option for an investor whose liabilities (i.e. future expenditure) are expected to increase with inflation.

- If you have a long time horizon and expenditure that rises much faster than official inflation, coupled with a low equity allocation, this will translate into a high probability of declining consumption in the long term (i.e. withdrawals will have to be reduced at some stage) to avoid the portfolio being exhausted.

● Expected final values are higher for portfolios with high equity allocations, but so is the likelihood of leaving a small legacy. This is a classic risk–return trade-off.

● Whether you adopt a static or dynamic withdrawal strategy, it is essential to review the withdrawal level periodically (no less than tri-annually) in the light of actual investment returns achieved and make adjustments as necessary. This is particularly important for portfolios with higher levels of withdrawals, regardless of their exposure to risky assets and to portfolios with high allocations to equities with moderate to high levels of withdrawals.

Adding risky assets to a portfolio is done in the expectation, but not the certainty, that it will generate real returns in excess of those available from cash and index-linked gilts. As an investor you need to weigh up the probability of running out of money in your lifetime against the alternative of a less expensive lifestyle.

The importance of rebalancing your portfolio

As we've already discussed, your portfolio's asset allocation is one of the most important decisions in the portfolio-construction process and is the major determinant of its risk–return characteristics. How the portfolio is taxed can also have a big impact on how much of those returns you keep. With a multi-asset class portfolio that uses collective funds, over time, each asset class will generate different returns, which will cause your portfolio's asset allocation and consequently its risk profile to change. This is known as portfolio drift and is unlikely to be consistent with your goals, preferences and tax position. The portfolio will, therefore, require some ongoing management and review to manage both risks and taxes.

Sometimes an asset class can experience significant volatility over a time period but end it at the same value as that at which it started. Take, for example, the Japanese stock market as represented by the Nikkei 225 Index for the 29 years ending 2013. As you can see from Figure 12.6, the index experienced many large rises and falls, some of which were more than 100%.

A disciplined rebalancing policy forces you to sell high and buy low. This doesn't remove risk but maintains the risk exposure (which is after all the source of additional returns) that you set at the outset. In order to re-establish the portfolio's original risk and return characteristics, it needs to be rebalanced so that each holding reflects the original asset allocation. All other things being equal, a regularly rebalanced portfolio will maintain the risk–reward characteristics of the target asset allocation compared with a portfolio that is never rebalanced. An optimally rebalanced portfolio is likely to produce a similar return to that of a non-rebalanced portfolio but at a lower level of risk. See Figure 12.7.

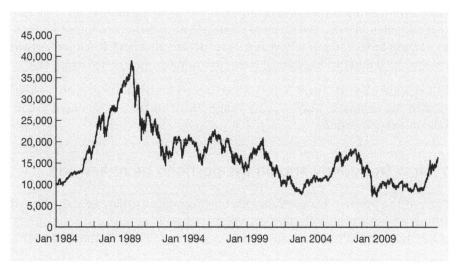

Figure 12.6 Performance of the Nikkei 225 Index (29 years ending 2013)

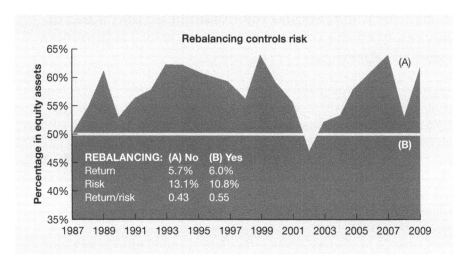

Figure 12.7 Comparison of rebalanced and non-rebalanced portfolios

An additional benefit of rebalancing a taxable portfolio is that it enables gains and losses to be crystallised, which can help with minimising tax. In practice, a sensible rebalancing strategy forces you to reduce exposure to those asset classes that have performed relatively well compared with the others you hold, in favour of asset classes that have performed relatively poorly and/or fallen in value. This 'sell high and buy low' discipline is the opposite of what most retail (and many institutional) investors do, because taking profits and buying more of an asset class that has fallen in value is difficult for most people to do, due to their emotional response to losses and gains. However, logically, if an asset has fallen in value, then its expected return increases, and if it has risen in value, its expected return falls.

In the same way that there is no 'perfect' asset allocation, there is no 'perfect' rebalancing approach. In developing your rebalancing strategy you need to consider three key questions.

1. How frequently should the portfolio be reviewed?

Most of the research on portfolio rebalancing suggests that the risk-adjusted returns are not significantly different whether rebalancing is carried out monthly, quarterly, bi-annually or annually. However, you need to balance the benefits arising from rebalancing against the practicalities of doing so and the associated costs and tax impact arising.

2. By how much should the holdings be permitted to deviate from the original allocation before triggering a need to rebalance?

The reason you should aim to have a threshold to trigger rebalancing is to minimise unnecessary transactions that may have unwelcome tax and cost consequences, not to mention unnecessary additional work. The most recent research[11] suggests that a threshold of between 5% and 10% of the weight of each asset in the portfolio would be optimum, assuming annual or semi-annual monitoring. In the case of a 10% tolerance, an asset with a target weight of 30% would be rebalanced if its actual weight in the portfolio fell to below 27% or rose above 33%. At a 10% tolerance the portfolio would require only 15 rebalancing events (trades) compared with well over 1,000 events for a portfolio with no threshold.

---

[11] Jaconetti, C.M., Kinniry Jr., F.M. and Zilbering, Y. (2010) 'Best practices for portfolio rebalancing', Vanguard, July, **www.vanguard.com/pdf/icrpr.pdf**

3. Should the portfolio be rebalanced exactly to the original asset allocation or a close approximation thereof?

If you pay transaction costs that are fixed (e.g. £20 per trade irrespective of size) and small in relation to the value of the rebalancing trades, then exact rebalancing is probably preferable as this reduces the need for further future transactions. However, if costs are a proportion of the transaction – which is usual in the case of commissions and taxes – then an approximation to the target asset allocation is probably desirable to minimise those costs.

The answers to the three rebalancing questions are mostly matters of investor preference. If you have a diversified equity and bond portfolio, pay a flat transaction fee and minimal tax (assuming reasonable expectations regarding return patterns, average returns and risk), then a sensible approach is to monitor your portfolio annually, use a tolerance trigger of 10% of the original allocation for each asset class and rebalance exactly to the preferred asset allocation. Variations will apply if your personal circumstances are different. Formulating a sensible rebalancing strategy will also provide the discipline to enable you to stick with your investment strategy through thick and thin. Regardless of whether markets are surging or plummeting, rebalancing helps you to avoid misplaced optimism or irrational fear.

The mechanics of rebalancing

The simplest way of rebalancing your portfolio is to use new cash to invest in those assets that are underweight. This cash might come from additional capital being added to the portfolio or, more likely, from accumulated interest and dividends arising from the portfolio holdings. For this reason it is important to avoid investing in any funds that automatically reinvest interest and dividends. By using cash to rebalance you will reduce the number of transactions that you or your adviser will need to carry out and, in the case of portfolios that are taxable, you'll avoid unnecessary crystallisation of taxable capital gains.

The other method of rebalancing is to realise cash from the overweight portfolio holdings to reinvest in the underweight holdings. In the case of taxable portfolios, this might be more attractive than using new cash if you need to crystallise gains to utilise your annual capital gains tax exemption or crystallise losses to offset against current year gains or to be carried forward for use in future tax years.

If a large, taxable capital gain would arise as a result of rebalancing back to the exact allocation, you might wish to rebalance to as near to the model as you can without crystallising the extra tax. Alternatively, you might wish to delay the rebalancing if you anticipate being able to add more capital to the portfolio in the near term or expect to be a basic-rate taxpayer in the next tax year, but don't fall into the trap of letting tax overly influence the need to rebalance. The most tax-efficient portfolio is one that makes only losses and if you don't rebalance, particularly when markets have risen sharply, you might see those gains evaporate, as we saw earlier with the Japanese stock market. I remember as far back as the late 1990s when many investors were unwilling to sell out of their technology stocks because of the tax they would have paid. Although continuing to hold them through 2001 certainly avoided the tax problem, the collateral damage to their portfolios when the sector corrected spectacularly may have given rise to a few regrets.

Most people with reasonable-sized portfolios are likely to have taxed and non-taxed elements. It is likely, therefore, that a combination of using cash (whether from interest/dividends or additional investment capital) and releasing cash from other holdings will be necessary to carry out rebalancing.

The use of debt with investing

Depending on your point of view, debt is either something to be avoided at all costs or a useful way of multiplying wealth and opportunity. The two most common questions about debt are:

1   Should I use capital/income to pay down debt or should I invest?
2   Should I use debt to augment my investment capital to leverage higher investment returns?

Debt is a negative bond (fixed-income) exposure, although the interest costs will invariably be higher than the interest rate earned on bonds. So if you have a £200,000 bond and £200,000 equity exposure in your investment portfolio, e.g. 50% to each asset class and a £50,000 mortgage, your actual bond exposure is £150,000 (the bond of £200,000 less the £50,000 mortgage). The result is that instead of having 50% of your portfolio allocated to risky equities you actually have 57%. This higher risk might be acceptable if you have a need and tolerance for a higher allocation to risky assets.

It is unlikely that you will be able to earn a higher rate of interest from cash or bonds in taxable accounts, particularly for higher- and additional-rate taxpayers,

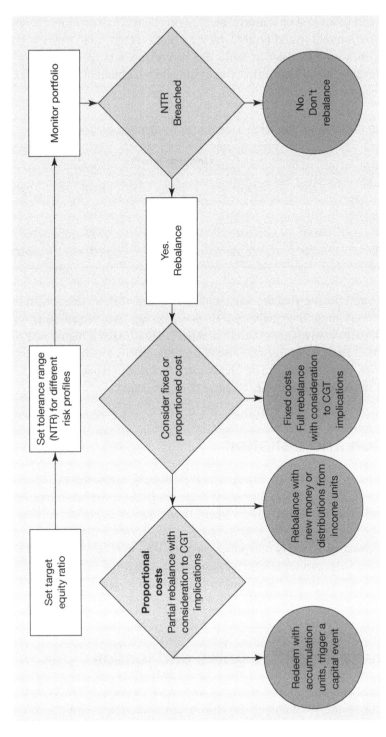

Figure 12.8 Portfolio rebalancing decision-making framework

than the cost of interest on a mortgage. Repaying debt is a risk-free return whereas a taxable investment would need to deliver a higher return than the risk-free rate and, as such, would be risky. In Table 12.5 you can see a range of mortgage rates and the taxable rate of return that you would need to obtain at different tax rates just to break even.

Table 12.5 Gross investment returns required to equal mortgage interest costs

Tax rate (%)	Mortgage rate (%)				
	3.00	**4.00**	**5.00**	**6.00**	**7.00**
20.00	3.75	5.00	6.25	7.50	8.75
40.00	5.00	6.67	8.34	10.00	11.67
50.00	6.00	8.00	10.00	12.00	14.00

In tax-free and tax-deferred accounts such as ISAs and offshore investment bonds, the position is more finely balanced. However, on tax-favoured accounts such as pensions, particularly where initial tax relief is obtained at a higher rate on the contribution than is payable on benefits and tax-efficient growth is achieved in the intervening period, it can be highly attractive not to repay debt and instead make pension contributions (see Chapter 17 on pensions).

Inflation and deflation

A variable-rate loan is fully exposed to inflationary pressures and one would expect rates to rise or remain high in an environment of rising or strong inflation. If you think that deflation is more likely, then a variable-rate loan makes more sense as the cost of borrowing is likely to fall to nil. However, in that situation, any real assets, such as property or equities, that the loan may have been used to purchase are also likely to experience a fall in value. A fixed-rate loan, meanwhile, is protected against rising inflation but will be exposed to deflation unless the loan includes the option to repay some of it or the entire amount early without penalty.

Leverage amplifies gains and losses

Borrowing allows you to leverage returns on investment capital. This is great when the asset or business is going up in value, because the return over the cost of the debt is added to the investor's capital as 'free' excess return. However, debt can also amplify losses, as many people and companies have found out since the financial crisis of 2007–2009 began to unwind.

For those with significant wealth, the most common use of debt is as investment in property, because fractional ownership of physical property is not feasible in most cases in the same way as it is with equities and bonds. In addition, debt can be introduced to a property portfolio, for example, to allow capital to be extracted tax-efficiently, with the rental income servicing the interest. If you want to retain the property as an investment but have a better use for some of the equity, this could be a good idea.

There is a multitude of packaged investments that come with inbuilt leverage, which serves to increase the relative risks compared with unleveraged investment in, say, an equity index fund. Examples of such investments are as follows:

- investment trusts (see Chapter 11)
- property funds
- property partnerships and syndicates
- enterprise zone property syndicates (no new schemes are available)
- business premises renovation allowance syndicates
- affordable housing partnerships
- film partnerships
- carbon/clean energy funds
- long/short 130 equity funds.

In some cases, the debt is required to obtain a tax effect, such as with business premises renovation allowance syndicates, whereas with others, such as the long/short 130 equity fund,[12] it is required to generate the expected return. The key point to remember is that once you adjust the expected return for the additional risk of debt, you are likely to end up with a return similar, or in some cases lower, than that from an unleveraged investment portfolio.

---

[12] A simple explanation of a long/short 130 equity fund is as follows: the fund typically borrows £30 for every £100 of investors' cash and then invests the combined amount, £130, in equities. At the same time the fund sells £30 of equities that it doesn't currently own, i.e. it goes 'short', in company shares that the fund manager thinks will suffer a fall, with the intention of buying the shares more cheaply to settle the short sale.

Later life needs

Debt can also be used as part of later life planning. Those who need to fund life-style expenditure and/or care fees funding, but who have insufficient liquid assets and/or income, could use what is known as a lifetime mortgage secured against their property. In most cases the interest is rolled up and added to the loan until the borrower's death, when the loan is repaid from the proceeds arising from selling the property. Most lenders active in this market give a guarantee that the loan and rolled-up interest will never be more than the value of the property, known as a 'no negative equity guarantee'. For this reason the maximum loan is usually less than 50% of the property value, but the actual amount depends on the borrower's age and the lender's interest rate.

Lifetime mortgages are a relatively expensive way of funding later life needs but can be a viable option for individuals who wish to remain in their own home, have no other assets on which to call and don't wish (or are unable) to borrow funds on similar terms from other family members. In addition to your willingness and need to take risks, using debt in your wealth plan boils down to your need to 'sleep well'. Those at the beginning of their earning capacity and those nearing the end of their life can usually cope with debt more than those with other age and wealth profiles. However, if you are looking to preserve what you have in real terms and want as few moving parts as possible in your investment approach, avoid debt as far as possible.

CHAPTER 13
THE ROLE OF INSURANCE

'Buy enough insurance for what can go wrong, so you can invest for what can go right.'

Nick Murray, financial commentator, author and speaker

The extent to which you need insurance will depend on a number of factors personal to you, including available financial resources, lifestyle spending, financial commitments and family health history. Perhaps a more important factor is your view on insurance and whether it is a good use of the family wealth to either insure or not insure and fund the consequences yourself (self-insuring). In addition, in the case of inheritance tax, much will depend on your views on wealth succession and whether you are concerned to replace any wealth lost to the state in tax upon your demise.

In the context of your wealth plan, there are six possible uses of insurance:

1 To protect against loss or damage to material assets such as property, vehicles and possessions using general insurance (GI).

2 To protect against unforeseen but financially significant expenditure on healthcare and/or long-term care using private medical (PMI) and long-term care insurance (LTC) respectively.

3 To protect against the loss of earned income as a result of being unable to work due to ill health using permanent health insurance (PHI).

4 To provide protection for your surviving family or business against a known liability such as a mortgage, business loan or business buyout that may be called in following your death or critical illness/permanent disability.

5   To protect against outliving your pension resources by transferring investment and longevity (living longer than average) risk to an insurance company
through the purchase of a traditional or limited-term annuity.

6   To replace the value of your estate that would be lost to inheritance tax (IHT)
following death through the use of either whole-of-life insurance or seven-year
level or decreasing-term insurance.

Insuring property and possessions

Most people under-insure their property and physical possessions, because they
underestimate the true replacement costs at the outset and/or because they fail to
update it against inflation. While price is often a major factor in choosing general
insurance, it really should be only one factor. While none of us expects to have to
call out the fire service, if we do so we want to know that they haven't gone for
the cheapest fire engine that fails to start when they get our call! General insurance is the same in the sense that if you need to claim you don't want to find that
the small print excludes your claim and/or getting paid out takes you ages (not to
mention wasted hours dealing with the claims department).

Higher-value homes, cars and possessions need to be covered by insurers that
understand and specialise in providing such cover. I recommend using the services of a reputable and experienced general insurance adviser to assess general
insurance coverage needs. A good adviser will be happy to visit you at your home
and carry out a proper assessment of your needs and suggest a comprehensive
solution. You'd be amazed at the real cost of replacing the contents of even a modestly furnished home and wardrobe.

A number of insurers in the higher-value market can provide a single insurance
policy that covers all property (including second homes and rental properties),
vehicles (including family members and staff) and travel insurance (including
business travel and winter sports). I can say from personal experience that having
one policy to cover these risks is much easier to administer and ensures nothing
'slips through the gaps'. See Figure 13.1.

Insuring against ill health

Private healthcare

While the National Health Service (NHS) provides comprehensive and generally good-quality healthcare, particularly for acute conditions, many families

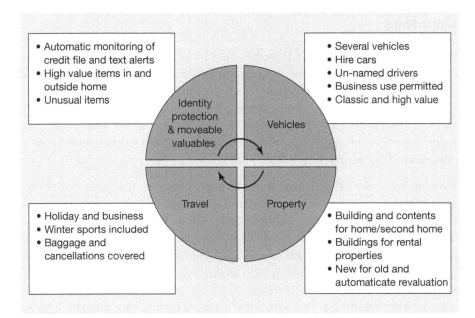

Figure 13.1 Combined high-value general insurance policy

like the choice, flexibility and speed associated with private healthcare. While it is perfectly possible to pay for private healthcare as it is needed, whether or not this is viable will very much depend on the level of your financial resources, your expected quality of health throughout your lifetime and the treatment required.

For most people it will be preferable to put in place some form of PMI to protect against large medical costs and, as a result, protect the family wealth. The problem with PMI is that it becomes quite expensive as you get older, given the higher risk of claims arising. There are several ways that you can minimise the cost of PMI, including having a high excess, accepting a restricted choice of hospitals, restricting certain medical conditions, and the last and probably most popular option being able to restrict private healthcare provision to instances in which care could not be provided by the NHS within a specified time period, typically six weeks.

Certain long-term health conditions are not treated by the NHS where the primary need is not nursing care. If you live in England or Wales you will be required to pay for any long-term care, whether this is in your own home or a residential care home. Long-term care is most likely to be required in older age and certain health conditions, which are not necessarily life-threatening, can last for many years, causing a serious drain on the family wealth. Long-term care is covered in more detail in Chapter 19.

Care fees

Long-term care insurance (LTCI) is similar to PMI in that it pays some or all of the costs of care but only if the insured is unable to perform a number of 'activities of daily living' (ADLs) or is permanently cognitively impaired (senile). ADLs include washing, moving, dressing, feeding, using the toilet and getting in and out of bed, and it is usual for the policy to require the policyholder to fail at least two, but more often three, of these before a claim will be paid. LTCI will continue to pay a claim until either recovery or death.

There are relatively few providers active in the LTC market, compared with other types of insurance, but those that are have a lot of experience and useful products. The only current LTCI policy available in the UK market is a care fees annuity – this is designed for those who need care immediately or on a deferred basis and wish to pay a single lump sum to pass the long-term liability for funding care costs to an insurance company. As with all annuities, those who live beyond the average will be better off and those who don't will be worse off. An immediate or deferred care annuity can be useful if it is essential to have certainty about being able to afford the cost of care but financial resources are limited. However, this still doesn't mean that all future care costs will be covered, particularly if care costs rise faster than the escalation factor (if any) added to the policy.

Critical illness

Critical illness (CI) insurance, originally known as 'dread disease' insurance, pays a lump sum on the diagnosis of any one of a range of serious illnesses or possibly in the event of suffering a permanent and total disability (PTD). However, it's important to note that some types of cancer are not covered and to make a claim for some illnesses, such as a stroke, you need to have permanent symptoms. For other conditions, such as a heart attack, the illness must be of a specified severity. Examples of conditions on which a valid claim would be paid are shown below:

Alzheimer's disease before age 65 – resulting in permanent symptoms.

Aorta graft surgery – for disease and trauma.

Aplastic anaemia – resulting in permanent symptoms.

Bacterial meningitis – resulting in permanent symptoms.

Benign brain tumour – resulting in permanent symptoms.

Benign spinal cord tumour.

Blindness – permanent and irreversible.

Cancer – excluding less advanced cases.

Carcinoma in situ of the breast – requiring mastectomy or lumpectomy.

Carcinoma in situ of the testicle – requiring surgery to remove one or both testicles.

Carcinoma in situ – urinary bladder.

Cardiomyopathy.

Cerebral aneurysm – treated by craniotomy or endovascular repair.

Coma – resulting in permanent symptoms.

Coronary artery bypass grafts – with surgery to divide the breastbone (a payment is available to pay for surgery after being placed on an NHS waiting list).

Creutzfeldt-Jakob Disease (CJD) – requiring continuous assistance.

Deafness – permanent and irreversible.

Encephalitis.

Heart attack – of specified severity.

Heart-valve replacement or repair – with surgery to divide the breastbone.

HIV caught from a blood transfusion, by physical assault or at work.

Kidney failure – requiring dialysis.

Liver failure – end stage.

Loss of independent existence – resulting in permanent symptoms.

Loss of hands or feet – permanent physical severance.

Loss of speech – permanent and irreversible.

Major organ transplant.

Motor neurone disease – resulting in permanent symptoms.

Multiple sclerosis – with persisting symptoms.

Multiple system atrophy – resulting in progressive and permanent symptoms.

Non-malignant pituitary adenoma with specified treatment.

Open heart surgery – with surgery to divide the breast bone.

Paralysis of limbs – total and irreversible.

Parkinson's disease before age 65 – resulting in permanent symptoms.

Pneumonectomy – for disease or trauma.

Pre-senile dementia before age 65 – resulting in permanent symptoms.

Primary pulmonary arterial hypertension – resulting in permanent symptoms.

Progressive supranuclear palsy.

Prostate cancer low-grade.

Pulmonary artery surgery – with surgery to divide the breastbone.

Removal of an eyeball as a result of injury or disease – permanent physical severance.

Severe lung disease/respiratory failure – of specified severity.

Stroke – resulting in permanent symptoms.

Systemic lupus erythematosus – of specified severity.

Terminal illness.

Third-degree burns – covering 20% of the body's surface area or 50% of the face's surface area.

Total permanent disability – unable before age 65 to look after yourself ever again.

Traumatic head injury – resulting in permanent symptoms.

This list of conditions, provided by Zurich Assurance Ltd (one of the largest critical illness insurers in the UK), is not a standard offering across all policies and providers – the list will vary in number and interpretation of each illness depending on the provider.

Sometimes CI and/or PTD benefit can be provided in addition to or in advance of normal life insurance via a single protection policy. Alternatively, CI/PTD can be provided as standalone cover. The cost of CI/PTD cover has risen quite sharply over the past ten years, and it becomes particularly expensive for those over the age of 45 and/or smokers, due to the increased risk of a claim arising. Whether or not you need CI/PTD cover depends on a number of factors, including the quality-of-life implications that would arise in the event of you suffering a serious illness or permanent disability. CI/PTD cover is a 'nice to have' once you've sorted out other insurance cover. Table 13.1 gives an example of the kinds of costs you could expect for £100,000 of cover.

Table 13.1 Illustrative cost of £100,000 CI/PTD cover – annual premiums

Age at outset	CI only	CI + PTD
30	£228.47	£238.16
35	£293.95	£306.87
40	£381.76	£399.70
45	£544.84	£570.67
50	£749.53	£786.94
55	£947.77	£996.48

Source: IRESS Exchange Comparison Services, May 2014 non-smoker, to age 60, class 1 occupation, non-smoker.

Insuring against loss of income

Permanent health insurance is neither permanent nor health insurance (which may explain why it is also referred to as income protection insurance) but provides a regular tax-free (as long as it is an individual and not a group policy) income if you are unable to work until recovery, death or the retirement age selected at the outset. The benefit is paid after a deferred period, which can be between 1 and 12 months, and is selected when the policy is established. Generally, the longer the deferred period and the earlier the retirement age, the cheaper the cover will be. Premiums are either guaranteed throughout the policy term or subject to review periodically, with guaranteed premiums being more expensive at the outset. It is also possible to have the income benefit increasing before and/or during a claim to provide some inflation protection. Table 13.2 illustrates the possible cost of £10,000 annual PHI cover.

Table 13.2 Illustrative cost of £10,000 pa PHI cover – annual premiums

Age at outset	3 months deferred	6 months deferred
30	£74.08	£68.02
35	£85.08	£75.79
40	£102.80	£86.30
45	£130.72	£104.09
50	£174.37	£142.37

Source: IRESS Exchange Comparison Services, May 2014 non-smoker, to age 60, class 1 occupation, own occupation work definition, non-smoker.

The basis on which benefits will be paid will also depend on the definition used to describe incapacity. Incapacity can be described as unable to perform:

● 'any occupation'

● 'any occupation for which you are suited or trained'

● 'your own occupation'.

The first definition is the widest and means that you can't do any work, whereas the last is the narrowest and means that if you can't do the job you were doing prior to the incapacity, the claim will be paid. If you have a very skilled or specialist occupation, 'own' occupation is preferable, but it is more expensive.

PHI is arguably one of the most underused types of policy, for reasons that have been attributed to the perceived time taken to underwrite benefits, complexity and a lack of awareness by individuals of the likelihood of needing to make a claim. Nevertheless, if you are dependent on earnings for your current and future lifestyle, it is the only insurance that can provide prolonged protection against their loss. While the UK consumer organisation Which? states that income protection is must-have insurance for most working adults,[1] apparently twice as many people choose to insure their pet or mobile phone instead.[2] Official 2013 statistics showed that 2.56 million people were claiming illness- or injury-related benefits from the government and, of those, 2.08 million people had been off work and claiming illness-related benefits for more than six months.[3] In 2011/12 in the UK 27 million working days were lost due to illness and injury and 212,000 injuries led to a three-day or longer absence.[4]

If you have income protection provided for you via your employment then the premiums paid by your employer will not be a taxable benefit in kind. However, if you make a valid claim under the policy, the benefit will be payable to you via the PAYE system and taxed as normal salary. Long-term claims are usually paid directly by the insurer, but they will still be taxed at source via the PAYE system.

If you are already financially independent but still generating income from employment or self-employment, there is no need for you to worry about insuring against the loss of that income in the event of ill health or disability. However, if you are using that income to make regular gifts to a family trust or one or more individuals, and you want to continue that in the event of ill health, or if you are not quite financially independent and are relying on future earned income to add to your financial resources, then insuring against loss of income should be a priority.

Insuring against liabilities arising on death

If you have not reached financial independence and have dependants, you will probably need life insurance to provide the financial resources that would not be generated following your death. If you are already financially independent, whether or not you are still working, there are also several situations in which life insurance might be required as part of your overall wealth plan, such as child maintenance obligations and/or covering any inheritance tax liability.

---

[1] www.which.co.uk/money/insurance/reviews-ns/income-protection/

[2] Think Tank Demos (2013) 'Financial protection', April.

[3] Department for Work and Pensions, March 2013.

[4] Health and Safety Executive Annual Statistics 2011/12.

Family income benefit

Family income benefit (FIB) is a special type of life policy that provides regular payments (free of income tax) in the event of the policyholder's death until the end of the policy term. In effect it is like life insurance in instalments. An FIB policy is likely to be cheaper than a term insurance or whole-of-life policy with the same term and total benefit level. This is because the insurer's risk gradually reduces as the policy progresses. For example, with a 20-year level-term policy of £500,000, if the insured died after 19 years and 330 days, the insurer would still have to pay out £500,000. With an FIB policy with £25,000 of annual benefit (a potential total payout of £500,000), if the insured died after 19 years and 330 days, the insurer would pay out only about £2,000, being 1/240th of the total initial benefit. Another benefit of FIB cover is that it avoids the need to have to invest funds to generate an income and therefore keeps things simple at what may be a very difficult time. Some policies allow future benefits to be paid as a discounted lump sum if necessary. Figure 13.2 gives an idea of how an FIB policy works while Table 13.3 illustrates the annual costs of FIB cover.

FIB offers very good value protection for those people still earning income and who want to replace it in the event of their death and where they do not want, or have insufficient resources, to self-insure. However, even if you are financially independent FIB might still be useful as part of an overall estate plan, particularly

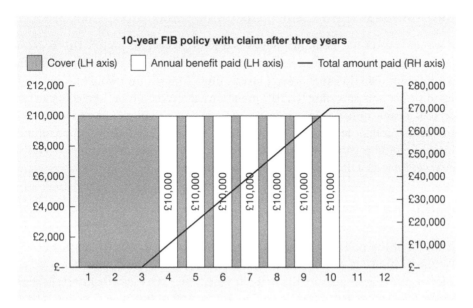

Figure 13.2 How a family income benefit policy works

if you have agreed to fund the education of family or friends or have other regular financial commitments, such as child maintenance payments, that you would like to continue in the event of your death. In this scenario an FIB policy provides a simple and targeted solution. Please note that to avoid inheritance tax it is usually advisable to assign life policies into a flexible trust. In Chapter 21 I explain the main types of trusts and their application.

Table 13.3 Illustrative cost of FIB cover – annual premiums

Age at outset	£10,000 p.a. payable within 20-year term	
	Death only	Death or earlier critical illness
30	£66.59	£184.20
35	£75.44	£254.91
40	£91.57	£366.05
45	£126.95	£557.90
50	£199.99	£903.30

Source: IRESS Exchange Comparison Services, May 2014 non-smoker, class 1 occupation, non-smoker.

Term policy

Another type of life assurance policy is a term protection policy. This type of policy has a set term of between 1 month and as long as 40 years, during which a lump sum (whether that is level, decreasing or increasing) would be paid out upon your death providing that the premiums are paid on time. The policy never accrues a value unless a claim is paid and premiums can be guaranteed to remain the same throughout the term. Alternatively, for a lower initial level of premium, future premiums can be subject to adjustment if the insurance company's rates change. Table 13.4 illustrates the cost of term insurance.

Whole life

A whole-of-life policy is designed to provide life cover, usually, until age 99. Premiums can be guaranteed or reviewable. If reviewable, premiums can be set at a lower initial level (usually the first ten years, then at five-yearly intervals), but expect steep increases in the future. The key benefit of this type of policy is that the cover continues as long as you pay the premiums.

Table 13.4 Illustrative annual costs of term insurance

Age at outset	£100,000 payable on death within 20-year term
30	£58.64
35	£73.22
40	£95.39
45	£135.61
50	£203.07

Source: IRESS Exchange Comparison Services, May 2014 non-smoker, class 1 occupation, non-smoker.

Relevant life policy

A relevant life policy (RLP) is essentially a life policy that is taken out by a company, limited liability partnership (LLP) or sole trader for the benefit of an employee. Subject to certain conditions, the premiums will be deductible against corporation tax (or profits in the case of a sole trader or members of a partnership) and not assessed as a benefit in kind for income tax and national insurance purposes against the employee. Partners, LLP members and sole traders are not employees for the purposes of an RLP. If, however, you run your business via a limited company and are also a director, then you are treated as an employee, whether or not you take substantial remuneration. This opens up the possibility of arranging your life insurance through your business and, as a result, lowering the cost substantially compared with a personal policy.

The company, as your 'employer', would apply for the RLP and as part of the application process would also complete special RLP trust documentation. The company would therefore be a trustee of the RLP, but it is perfectly acceptable to appoint additional individual trustees such as your spouse. The RLP benefit would be payable if you die before you reach age 75. Other benefits available are in respect of ill health, disablement or death by accident, but these benefits are payable only as long as you are still in employment. In the event of your death, the life policy benefit will be paid by the insurer to the trustees of the RLP. The trustees would have discretion as to who should receive the benefit from the classes of beneficiaries specified in the trust. If you have previously completed a nomination form addressed to the trustees of the RLP trust, this will give a non-binding expression of your wishes to them as to who you would prefer to gain from the death benefits. This is similar to the method of nominating beneficiaries under a registered pension scheme.

Any benefit payable for ill health or disability will be paid in the same way as the death benefit, i.e. to the trustees of the trust. As the employee is one of the trust beneficiaries, the trustees can make the payment either to the employee or to their family. The trustees will need to consider all the circumstances at the relevant time in order to decide who should receive the benefit. There is no statutory maximum amount that may be provided by an RLP. Insurers may have their own commercial maxima and associated underwriting/financial underwriting limits and the sum assured should be reasonable in relation to securing deductibility for premiums paid by the employer under the 'wholly and exclusively ' rules on the provision of benefits under the plan.

There are no other tax implications as long as the life assured is alive. Once the death benefit is paid to the trustees, as the trustees will hold the benefit subject to a discretionary trust, then the normal IHT rules that apply to the taxation of discretionary trusts (the 'relevant property regime') will also apply here. This will mean potential periodic and exit tax charges (see Chapter 21).

If the life assured leaves service and takes up a new employment, it may be that the new employer will be prepared to take over payment of the premiums and so keep the cover in force. Otherwise the policy would come to an end.

An RLP in practice

Darren owns a trading business called XYZ Ltd, of which he is also a director. As such he qualifies as an employee of XYZ Ltd and so the company can take out an RLP on his life. Darren takes a salary of £20,000 and regular dividends of £100,000 per annum. After taking into account his existing personal assets and the net value of the business if sold, it is determined that Darren needs life insurance of £2 million to meet his family's lifetime needs. XYZ Ltd applies for an RLP with ABC Life, which provides the necessary special RLP trust documentation. Because the sum assured is reasonable given Darren's historic earnings from the company and the RLP trust documentation complies with the RLP rules, the policy meets the 'wholly and exclusively' test. This means that the premium will be deductible from XYZ Ltd's profits for corporation tax purposes.

On the basis that the company's corporation tax rate is 20%, the cost of this policy when compared with arranging the same one personally funded from after-tax income would be as shown in Table 13.5. The annual cost differential in this example would be £1,333. Larger policies would generate even higher savings.

Table 13.5 Comparison of personal policy and relevant life policy

	Personal	RLP
Gross profit	£3,333	£2,000
RLP premium	Nil	£2,000
Corporation tax @ 20%	–£667	Nil
Net dividend as paid	£2,666	Nil
Income tax @ 25% of net dividend	–£667	Nil
Net cash available	£2,000	N/A
Effective cost	£5,555	£2,000

Note: these figures are purely to illustrate the cost differential between a personally funded policy and a company funded RLP. Actual cost will vary depending on age, benefit level, premium frequency and underwriting status.

In summary, an RLP offers the following benefits to employees (including controlling directors):

- tax relief on the premiums for the employer, subject to satisfying the 'wholly and exclusively' test

- no assessment of premiums on the employee as a benefit in kind

- premiums not taken into account in determining the available annual allowance for registered pensions

- no assessment for the purpose of employer or employee National Insurance contributions

- benefits arise free of income tax and inheritance tax

- benefits do not count towards the lifetime allowance for pension purposes.

If you qualify as an employee and need life insurance protection, then a relevant life policy is likely to be the most cost- and tax-efficient way of providing cover. It is also likely to be most cost-effective to arrange the policy on nil-commission terms and pay a fixed fee for advice and arrangement.

Loan protection

If you have any personal or business borrowing, check the position in the event of your death. Some loans have a clause that requires the loan to be repaid if the principal borrower or director dies. It is usually a better use of the family's or business's money to pay insurance premiums than to be scrambling around for cash to pay the bank at such times. Also check that you are getting good value for money as insurance offered by banks and other lenders is rarely the best value, particularly for large policies. The cost of life insurance has fallen a lot in the past ten years as life expectancy has increased. A term protection-only policy is usually the right type of policy in this situation.

Business protection

If you are a partner or one of several shareholders in an unquoted business, you need to ensure that your business or co-business owners have the means to fund any buyout of your share in the event of your death. There are two components to this planning: the agreement to buy and sell and the insurance or financial means to fund the transaction. A double-option agreement (which allows either party to enforce it) is usual in the case of individuals, giving both sides the option to buy/ sell and a life assurance policy to fund some or all of the buyout, without impairing the retention of business or agricultural property relief against IHT on the business assets – see Figure 13.3.

The life policy can either be owned by the other business owners or by you and written in a special business trust for their benefit. You need to make sure that you

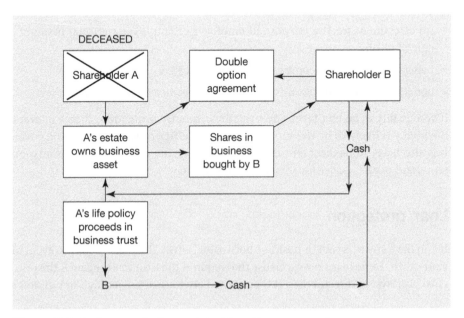

Figure 13.3 Business protection and double option agreement

have similar agreements and policies for your other co-owners. Where the company is to be the buyer of your shares in the event of your death, the life policy will be taken out by the company and the company's articles of association need to be checked to ensure that the company is permitted to buy its own shares. Term protection or whole-of-life is suitable to provide this cover, but they have different tax treatments on premiums and benefits. This is a complex area and specialist advice is required to ensure that things are structured correctly and the most beneficial tax treatment is secured.

Insuring against living too long

A traditional pension annuity is an insurance policy that allows you to exchange pension capital for a specified and usually guaranteed income throughout life. The life company usually prices an annuity based on four factors: general yields from long-term, fixed interest securities, life expectancy, administration costs and profit margin. Those annuitants who die earlier than the average subsidise those who live longer than average. Therefore those who do best from annuities are those who live the longest. The problem is that none of us knows exactly when we are going to die and so annuities are a bit of a lucky dip.

Henry Allingham is an extreme example of when buying an annuity with a pension fund can turn out to be a good choice. A veteran of the First World War, Henry died in 2010 at the age of 113, having received income from the pension annuity he purchased in 1962, aged 65, for 48 years. It was the insurance company that took the risk that Henry would live too long, which turned out to be a good deal for Henry and not such a good one for the annuity provider. Figure 13.4 shows average life expectancy for various age groups.

While they do provide certainty, traditional annuities lack flexibility and may be poor value for money if you die early or annuity rates improve in the future. As illustrated in Figure 13.5, annuity rates have actually been falling over the past few decades, mainly due to a fall in the yields available from long-term gilts and improving life expectancy. Whether this trend will continue is debatable, particularly if long-term interest rates rise in the future. As a general principle, it doesn't make sense to take longevity risk (i.e. the risk of living too long) and you should look to start purchasing an annuity or a series of annuities over time between the ages of 70 and 80 at the latest. We discuss the options for taking pension plan benefits in Chapter 18, where you will find a fuller explanation of the key factors that will influence your decision on whether or not, or the extent to which, you should buy a pension annuity with your pension pot.

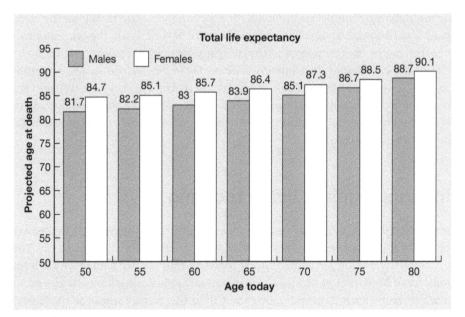

Figure 13.4 Life expectancy at different ages

Source: Office for National Statistics. Period expectation of life: based on unsmoothed calendar year mortality rates from 1981 to 2012 and projected mortality rates from the 2012-based national population projections.

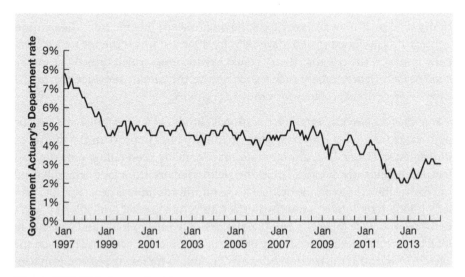

Figure 13.5 Historic annuity rates

Source: Scottish Life based on GAD tables.

Inheritance tax (IHT)

If you have an inheritance tax liability, which you can't or don't want to carry out any planning to reduce or avoid, or perhaps you've done as much planning as is practical or with which you are comfortable but you are concerned about the loss of your family's wealth to the Exchequer, you may want to consider the role of life insurance. Sometimes it is a better use of family money to buy life insurance equal to some or all of the IHT liability. While paying insurance is in effect the same thing as paying some of the IHT in advance, it does have the benefit, for those in reasonable health, of being simple and allows you to retain maximum flexibility and control over your wealth.

Table 13.6 illustrates the total cost of guaranteed whole-of-life insurance for different amounts of cover at various ages. A joint whole-of-life policy is usually the most competitive policy for couples, but single people might find a term policy better value. In any case the cost of the insurance is likely to be much less than the tax liability, in some cases a lot less. Insurance is not a panacea to IHT planning, but as one of a range of possible solutions it is worthy of consideration.

Table 13.6 Illustrative cost of £1 million long-term life cover – annual premiums

Age at outset	Whole-of-life policy to age 99
55	£8,375.28
60	£11,844.96
65	£17,756.04
70	£29,674.80
75	£43,473.25

Source: IRESS Exchange Comparison Services, May 2014 non-smoker.

If you've made an outright gift for which you need to survive seven years before it falls out of your estate, you may be concerned about the IHT liability that might arise should you not survive the required seven years. In this scenario a short-term life policy can be effected, with the cover equal to the tax liability. The policy, known as a gift *inter vivos* ('in life'), can be on either a level or a decreasing basis, depending on whether your nil-rate band is available (see Table 13.7). The policy is written subject to a trust to ensure that the benefit would remain outside your estate and be available to your beneficiaries. There are only a few insurers active in this market and the costs don't seem to be significantly different for those in good health, although if you have a health condition it is probably worth making

multiple, simultaneous applications (any medical examination required can usually be done once and the results shared between insurers) to see which provider
offers the best terms.

Table 13.7 Illustrative cost of £100,000 gift *inter-vivos* life cover

Age at outset	Annual premiums for £100,000 term insurance – 7 year term	
	Level cover	Decreasing cover
50	£127.04	£114.09
55	£187.32	£176.63
60	£299.44	£261.72
65	£503.18	£430.52
70	£878.12	£772.76

Source: IRESS Exchange Comparison Services, May 2014 non-smoker.

Buying any insurance involves a known cost in return for transferring a risk to an
insurance company. In the context of wealth planning the key issue is whether the
cost of insurance is a better use of family wealth compared with accepting the possibility of a high-impact but very low-probability risk.

PART 3
WEALTH ENHANCEMENT

CHAPTER 14
GENERAL TAX PLANNING

Intaxication (n.): Euphoria at getting a tax refund, which lasts until you realise it was your money to start with.

The main personal taxes

The following are the main taxes (and rates for 2014–2015) as they affect UK-domiciled and resident individuals:

- **Income tax** – levied on earnings, rental income, royalties, interest and dividends at rates between 20% and 45%.

- **Value added tax (VAT)** – levied on purchase of most goods and services, mainly at a rate of 20%.

- **Capital gains tax (CGT)** – levied on gains arising on disposal of assets in one's lifetime at either 18% or 28% depending on the income tax rate paid, although the rate is 10% for gains of up to £10 million arising from the sale of certain business interests and assets.

- **Stamp duty and Stamp duty land tax (SDLT)** – levied on most transactions involving the purchase of equities at a flat rate of 0.50% and transactions involving the purchase and sale of land and property at rates between 1% and 7% (15% where property is purchased by certain 'non-natural persons').

- **Inheritance tax (IHT)** – a flat rate of 40% levied on the death of a UK-domiciled individual (or a non-UK-domiciled individual who has become 'deemed' domiciled) on worldwide assets above £325,000 if not left to a surviving spouse/civil partner or charity/political party (36% where at least 10% of the taxable estate is left to charity). Non-UK-domiciled individuals who have neither been classed as 'deemed' domiciled nor elected to be treated as UK domiciled are subject to IHT only on most UK assets. A 20% rate is payable in lifetime on gifts to most types of trust above a limit (currently £325,000 every seven years).

Your tax risk profile

Just as we have our own individual investment risk profile we also all have our own tax risk profile. Knowing your tax risk profile is important because it will help you to determine what type of tax planning might be worth considering. Your tax risk profile will depend on a number of factors:

- **your desire to save tax** – most people understand that they have to pay a fair share of tax, although the top 1% of taxpayers pay nearly a third of all income tax[1]

- **your need to save tax** – what difference saving tax will make to you and/or your wider family

- **your capacity to understand** – being successful and creating wealth doesn't mean that you are necessarily able to understand complex planning ideas

- **your feelings about raising your tax profile** – the taxman uses a range of profiling techniques for taxpayers based on information gained from tax returns, land registry and various other data sources. Certain transactions and disclosures might increase your chances of an enquiry

- **whether or not you invest in professional and personalised advice** – employing a professional tax adviser can be a good 'investment', both in terms of avoiding pitfalls and securing tax savings many times the fee paid.

There are different degrees of tax planning, ranging from simple and tested through to highly aggressive and contentious:

- **low tax risk** – standard planning that is non-contentious such as making a pension contribution, offsetting losses against gains, using an investment bond to defer tax on gains, and using a limited company to control personal taxable income

- **high tax risk** – this includes aggressively marketed tax schemes that aim to achieve a tax saving. Examples of previous planning that would have fallen within this definition include double trust IOU home schemes – to achieve an inheritance tax saving, employee benefit trusts that used a sub-trust to obtain a corporation tax deduction, and certain qualifying recognised overseas pension schemes that offered the ability to give access to a 100% tax-free lump sum from UK-sourced pension funds.

---

[1]   HMRC, 'Income tax liabilities statistics 2011–12 to 2013–14', Table 2.4, p. 28 states that it is estimated that 28.3% of all income tax in 2013/14 was paid by the top 1% of taxpayers.

Attacking aggressive tax planning

HMRC estimates that the difference between the tax it receives and the tax it would have received as 'officially intended' is in the region of £35 billion.[2] Although illegal evasion and criminal activity represent the biggest element of this, a significant amount (c. £2 billion) relates to 'avoidance' and 'legal interpretation'. To counteract this loss of tax, a range of new rules and obligations has been introduced over the past decade.

Disclosure of Tax Avoidance Scheme (DoTAS)

Since 2004 promoters of tax 'schemes' to UK residents which meet certain conditions are required to notify HMRC of the existence of such schemes by quoting a Disclosure of Tax Avoidance Scheme number. There are high penalties for non-disclosure and the stated policy objective is to dissuade promotion and use of arrangements deemed aggressive and motivated mainly or partly by a tax advantage that Parliament did not intend. The taxpayer is then obliged to notify HMRC of their use of the scheme by disclosure of the DoTAS number on their self-assessment tax form. HMRC has taken an increasingly robust approach to challenging a significant number of arrangements that have been notified to them under DoTAS, and it has been claimed that it has been successful in about 80% of tax-avoidance cases.[3]

General Anti-Abuse Rule (GAAR)

In July 2013 the UK also introduced a General Anti-Abuse Rule (GAAR) to give HMRC wider powers to attack those arrangements it believes are abusive and to discourage taxpayers from using such arrangements. While it is too early to tell how effective the GAAR has been, you need to think carefully about how vulnerable to attack would be any tax planning you undertake. If the arrangement hasn't been specifically sanctioned by legislation and represents an interpretation or an exploitation of a loophole, you need to be ready for challenge by HMRC. Remember that in attacking any tax planning, HMRC is spending taxpayers' money and it has much deeper pockets than its 'customers'.

---

[2] HMRC, 'Measuring tax gaps – 2013 edition', **www.hmrc.gov.uk/statistics/tax-gaps/mtg-2013.pdf**

[3] As reported by Reuters, 'Britain seeks to take the shine off tax-avoidance schemes', 19 March 2014.

Accelerated tax payments

At the time of writing, the government had announced its intention to introduce a requirement for taxpayers to pay on account any disputed tax relating to:

a an avoidance scheme that is the same or similar to one that has been defeated through litigation with another taxpayer

b schemes that have been disclosed under DoTAS or

c schemes that have been counteracted under the GAAR.

Once the formal notification is given by HMRC, together with a request for the accelerated payment, the taxpayer will have 90 days to pay the tax in dispute. This won't affect the taxpayer's right to make their case through the tribunal process, but it does mean that there will be no cashflow advantage to the taxpayer in the meantime. If the taxpayer wins their case, HMRC will repay the tax, together with interest.

Capped income tax reliefs

Since 6 April 2013 there is a limit on the amount of tax relief that a taxpayer can claim against income tax as a result of losses, set at the greater of £50,000 or 25% of the individual's total annual income liable to income tax. Total income is adjusted to include an individual's charitable donations made via payroll giving and to exclude pension contributions, to create a level playing field between those whose deductions are made before they pay income tax and those whose deductions are made after tax.

The tax relief limit does not apply to:

- losses offset against profits from the same trade or property business
- losses attributable to overlap relief and Business Premises Renovation Allowances (BPRA) investment
- gifts to charity
- tax-relievable investments that are already capped, such as registered pensions, enterprise investment schemes (EIS), venture capital trusts (VCTs), Seed EIS (SEIS) and social impact investments.

Losses[4] that are subject to the limit include:

---

[4] There are several other losses that are included in the cap and these, together with helpful examples, can be found at **www.hmrc.gov.uk/budget-updates/march2013/limit-relief-guidance.pdf**

- qualifying loan interest – which relates to loans to buy an interest in certain types of company or to invest in a partnership
- total losses arising on shares bought at issue
- losses arising in the early years of a new business where those losses are being claimed against income arising from that business
- claims relating to property capital allowances and agricultural expenditure.

Some limited losses may be carried forward for future use, whereas others, such as qualifying loan interest, may not, so make sure that you claim loan interest first and carry forward other losses to relieve against future income.

Tax planning principles

There are a number of basic principles that you need to be aware of to minimise taxation.

1 Know your personal allowances – this is the amount you can earn or capital gains that you can realise without paying tax.

2 Know your income tax band – official figures show that the number of higher-rate taxpayers in the UK has almost doubled since 1998/99.[5]

3 Take action – make use of tax-efficient savings schemes, allowances and reliefs.

4 Deferring tax – even if you can't avoid tax, deferring when you have to pay it can enable you to generate additional returns in the meantime.

5 Integrated planning – your spending, earning, investing and lifestyle decisions all need to be taken into account to determine how best to minimise taxation.

6 Too good to be true – if something looks too good to be true it probably is.

7 Know what you are doing – if you don't understand it (having at least tried to), then don't do it.

8 Tax schemes – be wary of expensive tax schemes with large up-front fees from organisations with which you have no existing relationship and that require a DoTAS number to be entered on your tax return.

9 Be wary of any arrangement that involves overseas entities or structures and/ or that passes through several entities before ending in a final structure, as your money usually feeds many hungry mouths.

---

[5] HMRC, 'Income tax liabilities statistics 2011–12 to 2013–14', Table 2.1, p. 21 states that in 1998/99 there were 2.3 million higher-rate taxpayers compared with the estimate of 4.4 million in 2013/14.

10 Nothing is certain – remember that the rules can and do change, although retrospective changes are the exception and not the rule.

11 Your residence status affects your liability to most UK taxes except inheritance tax, so bear in mind the rules that determine this because they changed a few years ago (see later in this chapter).

12 Tax isn't everything – be careful not to let the tax tail wag the lifestyle planning dog. Moving abroad, for example, might help you to avoid tax but might have an adverse effect on your family and other personal relationships.

Practical ways of saving tax

For the rest of this chapter I'm going to set out a range of tax planning ideas so that you can check to see you are taking advantage of all the key tactics. I have not included any planning that is a 'scheme' or that one could view as 'aggressive'. That being said, you must always bear in mind that what is acceptable to the tax authorities today may well be unacceptable to them in the future. HMRC has been given significant targets to reduce the tax gap and substantial funding to achieve this by tackling tax-avoidance activities.

Closing interest deposit accounts

These are deposit accounts (usually offshore) that pay interest when you close the account and thus no tax liability can arise until then. Such accounts are useful if you want to avoid incurring taxable interest on cash until a future date, perhaps because you will then have your basic-rate income tax band available, you might have allowable capital allowances to offset or you might then be non-UK resident. If you are UK resident but non-UK domiciled, you could time the closure of an offshore account, and the addition of the accrued interest, to a tax year when you also pay the remittance basis charge, if this would be cheaper than paying UK income tax on the interest earned.

Use the tax-free savings band

From the 2015–2016 tax year, the starting rate of tax that applies on up to £5,000 of savings income is nil. The nil savings income band is lost if non-savings income (for most people, their pension or wages) exceeds their personal allowance (£10,500 in 2015–2016) plus the £5,000 savings band. This means that up to £15,500 p.a. of interest could potentially be received tax free. As well as interest from cash deposit accounts, this includes income arising from fixed income holdings such as gilts and corporate bonds, and 'gains' arising from offshore single-premium investment bonds.

Because an investment bond can be assigned to another person without causing an immediate tax charge, the gain will become assessable to income tax only when the recipient cashes in some or all of the bond. As long as the gain, when added to any other savings and non-savings income, is below £15,500, no tax will be payable. Figure 15.2 in Chapter 15 shows how this could work in practice.

Use other family members' income tax bands

If your spouse/civil partner doesn't use their personal income tax allowance or pays a lower rate of income tax than you, consider transferring sufficient savings or investment capital to them to enable any taxable income arising to be taxed at either nil or the lower rate. The transfer must be irrevocable and with tax saving not as the sole motive. Transfers of assets between spouses or civil partners who are living together are exempt from capital gains and as such may be arranged without triggering capital gains tax.

You could extend this concept to using other family members, such as a life 'partner', parents, children (aged 18+), brothers or sisters who are not using their full income tax band but share the same household. Make sure that your paperwork is in order, just in case you have to justify or substantiate any transfers.

Make maximum use of tax-free accounts

Make sure that you utilise your and your spouse's/civil partner's ISA allowance each tax year. Currently you may each contribute up to £15,000 per tax year to an Individual Savings Account and invest in cash deposits and/or stocks and shares, with all income and gains being tax-free. It is also possible to invest up to £4,000 per annum into a cash or stocks and shares Junior ISA for those under 16, and up to £15,000 p.a. into a cash-only ISA for those aged between 16 and 18.

Use National Savings products

Make use of National Savings Certificates when they are available as these provide tax-free, albeit low, returns (both nominal and index-linked) and security of capital. Premium bonds also provide tax-free returns by way of prize draws each month. Although the average return is usually quite low compared with most deposit accounts, the two top prizes each month are £1 million, so it's a reasonable choice if you have significant capital to place in low-risk holdings and/or you have other taxable income subject to higher- or additional-rate income tax.

Make a personal contribution to a pension

A personal contribution to a pension scheme is paid net of basic-rate income tax (currently 20%) and has the effect of expanding your basic-rate income tax band accordingly. For example, an £800 contribution would gross up to £1,000 received by the pension fund and your basic rate income tax band would increase accordingly. This means that, to the extent it falls below the threshold at which higher- and additional-rate income tax is payable, taxable income from earnings, savings or investment will be taxed at the basic rate (20%) rather than at the higher (40%) or additional rate (45%).

A pension contribution can also enable you to:

- restore the loss of personal allowance where total taxable income is between £100,000 and £120,000 and obtain effective tax relief of 60% (see the example that follows)
- enable taxable capital gains arising in the same tax year, in excess of the annual exemption of £11,000, to be taxed at 18% rather than 28%, to the extent that such gains fall below the threshold at which higher-rate income tax is payable
- reduce your net adjusted income to below the £60,000 threshold at which child benefit is completely lost, with income below £50,000 enabling the full benefit to be paid
- reduce the amount of income tax payable on taxable gains arising from single-premium investment bonds (see Chapter 13 for more details).

60% income tax relief

In 2014/15 John has income of £119,000, all of which consists of earnings and interest. His current pension contributions are under £20,000. He can thus make an extra £19,000 gross pension contribution without tax penalty because the aggregate contributions of £39,000 would still fall within the £40,000 annual allowance. Depending upon whether he makes the pension contribution, his tax bill would be:

	No pension contribution		Pension contribution	
	£	£	£	£
Gross income	119,000		119,000	
Pension contribution	–		19,000	
Personal allowance	500		10,000	
Taxable income	118,500		90,000	
Basic-rate tax	31,865 @ 20%	6,373	31,865 @ 20%	6,373
Higher-rate tax	86,635 @ 40%	34,654	58,135 @ 40%	23,254
Total tax		41,027		29,627

Thus, a gross pension contribution of £19,000 will save John £11,400 in tax, an effective 60% rate of relief.

Have your employer make a pension contribution

If you are employed (including by a company owned and controlled by you) your employer could contribute to a pension scheme for you. This could also be funded by you giving up a right to salary or bonus (this is known as salary sacrifice). If salary or bonus is sacrificed in favour of a pension contribution before it has been contractually earned, no income tax or employer's or employee's National Insurance contributions will be due. Most employers are prepared to add the National Insurance saving to the contribution on the basis that it costs them no extra than the salary or bonus.

Employer contributions, unlike personal contributions, do not require a corresponding amount of 'relevant' earnings to justify the contribution. Employer contributions will be tax exempt as long as they are within your unused annual allowance (including any carried forward from the previous three tax years).

Claim capital allowances on property

It is possible to claim capital allowances on the purchase price of certain types of property, including holiday lets, residential (as long as at some stage it has been let to multiple households at the same time) and commercial property. The allowance you can claim will depend on the type of property and varies between 5% and 30% of the purchase price, which may be offset against taxable income arising in the current, previous or future tax years. Capital allowances are a specialist area of tax and you should take appropriate advice from an expert in this area.

Rent a room in your home when you are away for tax-free income

If you rent a room (or an entire floor) in your home to a lodger you can receive up to £4,250 per annum tax-free (or £2,125 if shared without your partner or someone else). The legislation does not say the room or rooms have to be rented to a lodger staying in your home all year, so it would be perfectly acceptable for you to go away for a long summer break and to rent out your home to someone while you are away.

There are four basic rules you must follow in order to qualify for the relief:

1   The room or rooms must be within your 'only or main residence'.

2   The letting must be for living accommodation, not for use as an office, for example.

3   The relief is limited to £4,250 gross receipts in the tax year.

4   The relief applies to individuals only, not to companies or partnerships (although it does apply where individuals share the income other than as a business arrangement, for example husband and wife).

The 'only or main residence' is not the same definition as for capital gains tax relief but a simpler interpretation of where your friends would expect to find you. This means you cannot take advantage of the capital gains tax rules that allow you in certain circumstances to treat a property as being your main residence even though you do not currently live there. You do not have to own the property, although subletting rooms in a rented property would need the landlord's agreement. The definition of 'living accommodation' does not have to mean place of permanent residence. It would be permanent in the case of a lodger, but the law does not specify permanence as a requirement. A holidaymaker living there for only one or two weeks would be perfectly acceptable under the law. If your tax inspector does try to claim you cannot use the relief for temporary lettings or says you cannot let the whole of your home, as then it could not be your 'only or main residence', point out that nowhere in the legislation[6] does it say your home ceases to be your 'only or main residence' when you go on holiday.

---

[6] Section 784 of the Income Tax (Trading & Other Income) Act 2005 dictates exactly how the rent-a-room relief must be applied.

Make a gift to charity

Cash donations to registered charities have the effect of expanding your basic-rate income tax band. This provides higher-rate tax relief on any taxable income above the threshold at which higher-rate tax becomes payable. It can also reduce your adjusted net income to below the £60,000 threshold at which child benefit is lost. In addition, it may also allow capital gains to be taxed at 18% rather than 28%.

Gifts of property or investments have the effect of reducing your taxable income, and as such offer the highest personal cashflow benefit for the person making the gift. In this way it may also increase the amount of your surplus annual income for the purposes of making immediately IHT-exempt gifts (see Chapter 20). For a more detailed explanation of the tax treatment of charitable gifts, see Chapter 24 on philanthropy.

Become a non-UK tax resident

Income

If you become a non-UK resident then no UK income tax is usually payable on income arising while you are non-resident. It is usually best to avoid holding UK shares or equity funds that generate income while you are a non-UK resident, due to the imposition of unreclaimable withholding tax.

Chargeable event gains from bonds

Gains arising on life insurance investment bonds are treated as income for tax purposes when a chargeable event occurs and this offers two potential planning opportunities for non-UK resident investors.

First, an investor who has been non-UK resident for part of the investment period can claim a reduction against the 'chargeable gain' when they resume UK residence. This was formally known as 'time apportionment relief'. The gain calculated can be reduced by the total number of days spent out of the UK as a proportion of the total number of days the investment bond has been held. Previously, only offshore bond gains could be reduced for periods of non-UK residence, but this relief was extended to onshore bonds that commence after 5 April 2013 or existing onshore bonds that are assigned after this date. See Chapter 15 for more details on this tax treatment.

Second, if the bond is encashed when the investor is long-term non-UK resident, any gain will not be subject to UK income tax, although it may be taxable in the investor's country of residence. Do note, however, that anti-avoidance rules introduced in 2013 mean that chargeable event gains arising on an investment bond during a temporary period of non-residence will be taxable on the individual's return. This will be similar to the current CGT rule and will apply where an individual:

- has been resident in the UK for a period of at least four of the last seven tax years, and
- becomes UK-resident again within five years of leaving.

Capital gains

If you have assets that you acquired while a UK resident and on which you crystallise a capital gain after you become a non-UK resident, you must remain a non-UK resident for at least five years to avoid capital gains becoming payable retrospectively. If you acquire an asset after you have become a non-UK resident, you may crystallise any capital gains while you remain a non-UK resident and you will usually avoid UK capital gains tax, even if you return to the UK within five years of leaving.[7] An exception to this rule is expected (at the time of writing) to apply from 6 April 2015 for non-UK residents who dispose of UK residential property. Gains apportioned to the period from that date will be subject to tax, regardless of residence status.

The UK, in line with many countries around the world, now has a Statutory Residence Test, which is designed to give taxpayers more certainty about their residence status and what they need to do to ensure that they are non-UK resident. In broad terms, if you've never been UK resident then it is now harder to become tax resident, whereas if you have been UK resident it is now harder to lose that status. Figure 14.1 gives more information on residence, but bear in mind that if your circumstances are complicated, you should seek specialist tax advice on your status.

Offset trading losses against income

Business trading losses incurred personally,[8] whether as a sole trader or as a partner or member of an LLP, can be claimed against your other income, from

---

[7]   Where an asset has been acquired by an individual when non-UK resident, but which is classed as a replacement asset for an asset previously acquired while UK resident, capital gains can become payable on the disposal of the asset acquired while non-UK resident.

[8]   Where the claimant works in the trading business for less than ten hours per week on average over a six-month period, the trade will be treated as 'non-active' and as such any losses arising will be subject to a cap of £25,000 per annum.

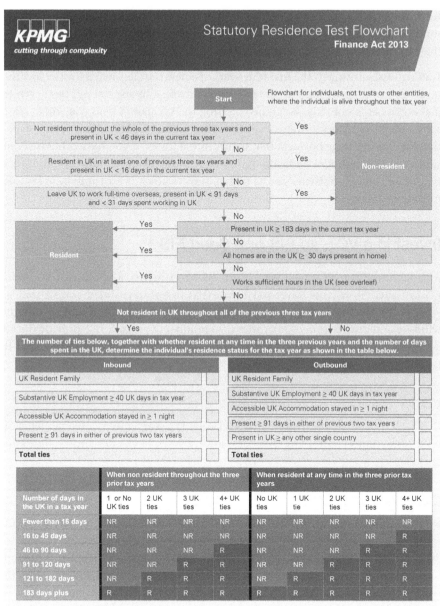

Figure 14.1 UK statutory residence flowchart

Source: KPMG.

whatever source, in the same year as the loss or the preceding year. Loss relief can similarly be claimed against capital gains, which is likely to be more useful now that the top rate of capital gains tax is 28%.

Trading losses arising in the first four years of a new business may be offset against taxable income going back up to three years on a first in and last out basis. While making losses is not to be welcomed, getting the taxman to help you will at least soften the blow. This illustrates a key benefit of using an LLP as the primary structure for an early-stage business that incurs initial losses, if you have other income subject to the higher or additional income tax rate. Do note, however, that this type of loss relief is restricted to the higher of £50,000 or 25% of your total taxable income each tax year.

Invest in a VCT, an EIS or a Seed EIS

Although traditionally these were high-risk investments, a number of VCT and EIS providers now issue lower-risk funds that invest in cash-generative trades, where the objective is to return the original capital invested through an orderly wind-up and distribution of cash after a set number of years. A SEIS provides more generous tax benefits but is generally much more risky due to the fact that it invests in very small start-up ventures.

VCT

Up to £200,000 may be invested in a VCT each tax year, with income tax relief of up to 30%, subject to holding the shares for five years. Dividends and capital gains are tax free.

EIS

Up to £1 million may be invested in a qualifying EIS each tax year (and a further £1 million can be carried back to the previous tax year), with income tax relief of up to 30%, subject to holding the shares for three years. The income tax relief is limited to the extent of your tax liability and if you make a loss from an EIS, in excess of the initial income tax relief, this may be offset against other taxable income in the tax year of loss and/or carried back to the preceding tax year. Any subsequent capital gains are tax-free, and for this reason it is rare for the EIS to pay dividends that would be taxable. However, unlike a VCT, any future losses in excess of the initial income tax relief are allowable as a deduction against other taxable income.

A lower-risk EIS, which returns just your initial investment, can offer a highly attractive return, purely on account of the initial tax relief. Figure 14.2 sets out the projected internal rate of return from an EIS based on a number of scenarios. The breakeven point for you to be no worse off is realising 70p for every 100p invested if you can't offset the loss against other taxable income, or 42p if you can (at the rate of 40%).

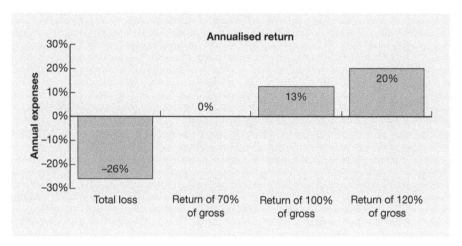

Figure 14.2 Internal rate of return from range of EIS outcomes

SEIS

Up to £100,000 can be invested into small start-up companies each tax year (and a further £100,000 can be carried back to the previous tax year), with income tax relief of up to 50%, subject to holding the shares for three years. In addition, other taxable capital gains may be reinvested into a SEIS and 50% of this amount will be permanently exempt from tax when the SEIS is eventually realised. Gains arising in the previous tax year also qualify for this treatment. SEIS are unlikely to appeal to many investors due to the extremely high-risk nature of the types of businesses that would qualify for investment. However, if you have a friend or relative who wants to start up a business that qualifies as a SEIS, the tax reliefs will reduce the effective cost.

Table 14.1 compares the main features of VCTs, EIS and SEIS.

Table 14.1 Comparison of the main features of VCTs, EIS and SEIS

	VCT	EIS	Social impact	SEIS
TAX ASPECTS				
Income tax relief	30%	30%	30%	50%
Maximum personal investment per tax year	£200,000	£1m for income tax relief, no limit for CGT deferral relief	£1m for income tax relief	£100,000
Tax relief clawback	5 years	3 years	3 years	3 years
Backdating to previous tax year?	No	Yes, up to 100% of investment	Yes, up to 100% of investment	Yes, up to 100% of investment
CGT reinvestment relief	No	Yes, deferral for gains made 1 year before/3 years after EIS investment	Yes, deferral for gains made 1 year before/3 years after EIS investment	Yes, 100% exemption for gains realised and reinvested in 2012/13, 50% for gains reinvested in 2013/14 or 2014/15
Investor capital gains tax liability	Nil at any time	Nil after 3 years, except for reinvested gains	Nil after 3 years, except for reinvested gains	Nil after 3 years
Dividends	Tax-free, but no tax credit reclaim	Taxable	Taxable	Taxable
IHT Business Property Relief	No	Yes, after 2 years	Yes, after 2 years	Yes, after 2 years

INVESTMENT ASPECTS

Structure	Approved investment trust company	Unlisted company	Unlisted company	Unlisted company less than two years old
Listing	Must be listed on main market	May be listed on the AIM, not main market	No	May be listed on the AIM, not main market
Liquidity	In theory tradeable as listed shares, in practice market may be very thin: wide price spreads	Usually nil unless AIM listing. Exit may be by takeover or liquidation	Usually nil. Exit usually via repayment of loan capital by social organisation after agreed investment period	Probably nil
Qualifying companies for investment	Unlisted small trading companies, subject to various restrictions	Unlisted small trading companies, subject to various restrictions	Equity or loan capital to charitable and social enterprises	Unlisted small trading companies, subject to various restrictions
Investments in qualifying companies	At least 70% of qualifying investments must be in shares. Balance can be debt	100% shares	100% shares	100% shares
Maximum holding in any one company	15% of value	100% – Single company structure	100% – Single company structure	100% – Single company structure
Non-qualifying investments	Up to 30%, e.g. in gilts	Ultimately none	No	Ultimately none
Maximum period to apply funds to qualifying investments	3 years	80% 1 year, Balance over 2 years	28 months from date of investment	3 years

Source: Technical Connection: Techlink Knowledgebase

Invest in a social impact investment

Social impact investments provide tax benefits that are virtually the same as EIS. However, because the return is primarily by way of positive outcomes for society, the investment return to you as an investor is likely to be minimal, if any. If you pay income tax, have other taxable capital gains subject to 28% tax, have maximised all the other non-aggressive planning options (or don't wish to) and are interested in making a difference to society instead of or in addition to any charitable giving, this could be an interesting addition to your plan. The following example shows that an internal rate of return of over 25% p.a. is possible with just a return of capital.

Social impact investing – an example

Sally has paid income tax for several years, up to and including the 2015–2016 tax year, of just over £15,000 per year. In the 2015–2016 tax year she also realised taxable capital gains (i.e. in excess of her capital gains tax exemption) of £100,000 from selling a rental property. Because she has no basic-rate income tax band, it having been used up by her taxable income, the tax would be due on the gains of £28,000 (£100,000 × 28%). Sally is interested in backing a broad range of social impact activities.

Sally invests £100,000 into the Make It Better social impact bond on 1 April 2016, (i.e. the 2015–2016 tax year) and elects to carry back £50,000 of this to the 2014–2015 tax year. In addition, she applies to hold over the capital gain arising from the property sale.

Gross investment	£100,000
Income tax relief (15/16)	(£15,000)
Income tax relief (14/15)	(£15,000)
Capital gains tax deferral (15/16)	(£28,000)
Net outlay	£42,000

On 5 April 2019 (i.e. 2018–2019 tax year) Sally encashes half the bond to receive half her original capital. She then encashes the other half on 6 April 2019 (i.e. 2019–2020 tax year). She has her full capital gains tax exemption available in both 2018–2019 and 2019–2020. Because she has retired, she also has £20,000 of her basic-rate income tax band available in both 2018–2019 and 2019–2020.

Realisation from investment		£100,000
Tax on original gain (18/19)	(£8,780)	
Tax on original gain (19/20)	(£8,780)	
Total capital gains tax due		(£17,560)
Net value		£82,440
Total cash benefit	(£82,440 – £42,000)	£40,440

Based on the projected cashflows the internal rate of return is 25.2% p.a.

Employing family

If you run your own business and have a lower tax-paying spouse/civil partner or other family member, you might consider employing them in your business. As long as you pay them below the thresholds at which income tax and National Insurance are payable (about £8,000 per annum should be fine), no tax will be payable, but valuable state benefits will be accrued. Make sure, however, that they actually do sufficient work to justify the income and that the rate is not less than the national minimum wage.

If you find that you need to cut expenses in a few years' time you could, of course, make these family members redundant and choose to pay them a non-contractual termination payment. Currently this is tax deductible for the employer and up to £30,000 is tax-free to the employee. If the termination of family employees happens to coincide with when they need a deposit for a new home, it might just work out nicely for all concerned.

Share the business

You might also give your spouse/civil partner, and possibly your children, shares in your company or partnership so that profits can be distributed to them. Although the shares need to have full voting rights, you could restrict these to a very small amount and you could then pay higher proportionate dividends to those shares. Do be careful if your business is already worth a lot, and avoid giving your children (or the bare trustee who will own the shares for a minor child) any cash used to subscribe for the shares, and make sure you take proper tax advice.[9]

Turn your investment property portfolio into a trading business

If you own property as part of a trading activity there are several tax advantages:

- Losses can be relieved against other income.
- Unrealised losses can be relieved against income.
- Rollover relief on capital gains arising from sale of fixed assets used for the trade.
- Tax of only 10% on the sale or wind-up of a company.
- The value should qualify for business property relief and as such be exempt from inheritance tax (see Chapters 20, 21 and 22).

Turn your hobby into a business

You'd be surprised how many hobbies could be turned into a trading business:

- travel – travel writer or reviewer, TV/film location scout
- country home – smallholding/farming business
- music – music label, promoter, reviewer, performer
- flying – teaching, transporting, fun flights
- history – lecturing and writing on historic matters
- cars – provide classic/high-value cars for hire to weddings, film production companies and other suitable hirers.

A business must be commercial and run with a view to making a profit, so you'll need to create a business plan setting out your aims and trading activities. Assuming that the commercial intention is clearly established, most of your setup and running costs will be tax deductible against your other taxable income. Don't forget that in the first four years of a trade you can carry back trading losses up to three years prior to the year of loss. A travel business, for example, will clearly involve flights, accommodation, travel and subsistence, a laptop computer, smart

---

[9]   The Children's Settlement rule applies where income arises from capital gifted by parents to be held on bare trust for their minor children such that any income arising would be taxed against the parent. It is therefore essential that you take expert tax advice when considering any income tax planning involving minor children. Capital gains arising, however, are still taxed against the child.

phone and stationery, so it's nice to know that the taxman will be helping towards these costs.

Invest in commercial woodland

Whether you invest via a fund, a syndicate or directly on your own, woodland that is managed commercially benefits from several tax advantages, including:

- income arising from the trade is exempt from income or corporation tax
- capital gains arising from the sale of trees (not the land) are exempt from tax
- other taxable capital gains may be deferred by being reinvested into woodland
- the value is exempt from inheritance tax after two years' ownership.

Become an owner in your friend's or relative's business

If you want to provide some financial assistance to a friend or relative, from a tax perspective it is likely to be more effective if you become a general partner or limited liability partner, rather than loaning them money. Any losses arising will be allowable against other taxable income (subject to limits), but as and when you want your capital back, this can be done without any tax implication as it will be treated as a repayment of your capital account. In addition, after two years your holding will qualify (as long as the business is not carrying out an excluded activity) for inheritance tax exemption under business property relief.

If your friend or relative's business is a limited company, make sure that you subscribe for new shares, not buying existing ones from existing shareholders. This is because only new shares qualify for income loss relief in the event that the company goes bust with no value.

Turn a second home or investment property into a furnished holiday letting property

Losses arising from a furnished holiday let (FHL) property, including those arising from mortgage interest, are allowable against the same FHL income. The FHL business could include several FHL properties held as a sole trader or within a limited liability partnership structure. The eligibility rules for a property to qualify as an FHL have been toughened up over the past few years. The property must be available for letting for at least 210 days/30 weeks (increased from 140 days/20 weeks) and must be actually let for at least 105 days/15 weeks (increased from 70 days/10 weeks) of the tax year. It should be noted that the tax treatment of FHLs applies to property situated anywhere in the European Economic Area (EEA).

Interest on a new mortgage taken against the FHL property will usually qualify as deductible against current and future FHL income as long as the loan is equal to or less than the original purchase price plus the cost of any improvements made since then and any profits are retained in the FHL business. It may be possible to claim capital allowances on certain aspects of the property, such as furniture and plant and machinery, and in some cases this can amount to as much as 15% of the property value. The availability of capital allowances on an FHL property depends on when it first qualified as an FHL based on the current eligibility rules referred to earlier.

Another point worth remembering is that all taxable earnings arising from an FHL qualify as relevant income for pension contribution purposes. Therefore, provided that you have sufficient unused pension annual and lifetime allowance, you could make a contribution and obtain tax relief at your highest rate. If only one of you has unused pension lifetime allowance but you own the FHL jointly, there is nothing to stop you from allocating the bulk of the profits to the one who has unused pension lifetime allowance so they can make the pension contribution.

Any capital gains arising on disposal of an FHL should qualify for entrepreneurs' relief. As such, as long as total gains from business holdings have not exceeded £10 million in your lifetime, the taxable gain on an FHL will be subject to only 10% tax. Alternatively, you might be able to apply for Business Asset Rollover relief, if you reinvest the proceeds of one FHL into another FHL (although it could be another non-FHL business asset). An FHL may qualify for exemption from inheritance tax, providing that it is treated as 'trading' rather than being held as purely an investment. The more actively you are involved in managing an FHL, the more likely you are to secure IHT exemption.

Minimising capital gains tax

- Use your annual exemption to crystallise gains (£11,000 in 2014–2015 and £11,100 in 2015–2016).
- Hold capital growth assets within an ISA (up to £15,000 per tax year).
- If your gains exceed the capital gains tax exemption each tax year, consider crystallising sufficient losses to offset those excess gains.
- Make an irrevocable transfer of assets to your spouse/civil partner prior to realising capital gains if they are a non/basic-rate taxpayer and as such would pay tax at 18% rather than 28% and/or they would fall within their unused annual capital gains tax exemption.

▶

- Make a pension contribution and/or a charitable gift. This will expand your basic-rate income tax band, so that taxable capital gains are taxed at 18% rather than 28%, to the extent that the gains fall within the unused basic-rate income tax band.

- Gift property and/or investments to a charity to reduce your taxable income to enable you to have gains taxed at 18%, to the extent that they fall within the unused basic-rate income tax band (c. £42,000 with personal allowance).

- If you do crystallise some capital gains, be careful about also realising losses before 6 April. Capital losses made in a tax year first have to be offset against gains made in the same tax year, with any extra losses carried forward to offset against gains arising in future years. If your gains alone would have been within your annual exemption, the losses are effectively wasted. Losses arising from previous tax years may continue to be carried forward indefinitely until taxable gains arise.

- Become non-UK resident before realising taxable gains, but remember to remain so for five years.

- Consider reinvesting the taxable gain into a qualifying trading investment, such as a lower-risk EIS or commercial woodland (or fund).

- Set up your own EIS company that carries out a qualifying trade (specialist advisers can help you with this), funded by reinvestment of other taxable capital gains to defer paying tax. As long as you aren't claiming income tax relief you can own 100% (not just 30%) of the shares and after three years you can change the trade to any activity (including becoming a family investment company) without the deferred capital gains becoming chargeable (see Chapter 22).

- Hold the asset until you die, as CGT is washed out on death.

Trading assets

Subject to the normal caveats about risk and liquidity, consider investing in a trading business so that disposal of the business would be eligible for entrepreneurs' relief, giving CGT at 10% on up to £10 million of gain. The main requirement is that the business must be trading and you have owned your stake for at least 12 months. In the case of a limited company you must be an employee (not necessarily full time) or officer of the company (i.e. a director but not necessarily paid) with at least 5% of the ordinary share capital and voting rights.

Business profit entity

Choose your business entity and method of profit extraction carefully. The choice is between sole trader, general partnership, limited liability partnership and limited company (UK or overseas) and each has a different tax effect. Don't assume that a limited company is the correct choice because this effectively creates an artificial tax barrier around profits and assets that can reduce flexibility. An LLP structure is transparent for tax purposes but does mean you can end up paying income tax on profits retained for use by the business.

Limited company directors – salary/bonus or dividends?

Unless you are a non-taxpayer or have losses that you are permitted to offset against income, a dividend usually provides a shareholding director with the highest net-of-tax cash. Bear in mind, however, that dividends won't contribute anything towards your state pension and other National Insurance contribution-based benefits. Table 14.2 shows the tax cost of extracting cash as salary/bonus or dividends for a basic-rate and higher-rate taxpayer.

Table 14.2 Net cash from salary/bonus or dividends for basic and higher-rate taxpayer

	Bonus £		Dividend £	
Marginal tax rate	20%	40%	20%	40%
Marginal gross profit	10,000	10,000	10,000	10,000
Corporation tax	N/A	N/A	(2,000)	(2,000)
Dividend	N/A	N/A	8,000	8,000
Employer's NI	NIL	NIL	N/A	N/A
Gross bonus	10,000	10,000	N/A	N/A
Employee's NICs @ 12%	(1,200)	(1,200)	N/A	N/A
Income tax	(2,000)	(4,000)	(Nil)	(2,000)
Net benefit	6,800	4,800	8,000	6,000

The need for professional advice

The UK tax system is intricate and constantly changing, so your planning needs to be reviewed regularly in the light of the applicable rules and legislation. Depending on the magnitude of your wealth and how complex your affairs are, you may need to employ a tax adviser. Minimising tax usually requires a coordinated approach and a mixture of planning tactics. This has never been more so than in today's taxation environment.

A common mistake is to confuse having an accountant with having a tax adviser. The majority of accountants are not tax advisers but are, in all truth, better described as tax and accounts compliance experts. A decent accountant will make sure that you prepare your tax information, make the correct disclosures and submit your tax return within the appropriate timescales. Because of their personality traits and business model, a substantial proportion of accountants are keen to preserve their regular fee income arising from tax compliance and audit work. While some do look to provide added-value services such as tax planning, for many it is not their focus and they often see it as a risky activity.

A qualified tax adviser, meanwhile, understands the detail of tax legislation/ practice and is constantly seeking out ways to arrange clients' financial affairs to minimise taxation. A tax adviser's business model may include a tax compliance service, but many of the best advisers do not get involved in compliance, preferring to work with clients' existing accountants. The best tax advisers are creative, proactive and generate fee income from delivering real tax savings that repay their fees many times over.

Tax is a complex area and not something that you should approach lightly. HMRC's current assertive and aggressive approach, together with the demands for tax revenue, is likely to see high-value taxpayers targeted more and more for investigation. It makes sense, therefore, to ensure that you have your tax affairs in good order.

CHAPTER 15
SINGLE-PREMIUM INVESTMENT BONDS

'Non-qualifying life insurance policies can also have tax advantages.'

Money Advice Service[1]

Investment bonds are single-premium life insurance policies issued by either a UK (onshore) or overseas (offshore) life assurance company. While the policy usually pays a slightly higher amount than the policy value on the death of the bond life assured, this is usually very small (typically 1% of the value).

Capital gains arising within an onshore bond will be subject to the life company's tax rate (currently 20%) after allowing for indexation relief and expenses. Gains arising within an offshore bond will be exempt from tax. UK dividends received inside a UK life fund bear no further tax and the investor has no tax liability on reinvested dividends either. Under an offshore bond the dividends will be received and no further tax will be payable, but there will be no reclamation of the tax credit either.

Foreign dividends will be subject to tax inside a UK life fund but typically not inside an offshore bond. In practice, however, the average yield on foreign equities and funds tends to be comparatively low and in any event, there are often non-reclaimable withholding taxes applied before receipt. The terms of any relevant double tax treaty may be helpful where the withholding tax is reclaimable.

Interest received by a UK life fund will be taxed at 20% – the life company tax rate. Interest received inside an offshore bond will not be subject to tax and the benefits of almost gross roll-up will be most keenly seen in connection with interest-bearing assets.

---

[1] www.moneyadviceservice.org.uk/en/articles/tax-and-qualifying-life-insurance-products

Unlike collective funds, on which the investor suffers income tax on dividends and interest on an arising basis and capital gains tax on eventual encashment, the tax treatment of an investment bond means that the investor potentially pays income tax upon encashment, on any gain, whether arising from accumulated interest, dividends or capital gains. This gives the investor a fair degree of flexibility over the timing of such liability, although with the disadvantage, for higher and additional-rate taxpayers, that the income tax rate payable may be higher than the highest capital gains tax rate of 28% at the time of writing.

With an onshore bond, because the taxable return is assumed already to have borne basic rate tax at 20%, there is no further tax liability upon encashment for nil and basic-rate taxpayers. The whole net gain arising on encashment is added to the investor's other taxable income arising in the same tax year and subject to a further 20% income tax for a higher rate and 25% for an additional-rate taxpayer. With an offshore bond the gross gain will be taxed at nil, 20%, 40% or 45% for nil, basic, higher and additional-rate taxpayers respectively. Figures 15.1, 15.2 and 15.3 show the projected values of a UK and offshore bond both before and after encashment for different taxpayers.

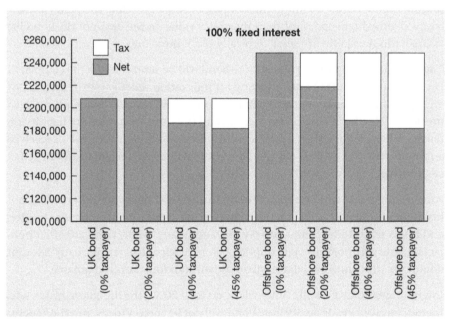

Figure 15.1 Projected values of onshore and offshore investment bonds – 100% fixed interest

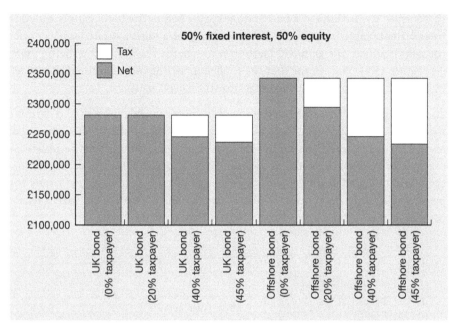

Figure 15.2 Projected values of onshore and offshore investment bonds – 50% fixed interest/50% global equities

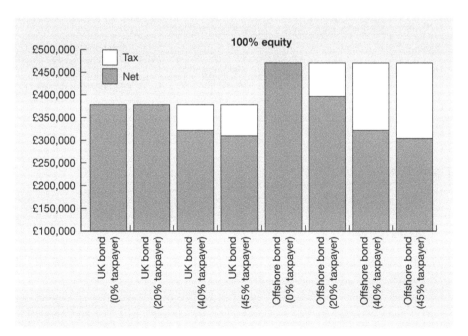

Figure 15.3 Projected values of onshore and offshore investment bonds – 100% global equities

If, however, the investor is a basic-rate taxpayer before the bond gain is added to their other taxable income, but becomes a higher/additional-rate taxpayer once the gain is added, the gain will be subject to what is known as 'top slicing' relief (see Figure 15.4). This means that the total gain arising on encashment is divided by the number of policy years to determine the 'sliced' gain.

The sliced gain is then added to the investor's other taxable income to determine whether it still exceeds the higher-rate income tax threshold. To the extent that each slice does exceed the higher-rate tax threshold, an onshore bond will be taxed at 20/25% on the net gain for each 'slice' above the threshold. An offshore bond will be taxed at nil/20% on the amount of each slice that falls below the personal allowance/threshold for higher-rate tax and 40/45% to the extent that it exceeds it.

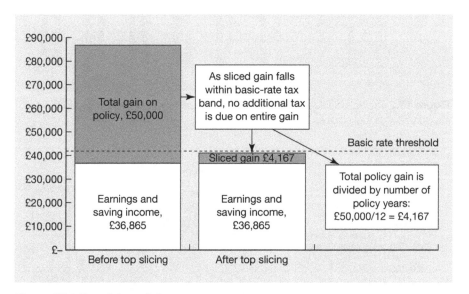

Figure 15.4 Top slicing relief

Example

Trevor originally invested £100,000 in a UK investment bond, which he has held for exactly 12 years. The value of the bond is currently £150,000 and Trevor has made no previous withdrawals. Trevor has £5,000 of his basic-rate income tax band available, due to taxable income from his employment and savings. He decides to encash the bond and as a result crystallises the £50,000 gain.

Because the gain exceeds the higher-rate income tax threshold, the £50,000 gain is divided by the 12 years that Trevor has owned the bond, to create a 'top slice' of £4,166.67 (£50,000/12). Because the sliced gain falls entirely within Trevor's unused basic-rate income tax band, no further income tax is payable.

Tax deferral

Personal income tax is payable only on investment returns arising within an investment bond when what is known as a 'chargeable event' occurs, which is:

- full encashment
- the death of all lives assured on the bond
- partial encashment that exceeds 5% p.a. of the original investment (the allowance is cumulative)
- assignment for money or money's worth.

When the bond is eventually encashed, any previous withdrawals that have not been taxed will be added back to work out the amount of taxable gain. However, this is where another feature, called assignment, becomes useful (see Figure 15.5).

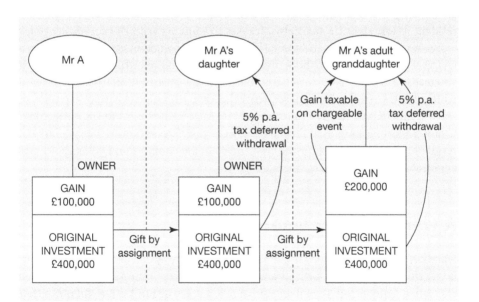

Figure 15.5 Deferring or avoiding tax on gains via assignment.
Source: Bloomsbury Wealth Management.

A transfer of shares or collective funds, by way of gift to a third party other than a spouse or civil partner, will give rise to capital gains tax unless it is to trustees and an election is made to 'hold over' the gain to the trustees. All or some of the segments of a bond, in contrast, may be assigned to a third party as a gift and there is no immediate tax charge on any gain. The gain is also gifted to the recipient and becomes subject to their own tax position.

In effect, the new owner takes on the base cost of the bond and any subsequent tax liability is assessed against them, not the original owner, when a future chargeable event occurs. The new bond owner could also, at some stage in the future, assign the bond to another person or to trustees and obtain further deferral of income tax.

Assignment makes a lot of sense if the new owner is someone who would be able to crystallise the gain within their personal allowance. In addition, from the 2015–2016 tax year, the first £5,000 of savings income is tax free where the individual has other non-savings income below the personal allowance. This means that potentially up to £15,500 of bond gains could be crystallised each tax year by someone to whom an investment bond had been assigned, perhaps while they are at university.

Assignment also works well if the person to whom the bond is being assigned qualifies as a non-UK resident in the tax year of encashment and their country of residence does not seek to tax (or taxes at a lower rate than the UK) the eventual gain arising. The new Statutory Residence Test makes it harder for a long-term UK resident to lose their UK tax status. It takes five full tax years of non-residence for a previously UK-resident individual[2] to avoid income tax on gains arising from a chargeable event on an offshore investment bond acquired while a UK resident. If you realise gains (or cause any chargeable event) by encashing an investment bond while non-UK resident, but subsequently become UK resident within five years of leaving the UK, any realised gains will be retrospectively subject to UK income tax. Chapter 14 has a simplified flowchart to help you determine whether you are UK resident or not, but bear in mind that the rules are complex and you should take advice on your individual circumstances.

A warning on adviser charges

Since 6 April 2013, if you pay financial advice fees by way of a deduction from your bond, this sum counts as a withdrawal for the purposes of the 5% p.a. tax-deferred allowance. Thus, an adviser charge of, say, 1% p.a. of the fund value will mean that

---

[2]   For this purpose UK residence means having been UK resident in at least four of the last seven tax years.

your tax-deferred withdrawal allowance will be progressively reduced each year. This is because your withdrawal allowance is based on the original investment, whereas typically the adviser charge is based on the (hopefully increasing) fund value. Discretionary investment manager fees are treated as an expense of the bond provider and as such are *not* treated as a withdrawal for the purposes of determining your 5% annual tax-deferred withdrawal allowance.

Practical application

Instead of holding an investment portfolio in your own name, you could hold it via an investment bond. As well as minimal or no tax arising within the bond, this leaves your personal income tax allowance, basic-rate band and capital gains tax exemption available to minimise taxation on other assets you may own. In the meantime you may withdraw the investment returns arising (up to 5% p.a. of the amount invested) without immediate tax. This could mean a substantial uplift in yearly cashflow and/or a lowering of tax on personally held assets.

Dividend income

The main problem with dividends, whether via direct holdings or from an investment fund, is the significant tax liability that higher-rate and additional-rate taxpayers incur, even if they accumulate the income. A 40% taxpayer will pay 25% and an additional-rate taxpayer will pay 30.55% on the net dividend received. This is where using a UK single-premium investment bond might be useful, as part of a balanced portfolio tax-planning strategy. Investment bonds come in two forms: self-select and restricted. The self-select version allows you, or the investment manager you appoint, to choose from a very wide range the investment funds or securities that you wish to use.

Dividend income received within a UK insurance company bond does not suffer corporation tax, having received an internal tax credit of 10% on the dividend. Therefore the compounded returns, particularly over very long time periods, will be greater than if a higher or additional-rate taxpayer received the dividends personally. The accumulated dividend income will eventually be taxed on the policyholder if they are a higher or additional-rate taxpayer on encashment but at a lower rate than you might think.

Consider Peter, a higher-rate taxpayer, who invests £1 million in a portfolio of equities that produces a high dividend yield of 4.5% net. As a higher-rate taxpayer he will pay the following income tax on these dividends:

Net dividend received	£45,000
Grossed-up dividend of	£50,000
Income tax @ 37.5% on gross	(£18,750)
Less dividend tax credit @ 10%	£5,000
Net additional tax payable	£13,750
Net dividend in Peter's hands	£31,250

This compares with no tax on the net dividends received inside the wrapper of the bond.

Disregarding the benefits of compounding returns subject to lower tax within the bond, let's assume that Peter encashes the bond after one year's ownership. Although this isn't likely, it allows us to make a clear comparison with the taxation position if held personally. Peter will pay income tax on the accumulated gain at 25% as follows:

Chargeable event gain	=	£45,000	
Additional-rate income tax @ 25%	=	(£11,250)	
Net gain in Peter's hands	=	£33,750	
Increase in return to Peter	=	£ 2,500	(+8%)

Peter retains 8% more of the dividend via the bond because the gain on the bond is not grossed up as it is with the direct receipt of a dividend and he is given credit for the bond having paid basic-rate tax already, when in fact the dividend tax credit was only 10%. In addition, the higher net dividends retained within the bond will compound each year to increase the terminal value of the portfolio still further.

Additional tax benefits of a single-premium bond include:

- facility to withdraw up to 5% p.a. (cumulative) of the original investment, tax-deferred
- may allow other taxable income to be brought below the £150,000 additional-rate threshold
- may allow personal allowance to be partially or fully reinstated if taxable income is below £120,000
- may bring adjusted net income below £60,000 and so reduce or avoid the child benefit tax charge
- one or more segments could be assigned to a basic-rate taxpayer before encashment, to avoid additional income tax arising on the gain

- if encashment arises when the policyholder qualifies as non-UK resident, no UK income tax liability will arise

- potential to reduce tax on encashment if the policyholder, before encashment, has any unused basic-rate income tax band.

A UK insurance bond can be cost-effective at any level from £100,000 upwards, but clearly the larger the investment and resulting yield, the bigger the benefits. Although the use of an investment bond is not a panacea to the problems of high taxation, as part of a balanced tax wrapper allocation strategy, and subject to the impact of charges, it could offer valuable benefits.

Using with trusts

Because investment bonds are deemed, for tax purposes, to be non-income producing and it is possible to choose when gains are taxed, they are particularly useful for trustees of discretionary trusts to use to hold investment capital on which they would otherwise pay income and capital gains tax at the higher rate. For example, you could set up a trust (under which the settlor is excluded from benefit) and then loan your capital to the trustees so that they can invest in an investment bond. The trustees could then repay you over a period of time using the 5% tax-deferred withdrawal facility to avoid an immediate income tax charge. See Figure 15.6.

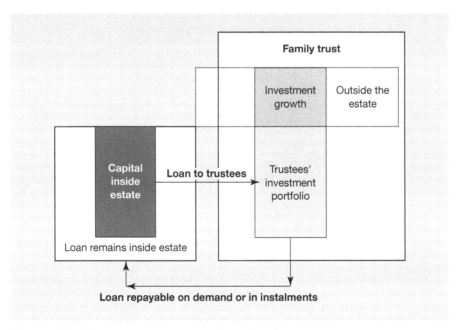

Figure 15.6 Gift and loan arrangement with an investment bond
Source: Bloomsbury Wealth Management.

Bespoke investments

Some offshore bonds provide the option of what is known as an 'internal linked fund' (ILF) (see Figure 15.7). An ILF can often be considered as an alternative to, or in addition to, a personalised open-ended investment company. An ILF must fulfil certain statutory criteria, which include the requirement that the fund be available to investors at large or to a class of investors, membership of which is determined by the insurer. If the option to invest in the fund is available to a class, that option must also appear in the insurer's marketing material.

ILFs can provide access to a variety of assets that could otherwise render an investment bond as 'highly personalised' for income tax purposes. Highly personalised bonds suffer an annual income tax charge of 15% of the bond's value, regardless of returns, so you need to avoid this treatment at all costs. Alternative assets such as hedge funds, shares, gilts and derivatives can be included in an ILF's investment portfolio without triggering the personalised bond tax charge.

Each ILF must be managed by a discretionary investment manager, appointed by the insurer, although the policyholder can pick their preferred manager. The insurer monitors future performance against the agreed strategy, benchmark and objectives.

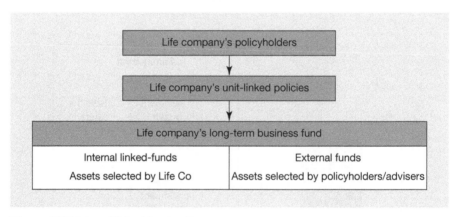

Figure 15.7 Internal linked fund option
Source: Bloomsbury Wealth Management.

Offshore bonds sold outside the UK

Many high-earning UK expatriates buy non-UK investment bonds that would be classed as highly personalised in the UK. While the investor remains non-UK tax resident, this is not a problem. However, to avoid the 15% annual tax charge arising on the bond when the investor becomes UK-tax resident, either the policy needs to be endorsed to restrict the offending investment options so that it would *not* be classed as highly personalised, or the bond will need to be encashed before the investor returns to the UK.

Discounted value arrangement

Bonds can also be set up with special conditions that have the effect of immediately reducing the value of the bond for IHT by up to 60%, but that permit the investor to retain access to as much as 10% p.a. of the original investment. See Chapter 22 on non-trust structures for estate planning application.

Accumulation and maintenance (A&M) plan

Another type of offshore bond has special policy conditions that restrict the right to encash to a date or dates in the future and then gift this to younger generations. This allows you to make a potentially exempt transfer for IHT purposes, while restricting when the new owners can access the funds and avoiding the hassle and tax complication of a trust.

You would invest into a specially modified offshore insurance bond, with a wide choice of investments, which you then assign as an outright gift to your chosen beneficiary or beneficiaries. The policy conditions are such that the surrender value of the bond is suppressed until a future date stipulated by you at the outset, to coincide with the age that you feel comfortable with the beneficiary or beneficiaries having access to the bond. This solution is ideal where you wish to make an outright gift now but want to avoid the recipient gaining access at a young age and either do not want, or are unable, to gift to a discretionary trust (because you have already made a gift to trust to the nil-rate band within the past seven years). See Chapter 22 for a more detailed explanation of this structure.

Private placement life assurance

Another version of investment bond is called private placement life assurance (PPLA). This allows the policyholder to obtain life cover, either on top of (additional cover) or instead of (integrated cover) the bond's surrender value. The cost of the life insurance is deducted from the bond but does not count towards the 5% tax-deferred withdrawal allowance and enables this to be funded from tax-free returns. Table 15.1 shows both types of cover for a £2 million PPLA bond.

Table 15.1 Private placement life assurance bond

Premium	Integrated cover	Additional cover
Life cover	£10m	£10m + surrender value
Projected encashment value – 20 yrs @ 5% pa growth	£2.5m	£2.2m

Source: Bloomsbury Wealth Management.

It is possible to arrange the policy in trust. This is achieved via a loan of capital to trustees who then invest in the bond. The loaned amount will remain in the donor's estate but the life cover will not.

Non-UK domiciled individuals

An investment bond that is funded by clean capital (i.e. that does not contain accrued income) allows a UK resident but non-UK domiciled individual to avoid having to pay the £30,000/£50,000 p.a. remittance basis charge, and as such benefit from use of their personal income tax allowance and capital gains tax exemption in respect of UK income and gains. This is because the bond is deemed to be non-income producing and as such not subject to UK income tax. Annual withdrawals of up to 5% of the original amount invested may also be remitted to the UK without tax charge.

Whether the current well-established tax treatment of investment bonds will continue is anyone's guess, but, if it doesn't, having all investment returns classed as income rather than capital gains might turn out to be rather expensive. For this reason, it probably makes sense to avoid holding your entire portfolio in an investment bond.

CHAPTER 16
MINIMISING
PORTFOLIO TAXATION

'An income tax form is like a laundry list – either way you lose your shirt.'

Fred Allen, American comedian

If your investment capital is not held in a tax-free or tax-deferred account such as an individual savings account (ISA), self-invested personal pension (SIPP), small self-administered scheme (SSAS) or offshore portfolio bond (OPB), then tax will be due on interest, dividends and capital gains to the extent that they exceed your individual personal allowance and gains exemption.

To determine whether total capital gains are taxable you need to first deduct all capital losses arising within the same tax year. Net capital gains in excess of the annual exemption can also be reduced by offsetting any carried forward losses available from previous tax years. Any net gains remaining, which exceed the annual exemption, are then taxed at either 18% or 28% depending on whether or not there is any unused basic-rate income tax band available.

Claiming losses

Losses relating to tax years prior to 1996/97 don't have a time limit for claim and can be claimed when you need to use them. For losses that arose in the 1996/97 tax year or later, you must have first submitted a claim to HMRC via your self-assessment tax return or, if you don't complete one of those, by writing to HMRC, within a time limit. The time limits are as follows:

a Losses arising from 1 April 2012 – four years from the end of the tax year in which the losses arose.

b Losses arising from before 1 April 2012, either:

   i four years from the end of the tax year in which the losses arose where you completed a self-assessment tax return for that tax year, or

   ii five years from 31 January following the tax year of loss if you didn't complete a self-assessment tax return for that tax year.

Please note that carried forward losses *must* be used where there are taxable gains. You can't decide not to use them because, for example, you'd rather pay capital gains tax at 10% on gains subject to entrepreneurs' relief and 'save' the carried forward losses for use against future gains that might be subject to higher rates of tax.

Capital gains – the 30-day rule

If you crystallise a capital gain by selling and then immediately repurchasing an investment – what used to be called bed-and-breakfasting – it will be treated as having no effect for CGT purposes. However, there are other ways of achieving similar results:

- Bed-and-ISA: you can sell an investment, e.g. shares in an open-ended investment company, and buy it back immediately within an ISA. For 2014/15 the maximum ISA investment is £15,000.

- Bed-and-SIPP: this is a similar process to bed-and-ISA, but the cash realised is used to make a contribution to a SIPP or any other suitable pension plan. The reinvestment is then made within the pension. This approach has the added benefit of income tax relief on the contribution and may also offer a higher reinvestment ceiling than an ISA, depending on your earned income and other pension contributions.

- Bed-and-spouse: you can sell an investment and your spouse can buy the same investment without falling foul of the 30-day rule. However, you cannot sell your investment to your spouse – the two transactions must be made separately through the market.

- Bed-and-something-very-similar: the growing number of funds that track UK and international stock market indices has created an opportunity to replicate the tax benefit of the old bed-and-breakfast strategy. For example, if you hold the ABC UK FTSE All-Share unit trust, you could sell it and immediately reinvest in the XYZ FTSE All-Share Exchange Traded Fund. Your underlying investment – shares in the constituents of the FTSE All-Share Index – will not alter but, because the fund entity (not necessarily the fund provider) has changed, you will escape the 30-day rule.

While your total taxable income now determines the rate of CGT you pay, capital gains do not impact on the amount of income tax you pay. Therefore, it is now important to carefully manage taxable income, as far as possible, to allow any taxable capital gains to benefit from the lower 18% tax rate, to the extent that taxable capital gains fall below the higher-rate income tax threshold of circa £32,000 in excess of the personal income tax allowance.

The way that investments are taxed can have a significant impact on overall returns. This is particularly relevant where the differential between income tax and CGT is wide, with the top rate of income tax currently 45% (the effective rate is 60% for income between £100,000 and £120,000), compared with CGT of up to 28%.

Understanding the composition of portfolio returns – interest, dividends or capital gains – helps us to consider how the returns will be taxed using different tax structures. Although there have been major changes to investment taxation over the past few years, for UK-resident and domiciled individuals these apply at the investor level, not the tax wrapper level, and relate to the income and CGT arising. All companies (including UK life insurers) continue to be taxed under the existing rules and as such will qualify for indexation allowance on capital gains.

The key factors that need to be taken into account when considering investment location are as follows:

- use of your personal CGT annual exemption
- whether or not you have any unused basic-rate income tax band
- your need for regular withdrawals to meet expenditure needs
- the amount of periodic rebalancing likely to be necessary to keep your portfolio consistent with your risk profile
- whether or not you have a spouse or civil partner with whom you can share the portfolio taxation options
- whether and to what extent the portfolio is to be held within a trust or pension structure, perhaps as part of other tax planning components
- the ability for CGT to be 'washed out' on your death, i.e. extinguished
- the product or tax wrapper charges incurred
- the type of asset held, i.e. deposit, fixed interest, equity income or growth, or real estate investment trust shares
- the type of investment required – some types of investments and funds are not permitted to be held within certain tax structures
- the administrative work and professional costs associated with tax reporting
- the holding period of the portfolio, because compounding works best over the long term
- whether or not you also wish to integrate inheritance tax planning with your investment capital.

The individual savings account (ISA) allowance

This allows a UK resident[1] to hold cash, fixed interest or equity investments in a tax-free environment, although withholding tax on dividends may not be reclaimed. The limit is £15,000 per person per tax year for those aged 18+, so couples can shield £30,000 p.a. from the taxman if both invest in an ISA. An ISA is most attractive for those who pay higher-rate income tax and who would generate capital gains of more than £11,000 per tax year. Having said that, it is often possible to invest in funds via an ISA at no extra charge, so just from an administration perspective an ISA is likely to be the foundation of your portfolio tax management strategy.

The four main non-pension investment tax wrappers

Beyond ISAs, the four types of tax wrapper most commonly used to hold an investment portfolio are:

1   Collective funds held via a nominee account or in own name.

2   An onshore investment bond.

3   An offshore investment bond.

4   A family investment company.

If you have a substantial portfolio, it is likely that a combination of these tax wrappers might be the best solution, but it will be influenced very much by the underlying investment strategy. The tax treatment of each wrapper is set out in Table 16.1.

Collective funds

Onshore open-ended funds and investment companies are exempt from CGT on disposals arising within the fund and generally corporation tax is not payable, provided that income is distributed to investors. At the investor level, a flat CGT rate of 18% or 28% (depending on the investor's taxable income) is charged on disposals of units or shares in such a fund. CGT is payable only if such realised gains exceed the investor's annual exemption, after first taking into account any losses

---

[1]   You must be UK resident at the time that you invest capital into an ISA, but you are permitted to retain the account and its UK-tax-exempt status if you become non-UK resident. The ISA may be taxable in your new country of residence.

Table 16.1 Comparison of tax treatment of main non-pension tax structures

	Collective fund (unit trust/OEIC)	Onshore investment bond	Offshore investment bond	Family investment company
Capital gains while invested				
	None	Taxed at insurers' rate (maximum 20%) after indexation relief and expenses	Exempt from UK tax	Taxed at corporate rate (20%) after indexation relief and expenses
UK dividends				
	Investor taxed on an arising basis	No further tax; investor has no further liability	No further tax but no reclamation of tax credit	No further tax; investor has no further liability
Non-UK dividends				
	Investor taxed on an arising basis	Subject to tax but liability may be accounted for by withholding tax in jurisdiction of origin	Typically not subject to further tax	Subject to tax but liability may be accounted for by withholding tax in jurisdiction of origin
Interest				
	Investor taxed on an arising basis	Taxed at insurers' rate (20%)	Not subject to tax	Taxed at company rate (20%)
Capital gains when wrapper encashed				
	Subject to capital gains tax (CGT) at 18–28% after annual exemption and allowable losses	Subject to income tax. No further tax liability for nil and basic-rate taxpayers. Entire net gain added to the investor's other taxable income arising in the same tax year and taxed by a further 20% for a higher-rate (40%) taxpayer and 25% for an additional-rate (45%) taxpayer. If, however, the addition of the gain to the taxable income of a basic-rate taxpayer makes them a higher-rate taxpayer, the gain will be subject to 'top-slicing' relief.*	Subject to income tax. Gross gain taxed at nil, 20%, 40% or 45% for non-, basic-rate, higher-rate and additional-rate taxpayers respectively. If, however, the addition of the gain to the taxable income of a basic-rate taxpayer makes them a higher- or additional-rate taxpayer, the gain will be subject to 'top slicing' relief.*	Subject to capital gains tax (CGT) at 18–28% after annual exemption and allowable losses

* For a detailed explanation of top slicing relief, please see Chapter 15.

arising in the current tax year or those carried forward from previous tax years. Non-, basic-rate and corporate taxpayers receive dividends from equity-based collectives free of any additional tax liability, although withholding tax on those dividends may not be reclaimed. Higher-rate (40%) and additional-rate (45%) taxpayers pay an effective tax of 25% and 30.55% respectively of the net dividend paid.[2]

Offshore investment funds are deemed to be either 'reporting' or 'non-reporting' for tax purposes. A reporting fund declares the income arising within the fund, whether this is paid out to investors or not. The investor is then responsible for paying income tax, at their highest rate, on that reported income. Depending on the nature of the underlying holdings, this income will be taxed as either interest or dividends. When the investor comes to dispose of their holding, any increase or decrease in value is then subject to CGT treatment.

Sometimes, the reported income in a tax year is higher than the income that has been distributed to the investor. If the fund is held in a nominee or other type of investment platform, the investor may mistakenly assume that the tax voucher issued by the nominee or investment administrator is equal to the total income reported by the fund manager. However, unless the investor checks the investment fund's annual report, they will not know if the reported income is higher than the distributed amount received by the nominee. If you hold reporting funds, either direct or via nominee, you must check the fund's annual report to make sure that you have declared all reported income, not just what you have received as dividends or that has been detailed in the nominee's consolidated annual tax report.

An offshore non-reporting fund is any fund that does not have reporting fund status, usually because it declares neither income arising within the fund nor any capital gains. As such no tax is payable by the investor until the holding is disposed of. If they are a UK-resident and domiciled person then income tax will be paid on the entire uplift in value of their holding, although no allowance is provided for losses against other taxable income. Many ETFs and most alternative investment strategies such as hedge funds and structured products are offered through non-reporting funds. This adverse tax treatment makes non-reporting funds unsuitable for most taxable investors, unless the fund is held within a tax wrapper such as a pension or an offshore bond.

---

[2] Dividends come with a non-reclaimable tax credit equal to 1/9th of the net dividend paid. So a £9 dividend would come with a £1 notional tax credit, making the gross dividend £10. The non-taxpayer cannot reclaim the notional tax credit, whereas it settles the liability of the basic-rate taxpayer. The higher-rate and additional-rate taxpayer, meanwhile, is required to pay 22.5/27.5% respectively of the grossed-up dividend not represented by the notional tax credit. This is equivalent to 25/30.55% respectively of the net dividend paid.

Figure 16.1 shows the optimum value of a taxable investment portfolio, based on three investor tax profiles, depending on how the returns arise.

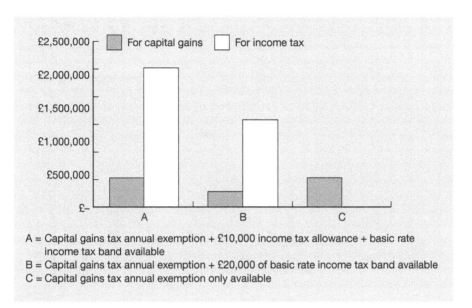

A = Capital gains tax annual exemption + £10,000 income tax allowance + basic rate income tax band available
B = Capital gains tax annual exemption + £20,000 of basic rate income tax band available
C = Capital gains tax annual exemption only available

Figure 16.1 Optimum value of taxable investment portfolio

Investment bonds

We looked at investment bonds in detail in Chapter 15.

Family investment company

Dividend income arising from the company's investment portfolio would be exempt from further tax, as the withholding tax attaching to dividends is deemed to have settled the corporation tax liability. Interest income would be subject to the main corporation tax rate of 20% (21% until April 2015).

For CGT purposes, the acquisition cost of the company's holdings would benefit from indexation allowance, which removes any inflationary gains arising. Any indexed gains realised within the portfolio would be subject to corporation tax of 20% (21% until April 2015). Care is required where the company holds large amounts of cash and fixed interest investments, as special rules called 'loan relationship' might cause unnecessary additional annual tax charges.

Although CGT, currently up to 28%, would be charged on the ultimate disposal of the FIC shares, this may not be for many years, if ever. If the shares in the FIC are

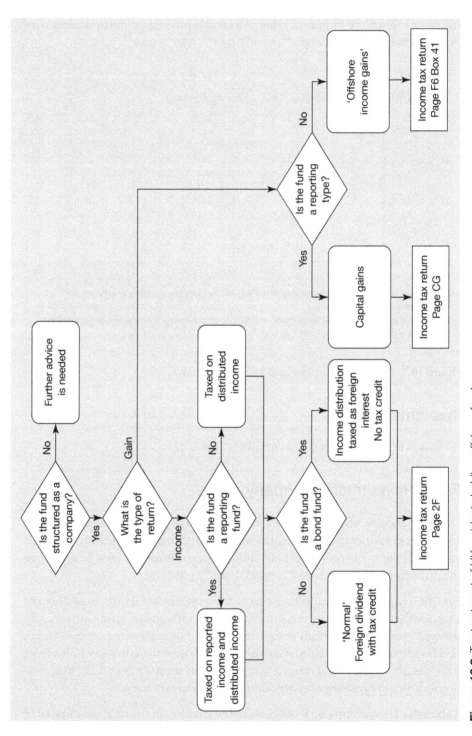

Figure 16.2 Tax treatment of UK residents holding offshore funds

held at death, then no CGT will be payable by the estate. In the meantime, the FIC would enable the family to accumulate wealth net of relatively low tax rates, compared with up to 27.5% on dividend income and 28% on unindexed gains arising if held personally (indexation allowance was abolished many years ago for personally owned investments).

Side by side

The balance between capital gains and reinvested income can have a big effect on the relative merits of the available investment tax wrappers, as well as the investor's rate of tax paid on encashment of the portfolio (if that ever happens in practice). In addition, the charges associated with setting up and maintaining the tax wrapper can have a significant impact.

Figures 16.3 to 16.5 show different investment strategies held via the main tax wrappers. The projected terminal values net of tax vary considerably. A point to

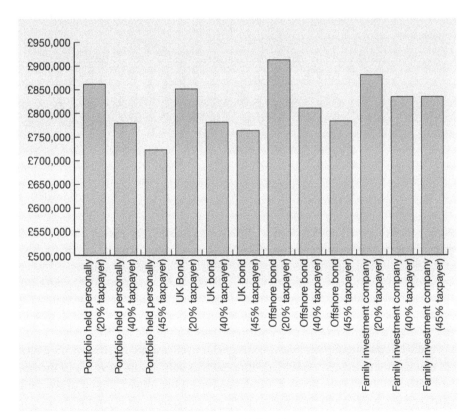

Figure 16.3 Projected portfolio values – 100% fixed interest

Asset class returns are based on those set out in Figure 3.3 of chapter 3.

bear in mind is the probability of actually paying the tax shown in the examples. A transfer of directly held funds by way of gift to a third party other than a spouse or civil partner will give rise to CGT unless it is to trustees and an election is made to 'hold over' the gain to the trustees. However, it may be possible to gift some shares with different rights, before any gains have accrued.

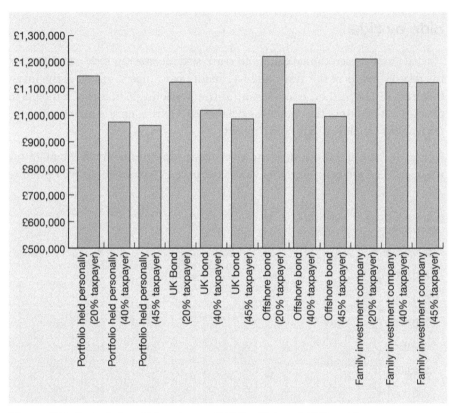

Figure 16.4 Projected portfolio values – 50% fixed interest, 50% equity

Asset class returns are based on those set out in Figure 3.3 of chapter 3.

An investment bond, in contrast, may be assigned to a third party as a gift and there is no immediate tax charge on any latent gain. The gain is also gifted to the recipient and subject to their own tax position on eventual encashment. It may be that you are a higher-rate taxpayer during some or all of the holding period of the portfolio but become a basic-rate taxpayer prior to encashment. This is where careful management of your taxable income, such as controlling how much income you withdraw from your pension fund, can have a big impact. If you or a person who receives assignment of some or all of the bond as a gift crystallises the gain when they are non-UK resident, they may avoid UK income tax completely.

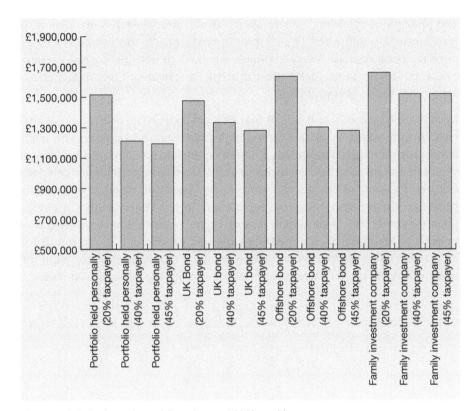

Figure 16.5 Projected portfolio values – 100% equities

Asset class returns are based on those set out in Figure 3.3 of chapter 3.

A family investment company funded substantially by way of a loan could provide tax-free cash to the original investor through loan repayments, rather than
being subject to higher-rate tax as would be the case had dividends been taken. An
investment bond can provide tax-deferred withdrawals of 5% p.a. of the original
investment.

No silver bullet

Given the many variables to take into account and the inherent uncertainties
with regard to the future (e.g. in respect of actual performance, individual investor tax rates and what the tax system will look like), you need to bear in mind that
there is an element of risk in choosing how best to hold investments from a tax
perspective, given that the assumptions used are highly likely to turn out to be
wrong. Asset allocation is the way investors minimise investment risk (for what
will always be an uncertain future) by diversifying across different asset classes.

This principle of 'spreading' or 'allocation' can also be applied in connection with tax wrapper selection where there is some uncertainty as to the future. Where this uncertainty could make a decision made on an 'all or nothing' basis the wrong one, it may make sense to diminish this risk by spreading investments across appropriate investment wrappers.

In addition to pensions and ISAs, it may be most appropriate to ensure that low-yield investments are held directly and high-yield funds held within investment bonds. For portfolios that include a mix of equity and fixed interest holdings it will be important to strike a balance and so across a whole portfolio one could see (subject to control of charges and unnecessary complexity) a range of wrappers being selected. It is also worth bearing in mind the need to rebalance the portfolio in the future. This would entail moving capital between different asset classes in order to maintain the required risk exposure, which can be compromised if each asset class is held within a different wrapper type. Choosing the right tax wrapper(s) needs careful analysis of the facts and your likely future circumstances.

CHAPTER 17
STATE AND PRIVATE PENSIONS

'My dad loves what I do and I support my parents financially because they didn't have a job that gave them a pension.'

Marilyn Manson, American musician, songwriter, actor, painter

There are two government-administered state pensions in the UK – the basic and additional state pensions.

Basic state pension

The basic state pension (BSP) is a taxable, flat-rate pension payable from state pension age (SPA) to anyone who has built up a sufficient number of qualifying years through payment of National Insurance contributions (or received National Insurance credits – NICs). The maximum (sometimes referred to as 'full') BSP for a single person in 2014/2015 is £113.15 per week.

People retiring between 6 April 2010 and 6 April 2016 must have 30 qualifying years for full entitlement to BSP. Entitlement is reduced by 1/30th for each qualifying year below 30. Qualifying years relate to National Insurance contributions (or credits) having been paid. People retiring from 6 April 2016 must have 35 qualifying years for full entitlement to BSP. Entitlement will be reduced by 1/35th for each qualifying year below 35.

Married couples (and civil partnership)

Where a spouse does not have sufficient qualifying years for a full BSP in their own right they can apply, on reaching SPA, for a BSP based on their spouse's National

Insurance record. The spouse with insufficient National Insurance will obtain 60% of the contributing spouse's BSP (if the contributing spouse has a reduced BSP then it is 60% of the reduced rate). Since 6 April 2010 it has no longer been a requirement that the contributing spouse has claimed their BSP; they must just be eligible to do so for the spouse with insufficient qualifying years to claim theirs (e.g. a wife reaching SPA at 62 can make a claim based on her husband's National Insurance record provided that he has also reached SPA, regardless of whether he is claiming or has deferred claiming BSP). Where a married woman has some qualifying years in her own right she can use her husband's National Insurance record to increase her own BSP by the lesser of:

- the shortfall between her reduced-rate BSP and the full-rate BSP, and
- the amount of BSP her spouse's record will provide.

This also applies to married men and civil partners, but only where their wife/civil partner was born after 6 April 1950.

State pension age (SPA)

The state pension is not paid automatically at SPA, but must be claimed on or after reaching SPA. The SPA is currently 65 for men and is being raised gradually to 65 for women by December 2018. The SPA for both men and women will then be raised gradually until it is 66 by October 2020. At the time of writing (May 2014) it was announced that the SPA will be raised to 67 for men and women between 6 April 2026 and 2028. Figure 17.1 shows these changes graphically. If you have not reached SPA already you can check your SPA by visiting **www.gov.uk/ calculate-state-pension**

It is interesting to note that in 1981 individuals received the state pension for 25% of their adult life but by 2000 this had increased to 30% and by 2010 it had risen to 33%. To keep the proportion of adult life in receipt of the state pension constant at the 2010 level (33%), the SPA would need to be 66.5 by 2030; at the 2000 level (30%) it would need to rise to 68 by 2030; and to get back to the 1981 level (25%) it would need to rise to 72 by 2030.[1] This suggests that the current intention to raise the SPA to 68 between 2044 and 2046 is highly likely to be brought forward.

Annual increases

For those living in the European Economic Area, the BSP is increased every year by whichever is the highest of:

---

[1]   Pensions Policy Institute (2010) 'Submission to the Work and Pensions Select Committee on the government's pension reforms', p. 4.

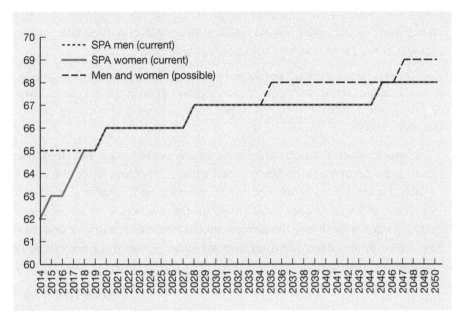

Figure 17.1 The changing state pension age

- the growth in average earnings
- the growth in prices
- or 2.5%.

For those living elsewhere, the BSP remains level and so will lose its purchasing value over time.

Deferring state pension

It is possible to defer taking your state pension, in which case it will be increased by a factor of 0.20% for each week of deferral, equivalent to 10.4% a year (with no compounding, unfortunately). This factor was last reviewed in April 2005 when the banks' base rate was 4.75%, a figure closely matched by the yield on short-dated gilts, meaning that the deferral offer was attractive but not a great deal.

Since 2006 there has also been the option to defer the state pension in return for a lump sum and this is calculated on the basis of accumulating the pension payments not made (subject to this being at least 12 months of continuous deferment) at a gross interest rate of bank base rate + 2% (i.e. 2.5% at present). The lump sum is fully taxable but taxed at your marginal rate, not simply added to your income. This treatment means that basic-rate taxpayers can avoid a possible one-year trip into the higher-rate income tax band when they draw their state pension lump sum. It also protects against the loss of age allowance.

There are several factors that you need to take into account when considering whether to defer taking your state pension. Before I explain these, consider what the government minister in charge of pensions had to say about state pension deferment choices:

> 'The way in which the deferral increments are worked out means that there is an extra percentage on the pension when it is drawn, while the way in which the lump sum is worked out is different and, bizarrely, relates to the Bank of England base rate. There are times when, if an actuary were making such a decision, the person should choose increments and there are other times, depending on interest rates, when the person should choose the lump sum.'

Steve Webb MP[2]

Deferral for an increased pension

This option now looks very appealing, particularly for shorter terms where the lack of compounding is of less import. For example, using figures from the DWP's guide, deferring a £100 per week state pension for a year currently provides either:

- a taxable lump sum of £5,270, or
- an increase in taxable pension of £10.40 per week (£540.80 a year), possibly with a corresponding increase to any dependant's pension.

For a person aged 66, that extra pension (on a single life basis) would cost about £15,000[3] to buy on the open market. It is worth noting, too, that for the basic state pension, a 'triple lock' now applies to increases, i.e. the greater of 2.5%, CPI and average earnings increases. In theory this should have prompted the DWP to worsen the deferral terms. For other state pensions, CPI sets the increase basis, which arguably would require an adjustment in the opposite direction. Deferment will not suit everyone and if you are single you need to be aware that if you die while deferring state pension, your estate can benefit from only a maximum of three months' unpaid pension.

---

[2] Public Bill Committee on the Pensions Bill 2013 (transcript), 4 July 2013.

[3] Money Advice Service – Annuity comparison service for best standard RPI linked annuity for person aged 66 (accessed 25 March 2014).

The increase rate for deferring the state pension will be reduced from April 2016 to about half the current rate, which is still not a bad deal. Using a similar calculation to the earlier example, the new increment basis implies an extra £5.20 a week for each year's deferral of £100 a week state pension. That extra £5.20 a week for a single person aged 66 (i.e. 65 + 1 year's deferral) would cost about £7,600[4] to buy on the open annuity market, assuming RPI linking, against a year's pension forgone of £5,200.

Deferral for a lump sum

When the lump sum option was introduced in 2006, the Government Actuary's Department calculated that deferral would be of financial benefit to the Treasury, which rather gives the game away. Finding more than a 2.5% gross return for savings is possible via cash ISAs, so the logical thing to do would be to draw the pension and use it to feed an appropriate savings account. This has the added benefit of avoiding some of the problems that deferral can create, e.g. where a wife has entitlement both in her own right and via her husband's contributions and gains nothing from deferral.

There are two obvious situations where lump sum deferral is preferable to the draw-and-save approach:

- For someone whose total income is over £27,000, removing entitlement to the full age allowance, deferring state pension can produce a useful tax saving that more than compensates for the modest interest rate. For example, if £5,000 is taken out of the total income figure by pension deferral, this could result in an increase of up to £2,500 in allowances and thus up to a £500 tax saving – effectively a 10% net return.

- For someone whose income will fall into a lower tax band at some point after state pension age, the marginal rate tax treatment described above will normally make lump sum deferral more attractive. It might be possible to achieve this band shifting temporarily via carefully timed income withdrawals.

The lump sum deferment option is due to be abolished in April 2016.

Additional state pension

The additional state pension is an earnings-related pension, payable on top of the BSP, at SPA, where this is reached before 6 April 2016. Until April 2002, the

---

4   Money Advice Service annuity comparison April 2014.

additional state pension for employees was called the State Earnings-Related Pension Scheme (SERPS). The amount of SERPS pension you received was based on a combination of your NICs and how much you earned. In April 2002, SERPS was reformed and renamed the State Second Pension (S2P). It now gives a more generous additional state pension to low and moderate earners, certain carers and people with a long-term illness or disability. If you have joined an employer's pension scheme you may have been 'opted out' of the additional state pension automatically. You can find out more from your scheme administrator or by obtaining a state pension forecast.

Additional state pension can arise from various state pension schemes, each with its own different and complicated set of calculations as to benefits payable:

- the Graduated Retirement Pension (GRP) – for earnings between 6 April 1961 and 5 April 1975
- SERPS – for earnings between 6 April 1978 and 5 April 2002[5]
- S2P – for earnings since 6 April 2002.

Once in payment the additional state pension is increased in line with the RPI, but this is due to change from April 2016.

The Directgov website provides further information about basic and additional state pensions, and gives a quick estimate state pension profiler tool that calculates the BSP earned to date (see **www.direct.gov.uk/en/Pensionsandretirementplanning/ StatePension/DG_184319**).

The basic and additional state pensions are dependent on an individual's NICs and earnings over their working life. Additional state pension calculations are extremely complex and may be made up of a combination of GRP, SERPS and/ or S2P. A comprehensive forecast based on an individual's National Insurance record can be obtained from the Pension Service part of the Department for Work and Pensions (see **www.direct.gov.uk/en/Pensionsandretirementplanning/ StatePension/StatePensionforecast/DG_10014008**).

Inheriting SERPS/S2P

The surviving spouse of a contributor to SERPS/S2P can, on the contributor's death, inherit a percentage of their SERPS/S2P entitlement. For SERPS the maximum percentage payable is dependent on the date the contributor reaches SPA

---

[5] Following a change of government in 1975 no additional state pension was provided until SERPS started on 6 April 1978.

– for a contributor reaching SPA after 6 October 2010 the maximum SERPS their surviving spouse can inherit is 50%. For S2P the maximum amount is 50%.

Single-tier state pension

A new single-tier state pension will be introduced for those reaching SPA from April 2016. The pension will be set at a rate no less than the basic level of means-tested support (i.e. the Pension Credit guarantee credit, which is £148.35 per week for a single pensioner in 2014/15). It will replace entitlement to the BSP and additional state pension (including shared additional pension and graduated pension).

Other features of the new single-tier pension include:

- minimum period of National Insurance contributions to qualify for any benefit to be set at ten years
- maximum benefit requires 35 years of contributions (this compares with 30 years under the existing state pension)
- entitlement will be assessed on an individual basis, without the current facility to inherit or derive benefit rights from a spouse or civil partner. However, there will be transitional provisions to recognise shared or inheritable additional state pension accrued before the start date and also for certain married or formerly married women who paid reduced-rate National Insurance contributions
- income will be no less than the present state scheme
- income will be revalued under the 'triple lock' approach of the higher of earnings, prices or 2.5%
- option to defer but only for higher income, not a lump sum. The increase in the deferred pension will be at a rate about 50% of the current factor
- transitional arrangements to protect state pension rights accrued up to the start date of the new single-tier pension
- those with rights that are higher than the single-tier pension will retain these, called 'protected benefits', but they will only be increased by the CPI before and after SPA.

Where an individual's existing benefits prior to April 2016 are less than the full single-tier pension, each additional year of qualifying service after the start date before they reach SPA will accrue further state pension entitlement of 1/35th of the full amount of the single-tier pension (i.e. £4.11 per week (£144/35) in current terms for each additional qualifying year), subject to their aggregate entitlement not exceeding the full single-tier amount.

For example, if Cindy had an existing entitlement (this is known as the 'foundation amount') of £50 per week, she could accrue additional state pension for each post-implementation qualifying year up to SPA subject to her aggregate entitlement not exceeding the full single-tier amount. In Cindy's case this implies a further 23 years (£50 + (£144 x (23/35)) = £144), so if she is more than 23 years away from SPA, her final years of contribution will earn no extra pension benefit.

Private pensions

Registered pension schemes are subject to limits on funding and benefits, with tax charges levied on any excesses. Below is an outline of the main features of the different types of scheme, followed by the funding limits and planning considerations.

Defined benefit schemes

Where retirement benefits are provided by an occupational pension plan, whether a private- or public-sector type, and calculated on the basis of service, salary and an accrual rate, it is the pension scheme and, by association, the sponsoring employer that bear most of the risk and costs associated with providing the pension benefits. In this sense the overall benefits are predictable, but the future costs of providing them are not. For this reason most defined benefit schemes have closed to new members and many have closed to further benefit accrual for existing members as employers seek to minimise their future funding liabilities. Most public-sector schemes are not underpinned by financial assets to fund pension benefits and are therefore known as unfunded. Most private-sector schemes are supported by financial assets (to a greater or lesser extent) and are known as funded.

If your benefits have yet to be paid out, either because you are still working and accruing service or because you have left service before the normal retirement age, you need to check the financial position of the scheme and the commitment and financial capability of the sponsoring employer to continue to fund the scheme. Every three years the scheme trustees are required to provide an assessment of the scheme's financial position and whether there are sufficient assets to secure all members' pension benefits through an insurance company if the scheme were wound up at that time.

While this assessment can be seen as the worst-case scenario, it can often suggest that a scheme is underfunded when, on a going-concern basis, it is not. This is because securing pensions with insurance companies is very expensive. In addition, if the assessment has been carried out when investment markets have fallen sharply, this will overstate the underfunding, when in reality members take benefits at different times, thus providing the trustees with some flexibility to ride out short-term investment volatility.

If the pension scheme fails and is unable to pay out existing or future pension benefits, a government-sponsored scheme known as the Pension Protection Fund (PPF) will step in and provide benefits. If you have reached the scheme's retirement age or are in receipt of an ill-health pension or where a survivor's pension is in payment, the protected amount will be 100% of the pension in payment. Otherwise the protected amount will be 90% of the pension benefit, whether or not you have reached the scheme's normal retirement age. The maximum protected pension payable is currently about £31,400 at age 65 but is lower for younger ages and higher for older ages.

Clearly, if you have a deferred defined benefit pension that is significantly in excess of £30,000 and/or the pension benefit represents a significant amount of the income that you expect to fund your lifetime spending, you need to be more concerned about the financial health of the scheme and possibly investigate whether it makes sense to transfer the cash value of your benefits to either your personal pension or your current employer's pension scheme.

Other reasons why you might wish to transfer benefits, regardless of whether or not the scheme is in good financial health, include the following:

- You do not need the guarantees that the scheme provides and/or the benefits are insignificant in relation to your overall wealth and you are comfortable with taking on the investment and longevity (living too long) risks yourself.

- You envisage living abroad when you take benefits and wish to mitigate the currency risks by investing and eventually taking benefits in the currency of your new country of residence.

- You do not need some of the benefits that the scheme provides, such as spouse's and dependants' pensions, and would prefer to have a higher pension instead.

- You would like flexibility as to the level of benefits that you take from year to year, with the ability to vary these to suit your spending needs.

- You have little confidence in the scheme trustees and/or the employer to pay the expected benefits.

- You believe that you (or an investment manager) can obtain a better return on your share of the value of the pension fund than the scheme trustees.

- You wish to use your pension benefits to invest in a commercial property, possibly to be used by your business.

- You wish to access the capital value by way of regular or lump sum drawdown (see Chapter 18).

A defined benefit pension is potentially a very valuable benefit and can provide a good foundation to your wealth plan. However, if benefits have yet to come into payment, it will certainly be advisable to review regularly both how the scheme fits into your overall planning and the financial strength of the scheme and the sponsoring employer. Because assessing the merits of transferring a defined pension benefit can be complex, you will almost certainly need to consult an independent financial adviser who is qualified and authorised to give such advice. The fees for this type of advice can be quite high, particularly where the deferred benefits are significant, as this reflects the complexity of the work and additional risks to the advice firm.

Defined contribution schemes

In contrast to a defined benefit scheme, with a defined contribution (DC) scheme the contribution levels are known (if continuing), whereas the eventual benefits are not. The benefits that the scheme can provide will depend directly on the size of the fund (influenced by both contributions made and investment returns achieved) as well as mortality and long-term interest rates. Interest rates affect annuity rates, particularly at younger ages, which in turn will dictate the level of guaranteed income that can be secured with the fund or, alternatively until 6 April 2015, the maximum level of income that can be withdrawn directly from the fund. The member of a DC pension scheme, therefore, takes on all the investment and longevity risks themselves.

A registered pension scheme may invest up to 5% of its funds in the ordinary share capital of a sponsoring employer, up to four, as long as the total holdings in them are less than 20% of the fund value in total. The value is tested only at the time the investment is made and not subsequently. There is no restriction on how much of the sponsoring company's shares may be owned by a pension plan and this could, in theory, be 100%.

There are two types of DC pension scheme: occupational and personal.

Occupational schemes

An occupational scheme is designed to provide benefits for the employees of a sponsoring employer and is subject to a detailed set of scheme rules and a trust deed. The benefits that the scheme can provide will be based on the value of funds earmarked for individual members, but will be subject to overall limits set by HMRC.

Another type of occupational DC pension is the small self-administered scheme, which was originally designed for controlling directors so that they could combine the benefits of pension tax relief with some flexibility to use their pension funds for business purposes. An SSAS must be established by a sponsoring employer for up to 12 employees, all of whom have to be trustees and who must make unanimous investment decisions. For this reason, an SSAS can be established by a company only if the members are also the owners of the business, because a sole trader or members of a partnership are classed as self-employed.

The scheme's assets are pooled together and then allocated as required to cash deposits, commercial property, an investment portfolio or individual investment. Unlike a personal pension, an SSAS may lend up to 50% of the fund to the sponsoring employer for commercial purposes, subject to taking adequate security, the loan being repaid in regular instalments over a period not exceeding five years and the interest rate being at least 1% over the bank base rate. A loan may not be given for the purposes of keeping an ailing business afloat. An SSAS may also borrow (on normal commercial terms) up to 50% of its assets, which can be useful to help fund property acquisition.

Personal schemes

A personal scheme is an individual plan in the member's own name and contributions can be made by the member, their employer, a third party or a combination of all three. There is no need for a sponsoring employer and all compliance with HMRC rules is handled by the pension scheme provider, not the employer. As a result, an increasing number of employers have put in place group personal pension schemes (GPPS) that combine the benefits of individual pension accounts with centralised payment and administration. Due to the obligations following the introduction of auto-enrolment in 2012 (more of which later), more group schemes are now being established.

Usually the plan is derived from a master scheme trust, from which it takes its rules and compliance with the tax rules for registered pensions. However, a small number of personal pensions can be established under an individual trust arrangement that has its own set of individual scheme rules, although in practice these are based on 'model' trust wordings. I'll explain more about how and why you might want to use an individual trust scheme shortly.

Personal pensions can be provided by a wide range of suppliers, including investment groups, insurance companies and professional trust companies. Increasingly, schemes are being offered on what is known as a self-invested basis, otherwise known as a self-invested personal pension. This allows members a wide choice of investments for their fund, including commercial property.

Alternatively, a member may appoint a professional investment manager to manage the investment of some or all their pension fund.

Auto enrolment

Pensions auto enrolment (AE) is a legal requirement on employers to ensure that all eligible employees are automatically enrolled into a pension scheme (known as a qualifying workplace pension scheme) with mandatory minimum contributions from the employer and the employee. Employers are required to do the following:

- assess eligibility of all employees
- register with the pensions regulator
- ensure that their pension schemes comply with all regulations
- manage the enrolment process for all employees
- manage and update the opting in and out of employees
- manage contributions
- ensure that inducements to opt out of auto enrolment are not offered
- provide regular updates and employee communications
- re-enrol opted-out employees on a regular basis
- keep accurate records of all the above.

Auto enrolment commenced in October 2012. However, to help businesses to prepare for the administration changes and costs, it is being introduced in stages (see Table 17.1). By March 2017, all employers will be required to auto enrol their employees into a qualifying scheme.

Table 17.1 Staging dates for auto enrolment

Employees	Date
4,000–4,999	01-Jun-13
3,000–3,999	01-Jul-13
2,000–2,999	01-Aug-13
1,250–1,999	01-Sep-13
800–1,249	01-Oct-13
500–799	01-Nov-13
350–499	01-Jan-14
250–349	01-Feb-14

Employees	Date
160–249	01-Apr-14
90–159	01-May-14
62–89	01-Jul-14
61	01-Aug-14
60	01-Oct-14
59	01-Nov-14
58	01-Jan-15
54–57	01-Mar-15
50–53	01-Apr-15
Test for fewer than 30	01-Jun-15 to 30-Jun-15
30 to 49	01-Aug-15 to 01-Oct-15
Fewer than 30	01-Jan-16 to 01-Apr-17

The eligibility criteria are based on a combination of the employee's age and amount of earnings, as shown in Figure 17.2, based on the 2014/15 tax year. Future tax years will clearly have higher earnings figures and the SPA will increase over the next few years, as explained earlier.

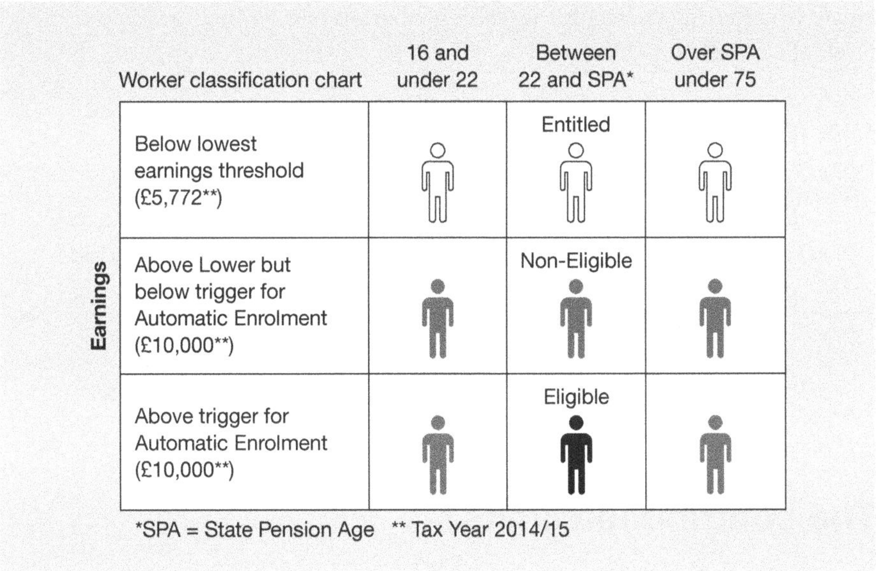

Worker classification chart	16 and under 22	Between 22 and SPA*	Over SPA under 75
Below lowest earnings threshold (£5,772**)	○	Entitled ○	○
Above Lower but below trigger for Automatic Enrolment (£10,000**)	●	Non-Eligible ●	●
Above trigger for Automatic Enrolment (£10,000**)	●	Eligible ●	●

*SPA = State Pension Age   ** Tax Year 2014/15

Figure 17.2 AE employee eligibility and entitlement
Source: TAP Assist Limited.

Under AE the total contribution starts at an initial level of 2% of earnings, with 1% of this being an employer contribution (see Table 17.2). The contributions will increase in stages to 8% of earnings, with 3% of this being contributed by the employer by October 2018.

Table 17.2 AE contributions rates

	Oct 12 – Sep 17	Oct 17 – Sep 18	Oct 2018 onwards
Minimum employee rate*	1%	3%	5%
Minimum employer rate	1%	2%	3%
Combined total rate (employee and employer)	2%	5%	8%

* including tax rebate on pension contributions

Employers have to certify that they are meeting the minimum contribution requirements for a scheme under their AE requirements, where there is a mismatch between the definition of pensionable pay under an employer's defined contribution pension scheme and that of qualifying earnings under the AE requirements. This quality test (see Table 17.3) runs for 12 months from the employer's pension staging date to the anniversary, taking in all earnings types (basic pay, commission, bonus and overtime), and will allow the employer to calculate whether they have hit the 8% contribution rate on the threshold earnings levels of £5,772 and £41,865.

Table 17.3 AE quality test for contributions

Total contribution	Employer contribution	Pensionable pay
9% of pensionable pay	4%	No quality test required
8% of pensionable pay	3%	Pensionable pay is at least 85% of the total pay bill for the workers
7% of pay	3%	All pay is pensionable

The contribution limits

The annual allowance is the annual limit to the amount of tax-relieved pension contributions or benefit accrual that you can have through all pension schemes in a tax year. For the purposes of the annual allowance limit defined contributions or defined benefit accrual fall within a 12-month period known as a payment input period (PIP), which ends in a particular tax year. With new personal pension plans the PIP always runs in line with the tax year, but it can be changed by the member if desired. With occupational pension plans the PIP will be set by the scheme trustees and can't be changed by the member. This can cause complications if, for example, the PIP of an occupational scheme ends on 30 September and the member wishes to also make contribution to a personal scheme which has a default PIP end date of 5 April. Because the occupational scheme PIP straddles two tax years, care is needed to ensure that the available annual allowance is correctly calculated. Figure 17.3 illustrates how this works in practice.

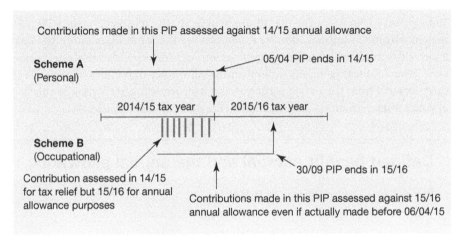

Figure 17.3 How the pension payment input period (PIP) works

The annual allowance is £40,000 for PIPs ending in the 2014/15 tax year and beyond, but previously it was £50,000. With defined contribution pension plans, the amount of any personal and/or employer's contributions in a PIP ending in the tax year is the amount tested against the annual allowance. With a defined benefit pension scheme the benefit accrued in a PIP ending in the tax year is multiplied by 16 to determine the value for annual allowance purposes (with allowance given for inflationary increases).

Where you wish to make a contribution in excess of the current tax year annual allowance (currently £40,000), carry forward is available to the extent that, in any of the previous three years, you had a registered pension scheme and had unused annual allowance. The unused allowance is available regardless of whether you were permitted to make contributions in those years or not (perhaps because you had insufficient earnings or were non-UK resident). The surplus (starting with the

earliest year) is then rolled forward to the current year to enable relief to be provided on the contribution made in the current tax year, to the extent that it exceeds
the annual allowance. For the three years prior to 2014/15 the annual allowance was
£50,000 and this amount may still be carried forward beyond 5 April 2014.

Although active (i.e. still accruing benefits) membership of defined benefit pension schemes is becoming rarer and mainly the preserve of public-sector workers,
about 28% of UK employees are members of such schemes (whether active or
deferred),[6] so there is a fair chance of them featuring in many people's wealth
planning. A defined benefit pension is potentially a valuable financial resource,
but it can cause complications with the annual allowance limit, particularly if you
have a high salary and/or high accrual rate. If you exceed the annual allowance,
this will cause a tax charge that negates the income tax relief given.

To help you to work out the maximum benefit that you can accrue in a PIP and
remain within the annual allowance, you can use the formula set out in the box.
If benefit accrual results in a pension input amount that exceeds the annual allowance (after accounting for any unused annual allowance that might be available to
carry forward from the previous three years), you are required to disclose this fact
in your self-assessment tax return and pay the associated tax charge.

Defined benefit accrual and the annual allowance

FORMULA $I = (PIA)/16 + (C \times Pension)$

I	= increase in pension in a payment input period
PIA	= payment input amount (increase in accrued benefits)
C	= Consumer Price Index increase rate in the September before tax year in question
Pension	= pension accrued at end of previous PIP

Example

Hope had accrued £38,000 of benefit in the previous PIP ending 31 March 2014.
The annual rate of the CPI to the previous September was 2%.

1 $(£40,000/16) + (0.02 \times £38,000)$

2 £2,500 + £760

3 £3,260

Hope can therefore accrue up to £3,260 of additional benefit in the PIP ending on
31 March 2015, i.e. the 2014/15 annual allowance.

---

[6] Office for National Statistics, *Pension Trends* – Chapter 7: Private Pension Scheme
Membership, 2013 Edition, p. 11.

Any personal contributions must not exceed 100% of earnings, although up to £3,600 per year can be contributed without any earnings. Employer contributions may be made without reference to the member's earnings, although contributions to defined contribution schemes are, in aggregate with personal contributions, subject to the annual allowance (including any carry forward of unused annual allowance available). Tax relief on personal contributions is given at your highest rate by extending the basic-rate income tax band. A personal contribution can thus be used to:

• bring a 40% or 45% taxpayer below the threshold at which that rate is paid

• enable capital gains otherwise taxable at 28% to be taxed at 18%

• enable taxable gains arising on encashment of life insurance bonds to be taxed (in whole or in part) at nil, 20% or 25% depending on the size of the gain and whether the policy is an offshore or onshore type

• retain the personal allowance by bringing income below the £100,000 threshold.

Putting aside for one moment any investment returns arising, making pension contributions to a defined contribution scheme can be highly attractive for certain taxpayers due to the availability of a 25% pension commencement lump sum (PCLS) that is currently tax-free. Table 17.4 shows the uplift in value for different taxpayers, disregarding any investment returns. The best effect is where tax relief is obtained at a rate of 40% or more but benefits are taxed at 40% or less. Someone obtaining effective tax relief of 60% (those with taxable income over £100,000) but who pays only 20% on those pension benefits would obtain a staggering 113% uplift by making a pension contribution.

Table 17.4 Uplift in value of pension contributions assuming 25% tax-free lump sum

Tax relief on contribution	% return on fund for different taxpayers after 25% tax-free cash			
	20%	40%	45%	60%*
20%	6	−13	−17	−13
32.5%	26	4	−2	−19
40%	42	17	10	−8
45%	55	27	20	0
60%*	113	75	66	38

* This is the effective income tax rate for those with taxable income of between £100,000 and £120,000 due to the loss of personal allowance (2014/15 tax year)

Contributions in excess of the current tax year's annual allowance may incur a tax charge if there is no unused annual allowance to carry forward from the previous three tax years, which has the effect of clawing back any tax relief provided (see Figure 17.4).

Figure 17.4 How tax relief (40%) is given on pension contributions

Figure 17.5 illustrates the position for Charlotte, who is a company director and has had a SIPP since 2008. She has a total of £90,000 unused relief available to carry forward to 2014/2015, allowing a maximum contribution of £130,000 to be made in that tax year.

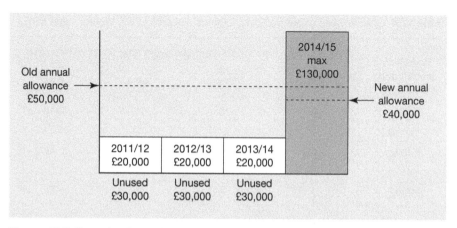

Figure 17.5 Example of carry forward of unused pension allowance – 2014/15

As time goes on the carry forward calculations could become complicated. Let's assume that Charlotte or her employer made a contribution of £90,000 in the 2014/15 tax year, making use of carry forward of unused annual allowance of £50,000 (£30,000 from 2011/12 and £20,000 from 2012/2013). In the 2015/2016 tax year she can still carry forward unused annual allowance of £40,000 (£10,000 from 2012/2013 and £30,000 from 2013/2014 tax years to enable her employer or herself (if she has sufficient earnings) to make a contribution of £80,000 (£10,000 + £30,000 + £40,000). See Figure 17.6.

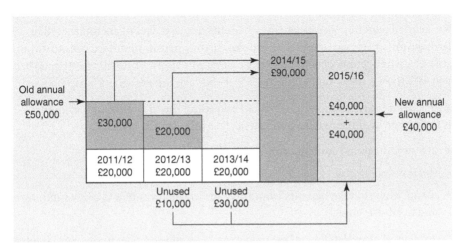

Figure 17.6 Example of carry forward of unused pension allowance – 2015/16

This is a simplified example of how carry forward works. In practice, different circumstances will cause different outcomes and considerations, particularly if you have more than one pension scheme, and/or you have defined benefit pension schemes, and/or your historic contributions include one or more years in which you or your employer contributed more than £40,000. Great care is required to ensure that you do not inadvertently incur an annual allowance tax charge and this is an area where a good adviser can be very helpful. If you want to work out your available annual allowance, HMRC has a useful pension annual allowance online calculator tool at **www.hmrc.gov.uk/tools/pension-allowance/index.htm**

The lifetime limit

The total amount of benefit that you may accrue within all registered pension schemes is limited to an upper limit known as the lifetime allowance (LTA). There are several types of lifetime allowance:

1   Standard – £1.25 million (from 6 April 2014).

2   Individual protection 2014 – between £1.25 million and £1.5 million (must be applied for between 6 April 2014 and 5 April 2017).

3   Fixed protection 2014 – up to £1.5 million (from 6 April 2014).

4   Fixed protection 2012 – up to £1.8 million (from 6 April 2012).

5   Enhanced – no limit (if applied for between 6 April 2006 and 5 April 2009).

6   Primary – limit is the amount that the fund exceeded £1.5 million on 6 April 2006, increased by 20%.

For defined benefit pension schemes, benefits not in payment are multiplied by 20 to determine their value for LTA purposes. If your pension fund exceeds the available LTA when you take benefits, a tax charge will apply. This will be either 25% if you take the excess as an income, or 55% if you take the excess as a lump sum.

As a general rule it makes sense to avoid exceeding the LTA (although sometimes it is less of a problem) and therefore you need to monitor the effect of:

● any new proposed contributions

● the investment strategy and returns arising

● if and when to take benefits from the plan in the form of a tax-free lump sum and taxable income.

I'll explain in more detail how best to manage your pension plan in the next chapter, but for now I just want to consider the lifetime allowance in the context of whether or not you make any new contributions. As illustrated in Table 17.5, if you have no existing pension provision, it is unlikely that you will exceed the lifetime allowance unless you contribute near to the annual allowance maximum and/or have a long time horizon before taking benefits and/or achieve quite high investment returns.

Table 17.5 Summary of growth required to reach standard lifetime allowance assuming no existing pension fund

Age	Annual contribution			
	£10,000	£25,000	£40,000	Term
30	7.07%	2.82%	–0.64%	35
35	9.5%	4.16%	0.28%	30
40	12.05%	6.21%	1.65%	25
45	16.39%	9.61%	4.08%	20

Age	Annual contribution			Term
	£10,000	**£25,000**	**£40,000**	
50	25.98%	16.02%	8.75%	15
55	47.70%	31.38%	20.08%	10
60	145.98%	93.45%	63.91%	5

This is the effective income tax rate for those with taxable income of between £100,000 and £120,000 due to the loss of personal allowance (2014/15 tax year)

Figure 17.7 shows the annual investment return required to reach the lifetime allowance at different levels of existing pension benefits and terms assuming that ongoing contributions are made to a defined contribution scheme equal to the annual allowance of £40,000. Fund values in excess of about £600,000–700,000 with a term of more than five years need either low or negative returns to avoid breaching the lifetime allowance.

Term to retirement / Existing fund	5 years	10 years	15 years	20 years
£100,000	42.73%	13.97%	6.20%	2.76%
£200,000	30.89%	10.34%	4.45%	1.76%
£300,000	23.38%	7.75%	3.12%	0.97%
£400,000	17.94%	5.74%	2.04%	0.30%
£500,000	13.72%	4.10%	1.14%	−0.28%
£600,000	10.29%	2.72%	0.35%	−0.78%
£700,000	7.41%	1.53%	−0.33%	−1.23%
£800,000	4.94%	0.48%	−0.95%	−1.64%
£900,000	2.79%	−0.46%	−1.50%	−2.01%
£1,000,000	0.88%	−1.30%	−2.01%	−2.35%
£1,100,000	−0.83%	−2.07%	−2.47%	−2.67%
£1,200,000	−2.38%	−2.77%	−2.90%	−2.96%

Highlighted figures represent realistic returns for typical balanced portfolio

Figure 17.7 Annual growth required to fund £1.25 million lifetime allowance assuming £40,000 annual contributions with existing fund value

Qualified non-UK pension scheme (QNUPS)

This is the term given to most overseas pension plans that meet certain rules set down by HMRC. QNUPS fall into two types:

1 Those that are classed as qualifying recognised overseas pension schemes (QROPS) because they qualify to receive a transfer of benefits from a UK pension scheme.

2 Those that are not a QROPS because they do not qualify to receive a transfer in of benefits from a UK pension scheme.

The key benefits of a QNUPS, which is not also a QROPS, are as follows:

- There is no limit on the amount that may be contributed, although no tax relief is given.
- Non-UK-sited investments usually grow free of UK taxes.
- Potential to avoid tax on amounts taken as a lump sum.
- Potential to borrow between 25% and 50% of the fund, depending on the jurisdiction.
- Ability to invest in a wide range of investments, including residential property.
- No UK inheritance tax on the value of the fund as long as it is being used as a proper retirement plan.

> In the 2014 budget, the government announced that it would consult on the tax treatment of QNUPS, with the intention of preventing inheritance tax avoidance.

With the exception of defined benefit plans, pension plans are merely tax wrappers within which one can hold some wealth to achieve a tax effect. The tax reliefs on offer – income tax relief on contributions, largely tax-free growth and freedom from inheritance tax – are very attractive. In the next chapter I'll explain how best to manage pension assets in the context of your overall wealth plan.

CHAPTER 18
MANAGING YOUR PENSION PORTFOLIO

'Pensioners will have complete freedom to draw down as much or as little of their pension pot as they want, anytime they want. No caps. No drawdown limits ... No one will have to buy an annuity.'

George Osborne[1]

For many people the value of their pension represents a significant element of their wealth and one that needs to be factored into a comprehensive wealth plan. In Chapter 12 we looked at the issues relating to taking regular withdrawals from an investment portfolio and the potential problems associated with funding a constant expenditure with volatile investment assets. Similar considerations apply to managing the investment strategy of your pension plan(s) and deciding how and when to take benefits, but with the added complication of the tax treatment being affected by how benefits are taken, particularly with larger funds.

The main factors that you need to consider in the management of your pension assets are as follows:

- your cashflow needs
- your life expectancy and any dependants' circumstances
- your income tax, capital gains tax and residency status
- the pension lifetime allowance
- investment risk and taxation of non-pension investments
- taxation of the payment of pension benefits on your death
- estate planning considerations.

---

[1] UK Budget speech, 19 March 2014.

Cashflow needs

As we saw in Chapter 3, having an idea of your cashflow needs is likely to help you to make better financial decisions and should form the cornerstone of your wealth plan. With pensions this is even more important so that you can determine how and when to take benefits, what risks you need to take and how best to minimise or avoid tax. It is essential to bear in mind that your pension fund should not be looked at in isolation. You will also need to consider the level of net-of-tax cashflow that your non-pension investment portfolio can provide. If your investment portfolio were established in the expectation of no withdrawals being required, it may need to be reviewed if it is tax-inefficient or unfeasible for your pension portfolio to meet all your lifestyle costs.

The earliest age at which you can take benefits from your pension is usually 55, unless you were in a special occupation and had pension arrangements in relation to that occupation, which permitted earlier access (e.g. sports person, model, diver, etc.) before 6 April 2006 or you qualify for a severe and permanent ill-health pension. There is no longer an upper age limit by which pension benefits must be taken, whether that is as an income or a lump sum.

Life expectancy and dependants

How long you expect to live has important implications for how you manage your wealth because it dictates the time horizon that your resources need to last. As I explained in Chapter 3, life expectancy has been rising in the UK over the past 50 years. Unless you have a terminal health condition, or a family history of short life expectancy, it is impossible to know how long you are likely to live. All the evidence suggests that it will be a lot longer than you think. As a general rule it doesn't make sense to take on the risk of living too long (longevity risk), particularly if you expect above-average life expectancy. You might, therefore, find purchasing a guaranteed pension annuity a more attractive option for some or your entire pension-related wealth. In this context the annuity is insurance against living too long.

Income and capital gains tax

Pension benefits are usually available in the form of a taxable income and a tax-free lump sum, known as a pension commencement lump sum (in most cases this is 25% of the fund value). In the case of a defined benefits pension scheme, the lump sum can be in addition to the guaranteed pension income (most commonly in government-backed schemes or those operated by companies that were previously government-owned) or in return for giving up some of it, known as commutation (more of which later). From April 2015 you may also take the entire fund of a defined contribution pension scheme (after deducting the tax-free lump sum amount) as a taxable lump sum. Prior to that date, taking a taxable lump sum required the member to have a secure[2] pension income of at least £12,000 per annum.

State and private pension income, lump sum taxable pension fund withdrawals and income from employment and self-employment form the first slice of taxable income. To the extent that such income (or taxable capital pension withdrawals) uses up some or all of your lower- and/or higher-rate income tax bands, it can affect whether or not you retain your personal income tax allowance and the rate of tax that you pay on rental income, interest and dividends, which form the top slice of taxable income, as illustrated in Figure 18.1. With income tax rates as high as 45% and capital gains tax also affected by whether or not you are a basic- or higher-rate taxpayer, it makes sense to carefully consider the income tax effect of taking pension benefits. The tax rate applied to taxable pension lump sums is determined in the tax year in which you take the benefit.

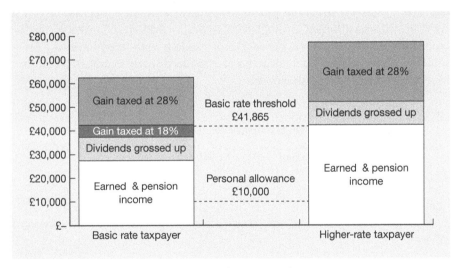

Figure 18.1 Order in which income and gains are taxed

It may be that you can take pension benefits gradually over a number of years and use tax-free lump sums to provide cash inflows to meet your lifestyle expenditure each year, together with taxable income either directly from the fund or from the

---

2   This means state pensions, guaranteed annuities and benefits from a defined benefits scheme.

purchase of an annuity. You could take the maximum pension commencement lump sum from your whole pension, and then have the choice of taking a taxable income or a taxable lump sum from some or all of the remaining fund. Taking the taxable portion of your pension as a single lump sum needs to be carefully considered in the context of:

- your other taxable income and capital gains
- whether you can mitigate any income tax arising on the withdrawal (i.e. investing in an EIS or similar tax shelter or offset trading losses)
- what you intend to do with the funds
- whether or not you want/need to remove longevity risk by buying a standard or enhanced annuity (i.e. which is higher due to poor health)
- whether and to what extent the withdrawn capital would give rise to a higher inheritance tax liability for your estate and whether this is a concern for you.

Figure 18.2 shows the cashflow position of a £250,000 taxable lump sum taken from a pension fund, compared with taking a withdrawal of £20,000 p.a. within the basic-rate income tax band. Disregarding investment returns and inflation, taking the regular withdrawals provides the higher amount of net cash after just six years. Clearly, different assumptions will produce different breakeven points, but the key point is that for many people, particularly with larger funds and other sources of taxable income, taking the pension as a single taxable lump sum is likely to result in a lower cash outcome.

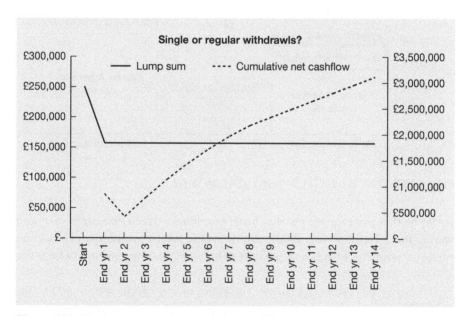

Figure 18.2 Single versus regular pension fund withdrawal

If you own investments that are held outside tax-efficient wrappers, and that generate realised capital gains in excess of your capital gains tax annual exemption, the rate of capital gains tax will be determined by the total amount of taxable income you receive from all sources, including your pension plan. If any part of the taxable gain, when aggregated with your taxable income, falls into the basic-rate income tax band, it will be taxed at 18%. Otherwise the capital gains tax rate will be 28%. It can be very useful, therefore, to have the flexibility to control how much taxable income and/or capital you receive from your pension portfolio, where you anticipate ongoing capital gains arising from an investment portfolio.

Pension lifetime allowance

When the UK pension regime was changed on 6 April 2006, a new control mechanism, the lifetime allowance, was introduced. There are several circumstances in which the total value of your accumulated pension benefits must be tested to see whether it exceeds the LTA. These include:

- taking benefits
- transferring benefits to another scheme
- attaining age 75
- death.

Taking benefits before age 75

In a money purchase pension scheme, any excess over the LTA will be taxed at the rate of 25% – the 'LTA charge' – and income tax levied on any income benefits. Alternatively, the excess over the LTA can be withdrawn from the pension fund as a lump sum, in which case it will be subject to a flat 55% tax charge and no further income tax charge. The standard lifetime allowance (SLA) is £1.25 million at the time of writing.

If an individual takes benefits under income drawdown (i.e. income is taken directly from the fund rather than via a guaranteed annuity purchased with the fund), a second test against the LTA will normally be made at age 75. If the value of the individual's pension fund at that time exceeds the amount that was originally put into income drawdown, the excess will be tested against the LTA. If it exceeds the individual's unused LTA then the excess will be subject to a one-off 25% tax charge.

In the case of defined benefit pension schemes, the accrued pension benefit is multiplied by 20 to determine its value for testing against the LTA. Thus, a pension of £100,000 would be valued at £2 million for this purpose. Any LTA tax charge can be paid by deduction from the individual's benefits by the scheme itself, the calculation being based on the same actuarial principles used to determine the rate for commuting the pension to a lump sum.

Scheme pension

Some money purchase pension funds, such as SSAS and family self-invested personal pension schemes (family SIPPS), allow the scheme trustees to pay a fixed pension directly from the fund. Known as 'scheme pension', the pension benefit is determined by reference to actuarial factors. The scheme pension is multiplied by 20 to determine its value for testing against the LTA, which can be much lower than the value of the fund that is used to provide it.

For the purposes of testing against the member's lifetime allowance, the value of the scheme pension is multiplied by a factor of 20 when it commences. Thus, someone subject to the standard LTA of £1.25 million could receive a fully inflation-protected scheme pension directly from the scheme of up to £62,500 per annum, without exceeding the standard lifetime limit. If fixed protection 2012 (£1.8 million) or 2014 (£1.5 million) applies, then a scheme pension of up to £90,000 or £75,000 per annum respectively is possible, without exceeding the protected LTA.

Consider the case of Douglas, who is single, aged 60 and in good health, with a directors' pension fund of £2 million and fixed protection 2014. The current open market annuity rate for a single life, guaranteed annuity with inflation protection would currently provide a starting pension of £57,975.

At the time Douglas's scheme secures the annuity, the value of his fund is tested against his available LTA, which in this case would be £1.5 million. Thus, £500,000 of Douglas's fund is in excess of his LTA, so he would incur a tax charge of £275,000 ((£2 million – £1.5 million) × 55%).

If, however, Douglas arranges for the pension trustees (of which he is one) to pay him a scheme pension that broadly mirrors that which he could secure from a guaranteed annuity but paid directly from the fund, the value of his pension benefits for testing against the LTA would be £1,159,500, being 20 × the starting pension of £57,975. As this is below his £1.5 million LTA, no LTA tax charge will arise.

Transfers

This is a complex area but in general terms a transfer to another UK pension will not be tested against the LTA if it is a 'permitted transfer'. Broadly speaking, a permitted transfer must be made to another approved or qualifying pension arrangement.

If UK pension benefits are transferred to a qualifying recognised overseas pension scheme (QROPS), then the value will be tested against the LTA at that time, regardless of whether or not benefits have previously been taken. Any excess over the available LTA that has not previously been tested will be subject to a tax charge of 25%. A QROPS will *not* then incur a further LTA test or charge, whether or not the member is a UK resident at the time benefits are taken or they reach age 75. This means that all post-transfer growth in the fund currently avoids a further LTA test. Table 18.1 shows the LTA charge position for a UK pension scheme compared with a QROPS.

Table 18.1 LTA and QROPS

Tax status when benefits taken	UK scheme UK and non-resident	Transfer to QROPS then take benefits			
		UK resident @ 45%	UK resident @ 40%	UK resident @ 20%	Non-UK resident/ Non-UK taxpayer
Gross fund	£100,000	£100,000	£100,000	£100,000	£100,000
LTA tax charge	(£55,000)	(£25,000)	(£25,000)	(£25,000)	(£25,000)
Net taxable fund	£45,000	£75,000	£75,000	£75,000	£75,000
Income tax	NIL	(£33,750)	(£30,000)	(£15,000)	NIL
Net fund	£45,000	£41,250	£45,000	£60,000	£75,000

Note: It has been assumed that there is no unused remaining LTA available and that the fund value shown has not previously been tested against the LTA.

The only circumstance in which the member would be worse off would be if they were a UK resident when they came to take benefits from their QROPS and they paid income tax of more than 40% on the net fund. If, however, investment returns have been high between the date of the transfer to the QROPS and the date benefits are taken, the benefit of nearly gross roll-up of returns might outweigh the current 45% additional (and currently highest) rate of UK income tax.

Not taking benefits by age 75

If income drawdown has not commenced by age 75 then at that age the whole of the individual's pension fund will normally be tested against the LTA and any excess will be subject to a one-off 25% tax charge (and there will be no subsequent test against the LTA). Alternatively, in most cases the excess over the LTA can be withdrawn from a money purchase pension fund as a lump sum, in which case it will be subject to a 55% tax charge.

Death

If a member dies before age 75 with a fund from which no benefits have been taken (uncrystallised benefits), the value will be tested against the unused LTA and any excess taxed at 25% if taken as income or 55% if taken as a lump sum. If a member dies before age 75 having taken benefits, there will be no further LTA tax charge but any lump sum death benefit will be taxed at the rate of 55%.

If a member dies at any age having taken benefits that are held within a QROPS, no further LTA charge applies to those benefits, regardless of residence status or growth in the fund. However, if the member does not meet the QROPS definition of non-UK resident at the time of death, there will be a 55% tax charge on any lump sum death benefit from the QROPS. The tax charge is based on the value of the amount originally transferred to the QROPS, less any benefits taken since the transfer, not (as is the case for a UK pension scheme) the value at death.

If a member dies after age 75, regardless of whether or not they have taken any benefits, there will be no further LTA charge, regardless of fund growth, as they would have been tested and taxed on any excess as appropriate at age 75. However, there will be a 55% tax charge on the value of any lump sum death benefits paid (although this is currently being reviewed by the UK government with a view to lowering it, probably to be the same as income tax on benefits taken during lifetime). See Figure 18.3.

Impact of the LTA tax charge

Even if the LTA tax charge is payable, it may not, in some scenarios, lead to such a bad outcome. Figures 18.4 and 18.5 compare the terminal values of receiving income net of income tax and investing that in a taxable portfolio, with making a pension contribution of £100,000, on which tax relief is received of 40% or 45%, but which is then subject to the LTA tax charge of 55% on the lump sum eventually taken from the pension scheme.

The breakeven points at which the gross pension contribution, net of the LTA tax charge, produces a higher terminal value than the net income invested in a taxable portfolio is about 25 years for a 40% taxpayer and about 15 years for a 45% taxpayer. This assumes a gross annual investment return of 5% in the pension and 4% in the taxable portfolio, which equates to an effective tax rate on the taxable portfolio of 20%. The rate of investment return does not appear to have much impact on the net terminal value compared with the time horizon and the income tax paid or pension income tax relief obtained on the contribution.

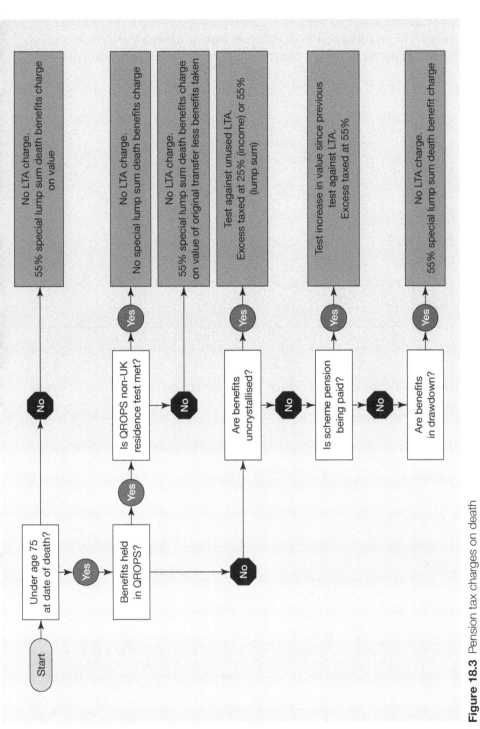

Figure 18.3 Pension tax charges on death

Source: Bloomsbury Wealth Management.

A 45% income tax payer with a time horizon of more than 15 years before they take benefits would appear to be better off making a pension contribution now, even if they expect to pay the LTA tax charge of 55% on the eventual fund resulting from it.

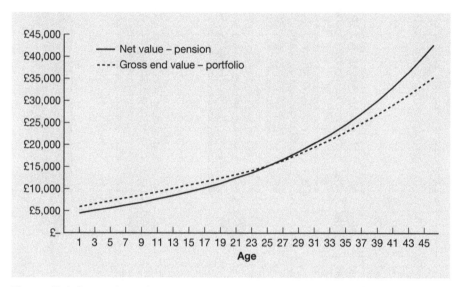

Figure 18.4 Comparison of net pension and non-pension portfolio value – 40% taxpayer
Source: Bloomsbury Wealth Management.

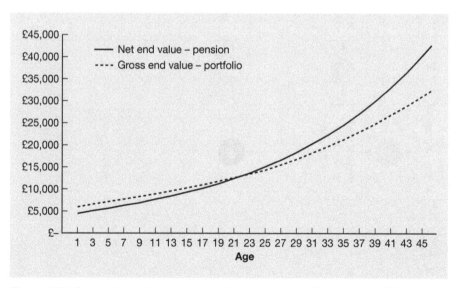

Figure 18.5 Comparison of net pension and non-pension portfolio value – 45% taxpayer
Source: Bloomsbury Wealth Management.

Protection against the LTA tax charge

Protection against the LTA charge was introduced on 6 April 2006 for those individuals whose pension benefits exceeded, or were expected to exceed, the then LTA of £1.5 million. There were two types of protection available – primary protection and enhanced protection – and they had to be elected for before 6 April 2009.

A third type of protection, fixed protection, was introduced when the LTA was reduced from £1.8 million to £1.5 million on 6 April 2012, which had to be elected for before that date. As a consequence of the LTA being reduced again, from £1.5 million to £1.25 million, on 6 April 2014, a fourth type of protection, fixed protection 2014, has been added and this had to have been elected for before 6 April 2014. A fifth type of protection, individual protection 2014, can be elected for between 6 April 2014 and 5 April 2017. Details of all these types of protection are set out in Figure 18.6.

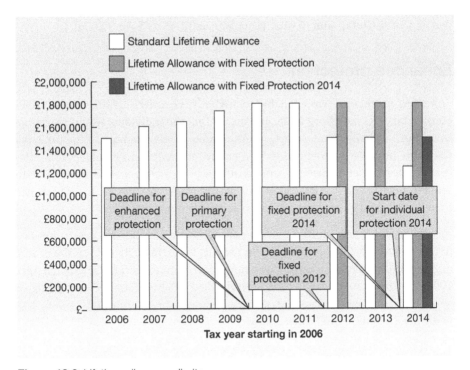

Figure 18.6 Lifetime allowance limits
Source: Bloomsbury Wealth Management.

Primary protection

Primary protection was available only if an individual's pension benefits exceeded £1.5 million on 5 April 2006, in which case the LTA is:

$$\frac{\text{Benefits value as at 5 April 2006} \times \text{Greater of current LTA and £1.8 million}}{\text{£1.5 million}}$$

Individuals who have primary protection can continue to accrue further pension benefits if they wish. They are subject to the normal maximum tax-free lump sum (of 25% of their pension benefits up to a maximum of 25% of £1.5 million or the standard LTA if higher) unless they were entitled to a lump sum of more than £375,000 on 5 April 2006, in which case their maximum tax-free lump sum is:

$$\frac{\text{LS} \times \text{Greater of standard LTA and £1.8 million}}{\text{£1.5 million}}$$

(where LS is the lump sum to which they were entitled on 5 April 2006).

Enhanced protection

Enhanced protection was available to anybody, regardless of the value of their pension benefits on 5 April 2006, and meant that the individual would be exempt from the LTA charge whatever the eventual value of their benefits at the time that they were put into payment. However, enhanced protection is subject to no further pension benefits (beyond limited inflationary increases for defined benefits schemes) being accrued for the individual after 5 April 2006. If this is breached then HMRC must be notified and enhanced protection will be lost.

Individuals with enhanced protection are subject to the normal maximum tax-free lump sum (of 25% of their pension benefits up to the higher of the SLA or £1.5 million) unless they were entitled to a lump sum of more than £375,000 on 5 April 2006, in which case they will have been notified of a lump sum percentage figure when they received confirmation of their enhanced protection from HMRC. This percentage will have been calculated as:

$$\frac{100 \times \text{Lump sum to which they were entitled on 5 April 2006}}{\text{Benefits value as at 5 April 2006}}$$

The lump sum to which they will be entitled when their benefits are put into payment will be their benefits value at that date multiplied by their lump sum percentage.

Fixed protection

The LTA gradually increased to £1.8 million for the 2010/11 and 2011/12 tax years but was then reduced to £1.5 million from 6 April 2012. A new form of protection, fixed protection, which allowed individuals to retain the £1.8 million LTA, was introduced for those individuals whose pension benefits exceeded, or were expected to exceed, £1.5 million.

Fixed protection is subject to no further benefits (beyond limited inflationary increases for defined benefits schemes) being accrued for the individual after 5 April 2012. If this condition is breached then HMRC must be notified within 90 days and fixed protection will be lost.

Fixed protection 2014

The LTA was further reduced from £1.5 million to £1.25 million on 6 April 2014 and yet another form of protection, fixed protection 2014, was introduced to allow individuals whose pension benefits exceed, or are expected to exceed, £1.25 million to retain the £1.5 million LTA. This had to have been elected for by 5 April 2014.

Fixed protection 2014 was not available to individuals who already had primary protection, enhanced protection or fixed protection and it is subject to no further pension benefits (beyond limited inflationary increases for defined benefits schemes) being accrued for the individual after 5 April 2014. If this condition is breached, then HMRC must be notified within 90 days and fixed protection 2014 will be lost. It is possible for an individual with enhanced protection to elect to HMRC to forgo it, but if they have primary protection this cannot be forgone.

Individual protection 2014

Individual protection 2014 (IP14) allows protection from the LTA charge for pension benefits valued at between £1.25 million and £1.5 million as at 5 April 2014. Individuals with total benefits greater than £1.5 million and who are not already registered for enhanced or primary protection can apply, but IP14 will be capped at £1.5 million. The IP14 amount will become the individual's standard LTA (SLA) amount.

Individuals with IP14 can continue to accrue future pension benefits without losing their entitlement to IP14. This is the critical difference when compared with fixed protection 2014, which can be maintained only if:

- no further contributions are received on the member's behalf by a defined contribution scheme on or after 6 April 2014

- individuals in a defined benefits scheme do not accrue further benefits above a 'relevant percentage' from 6 April 2014. This will normally be either the annual rate of increase specified in the scheme rules as at 11 December 2012 or the increase in the CPI over the preceding year (if no rate is specified in the scheme rules).

The personalised limit under IP14 is fixed and will not increase over time. However, it can reduce if there is a pension debit on divorce. IP14 cannot be given up by the individual but will automatically cease should the SLA increase to a higher level than the personalised allowance afforded by IP14. Under IP14 the maximum tax-free lump sum available will be 25% of the member's pension benefits to a cap of 25% of their personalised LTA. So if, for example, an individual's personalised LTA as at 5 April 2014 is £1.4 million, their maximum tax-free lump sum will be £350,000.

Another implication of having a personalised LTA under IP14 is that in cases where the member has taken (crystallised) some benefits before 6 April 2014, they may be able to avoid an LTA charge on benefits subsequently taken after that date compared with if they had taken all benefits before it. The previously taken benefits need to be revalued from the original value to the percentage of the new personalised LTA that they represent, as follows:

$$\text{Personalised LTA under IP14} - \frac{(\text{Value of previous crystallisation} \times \text{Personalised LTA under IP14})}{\text{LTA at date of previous benefit crystallisation}}$$

Example

Morris has IP14 and a personalised LTA of £1,333,333. This was calculated on the basis of benefits of £833,333 having been taken in the 2011/12 tax year (adjusted under the rules of IP14 from the actual £1 million value of the benefits that he took) and remaining benefits of £500,000. On the face of it one would think that Morris has unused personalised LTA of £500,000, but this is not the case.

If Morris takes his remaining benefits in 2014/15, the benefits that he took in 2011/12 will be revalued as if his personalised LTA were the standard lifetime allowance, as follows:

$$£1,333,333 - \frac{(£1,000,000 \times £1,333,333)}{£1,800,000^*} = £592,592$$

*This was the SLA in 2011/12 before the reduction to £1.5 million.

Thus, Morris will be able to take benefits of up to £592,592 before he exceeds his personalised lifetime allowance.

Combined fixed protection 2014 and individual protection 2014

Fixed protection 2014 takes priority over individual protection 2014 so an individual claiming both will have an LTA of:

- £1.5 million if no contributions are made and no benefit accrual occurs after 5 April 2014, or
- their total benefit value (between £1.25 million and the £1.5 million cap) as at 5 April 2014 if contributions and/or accrual take place after that date.

There is no downside in having both forms of protection. For individuals with defined contribution benefits, if the total value of benefits taken is below the individual protection 2014 figure it may be possible to top benefits back up to that level through additional contributions.

Example

Emma has no existing form of protection. The value of her SIPP as at 5 April 2014 is £1.4 million and she expects to take retirement benefits in the 2017/18 tax year. She opted for fixed protection 2014 before the deadline when contributions ceased. In January 2015 she also claims individual protection 2014 based upon the £1.4 million SIPP value at 5 April 2014.

Emma's SIPP has fallen to £1.3 million when she comes to take her benefits in 2017/18, due to poor investment returns in the interim. As she has individual protection 2014 she can make further contributions. Assuming that she has sufficient earnings and unused annual allowance to carry forward, she can make a contribution of £100,000 to bring her SIPP value up to her £1.4 million individual protection allowance. This will mean that fixed protection 2014 is lost. However, without the claim for individual protection 2014, she would be unable to replace the lost pension value, as paying a contribution invalidates the fixed protection 2014.

An election for individual protection 2014 will allow any employer's pension contribution to continue for her while providing LTA protection on £1.4 million of her funds. Without individual protection, continuing contributions would mean a reduction in her LTA to £1.25 million, making an additional £150,000 of Emma's pension fund potentially subject to the LTA charge. This is shown graphically in Figure 18.7.

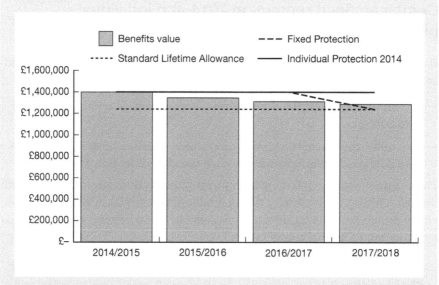

Figure 18.7 Lifetime allowance protection in action
Source: Bloomsbury Wealth Management.

Scheme-specific tax-free lump sum protection

Some pension scheme members had an entitlement, under the pre-6 April 2006 rules, to a tax-free lump sum that was higher than the 25% of the LTA that was subsequently introduced. These members were given automatic protection of this entitlement, whether or not they applied for primary or enhanced protection by 5 April 2009. The reduction in the SLA to £1.25 million from 6 April 2014 can, in certain circumstances, result in an increase of an individual's scheme-specific protected cash entitlement. A further case study may help to explain how this works in practice.

Example

Mike had a fund entitlement under a directors' pension scheme of £300,000 on 5 April 2006. He also had an entitlement to a cash lump sum of £100,000. Therefore, he would automatically be granted scheme-specific protected cash entitlement. His fund has since grown to £400,000 and he does not have enhanced, primary or fixed protection.

Table 18.2 shows the maximum amount that Mike could have taken as tax-free cash in 2013/14 compared with the 2014/15 tax year onwards. When Mike takes benefits, as he does not have fixed protection 2014, his tax-free lump sum entitlement would be £12,000 more than if he had taken it in 2013/14 and £27,000 more than if he had either form of fixed protection whenever he takes benefits.

Table 18.2 Protected lump sums

	2013/14	2014/15
Fixed protection 2012	£130,000	£130,000
Fixed protection 2014	N/A	£130,000
No fixed protection	£145,000	£157,000

Source: Bloomsbury Wealth Management.

LTA tax charge mitigation strategies

Individuals with scheme-specific protected cash lump sums as at 5 April 2006 and whose total benefits value is below £1.25 million on 5 April 2014 (and that value is itself greater than 83.33% of the 5 April 2006 fund value) should revoke any fixed protection because taking any tax-free lump sum after 5 April 2014 will be higher than if taken with fixed protection.

Individuals with benefits valued at more than £1.25 million at 5 April 2014 should claim individual protection 2014 whether or not they have claimed fixed protection 2014, as they will not be worse off by doing so. In the example given earlier of Emma, the position would be the same except that Emma's individual protection would be £1.4 million rather than £1.5 million if she has valid fixed protection 2014. IP14 allows the option of filling a shortfall at retirement or continuing to accrue employer-funded benefits while only reverting to an LTA of, in the Emma example, £1.4 million rather than the current SLA of £1.25 million.

Individuals who have taken some benefits before 5 April 2014 and who intend to apply for individual protection 2014 (whether or not they also have fixed protection) may have a higher unused LTA on benefits subsequently taken after 5 April 2014 compared with if they had taken all benefits before that date.

Individuals who are expecting to retire abroad should consider the merits of transferring UK pension benefits to a qualifying recognised overseas pension scheme to enable the fund to be tested against the LTA now (whether it is the standard £1.25 million or a higher protected amount) and allow future growth to arise free of any further LTA tax charges.

Individuals who are members of an SSAS or a family SIPP and who wish to take income benefits should consider taking those benefits by way of scheme pension, as this may be valued at a much lower amount than the actual fund value used to provide benefits by way of drawdown or annuity purchase.

Even if it seems likely that they will exceed the LTA, a 45% taxpayer with at least 15 years and a 40% taxpayer with 25 years before they expect their pension fund to be tested against the LTA should consider making an additional pension contribution if they can obtain tax relief of 45% or 40% respectively on it.

I will not pretend that the 'simplified' pension regime is simple and there are clearly many traps for the unwary. Each situation needs carefully reviewing based on a proper analysis of your objectives, preferences, tax position, pension benefits and employment/self-employment circumstances. This is an area where personalised advice is essential if you are to minimise tax charges.

Investment strategy

Investment returns arising within a pension plan grow free of tax. With the exception of withholding tax on dividends from equities, there is no tax on interest, dividends, property, rental income or capital gains arising within the fund. It is therefore most tax-efficient to hold interest-yielding deposits and fixed interest assets, rental-producing commercial property and capital gains-generating investments.

If you are not intending to withdraw the capital as a taxable lump sum, then your investment strategy for the pension fund needs to reflect the following:

- the amount of any regular income withdrawals
- the likelihood of your fund value exceeding the LTA and the possible tax impact if it does

- the death benefit position for any of your financial dependants
- whether you manage the portfolio yourself or outsource this to a third party.

Table 18.3 shows the annual investment returns required at different fund values to reach the current (2014/15) £1.25 million SLA. Unsurprisingly, the larger fund values and longer terms require the lowest annual rate of growth to reach the limit. If you benefit from enhanced protection because you had significant pension benefits before 6 April 2006, these considerations do not apply and you are free to pursue whatever investment strategy you wish. Other forms of LTA protection provide higher LTA limits than the standard one, so there may be more scope to generate investment returns without incurring the LTA tax charges, as set out in Tables 18.4 and 18.5.

Table 18.3 Ready reckoner – annual investment return required to fund for £1.25 million lifetime allowance with no new contributions

Existing fund value	Term to retirement 5 years	10 years	15 years	20 years
£100,000	65.72%	28.73%	18.34%	13.46%
£200,000	44.27%	20.11%	12.99%	9.60%
£300,000	33.03%	15.34%	9.98%	7.40%
£400,000	25.59%	12.07%	7.89%	5.86%
£500,000	20.11%	9.60%	6.30%	4.69%
£600,000	15.81%	7.62%	5.01%	3.74%
£700,000	12.30%	5.97%	3.94%	2.94%
£800,000	9.34%	4.56%	3.02%	2.26%
£900,000	6.79%	3.34%	2.21%	1.66%
£1,000,000	4.56%	2.26%	1.50%	1.12%
£1,100,000	2.59%	1.29%	0.86%	0.64%
£1,200,000	0.82%	0.41%	0.27%	0.20%

Note: Shaded area represents realistic returns for typical balanced portfolio

Table 18.4 Ready reckoner – annual investment return required to fund for £1.5m lifetime allowance with no new contributions

Term to retirement / Existing fund value	5 years	10 years	15 years	20 years
£100,000	71.83%	31.08%	19.78%	14.49%
£200,000	49.60%	22.31%	14.37%	10.60%
£300,000	37.95%	17.45%	11.32%	8.33%
£400,000	30.24%	14.12%	9.21%	6.83%
£500,000	24.56%	11.61%	7.60%	5.65%
£600,000	20.11%	9.59%	6.30%	4.69%
£700,000	16.46%	7.92%	5.21%	3.89%
£800,000	13.39%	6.49%	4.28%	3.20%
£900,000	10.76%	5.24%	3.47%	2.59%
£1,000,000	8.45%	4.14%	2.74%	2.05%
£1,100,000	6.40%	3.15%	2.09%	1.57%
£1,200,000	4.57%	2.26%	1.50%	1.13%
£1,300,000	2.91%	1.45%	0.96%	0.72%
£1,400,000	1.39%	0.70%	0.47%	0.35%

Note: Shaded area represents realistic returns for typical balanced portfolio

Table 18.5 Ready reckoner – annual investment return required to fund for £1.8m lifetime allowance with no new contributions

Term to retirement / Existing fund value	5 years	10 years	15 years	20 years
£500,000	28.20%	13.87%	8.81%	6.61%
£600,000	24.67%	11.81%	7.80%	5.85%
£700,000	20.78%	9.90%	6.60%	4.84%
£800,000	17.81%	8.45%	5.58%	4.14%
£900,000	14.87%	7.18%	4.73%	3.64%
£1,000,000	12.47%	6.06%	4.00%	2.68%
£1,100,000	10.35%	5.05%	3.34%	2.49%

Existing fund value \ Term to retirement	5 years	10 years	15 years	20 years
£1,200,000	8.45%	4.14%	2.74%	2.06%
£1,300,000	6.72%	3.31%	2.18%	1.64%
£1,400,000	6.16%	2.64%	1.69%	1.28%
£1,500,000	3.71%	1.84%	1.22%	0.82%
£1,600,000	2.88%	1.18%	0.78%	0.69%
£1,700,000	1.16%	0.67%	0.68%	0.28%

Note: Shaded area represents realistic returns for typical balanced portfolio

Estate planning

The value of pension funds is usually exempt from inheritance tax at all ages, provided that any contributions or a transfer in of benefits (from a previous pension scheme) did not happen within two years of death and/or you were aware that you had a terminal illness when you made the contribution or a transfer in of benefits from another pension scheme. Any lump sum that you take from your pension scheme in your lifetime (whether or not it is taxable) will immediately form part of your estate for inheritance tax to the extent that you do not spend it.

How death benefits are distributed will depend on the way the scheme has been set up and whether it has an integrated or master trust. Most schemes are established under a master trust and the member gives the trustees an 'expression of wishes' or nomination form specifying whom they would like to benefit in the event of their death. There could be advantages to setting up a special pension 'bypass' trust and nominating any death benefits to be paid to that trust (see Chapter 21 for more details).

Currently a flat rate tax charge of 55% is payable on lump sum death benefits paid from a scheme (or part of a scheme) from which benefits have been taken or for any scheme, regardless of whether or not benefits have been taken, where the member is aged 75 or over. At the time of writing the government has announced its intention to review the taxation of pension death benefits, indicating that this is likely to result in a reduction to bring the rate in line with the income tax treatment of withdrawals during lifetime.

Taking benefits

Extracting benefits from an approved pension scheme used to be straightforward – they were paid as an annuity, some of which could be commuted in exchange for a tax-free lump sum. Over the years the number of options has increased considerably, culminating in the introduction in April 2015 of lump sum withdrawal, which will provide even greater options to avoid annuity purchase altogether.

The following is a brief summary of the current options available to pension investors for the vesting of benefits. They are not mutually exclusive and, in many cases, a combination of them together, possibly with, ongoing earnings and/ or drawings from an investment portfolio or other assets will prove to be the preferred route to provide for ongoing expenditure requirements when full-time paid work has ceased to become a necessity or a possibility.

Annuities

Conventional annuity

An annuity is not an investment but an insurance policy against living too long. Although this is the most straightforward option, it is still worthwhile to use the open market option, which allows the annuity to be purchased from any provider, not just the one with whom the existing fund is held (assuming that the existing provider offers annuities, which it will not unless it is an insurance company and even then it may not do so).

Annuity rates depend on several factors, of which the most important are the level of long-term interest rates and expected mortality rates. Important factors to consider, then, are the following:

- Should you take the maximum pension commencement lump sum (i.e. tax-free cash)?
- Should you purchase a single life annuity or an annuity based on the joint lives of you and your spouse?
- In the event of your death, what proportion (usually 50%, 66% or 100%) of your pension should continue to your spouse?
- Should your pension increase each year and, if so, by how much, given that the higher the rate of annual increases, the lower the starting amount?
- Should you build in a guarantee period of five or ten years to ensure the continuation of payments for several years in case you die soon after commencement?
- How frequently do you want payments to be made? (Monthly, quarterly and annually are the usual options.)

- Do you want payments to be made in advance (more expensive) or arrears (less expensive)?
- Could you qualify for an enhanced or impaired life annuity because of your medical history or lifestyle (e.g. if you smoke or have a health condition)?

All of these options affect the income that you will receive. You need to know how much each one costs and find the right balance of benefits for your circumstances, as the extent to which you have other assets and sources of income will affect the suitability of each option – the pension income should not be considered in isolation from your other assets. I recommend a conventional level annuity as the default choice, against which all the other options are compared on the basis that it is the cheapest, simplest, lowest-risk and lowest-cost option for the majority of people. The UK financial regulator has endorsed this view.[3]

Figure 18.8 shows example rates for a guaranteed level and index-linked annuity at different ages, with and without a survivor's pension. Figure 18.9 compares a level and inflation-linked annuity for a 60 year old over the long term. At the 4% p.a. inflation rate used, it takes more than 22 years for the inflation-linked annuity to beat the level annuity. Clearly, the crossover point will be later for lower inflation and sooner for higher inflation.

The regulator's view

An increasing number of consumers, especially those moving from defined benefit to defined contribution pension schemes, may demand products that allow decumulation of capital. However, this is an area where consumer financial capability is particularly low.

For many, an annuity will be the most appropriate option. However, people approaching retirement may be more susceptible to sales of income drawdown because, as discussed earlier, annuity rates are lower and could generate an income below consumers' expectations. These factors create the conditions for potential misselling of products that generate higher fees or commissions than annuities, even when annuities would be more appropriate.

A related risk is that consumers who buy drawdown products do not understand the need for regular review or take the after-sales advice offered to them to help decide when to purchase an annuity. While the market for income drawdown is small, there has been a significant increase in the volume of sales in recent years.

---

[3] Financial Services Authority (2010) 'Financial risk outlook 2010', March, available at **www. fsa.gov.uk/pubs/plan/financial_risk_outlook_2010.pdf**

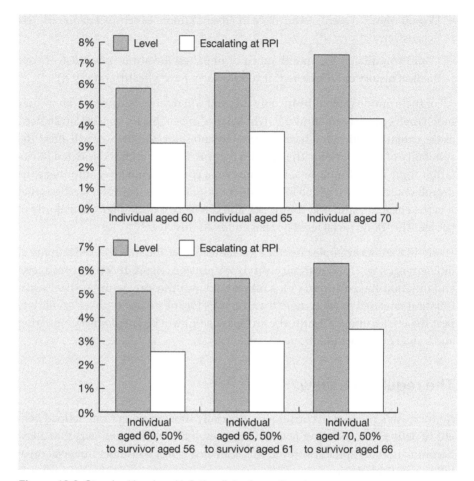

Figure 18.8 Standard level and inflation-linked annuity rates

Enhanced annuity

It is estimated that one in two people[4] could qualify for an enhanced annuity typically offering 15–20% more than a standard annuity, where they have lifestyle or health conditions that suggest lower life expectancy. Figure 18.10 compares standard and enhanced annuity rates for a 65-year-old smoker who has suffered a heart attack.

---

4   Partnership Life estimate stated on factsheet 'Annuities – still a core solution', April 2014.

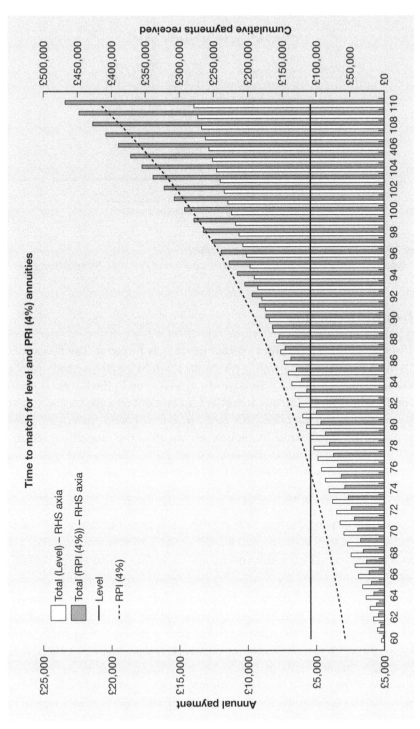

Figure 18.9 Comparison of projected benefits from level and inflation-linked annuities

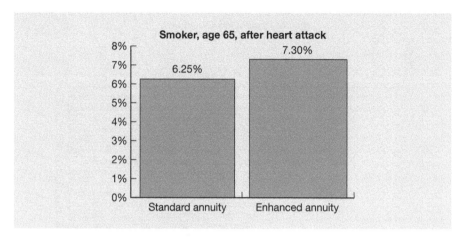

Figure 18.10 Standard and impaired life annuities

Source: Data from Money Advice Services, comparison service (accessed May 2014), Partnership Assurance.

With-profits annuity

A with-profits annuity provides an income that is linked to the investment returns of an insurance company's with-profits fund. As for all investment-linked annuities, the income payable can go down as well as up in the future. However, with-profit annuities do provide smoothed investment returns, so that in poor years, your income will not necessarily go down as much as the underlying investments have gone down, while in good years, not all of the investment return is necessarily paid out (as some is retained to cover the bad years). With-profit fund returns should therefore be less volatile than those of other investment funds.

Typically, income is made up of two parts:

1   A minimum starting income. This is set at a low level, but unless investment conditions are very bad, you will usually get at least this much income provided that you select a 0% anticipated bonus rate. Some with-profits annuities guarantee it.

2   Bonuses. The insurance company usually announces bonus rates once a year. Bonuses can be both 'reversionary' (usually announced once a year and then guaranteed to pay out for the duration of your annuity) and 'special' (which pay out for only a year or so until the next bonus announcement). The amount of bonuses depends on many factors, the most important of which is the performance of the underlying assets within the with-profits fund itself. However, the insurer's expectations for future mortality and its financial strength are also an influence.

When you start a with-profits annuity, you normally select an anticipated bonus rate. The minimum and maximum rates of anticipated bonus rate you can choose vary by provider, but typically the range is from 0% to 5% and normally once selected it cannot be changed. A cautious person wishing to use a with-profits annuity would choose a 0% anticipated bonus rate. Selecting a higher anticipated rate gives a higher initial income but lower future increases and the income could fall if actual bonuses do not match the anticipated ones.

Some providers allow you to convert to a conventional annuity (which must be purchased from the same provider) at given points in the future. This means that you can change your annuity to one that provides set income levels and no investment risk, which can be useful if your circumstances or conventional annuity rates change.

The main drawback of with-profit annuities is that the underlying asset mix is tailored to the liability stream of the insurer, not the investor. There is consequently no inherent relationship between the investment risk that you take and your risk tolerance or capacity, and the composition of the underlying fund can change quite dramatically over a relatively short period of time, often without it being obvious until some months later.

Unit-linked annuity

With a unit-linked annuity, your income in retirement will be linked directly to the value of an underlying fund of investments. Generally, you can choose the types of funds, for example:

- one or more managed funds whose managers select from a broad range of different assets and may vary the exposure to each over time
- one or more actively managed sector funds whose managers select investments from within particular countries or sectors
- index-tracking funds that track the performance of particular stock market indices.

The riskier the underlying fund you choose, the more your retirement income may vary – both up and down. Some unit-linked annuities work in a similar way to with-profits annuities, in that your starting income is based on an assumed growth rate and if the fund grows at that assumed rate, your income stays the same. If growth exceeds the assumed rate, your income increases. If growth is less than the assumed rate, your income falls.

A few unit-linked annuities offer access to a 'protected fund' that limits the fall in your income, although most unit-linked annuities do not guarantee any minimum income. The drawback is that you are restricted to the range of funds offered by the insurer whose annuity product you purchase. It may therefore be difficult or impossible to find a mix of funds that meets your requirements at a reasonable cost, if at all.

Third way products

A few providers now provide what are called 'third way' annuities that combine limited guarantees with some investment upside. While there may be some situations where these are useful, such as where someone needs more income than a guaranteed annuity but can't accept the full risk of income drawdown, their use by affluent and wealthy individuals is likely to be limited.

Self-invested annuities

If you transfer your pension to a QROPS you can use your fund to provide a non-UK self-invested annuity. The main benefit is that you can leave any residual fund available on death to an offshore trust and, as such, avoid the 55% flat rate death charge that would apply if in drawdown. Table 18.6 compares the death tax charge of a SIPP in drawdown and a self-invested annuity.

Table 18.6 Death benefits comparison of SIPP drawdown and EU open annuity

	Aged 65	Aged 70	Aged 75
SIPP drawdown fund value	£618,000	£692,000	£847,000
EU open annuity fund value	£540,289	£577,251	£624,888
Difference in fund value	−£77,711	−£90,829	−£222,112
SIPP lump sum dealth benefit paid to beneficiaries assuming 55% tax rate	£278,100	£311,400	£381,150
EU open annuity mortality profit paid to offshore trust upon death	£540,289	£577,251	£624,888
Difference	+£262,189	+£265,851	+£243,738

Note: Assumptions: age at outset 55, starting fund value £500,000, 7% p.a. growth; annual withdrawals taken of £25,000, does not include investment or advice charges.
Source: London and Colonial.

Phased retirement or staggered vesting

Phased retirement is the process of taking pension benefits (whether by way of annuity purchase or taking income directly from the fund) over a period of time rather than in one go. Although it used to be necessary for personal pensions to be arranged as a cluster of many separate plans or segments for phased retirement to be an option, the introduction of the pension simplification regime in April 2006 eliminated this requirement and even non-segmented plans can take advantage of the facility. Each time you use part of the fund to purchase an annuity or provide income withdrawals, you can first take part of it as a pension commencement lump sum of up to 25% of the total amount being vested. Repeating the process regularly means that you can effectively use the pension commencement lump sum as well as the annuity or income withdrawal to provide your cashflow for each year, as Figure 18.11 shows.

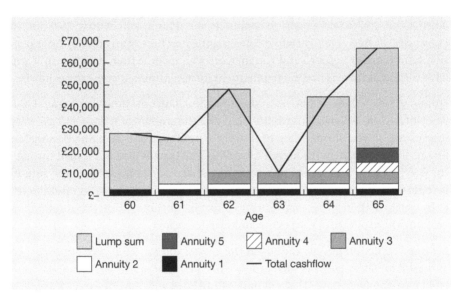

Figure 18.11 Phased pension benefit crystallisation

The drawback of this approach is that if you stagger the vesting of your pension fund in this way, you will not be able to take all of your pension commencement lump sum from your total pension fund at once. Phased retirement can be a useful financial planning tool, for example if you want to ease back gradually on work and start to replace your earnings with pension income. It also provides more flexible help for your survivors if you die before converting the whole of your fund to annuities. It is possible to vary the type of annuity that you purchase on each occasion and it need not be on the same basis as in previous years. You can also purchase each annuity from a different provider. Any unvested fund that has not yet been converted to annuities can provide a lump sum or a pension for your surviving dependants, depending on the terms of the pension scheme, although these may be subject to tax if the value of your total pension benefits exceeds the LTA.

Phased retirement is generally suitable only if you have a fairly large pension fund or have other assets or income on which to live. This is because the bulk of your pension savings remains invested, which may be riskier and more expensive than buying an annuity straight away.

Pension drawdown

Originally introduced in 1995 under the name of 'pension fund withdrawal', drawdown allows you to take a pension commencement lump sum of up to 25% and an *income directly from your fund* while deferring the purchase of an annuity. Your pension fund remains invested and you may draw an income from it each year if you wish, although there is now no requirement for a minimum income to be drawn.

From April 2015 there will be no maximum annual income limit requirement and you will have considerable flexibility in setting the amount you draw and can vary it from year to year (from nil up to the entire fund) to meet changing personal or financial circumstances throughout your life. The taxable element is paid through the PAYE system and, as such, will be taxed at your highest marginal rate of income tax. The advantage of being able to access your entire pension fund needs to be weighed against the disadvantages of paying income tax on the amount and bringing the capital into your estate for inheritance tax.

Because you do not buy an annuity at the outset, you can keep your options open as regards ancillary benefits such as survivors' pensions and escalation and do not end up paying for benefits that might not be needed (e.g. were one or more of your dependants to pre-decease you). The pension fund remains under your control, so can be invested according to your objectives and risk profile (need, capacity and tolerance). On death, the whole of your remaining pension fund, less a 55% tax charge, is available to provide lump sum benefits to your family or beneficiaries. This means that if you are under age 75, drawdown will reduce the potential fund value that could be passed to your heirs. For those who die aged 75 or over the fund is subject to the 55% tax charge regardless of whether or not drawdown has been activated. It may be possible for a dependant's pension to be payable, subject to the scheme provider offering this option. A dependant's pension will not attract a 55% tax charge until the fund is paid out as a lump sum.

If you are risk-averse and need a high level of income in retirement, you're unlikely to gain any benefit from taking income directly from your pension fund and may end up with an inferior pension to that which you could have had simply by purchasing an annuity at the outset. This is partly because the cross-subsidy from those who die early, which helps to support annuity rates, does not apply to drawdown pension (this is known as the mortality drag), as well as the additional costs involved in the ongoing portfolio management and advice. See Figure 18.12.

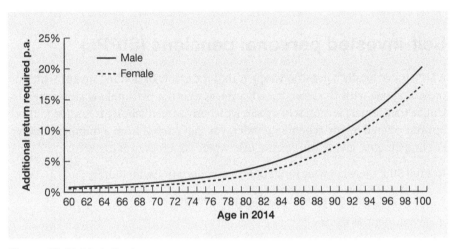

Figure 18.12 Mortality drag
Source: Office for National Statistics. Projected mortality rates (qx) for the 2012-based UK life tables.

The cost of mortality drag is less than 0.5% per year for someone effecting drawdown at age 60, but this rises to nearly 3% p.a. at age 75 and 5% p.a. by age 85. Therefore, unless there are other special factors, such as having no need to use the pension fund to fund retirement income or if you have health issues, you should buy an annuity, or start to buy a series of annuities, by the time you reach age 70. Drawdown is therefore most appropriate for those circumstances when financial planning concerns (such as cashflow and tax planning) are dominant.

Deferring annuity purchase in the expectation of annuity rates rising is unlikely to be an effective strategy as even if long-term interest rates do rise sufficiently to overcome the effect of increased longevity, the income forgone by deferral may never be recouped over the remainder of your lifetime.

Phased retirement and drawdown pension combined

Combining both phased retirement and flexible drawdown pension means that you would start to draw a taxable income or lump sum (whether taxed or tax-free) from just part of your pension fund on one date, leaving the rest of the fund intact. If, in the future, you wish to increase your income you could either increase the rate of withdrawal or start to draw an income from a further part of your pension fund. In the event of your death before age 75, any element of your pension plan from which benefits have not been drawn would be paid as a tax-free lump sum to your nominated beneficiaries.

Self-invested personal pensions (SIPPs)

A SIPP is essentially a pension wrapper that is capable of holding investments and providing you with the same tax advantages as other personal pension schemes. Unlike traditional pension schemes in which investment choice is limited to those options offered by the scheme provider, you can choose from a number of different investments, giving you control over where your money is invested.

In a full SIPP there is a wide range of investment options, including:

- stocks and shares, including exchange-traded funds
- government securities
- mutual investment funds (unit trusts and open-ended funds)
- investment trusts companies
- insurance company funds
- traded endowment policies
- deposit accounts with bank and building societies
- National Savings and Investments products
- commercial property (such as offices, shops or factory premises).

This level of choice can be expensive to offer and many people find that they do not need it, so lower-cost SIPPs have been developed that focus on investment funds only. These lower-cost SIPPs usually offer significantly more fund options than would a traditional pension scheme. If you are working with a wealth manager, they should integrate the management of your SIPP, including taking benefits over time, into the overall management of your wealth.

The family SIPP

A family SIPP is a pooled arrangement where all members may also be trustees if over the age of 18, as illustrated in Figure 18.13. The key aspect of this type of scheme is that all the members pool their capital for the purposes of investment, whether in funds, property or both, which is known as the 'common' fund. A family SIPP can also offer a scheme pension, which is not something available from standard SIPPs.

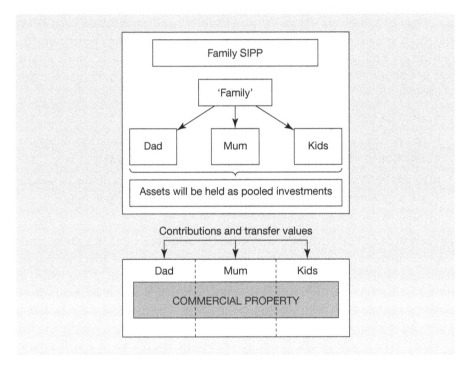

Figure 18.13 The family SIPP

Small self-administered scheme (SSAS)

An SSAS offers similar options for pooling investment and paying a scheme pension, but because it is covered by occupational rules, it has additional compliance obligations that mean external trustee services and running costs are likely to be higher. This higher cost is usually good value if you want to have your own pension scheme (and not be part of a master trust personal scheme) and take advantage of the SSAS's ability to lend funds back and/or investing shares of the sponsoring employer. In all other respects it will be broadly similar to a family SIPP.

Qualifying recognised overseas pension schemes (QROPS)

It is only possible to transfer benefits from a UK-registered pension scheme to an overseas pension scheme that meets strict rules set down by the UK tax authorities. Since 2006 overseas schemes that meet these requirements have been called QROPS. If you expect to retire abroad permanently (this means being non-UK-resident for a minimum of five complete tax years) or have already done so, you may benefit from transferring your UK pension benefits to a QROPS for a number of reasons:

- to avoid UK income tax on the income or capital withdrawn
- to remove the currency risk of receiving a pension denominated in sterling in a jurisdiction in which your expenditure is in a different currency
- to avoid the 55% tax charge payable on lump sum death benefits for those aged 75+ or for younger individuals who have taken benefits from their fund
- to improve investment flexibility.

The benefit of a QROPS depends on whether the member is non-UK resident when they take benefits or not and, if they are, the rate of income tax that they pay on the excess benefits taken as a taxable income and/or lump sum. If you return to the UK, or never ended up leaving, a QROPS could still be useful for two reasons. First, the pension fund is tested against the LTA only at the time it is transferred and thereafter any growth beyond the LTA would not currently be subject to the LTA tax charge. Second, a QROPS will allow the purchase of a non-UK self-invested annuity that offers the possibility to pass any residual fund value to your beneficiaries free of tax.

Using a QROPS to avoid the LTA and/or lump sum death benefit tax charges could be viewed as provocative by HMRC and future legislation nullifying the QROPS advantage for those continuing UK residence after transfer is a possibility. It is worth recalling what HMRC said in its December 2011 statement in which it announced a tightening up of the QROPS regime: 'The Government expects that individuals ... can use the QROPS regime to transfer their pension savings *where they leave, or intend to leave*, the UK permanently so that they can continue to save to provide an income when they retire' [my emphasis].[5]

HMRC reiterated this point in 2013: 'The primary objective of the QROPS regime is to enable individuals *leaving the UK permanently* to simplify their affairs by taking their pension savings with them to their new country of residence. This is intended to enable them to continue to save to provide themselves with a higher income when they retire. In particular it is not considered desirable for individuals to be able to use a transfer to an overseas scheme to facilitate the withdrawal of their savings as a large lump sum or to receive more tax relief than would have been available had the pension savings remained in the UK' [my emphasis].[6]

A QROPS provider must continue to report to the UK tax authorities on any benefits taken from a member's QROPS while they are UK-tax resident and for five tax years after the one in which they cease to be UK-tax resident. The QROPS provider is required to report all payment of benefits and transfers to other pension schemes for the first ten years since the transfer was effected regardless of the member's UK residence status.

---

[5]   HMRC (2011) 'Purpose of the QROPS regime', December, available from **www.hmrc.gov. uk/budget-updates/06dec11/pensions-hmrc-stat.pdf**

[6]   HMRC (2013) 'Pension schemes: Guidance on the taxation of unauthorised transfers to schemes included on the QROPS', November, list available from **www.hmrc.gov.uk/pensionschemes/transfers-to-qrops.pdf**

PART 4
WEALTH TRANSFER AND SUCCESSION

CHAPTER 19
LATER LIFE PLANNING

'One of the most attractive things about writing your autobiography is that you're not dead.'

Joseph Barbera, American animator, director, producer

As Chapter 3 showed, we are all living much longer and the outlook is for life expectancy to continue to increase, but perhaps not at the same rate as it has over the past 30 years or so. Increased life expectancy, however, also brings with it a multitude of issues that may have a bearing on your wealth planning and possibly that of your parents or relatives.

Dementia is one of the main causes of mental incapacity in older people in the UK, affecting about 800,000 people, and this number is set to rise to more than 1 million people by 2025.[1] The chances of suffering dementia increase significantly with age and roughly double with every five-year age group.

Power of attorney

A lasting power of attorney (LPA) is a legal document that provides one or more people (known as attorneys) whom you appoint to deal with your affairs as if they were you, subject to certain conditions and obligations. LPAs replaced enduring powers of attorney (EPA) in England and Wales in 2008 – although EPAs executed prior to the change remain valid, no EPAs may be created since 1 October 2007. In Northern Ireland LPAs are governed by slightly different rules. The equivalent in Scotland is known as a power of attorney and the rules are also slightly different to those applying in England and Wales.

---

[1] Alzheimer's Society (2013) 'Dementia – the hidden voice of loneliness 2013', infographic available at **www.alzheimers.org.uk/site/scripts/download_info.php?fileID=1409**

An LPA is arguably more important in your later life stages, given the higher likelihood of losing mental capacity compared with middle age. Ensuring that someone has the legal means to make important legal, financial and medical decisions on your (or your parents') behalf when you (or your parents) are not capable of making those decisions is a prudent and responsible piece of forward planning.

A person acting as an attorney must follow certain principles that govern what they can and cannot do. These principles include:

- acting only within the powers set out in the LPA
- acting in the best interests of the donor
- involving the donor in decision making as far as possible
- not taking advantage of the donor's situation to benefit the attorney personally
- keeping property and money separate from the attorney's.

In England and Wales an LPA must be registered with the Office of the Public Guardian (OPG) in order to be valid. However, because it can take up to four months to register an LPA I recommend that you register it at the outset to avoid delays if it needs to be used. LPAs can be wide-ranging, including allowing your attorney to sell property, operate your bank accounts or even provide guidance as to what type of health treatment you would like to receive in certain scenarios. Alternatively, you could make your LPA limited in scope to deal with only a narrow range of scenarios.

The old-style EPA needs to be registered with the OPG only in the event that it is to be used when the person subject to the EPA (known as the donor) has lost mental capacity. If the donor hasn't lost mental capacity, the EPA can be used without being registered, although there can be practical difficulties with banks and investment providers refusing to deal with an attorney where the EPA is unregistered.

In England and Wales there are two types of LPA: a property and affairs LPA, which covers financial and legal issues, and a personal welfare LPA, covering things such as where you will live and medical preferences. Since 2005 it has also been possible to create what is known as an advance decision to state preferences for medical treatment that one would like or not like if one were no longer able to decide for oneself.

If you have strong views on medical treatment, you should set these out in either a personal welfare LPA or an advance decision, but ensure that your general practitioner and your next of kin know about it. In most cases a personal welfare LPA will override an advance decision as long as the LPA is prepared after the advance decision and it specifically confers authority on the attorney.

If someone loses mental capacity but they have not established an EPA or LPA, it is possible for a friend or relative to make a deputyship application to the Court of Protection. The Court will then consider conferring specific powers on the prospective deputy making the application, to deal with the person's legal and financial affairs, together with various legal obligations. The Court also has power to appoint someone else as the deputy if they think the applicant isn't suitable (e.g. they have a criminal record).

In Scotland, a power of attorney (PA) can include powers to deal with financial assets (known as 'continuing powers') and/or personal welfare. While continuing powers can be conferred for use regardless of the mental capability of the person subject to the PA, they can be used for welfare-related aspects only if the subject has lost mental capacity to make such decisions. All Scottish PAs must include a certificate signed by a Scottish legal professional or medical practitioner to the effect that the person granting the PA is making the decision freely and understands the implications. Before it can be used the PA must be registered with the OPG in Scotland.

In Northern Ireland, an LPA must be registered with the Office of Care and Protection (OCP) if it is to be used when the subject of the LPA has lost mental capacity.

Making wills in old age

There are a number of potential problems associated with older people making wills, particularly when they deprive relatives of inheritance. The case of Golda Bechal highlights these.[2] Mrs Bechal left her £10 million estate to a couple who ran her favourite Chinese restaurant, to the detriment of her immediate family. The family contested the will on the basis that Mrs Bechal executed it without being fully aware of what she was doing. The case was eventually settled in favour of the beneficiaries of Mrs Bechal's will but not until after several years of legal wrangling.

Another case involved Dr Christine Gill, whose parents, John and Joyce Gill, had left their entire estate of more than £2 million to the RSPCA charity.[3] The court was told the Gills were a 'very close family' and there had been no major rifts to explain

---

[2] *London Evening Standard* (2008) 'Thanks for the tip: Restaurant keeps £9 million from favourite customer's £10 million contested will', 28 June.

[3] Brooke, C. (2009) 'Daughter wins back £2 million estate left to RSPCA after overturning parents' will', Mail Online, 10 October.

cutting their only child out of the will. Indeed, the daughter did thousands of hours of unpaid work helping to run the family's 287-acre farm and selflessly supported her troubled mother, Joyce, who suffered from various phobias.

Dr Gill argued in court that her mother had been coerced into making the will by her 'domineering' father, John, who died in 1999. Judge James Allen QC said Mr Gill was a bully and a 'stubborn, self-opinionated, domineering man, who was prone to losing his temper'. His wife, a shy woman, deferred to what he wanted, said the judge. In 1993 Mrs Gill signed a will leaving everything to the RSPCA, despite being said to have an 'avowed dislike' of the organisation. Judge Allen found that Joyce Gill had been coerced into making a will that was against her wishes and awarded the estate to the daughter.

To avoid disputes about your (or any elderly relative's) will after death, you need to prove that you (or your relative) had 'testamentary capacity' (i.e. you had the mental capacity to make decisions) at the time the will was made. Although the test for testamentary capacity is not quite the same as the medical test for mental capacity, it is still a good idea to obtain a statement from your family doctor that confirms you have mental capacity. In addition, to avoid legal claims from those with legitimate claims as your 'dependants', you should make reasonable provision for them in your will. Otherwise such individuals might be able to contest your will.[4]

Nevertheless, all is not lost if someone loses mental capacity to make a will as it is possible to create a statutory will providing that the person wishing to make the will is either an attorney under a registered EPA or LPA or has been granted a deputyship by the Court of Protection and subsequently applies to the OPG with a formal proposal for the terms of a statutory will. However, sophisticated estate planning is unlikely to figure highly on the list of permitted actions.

Long-term care fees

Much attention is focused on the issue of long-term residential care costs and the impact they can have on a family's wealth. The consensus of all the available research seems to be that one in three people will need some form of long-term care. In many situations, funding care fees while remaining in your own home can actually be more expensive than residential or nursing home care costs, because of the need to meet the cost of care and of running and maintaining the home. It

---

[4] The Inheritance (Family and Dependants) Act 1975 provides certain protections for family members and dependants who have not been adequately provided for financially as a result of the deceased's will.

has been estimated that the average cost of care at home for just two hours a day would amount to £7,300 per annum.[5] My own experience from working with clients is that 24-hour live-in care can easily cost more than £100,000 per annum.

On average, an individual can expect to pay around £27,612 a year for a residential care home, rising to more than £38,000 if nursing is required.[6] However, the cost of residential or nursing home care varies widely depending on the location, as illustrated by Table 19.1. The average life expectancy for those entering residential care is about 2.5 years.[7] However, if we remove from the statistics those severely sick and disabled people who are admitted to care homes straight from hospital, the average stay in a care home for a self-funder (i.e. someone not receiving state care fees funding) is actually closer to four years, with a one in eight chance of living more than seven years.[8]

Table 19.1 Average weekly care home fees around the UK 2012/2013

	Weighted average weekly fees by region – private homes for elderly people, UK 2012/2013	
Area	**Residential care home**	**Residential nursing home**
England – average	£532	£750
North East	£471	£597
North West	£468	£663
Yorkshire and the Humber	£463	£624
East Midlands	£506	£618
West Midlands	£495	£708
East of England	£564	£800
London	£598	£821
South East	£591	£869
South West	£551	£764
Scotland	£555	£685
Wales	£491	£650
Northern Ireland	£466	£570

Source: Laing & Buisson, 'Care of elderly people UK market survey 2012/13'.

5   Partnership Insurance estimate 2014.

6   Laing & Buisson, 'Care of elderly people UK market survey 2012/13', based on average figures for the UK.

7   Personal Social Services Research Unit (2011) 'Length of stay in care homes', January.

8   Partnership Insurance internal estimate.

Care costs are fully funded by the NHS if the 'primary' need is for healthcare. This is assessed by the NHS when the patient is discharged from hospital or moves into a care home and since 1 October 2007 has been covered by the National Framework for NHS Continuing Healthcare and NHS-funded Nursing Care. However, like hospital stays, such funding affects an individual's entitlement to a state pension and certain other benefits. In addition, the individual has no say in the choice of care provider or establishment.

Part-funded care: non-means tested

If a registered nurse assesses that an individual needs nursing care as part of their care needs, the NHS will, regardless of that person's wealth or income, contribute a flat weekly rate (at the time of writing this is £106.30 in England and £119.66 in Wales). If the assessment was carried out before 1 October 2007 and the person qualified for the higher rate of nursing care funding, this will continue (this is £146.30 in England and Wales).

The situation in Scotland is different in that those aged 65 and over who self-fund their care benefit from an NHS contribution towards nursing and personal care (this currently amounts to £222 per week). Those aged under 65 benefit from a contribution towards personal care only (this is currently £69 per week).

Means-tested care fees funding

Means-tested care fees funding is assessed and provided by the social services departments of local authorities. Each local authority can choose its own eligibility criteria, although national guidelines set out the core rules and legal obligations. As a general rule any person who is assessed with having more than a modest amount of income or capital is not eligible for means-tested care fees funding (see Table 19.2).

Table 19.2 Capital limits for care funding 2014/2015

	England	Scotland	Wales	Northern Ireland
Upper limit	£23,250	£26,000	£24,000	£23,250
Lower limit	£14,250	£16,000	£24,000	£14,250

Source: Department of Health (2014) 'Charging for Residential Accommodation Guide (CRAG)', April.

The current capital upper limit of £23,250–26,000 means that most affluent people will need to fund all of their care fees, at least until their capital falls below the upper limit. A reducing scale of support applies between the lower and upper capital limits, based on you contributing £1 a week for every £250 in assets over £14,250 (in respect of those living in England).

Certain assets are excluded from the means-tested care fees funding assessment, including:

- an individual's home that continues to be occupied by a spouse, civil partner or someone living with the claimant as a spouse or civil partner
- an individual's home that continues to be, or is intended to be, occupied by a relative aged over 60 or who is incapacitated
- the proceeds of the sale of the home to the extent that the capital is used to buy a replacement property for the resident spouse, civil partner or qualifying resident
- previous outright gifts to individuals or trustees as long as these were not, and can't be shown to have been, made with an intention to deliberately avoid paying care fees
- the surrender value of life insurance policies, including investment bonds but not capital redemption bonds.

Proposed changes to care fees funding

There are two major changes proposed for long-term care fees funding over the next few years. Starting from April 2015, individuals requiring care may defer paying towards their care costs, under a 'universal deferred payment' arrangement that will enable them to defer payment of care costs until after their death by taking a local authority loan that would be secured on their home. A number of local authorities already offer deferred payment arrangements on a discretionary basis.

The second and more welcome change relates to the roll-out of a national minimum eligibility assessment for support. The basis for assessing eligibility for care will be simplified and harmonised to stop the postcode lottery that currently exists. Whether this is achievable in practice, with hard-pressed local authorities, remains to be seen. No one aged over 65 will have to meet care costs if these first arise after April 2016 and they have assets worth less than £14,250. Those with assets between £14,250 and £118,500 will have to meet some of the costs of residential care up to a cap of £72,000 for 'eligible' care costs, which are within the local authority's assessment of what it will pay towards this cost. If the person requiring care cannot find a residential care home to deliver this care at this price, or they cannot find one they like within this budget, the individual or their family will have to 'top up' the difference. These additional payments will not count towards the care cap. In any case, those needing care will still have to pay towards the cost of food and accommodation, and this has been set at a maximum of £12,000 per annum. It is estimated that the new cap will benefit the 16% of older people who face care fees of more than £72,000.[9]

Figure 19.1 projects the cumulative care costs for someone who has capital above the proposed new upper limit of £118,000 throughout, based on the average annual care costs for England. Clearly, the length of time that care is required has a large impact on the cumulative total cost to the individual, with this varying from £120,000 for four years, £174,000 for eight years and £234,000 for 12 years in the projection. One point to note is that the proposed care fees cap of £72,000 is met only after just over 3.5 years, because I have assumed that the local authority definition of the individual's contribution to 'eligible care' is £20,000 compared with the actual cost of £28,000. This seems a reasonably prudent basis on which to assess the potential liability to personal wealth. An additional point worth making is that the cost of the better quality care homes and those in London and the

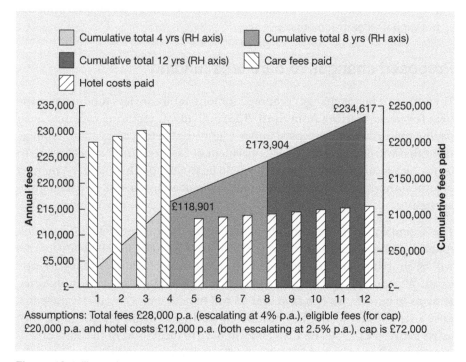

Assumptions: Total fees £28,000 p.a. (escalating at 4% p.a.), eligible fees (for cap) £20,000 p.a. and hotel costs £12,000 p.a. (both escalating at 2.5% p.a.), cap is £72,000

Figure 19.1 Illustrative cumulative care costs

9   Source: Department of Health (2013) 'Policy statement on care and support funding reform', February.

South of the UK will almost certainly be greater than the £28,000 used in the example, as will the difference between actual cost and 'eligible care' costs for the purposes of the cap.

Interestingly, parents of those under 18 requiring care will not have to meet any of their care costs because the care fees cap will be zero. People requiring care between the ages of 18 and 65 with assets above the £14,250 capital threshold will have to meet some of those costs but with a lower, yet to be decided, cap than the £72,000 that applies for those aged 65 and over.

Protecting assets from assessment

If the local authority can prove that the individual (or their attorney) deliberately deprived themselves of assets to avoid paying care fees, then the local authority can seek payment from the recipient of the capital, including placing a charge on any assets. Although any transfer of assets made by the individual within the six months before they required care will always be treated as a deliberate deprivation of assets, in theory the local authority can go back many years before that if it thinks it has sufficient evidence that avoiding care fees was the main motivation for giving away assets or capital.

The whole issue of deliberate deprivation of assets is a bit of a 'grey' area as the test will depend on the facts of each case as well as a degree of subjectivity. Any preventative planning needs to be done in the context of one's overall wealth plan and should avoid the accusation that '[while] avoiding the charge need not be the main motive . . . it must be a significant one'.[10] The guidelines state that it is reasonable to ignore disposals made when the individual 'was fit and healthy and could not have foreseen the need for a move to residential accommodation'. The length of time between any planning action and requiring care funding would seem to be an important element of any defence against a charge of deliberate deprivation of assets.

Maximising state funding of care fees

The following planning areas are worth considering as part of your wider wealth plan as they may minimise how much you and/or your spouse or civil partner have to pay towards care fees:

---

[10] Department of Health (2010) 'Charging for Residential Accommodation Guide (CRAG)', para. 6.062, The Stationery Office.

- Make gifts to a discretionary trust from which you can't benefit and which is done for the purpose of minimising inheritance tax while you are in good health.

- In your will, direct an amount equal to the available nil-rate band to a trust from which your surviving spouse (and wider family) can receive benefit, ideally by way of loans (as well as outright income and capital), for the purpose of providing flexibility over who can benefit and to minimise inheritance tax.

- Make a nomination for any uncrystallised pension lump sum death benefit to be paid to a pension bypass discretionary trust that will allow your surviving spouse (and wider family) to receive benefit, ideally by way of loans (as well as outright income and capital), for the purpose of providing flexibility over who can benefit and to minimise inheritance tax.

- Effect a discounted gift trust (which is explained in more detail in Chapter 21).

- Consider using your home and a trust structure to carry out inheritance tax planning, taking care that the main objective is inheritance tax planning and it is effective.[11]

- Hold capital within an onshore or offshore life insurance investment bond.

- Buy an immediate needs deferred care fees annuity from an insurance company to transfer the risk of living longer than average.

Protecting the family home against care fees

Where the family home is owned jointly by a married couple or civil partners as joint tenants, each person's share will, upon their death, pass automatically to the surviving spouse/partner, regardless of what their will states or the rules of intestacy. This means that any future means test for care fees funding for the survivor will be based on the entire property value, as and when they have been receiving residential care for six months.

If, however, the couple severs their joint tenancy in favour of owning it as tenants in common, on the death of the first of the joint owners to die, his or her share can pass, via their will, to a third party (or to a trust). This means that only the half share that is owned by the survivor will be taken into account for the purposes of any means test assessment should he or she subsequently need residential care. As no gift has been made by the surviving client, this strategy does not count as deliberate deprivation despite its effectiveness in ring-fencing the home.

The value of any property should also be disregarded for a residential care fees assessment if it is 'occupied in whole or in part as their home by the resident's

---

[11] The Law Society advises its members against planning using the family home but you might disagree.

other family member or relative who is aged 60 or over'.[12] However, the High Court recently prevented a local authority from selling an elderly lady's house to pay for her care fees, on account of the fact that the woman's daughter had demonstrated a degree of attachment to the property, despite not actually living there permanently.[13] The relative argued that, although she rented a studio flat in London (where she worked), she considered her mother's property to be her permanent home. This was evidenced by the considerable sum she had spent maintaining it, the fact that she had kept a bedroom, office and shed there for her own use, and her intention to retire there in the near future. The local authority rejected her arguments saying that her occasional occupation of the property could more accurately be likened to a person's occupation of a holiday home.

Defining home as 'a place to which a person has a degree of attachment both physical and emotional', the judge concluded that the local authority had incorrectly interpreted and applied the test (by apparently applying a test of actual occupation and/or permanent residence) and ordered it to 'redetermine' its decision in accordance with the terms of the judgment.

This is the first occasion that this particular issue has come before the courts and while the local authority was, at the time of writing, planning to appeal against the decision, the case may set a precedent for others if allowed to stand. Even then, however, the scope of similar claims is likely to be limited to children over the age of 60 who have invested in, or shown other forms of commitment to, the property.

Life assurance bonds

Although some local authorities do try to include investment bonds in care fees funding assessments, the legislation and guidance are quite clear that such capital must be disregarded.[14] However, any 'income' taken from an investment will be assessed as income for fees funding purposes, but if the 'income' is stopped when care fees start, such income will then cease to exist and, as such, will be disregarded under means testing. A capital redemption bond is not one that is treated as providing life insurance and therefore is not disregarded for care fees funding assessment.

---

[12] Paragraph 2(1)(b)(ii) of Schedule 4 to the National Assistance (Assessment of Resources) Regulations 1992 (as qualified by Section 7 of the CRAG (Charging for Residential Accommodation Guide) rules).

[13] *Walford, R (On the Application of)* v *Worcestershire County Council* [2014] EWHC 234.

[14] National Assistance (Assessment of Resources) Regulations 1992, Schedule 4, para. 13; Department of Health (2010) 'Charging for Residential Accommodation Guide (CRAG)', para. 6.002B, The Stationery Office.

Immediate care fees annuity

It is possible to take out care fees insurance by way of an immediate needs annuity when you know that you have to fund care fees. Whether buying a care fees annuity is a good use of family wealth or not depends on for how long care fees need to be paid, the cost of the care fees annuity, the impact that care fees will have on the family wealth and the extent to which preserving wealth for other family members is a priority. Immediate care annuities are useful if you would prefer to make a known payment up front in return for passing to an insurance company the risk of meeting the agreed level of fees for the rest of your life.

There are only a handful of insurers active in this market and the maximum amount of fees benefit is usually limited to £5,000 per month. While care fees benefit can also be protected against general inflation, care fees inflation has, historically, risen at a higher rate. Therefore, claims over the long term might see the cost of care exceed the insurance benefit.

The reality of care fees funding

Most people want to know that they will have a choice about the type and quality of care, if required, that they will receive in later life. Financial planning that has the effect of avoiding having to fund care fees means you will, to a large extent, give away your choice to the local authority. This may not be a desirable objective. However, you might be of the opinion that any planning that has, as a long-term additional benefit, the potential outcome of giving you and your family the choice of whether or not to use family wealth to fund care fees, either wholly or to top up local authority funding, is better than not having the choice.

The reality for most affluent and wealthy people is they will have to use their own income and capital to fund a substantial element, of the cost of any long-term care fees that might arise in later life. The important questions that you need to ask yourself are:

- What quality of care would you wish to have if you needed it and how much is it likely to cost?
- Would the anticipated care costs be higher than the amount your local authority would classify as 'eligible' care costs and if so how much would you be likely to pay in addition to the proposed eligible care cap of £72,000?
- What impact will funding capped and uncapped care fees and accommodation costs have on your overall wealth and your ability to leave a legacy to your family, friends and/or causes?

- What implications for your investment strategy arise from potentially funding long-term care fees?
- What risk does long-term care represent to you given your family history, current and anticipated health status, and your views about government-sponsored assistance?

A good wealth planning strategy, coordinated by a caring and knowledgeable financial planner, should help you to find the answers.

CHAPTER 20
WEALTH SUCCESSION

'Enough so that they can do anything they want, but not enough that they can do nothing.'

John C. Bogle[1]

Wealth succession is all about ensuring that the right people and/or causes receive the right amount of your surplus wealth, at the right time, in the most tax-efficient manner. It is not about giving away all your money to avoid inheritance tax, although that may well be a legitimate concern. If you've done your strategic wealth planning properly then you should have a good idea of whether you have any surplus capital or income available in your lifetime. However, before you start thinking of giving away any of your wealth or nominating beneficiaries in your will, I suggest that you consider what really matters to you and the impact that any gift might have on the recipient.

You might have concerns that your gift could have a detrimental effect on the recipient or cause tension within the family. Sometimes giving young people large amounts of money can have a negative impact on their motivation and life choices and lead to unhappiness. Treating beneficiaries differently can also cause friction between family members and you'll need to think through the implications carefully. Leaving any gifting until your death might not be the best approach if the beneficiaries are having a tough time now and a financial gift could have a positive impact on their life. The key is to strike the right balance between helping and hindering beneficiaries. See Chapter 23 for more insights into young people and money.

Some people are worried about their beneficiaries getting divorced and the gifted wealth disappearing in any subsequent financial settlement. In some cases your

[1]   Bogle, J.C. (2010) *Enough: True measures of money, business, and life,* Wiley.

intended beneficiary might not want your gift and/or it might exacerbate their own IHT exposure. Significant wealth can also have a negative impact. You might find it helpful to draw up a family mindmap or organisational chart like the one shown in Figure 20.1, noting all relevant facts and issues so that you can discuss these with your professional advisers and agree a plan that avoids, as far as possible, any potential problems.

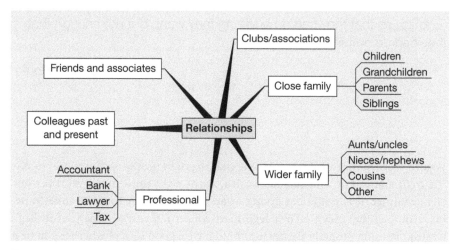

Figure 20.1 The family map

You might want to give directly to family members or a family trust during your lifetime and leave any charitable gifts to be made on your death, or vice versa. It is highly likely that one or more trusts would be required to help achieve your objectives. For many people, providing their children and grandchildren with a good education is an important priority, which is seen as a good 'investment'. In some cases parents and grandparents view funding school fees as a more practical and positive method of transferring wealth to the next generation than giving them money either during their lifetime or on death.

Funding a private education, however, is not an insignificant commitment and could well equate to more than £300,000 (about £250,000 in present-value terms) based on a cost of £5,000 per term. University fees and costs will add another £45,000 to that total cost. In addition, school fees inflation (see Figure 20.2) continues to be well above price inflation, with latest figures from the Independent Schools Council (ISC) showing this to be 3.9% in 2013.

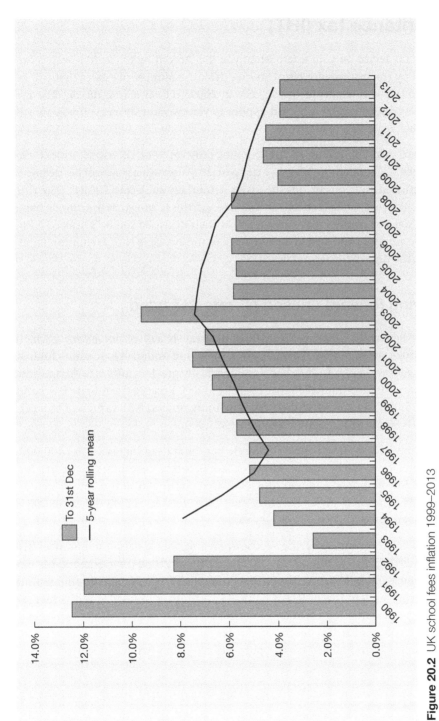

Figure 20.2 UK school fees inflation 1999–2013

Source: Independent Schools Council.

Inheritance tax (IHT)

IHT is a tax levied on your estate when you die. According to recent research carried out by the Institute for Fiscal Studies (IFS), the number of estates that will be liable to IHT will quadruple from 2.6% in 2009/10 to 10% in 2018/19.[2] The tax charge is currently a flat 40% and applies to your worldwide assets if you are UK domiciled, regardless of residence.

If you are non-UK domiciled, IHT applies only on your UK assets, unless you have been UK-resident in 17 out of the past 20 years, when you will be 'deemed' UK domiciled and your worldwide assets potentially subject to UK IHT. The first £325,000 of your estate is effectively tax-free and this is known as the nil-rate band (NRB). Married couples may carry forward their deceased spouse's unused NRB, with the amount expressed as a percentage of the available NRB exemption applicable at the time of the second death.

Carrying forward unused nil-rate IHT band

Andrew died in 2012, leaving £200,000 of his estate to a discretionary trust, which had a wide class of potential beneficiaries, including Andrew's four adult children and his widow, Sandy. Andrew had never made any previous gifts other than those that were classed as immediately exempt from IHT. Because the nil-rate IHT band was £325,000 when Andrew died, his remaining unused NRB expressed as a percentage is 38.5% ((£325,000 – £200,000)/£325,000).

Sandy dies in 2020 when the IHT nil-rate band has been increased to £400,000. Therefore, as well as her own NRB of £400,000, Sandy's executors may carry forward 38.5% of Andrew's unused NRB, but based on the NRB at the time of Sandy's death. Therefore, Sandy's executors may carry forward £154,000 (£400,000 × 38.5%) of unused NRB from Andrew's estate.

Any assets left to your surviving spouse or civil partner are also exempt from IHT as long as they are UK domiciled. If you are UK domiciled (or deemed to be) but your spouse or civil partner is non-UK domiciled, then the maximum amount you can leave them free of IHT is £325,000. A non-UK domiciled individual (or their legal personal representatives within two years of their death) who has a deceased UK-domiciled spouse/civil partner may make an irrevocable election to be treated as UK domiciled for IHT purposes only. This will retrospectively apply

---

[2]   Institute for Fiscal Studies (2014) 'Death to the death tax?' April, available at **www.ifs.org.uk/publications/7164**

to the previous seven years. This election will cease to apply if the surviving spouse making the election ceases to be UK tax resident for at least four successive tax years after the election.

Certain assets are exempt from IHT and these include holdings in unquoted trading businesses (including assets used by such a business), agricultural land and buildings and commercial woodland (but not the land). Gifts to political parties and registered charities are exempt from IHT, whether made in your lifetime or upon your death. In addition, where at least 10% of your taxable estate is left to a registered charity, the tax on the rest of your estate is reduced by 10% to 36%. This isn't sufficient to make your beneficiaries better off but it's useful if you intend to leave some of your wealth to charity.

As a general rule, you can give away any amount of your estate during your lifetime to individuals or bare/absolute trusts and as long as you derive no use or benefit from the gifted amount and survive for at least seven years afterwards, the gift will fall out of your estate for IHT purposes. This type of gift is known as a potentially exempt transfer (PET). However, there are ways of making gifts that are immediately exempt from IHT and that allow you to retain some benefit without offending these requirements.

If you do not survive a PET by seven years, then the PET will fail (known as a failed PET) and thereby be subject to IHT to the extent that it exceeds the available NRB at the time of death. Any tax due will benefit from a reduction (known as taper relief) on a sliding scale from 20% to 80% if death occurs after the first three years (see Table 20.1). Any gift made to a non-bare/absolute trust in the seven years prior to a failed PET will be taken into account in determining whether and if so to what extent the NRB is available.

Table 20.1 IHT taper relief reductions

Time between the date the gift was made and the date of death	Taper relief percentage applied to the tax due
3 to 4 years	20%
4 to 5 years	40%
5 to 6 years	60%
6 to 7 years	80%

Source: **HMRC.gov.uk**

Example

A failed PET

Andrea, who has never been married, died four years and two months after making a PET of £250,000. She had also made a gift of £250,000 to a discretionary trust seven years before her death. She had always used her annual and small gift exemptions separately and none of her assets or gifts was an exempt asset. Disregarding her remaining estate value, this is how the IHT position would be calculated:

Step 1 – PET was within seven years of death so fails with value of £250,000.

Step 2 – there was a chargeable lifetime transfer (CLT) of £250,000 within seven years of the original PET so this must be deducted from the NRB at the date of death.

Step 3 – the available NRB at date of death is therefore £75,000 (£325,000 – £250,000).

Step 4 – the failed PET is reduced by the remaining £75,000 unused NRB, leaving £175,000 taxable.

Step 5 – IHT on failed PET is £70,000 (£175,000 × 40%).

Step 6 – taper relief of 40% applies because the PET failed within years 4–5.

Step 7 – the IHT payable is £42,000, being 60% of the normal amount, after deducting the 40% taper relief.

Gifts to most types of trusts (other than bare/absolute trusts) are known as chargeable lifetime transfers (CLTs) and, as such, attract an immediate tax charge of 20% of the amount of the gift over the available NRB and the annual exemption(s). However, if the gift to the trust, together with any other gifts made to the same or other trusts in the past seven years, is equal to or less than the NRB (currently £325,000), no immediate charge to IHT is due. In addition, no immediate charge to IHT will arise if the gift to the trust is:

- of business or agricultural assets that qualify for 100% relief, or
- funded from regular gifts made out of surplus income, or
- paid from a pension trust that itself meets the IHT exemption rules.

As long as you derive no use or benefit from the gifted amount and survive for at least seven years afterwards, the gift will fall out of your estate for IHT purposes and no further IHT will be payable. All growth arising from the date of the gift will arise outside your estate. For this reason it makes sense to gift as much as you can up to the maximum of the NRB, whether to an individual(s) or to a trust every seven years if you can afford to do so.

Estate planning basics

Having a valid will is essential to help others deal with your affairs following your death. If you don't have a will in place when you die, you will die intestate. This means that your assets will be distributed in accordance with the rules of intestacy, which are set out in Figure 20.3. Depending on the amount of your wealth, the types of assets you own and the makeup of your family, dying intestate is unlikely to be recommended. For example, a spouse or civil partner is unlikely to inherit all your assets under the intestacy rules.

Although it is possible to effect a deed of variation to override the intestacy rules and vary the basis on which an estate is to be distributed, as it is with a will (more of which later), this relies on the various beneficiaries who are entitled to the inheritance all agreeing to the terms of any variation of intestacy. This is fine if everyone agrees but not if they don't. Also, if there are any minor beneficiaries involved, the variation has to be approved by the court, which is obviously expensive and uncertain.

Ideally, you need to have a will in any country in which you own real property as some countries like France have forced heirship rules that are different to the rules in the UK. If you need a will in more than one country, you should take legal advice to ensure that these are coordinated.

I do not recommend using a will-writing company to draw up your will unless your affairs are simple and modest. Many of the will-writing companies use non-legally qualified representatives to take instructions and see to the signing of documents. This can lead to mistakes and misunderstandings that can turn out to be costly and problematic further down the line. In addition, some will-writing companies have no or very modest professional negligence insurance cover.

There are a number of ways that you can increase the tax efficiency and flexibility of your will to deal with things such as business assets, second marriages, unequal gifts of property or other assets. A good lawyer is worth paying for and, as long as they have a clear grasp of what you own and the overall context of your wealth

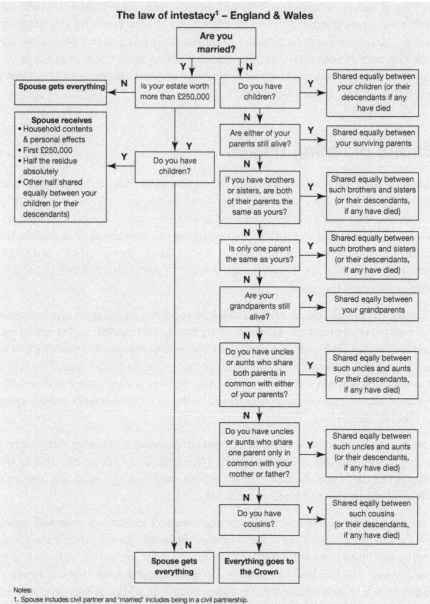

The law of intestacy[1] – England & Wales

Are you married?

- Y → Is your estate worth more than £250,000
  - N → **Spouse gets everything**
  - Y → Do you have children?
    - Y → **Spouse receives**
      - Household contents & personal effects
      - First £250,000
      - Half the residue absolutely
      - Other half shared equally between your children (or their descendants)
    - N → **Spouse gets everything**
- N → Do you have children?
  - Y → Shared equally between your children (or their descendants if any have died)
  - N → Are either of your parents still alive?
    - Y → Shared equally between your surviving parents
    - N → If you have brothers or sisters, are both of your parents the same as yours?
      - Y → Shared equally between such brothers and sisters (or their descendants, if any have died)
      - N → Is only one parent the same as yours?
        - Y → Shared equally between such brothers and sisters (or their descendants, if any have died)
        - N → Are your grandparents still alive?
          - Y → Shared eqally between your grandparents
          - N → Do you have uncles or aunts who share both parents in common with either of your parents?
            - Y → Shared eqally between such uncles and aunts (or their descendants, if any have died)
            - N → Do you have uncles or aunts who share one parent only in common with your mother or father?
              - Y → Shared eqally between such uncles and aunts (or their descendants, if any have died)
              - N → Do you have cousins?
                - Y → Shared eqally between such cousins (or their descendants, if any have died)
                - N → **Everything goes to the Crown**

Notes:
1. Spouse includes civil partner and 'married' includes being in a civil partnership.
2. Children includes adopted and illegitimate children, where intestate died after 2 April 1988, but excludes stepchildren.
3. Children receive their inheritance on reaching 18, or earlier marriage.
4. Descendants share equally the parts that the deceased parents would have taken.

[1]Created by the author based on the IHTM1211-(E &W): summary of the main rules of intestacy, **http://www.hmrc.gov.uk/manuals/ihtmanual/ihtm12111.htm** but incorporating changes arising from the Inheritance Tax and Trustees' Powers Bill (2014).

Figure 20.3 The law of intestacy – England and Wales

Source: Data sourced from 'IHTM12111–Intestacy (E&W): summary of the main rules of intestacy', available online at **www.hmrc.gov.uk/manuals/ihtmanual/ihtm12111.htm**

strategy and personal objectives, they can help to craft a more sophisticated will that reflects your wishes and is tax-efficient. The more wealth you have and the more complex your financial affairs, the more important and valuable this will be.

Deed of variation

Where property is inherited, whether under a will, under the intestacy rules or by survivorship (i.e. it is owned as joint tenants), it is possible to redirect the inheritance to achieve an immediate IHT saving by using a deed of variation.

Ordinarily the inherited assets will accumulate in the taxable estate of the receiving beneficiary, who may not want or need the inheritance. Instead of choosing to make a gift of the inheritance (which would be treated as either a potentially exempt transfer or a chargeable lifetime transfer), it is possible for someone to take advantage of the deed of variation option and achieve an immediate inheritance tax saving on their own estate.

In order to achieve the desired outcome, the variation must:

- be in writing
- contain a statement that the relevant legislation (s. 142 IHTA 1984) is intended to apply
- be made within two years of the death of the donor,[3] by the person(s) who would have benefited from the original gift.

In addition, the property must have been included in the deceased's estate at the date of death.

In practice, there is no requirement to vary the entire amount of the inheritance, which could enable the recipient to choose to vary only part of it. It is possible to vary an amount directly to an individual or to a trust. The option chosen will depend on the beneficiary's specific circumstances, of course, taking account of factors such as whether they are wealthy in their own right, whether they are likely to want to retain control and whether they may wish to benefit in future should the need arise.

A variation into a discretionary trust enables the original recipient to retain access by being named as a beneficiary. They can also maintain control by acting as one of the trustees. This is a viable planning option that does not fall foul of the gift with reservation provisions or pre-owned assets tax – the variation is effectively treated as having been made by the deceased for IHT purposes provided the necessary conditions are satisfied.

---

[3] Donor means the deceased individual who leaves assets.

Note that in cases where the variation is into trust and the original recipient of the legacy is included as a beneficiary, they will be taxable on any income arising within the trust (under what are known as the settlor-interested trust provisions).

Life and pension policies

If you have life policies or pension plans, you should ensure that these are written under an appropriate trust so that they do not form part of your estate for IHT and to enable the proceeds to be paid out quickly, side-stepping the process of probate on the rest of your estate. However, you need to be careful when putting existing policies into a trust in case they are deemed to have a value and, as such, could trigger an immediate tax charge. Most term policies with no cash in value will not cause a tax problem on transfer as long as you are in good health at the time. Some investment-based policies, particularly whole-of-life types, could have a significant value. However, any life policy could be deemed to have a value equal to the life assurance benefit if, at the time of transfer to trust, you are suffering from a terminal illness of which you were aware.

Mortgage protection policy held in trust

A debt is deductible from an individual's estate for IHT purposes only if it is repaid from the deceased's estate. Therefore, where a life policy has been taken out to repay a mortgage in the event of the borrower's death, but placed under trust for the benefit of relatives, those proceeds would not be available in the deceased's estate to repay the loan. In cases where there are no other funds available to repay the outstanding mortgage from the estate, HMRC may refuse to allow the mortgage to be deducted from the estate for IHT purposes. The solution to this problem is for the trustees of the life policy to lend the funds to the deceased's personal representatives, to meet the IHT liability that arises due to not being able to deduct the mortgage from the estate. This would mean that the estate passes to the beneficiaries encumbered with a new liability which would be IHT deductible in the future.

Although a trust will never fail because there is no trustee available to act, it is advisable to appoint at least two trustees other than yourself, so that there are no undue delays in distributing life policy proceeds to beneficiaries, if required. Your trustees should be people you trust to make good financial decisions and you should feel comfortable that they could deal with the trust's business.

Death-in-service benefits from occupational pension schemes and personal pension plans written under a 'master' trust-type arrangement usually pay out at the discretion of the scheme's trustees. However, you may complete a written nomination stating to whom you would like the trustees to consider paying out any lump sum death benefits. It is essential that you complete and keep up to date this nomination as it is the first thing that the trustees will refer to in the event of your death, although they will not be bound by it. Instead of nominating your spouse (or civil partner) or other beneficiaries as your preferred recipients, you might instead create and nominate a special trust known as a 'pilot' or 'bypass' trust to receive any death-in-service or pension plan death payment (see Figure 21.7 in Chapter 21). The benefit of doing this is that it enables the lump sum to be paid into the trust and avoids the capital falling into the estate of your chosen beneficiaries and thus avoids IHT being charged on that capital if any of your beneficiaries subsequently die. In addition, it will help avoid other potential creditors, including local authorities (care fees), ex-spouses or civil partners, or bankruptcy proceedings that may be experienced by your beneficiaries.

If, however, you have a personal or directors' pension plan from which you have taken taxable withdrawals and/or a tax-free lump sum, the payment of the remaining fund to a bypass trust would cause a 55% tax charge. This can be avoided if there is a spouse/civil partner and/or financial dependants to whom taxable income benefits can continue to be paid.

Digital and virtual assets

The growth in social media and cloud-based digital storage systems means that increasingly, people need to leave clear instructions as to what should happen to these 'digital assets' after their death. The Law Society recommends that, at the very least, an up-to-date list of online accounts, such as email, banking, investments and social networking sites, should be kept. Not only will this save executors time and money, it will make it easier for family members to recover important or sentimental material – such as photographs on social networks – that might otherwise be lost.

The growing trend for digital media also means that many people will have amassed valuable assets in the form of music and films, internet domains, YouTube videos and even computer game characters in online games. Without proper records, much of this can be lost on the owner's death.

While access to online accounts and other digital media could theoretically be provided by leaving details of passwords, access codes, etc. in a will, this is rarely a good idea. Not only does the will become a public document after death, this sort of information may change regularly, in which case successive codicils will be required to amend the will – leading to expense and inconvenience.

An online storage arrangement is potentially a good solution, but there are obvious risks with using this type of service as well. It may be that for the time being (or at least until the example set by Google – allowing users to specify which of their 'trusted contacts' can access their accounts after they die – is followed by other service providers), setting out express instructions in a Letter of Wishes will give the user the best chance of enabling their executors and loved ones to take the necessary steps to access and protect valuable digital content.

The licensing agreements attaching to some assets – such as iTunes and Kindle e-books – specify that the assets die with the original owner. However, as technology advances, wills may need to be reviewed to ensure that their provisions specifically cover the testator's digital estate. A general legacy of personal items may not be wide enough to cover assets that exist virtually only and specific 'digital asset' legacies may therefore need to be developed to cover this.

The box gives a quick checklist of the main planning points worth considering in your estate plan that will help minimise IHT and avoid other claims on your estate.

Checklist

- Use your current annual gift exemption of £3,000 (the previous year can also be used if you have not already done so).
- Make annual gifts of £250 capital to any number of beneficiaries (no one person can receive more than £250 unless this is part of the £3,000 annual exemption and you cannot add together these exemptions to give £3,250 to one person).
- Make gifts in consideration of marriage (£5,000 for your own children, £2,500 for grandchildren, £1,000 to anyone else) if relevant.
- Make regular gifts out of surplus income (see the following section) to individuals or, if the amounts are meaningful, a discretionary trust, as the gifts fall out of your estate immediately.
- Lend capital to individuals or a trust to 'freeze' the value for IHT purposes.
- Gift capital or assets up to the value of the nil-rate exemption band to a trust to freeze the value of assets, avoid future growth arising within your estate and remove the gifted value from your estate after seven years (currently the limit is £325,000 every seven years).

▶

- Invest in assets that qualify for business property relief or agricultural property relief (effective after two years of ownership) to avoid IHT on the value on death.

- Make gifts to charities or, if the amounts are significant and you have particular objectives, to your own charitable foundation to remove them from your estate immediately for IHT purposes.

- Effect a long-term insurance policy on your life in trust to pay out some or the entire IHT bill on your death (or the second of you to die if you are married or in a civil partnership).

Normal expenditure out of surplus income exemption

This is one of the most underused IHT exemptions but also one of the most effective and simplest to use. If you meet the conditions then the gifted amount falls out of your estate immediately and does not use up any of your nil-rate band. The conditions that must be satisfied are as follows:

- the gifted amount must form part of your usual expenditure

- it must be made out of income (whether or not it is taxable, but *not* income arising under a purchased life annuity)

- it must leave you with sufficient income to maintain your normal standard of living.

Using life insurance

If you have made a gift that is classed as a PET and might become taxable if you die within seven years of the gift, to the extent that it exceeds the available NRB on death, life insurance can provide the funds to enable the recipient of the gift (known as the donee) to meet the IHT that will become due. The NRB can also be used up for these purposes if you have made a gift to a trust (other than a bare trust) in the seven years prior to the PET. It is worth noting that responsibility to pay the tax due is in the following order:

1 donor (or their personal representatives)

2 donee

3 anyone in whom the property is now vested

4 any beneficiary of a trust who receives the asset in question.

If you still have a residual IHT liability and either can't or don't want to carry out other planning, and are in reasonable health, you (or your beneficiaries) could take out long-term life assurance for some or all of the tax liability to reduce the loss to your beneficiaries. The cost depends on your age, health and lifestyle factors. You should expect premiums to increase significantly once you reach age 75. The policy would need to be written under trust to avoid it forming part of your estate. Please refer to Chapter 13 for a fuller explanation of the role of life insurance in IHT planning.

Getting a bit more creative

There are numerous planning solutions that are usually (but not always) more complicated and costly than the standard planning referred to earlier. The benefits include quicker or higher IHT savings; being able to retain some use, enjoyment or benefit from the asset or capital; and/or greater flexibility in how and when wealth can be distributed to beneficiaries. The box shows a non-exhaustive list of some of the more widely used planning concepts, a number of which are explained in more detail in Chapters 21 and 22.

Some widely used planning concepts

- A discounted gift trust immediately removes a proportion of gifted capital from your estate while still allowing you to benefit from a preselected 'income' during your lifetime. As a general rule, the higher the amount of income and the lower your age, the greater the immediate discount.

- Use trusts to obtain IHT reductions on property, including your main home, second home and investment properties.

- Restructure businesses to maximise IHT exemptions, the main one of which is business property relief (BPR), which provides complete exemption from IHT once owned for two years.

- Loan capital on interest-free terms to a trust of which you are not a beneficiary in order to freeze the value of your capital for IHT purposes but allow yourself access to the capital through repayments of the loan on terms agreeable to you.

▶

- Do gifting in the right order to minimise IHT. The general order should be: 1) set up any lifetime pilot trusts (to receive pension death benefits, etc.); 2) make loans to individuals or trusts; 3) gift exempt assets; 4) make chargeable lifetime transfers; 5) make potentially exempt transfers.

- Gift assets to a special type of 'reversionary' trust that allows you to remove assets from your estate while still benefiting from some or all of the gifted capital by way of a future 'reversion' of the gifted asset.

- For mixed-domiciled marriages/civil partnerships, investigate how you can exploit the UK-domicile election rule to allow IHT exemption.

- If you are non-UK-domiciled and have not been a UK resident for more than 17 out of the past 20 years, consider putting non-UK assets in an excluded property trust before you become deemed UK domiciled, to avoid UK IHT on those assets subsequently applying.

- Via your will, pass a minority interest in a property to a trust that benefits unconnected beneficiaries, i.e. not your spouse or civil partner, so as to create a discount of the value of the surviving spouse or civil partner's retained share for IHT purposes.

- If you have a spouse or civil partner, create a nil-rate band trust on your death and have the trustees of your residual estate enter into a debt arrangement with the trustees of your NRB trust. With the passage of time during which your spouse or civil partner survives you, the debt has the effect of 'sucking' value out of their estate and placing it in the NRB trust.

- Borrow assets/capital from a trust interest-free and then gift those assets/capital to another trust so as to create a debt on your estate that reduces the value of your estate for IHT purposes, as long as you survive for seven years and the debt is actually repaid by your estate upon your death.

- Invest in assets, such as AIM shares, enterprise investment schemes and special inheritance tax investment services, which qualify for IHT exemption under BPR or agricultural property relief (APR) after two years.

- Leave any asset that qualifies for BPR/APR in a discretionary trust and have your surviving spouse/civil partner exchange an equivalent amount of their own assets for the BPR/APR assets so that they own IHT-exempt assets (after two years' ownership) and the trust owns the assets that would have been subject to IHT.

The key point to bear in mind about some creative planning, particularly that which involves the family home or other property, is that there is always a risk the tax authorities may change the rules to render the planning ineffective retrospectively. Over the past ten years alone we have seen a barrage of anti-avoidance rules that has removed any tax benefit from thousands of 'schemes'. In addition, new IHT planning 'schemes' are now included within the Disclosure of Tax Avoidance Scheme (DoTAS) rules that already apply to income and capital gains tax planning.

Ensuring that your financial affairs are well organised means that you will not leave a mess for your family to sort out if they have to deal with your financial affairs in the event of your death. Wealth succession planning can be as simple or complicated as you wish, but it must be viewed in the context of your own needs, values, resources and tax position. In any event, a decent private-client lawyer is essential to help you form a sensible wealth succession strategy that is in context with your financial needs and overall financial plan.

CHAPTER 21
USING TRUSTS

'Put not your trust in money, but put your money in trust.'

Oliver Wendell Holmes Sr, American physician,
poet, professor, lecturer and author

A trust is a set of obligations and duties, splitting legal ownership and economic benefits. A person, known as the settlor, transfers the ownership of their assets to another party – a trustee. The trustee holds the assets for the benefit of a person, group of people, charity or organisation – the beneficiaries – without giving them full access to the assets for the time being. Because children (those aged under 18) cannot own assets in their own name, these will always be held in trust until at least age 18.

As well as holding assets for children, trusts are used for a number of other reasons, including:

- reducing inheritance tax
- providing formal oversight and controls about how assets will be used
- providing flexibility to defer decisions about how assets will be distributed or otherwise to benefit different beneficiaries
- ensuring that assets are legally separated from one's personal assets, and thus potentially protected against unforeseen situations such as divorce or bankruptcy
- providing protection for vulnerable beneficiaries
- providing a means for managing assets for those unable to do so themselves.

A trust can be created either in your lifetime or through your will. Sometimes a trust can arise through your action, without any formal documentation. Changes in the tax treatment of trusts over recent years have seen a reduction in the types of new trust that may be worth establishing, although many of the other types remain in existence.

There are three parties involved in setting up a trust:

1   The **settlor** gives away an initial asset (e.g. cash, a property, an insurance or pension contract) and then transfers the ownership of the asset to one or more trustees.

2   The **trustee** is the legal owner of the assets who holds and manages them for the benefit of the beneficiaries according to the terms of the trust deed or trust law.

3   The **beneficiaries** are the individuals or groups of people selected by the settlor to receive the benefits of the trust.

A trust is typically a single-settlor trust or a joint-settlor trust with two settlors. The settlor can appoint individuals as trustees, a corporate trustee or a trust corporation (a company constituted to carry out trustee duties with several authorised directors). If the trust holds land, you will need to appoint at least two individual or corporate trustees or a single trust corporation. Individual trustees could be another family member, a close friend or someone else you trust to deal with financial and legal issues. The basic rule is that a trustee must be at least 18 years old and of sound mind. The named trustees must also accept the appointment for it to be valid. A settlor can, and almost always does, appoint themselves as a trustee and this gives them some control over the trust property during their lifetime.

The trust deed will set out the basis on which trustees can be changed and it is usual to give the power to change a trustee to the settlor in their lifetime. If the trust deed is silent on who has power to appoint and remove trustee, trust law provides for current trustees to appoint their own replacements. The trustees must also take minutes of a meeting regarding the change of trustee. The legal rules relating to appointing and retiring trustees are strict and must be followed carefully.

The two main types of trusts

The two main types of trusts that are most likely to be created today are a bare/absolute trust or a discretionary trust.

Bare/absolute trusts

This type of trust is the simplest and is used to hold assets on behalf of someone else where it is intended that the beneficiary has the definite right call for the asset. The trust is called a bare trust where the beneficiary is aged under 18 and is called an absolute trust where they are 18 and over. The asset will form part of the beneficiary's estate for IHT purposes and they have a legal right of ownership at age 18.

Gifts to a bare or absolute trust are treated as a potentially exempt transfer for IHT purposes, in the same way as gifts of assets to individuals. This means that no IHT is due at the time the gift is made to the trust and, as long as the person making the gift survives for seven complete years, the gift will fall out of account for IHT purposes. There is also no periodic (ten-yearly) charge on the trust's assets (see below). However, the assets subject to a bare or absolute trust will count as the beneficiary's for IHT purposes and will also be exposed to other potential 'hostile' creditors such as divorce and bankruptcy proceedings that might be brought against them in the future.

Income and gains arising from assets held in a bare trust are taxed as if they were the beneficiary's, subject to them having full use of their personal income and capital gains tax allowance. The tax rate paid will therefore depend on the beneficiary's other taxable income and capital gains. However, if the capital within the trust was provided by a parent (or joint parents), then while the child is aged under 18, any income arising from that capital over £100 per tax year (£200 if joint parents) would be taxed at the parent's (or parents' if jointly gifted) highest marginal income tax rate.

Where you are comfortable to make an outright gift to someone but they are under 18, you will have to own it (or have someone else own it) as a bare trustee. This can be as simple as opening a savings or investment account in your name with the child's initials to signify you are not the beneficial owner. In this case the arrangement will be governed by the Trustee Act 2000, which includes rules on investments and how the trust should be managed. Alternatively, you could have a formal trust deed drawn up to override the Trustee Act's default provision. As a general rule, for small amounts and simple assets such as a savings account or investment funds, a simple designation (initials) should be adequate. However, for more significant amounts, or in the case of land or other more complicated assets, a formal deed is likely to be desirable.

Clearly, the larger the amount, the greater the potential problem. If you have already made a gift to a discretionary trust up to the nil-rate band, which is currently £325,000, a bare trust is the only way that you can make a gift of non-IHT exempt assets without an immediate charge to IHT. One of the potential problems with a bare trust is that the beneficiary has an absolute right to the trust's assets at age 18; many people are uncomfortable at the thought of an 18 year old having access to capital without any restrictions.

One potential solution to this problem for larger amounts (£100,000 or more) is to invest in a special type of offshore insurance bond, which has specific policy conditions that govern when the policy may be encashed and the values available. So while the beneficiary would have the right to the capital at 18, in fact all they would have a right to is an offshore insurance bond/policy that has prescribed policy conditions. The conditions of the policy are set at the outset but can, for example, stipulate that the policy has no cash in value until, say, the beneficiary's 25th or 30th birthday. This enables you to combine the benefits of a PET and restrict access to the capital until the beneficiary is older. See Chapter 22 for a more detailed explanation of this solution.

A bare trust is usually preferable for people:

- who wish to make modest gifts
- who are happy for the child to have access to the cash at 18
- who require the investment strategy to be capital growth orientated and thus able to benefit from both the child's capital gains tax allowance and 18% flat rate on any excess gains within their basic-rate income tax band
- for whom the £100 rule on income will either be insignificant or does not apply as the donor is not the parent.

Discretionary trusts

This type of trust, also sometimes known as a flexible trust, allows the trustees to choose who can benefit from the trust, from a wide class of potential beneficiaries, including those yet to be born, such as future grandchildren, etc. As well as giving the trustees maximum flexibility over who can benefit, in what proportions and when, this type of trust offers the possibility of avoiding IHT both against the estate of the person making the gift (known as the **donor**) and the estate of beneficiaries (known as **donees**).

All discretionary trusts created after 5 April 2010 may continue in existence for up to 125 years. In addition to providing flexibility over who might receive outright distributions of trust capital and/or income, trustees of a discretionary trust might prefer to lend capital to beneficiaries, provided that the trust powers permit this.

Lending capital to beneficiaries can sometimes be a better way of protecting the family wealth from creditors such as bankruptcy or divorce proceedings being brought against a beneficiary because, being a loan, the capital is not assessed as part of the beneficiary's personal assets. Loans can also preserve beneficiaries' entitlements to means-tested state benefits, including long-term care fees, assuming that any loan were called in by the trustees. Any loan owed by beneficiaries to a trust is also deductible from each beneficiary's estate for IHT purposes, providing that it is actually repaid by the deceased's estate and was not used by the deceased to acquire exempt assets such as business or agricultural assets, thus potentially saving up to 40% in IHT.

Borrowing to buy exempt assets

If you take out a loan to buy agricultural property and/or shares in a trading company (which can include shares in AIM-listed companies and EIS), once they have been held for two years they should qualify for exemption from IHT under agricultural property relief or business property relief rules. Because the loan was used to buy the property or shares, it will not normally be deductible for IHT purposes in the event of your death and the relief will be restricted to the net amount of the agricultural or business asset.

Alternatively, if you gift your agricultural property or shares to your spouse during your lifetime, the loan used to fund the original purchase would be deductible from your estate for IHT purposes because you no longer own the acquired exempt asset upon your death; your spouse does. This planning is not aggressive as it is actually clearly set out in HMRC's tax manual.

It is worth pointing out that the main reasons to use borrowing to acquire exempt assets are if you do not have sufficient liquid capital available and/or you can obtain income tax relief at 40% or 45% on loan interest arising.

Tax charges on transfer to a discretionary trust

As explained in Chapter 20, the transfer of most assets to a discretionary trust will be treated as a chargeable lifetime transfer for IHT purposes. As long as there have been no other gifts to a discretionary trust in the previous seven years, the gift to this trust is within the NRB (currently £325,000) and any unused current and previous annual gift exemption (£3,000 per year), no immediate charge to IHT will arise. However, if the settlor dies within seven years of the date of the transfer to the trust, the gift will become chargeable and utilise some or the entire NRB applicable at the date of death, effectively pushing other assets into charge.

If the gift, when made to the trust, exceeds the available NRB, the excess will be subject to an immediate charge to IHT of currently 20% (i.e. half of the normal rate) if paid by the donee or 25% if paid by the donor. The available NRB will be the current NRB, less any other CLTs that have been made in the previous seven years. Whether or not the gift is subject to tax at the outset, after seven years, assuming no other gifts have been made, the gift will fall out of account for IHT purposes and the NRB will become available again to enable further lifetime gifts or a tax-free amount of the estate to pass free of IHT on death.

Certain assets, however, are *exempt* from IHT, such as qualifying business assets, qualifying agricultural property, commercial woodland and lump sum death benefits from registered UK or qualified non-UK pension schemes. If this is the case, no immediate charge to IHT can apply on the initial transfer value transferred to a trust. In the case of exempt assets gifted during lifetime, as long as the settlor survives for seven further years, the asset will fall out of their estate completely for IHT purposes, assuming that they can't benefit from the trust.

It is possible, however, for a settlor's spouse or civil partner to be a beneficiary of that same trust during the settlor's lifetime, but this will cause the income and capital gains arising within the trust to be taxed on the settlor during their lifetime. If the spouse or civil partner is entitled to benefit from the trust only after the settlor's death, i.e. as a widow or widower, income and gains arising will not be taxable against the settlor during their lifetime. Exempt assets can also be passed, free of IHT, to a trust via your will, whether that trust is an existing one or created within your will.

The discretionary trust periodic charge

If the value of the trust exceeds the available NRB at the time (currently a maximum of £325,000), on each ten-year anniversary of the trust or when capital is distributed out of the trust, the trustees may incur a tax charge of up to 6% of the value above the available NRB at the time. For example, if the trust fund were £100,000 above the NRB, £6,000 could be payable every ten years by the trustees. However, this needs to be weighed up against the 40% IHT charge that would otherwise have applied.

Each discretionary trust established or to which property/assets have been added on or before 6 June 2014* benefits from its own periodic charge allowance, as long as each trust was established on a different day and there were no prior gifts that used up some or all of the NRB. This can be very useful where trusts have been established, for example, to hold large life insurance policies or assets have been transferred to trusts that do not attract an immediate charge to IHT but that are subsequently sold and become chargeable assets. Any asset owned by the trust that is treated as exempt, such as a trading business, will also avoid the periodic charge.

Discretionary trusts created by a will, no matter what date they come into effect, are treated as being created on the same day (the date of death) and thus are subject to one NRB for all trusts created this way for the periodic charge every ten years. The exception to this rule is where the trust created via the will is specifically designated to receive only lump sum death benefits from a pension trust. In this situation the will trust is deemed to have been created on the date that the deceased joined the pension scheme. Therefore, for periodic charge purposes, the ten-year anniversary may be much sooner than ten years after death.

---

*Changes to taxation of discretionary trusts

In June 2014 HMRC issued a third and final consultation on proposals to reform the taxation of trusts, including the periodic tax charge. The main proposed new rule is that the NRB will be shared between all trusts that have been created by an individual after 6 April 2014. Each trust can be allocated a proportion of the NRB (known as the settlement nil-rate band (SNRB)), as long as the settlor elects this before the ten-year anniversary or when property exits the trust. Figure 21.1 illustrates how this might apply in practice.

It is anticipated that the new rules will come into effect in the 2015/16 tax year, backdated to 7 June 2014. In this case there would be no tax benefit in having multiple trusts, although trusts in place prior to 7 June 2014 will continue to be treated under the old rules.

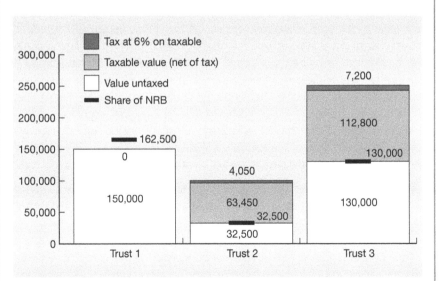

Figure 21.1 Trust periodic charge and the settlement nil-rate band

Prior lifetime gifts

If you make a gift to a non-bare trust in your lifetime, which counts as a CLT, but you subsequently die within seven years of that gift, the NRB will have been used up to the extent of that gift. Where you have established one or more pilot trusts in your lifetime on or before 6 June 2014, when each of these trusts reaches its ten-year anniversary, they will benefit only from the available NRB, which may be less than the full NRB amount, and this can lead to much higher ten-yearly tax charges than anticipated.

Example

Sheila is a widow who made a £325,000 lifetime gift to a discretionary trust (classed as a chargeable lifetime transfer), being the maximum amount she could gift without incurring an immediate tax charge. This was followed by further gifts of £10 to ten additional discretionary trusts, each created on different days but before the 7 June 2014 NRB anti-forestalling rule was announced in the trust taxation reform consultation. The large cash gift is within her NRB and the smaller initial gifts for each trust are within her annual gift exemption. In her will Sheila leaves her net residual estate equally to the ten pilot trusts.

Sadly Sheila dies three years later when her estate is worth £3.25 million (after IHT). Seven years after her death each of the pilot trusts reaches (on different days) its ten-year anniversary for periodic tax charge purposes. Regardless of whether or not Sheila survived the original £325,000 gift to the first trust ten years previously, each pilot trust would only have available, at the ten-year anniversary, an NRB to the extent that the NRB at that time exceeds the value of the original NRB at the time of the first, larger gift to trust. Thus, if the NRB remains at £325,000, then none of the pilot trusts would have a tax-free amount at the ten-year anniversary. Even if the NRB is increased by that time, the first £325,000 will always have been used by the lifetime gift made within the seven-year period prior to the establishment of the pilot trusts. Figure 21.2 illustrates this graphically.

Let's now assume that Sheila had created the ten small trusts with the initial £10 each on different days, *before* the trust with the large £325,000 gift to the discretionary trust. The trustees are permitted, as in the previous scenario, to deduct the available NRB from the trust's value, when working out whether any tax is due on the pilot trusts' assets at the ten-year anniversary. However, because Sheila did not survive the £325,000 gift to the first discretionary trust by seven years, each of the pilot trusts will not have any tax-free amount (£325,000– £325,000) to deduct from the trust fund for periodic charge purposes, unless the NRB has been increased by then.

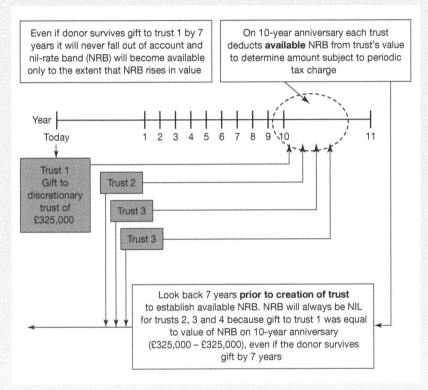

Figure 21.2 IHT position of pilot trusts created after CLT

However, if Sheila had survived at least seven years after the £325,000 gift to the first trust, the entire NRB would be available for each of the pilot trusts. If the value of each pilot trust at the ten-year anniversary was below the value of the NRB applicable, no tax would be due. This illustrates the importance of pre-7 June 2014 pilot trusts being created *before* any subsequent lifetime gifts to a trust, even if this is by just a few days. As long as you survive the lifetime gift to trust by at least seven years, each pilot trust will have the full NRB to deduct for the purposes of calculating the periodic tax charge. Figure 21.3 shows the IHT position of pilot trusts created before CLT.

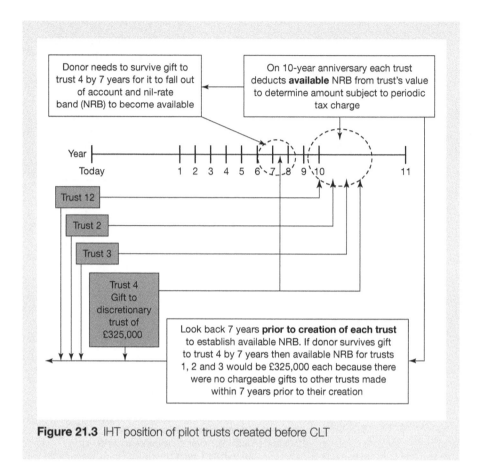

Figure 21.3 IHT position of pilot trusts created before CLT

Distributing capital before first 10-year anniversary

Tax is charged (the exit charge) on any capital distributed to beneficiaries based on a proportion of the rate that was paid at the last 10-year anniversary. Thus a distribution made 5 years since the last 10-year anniversary would be charged at half the 10-year rate.

Where capital passes out of the trust before the first 10-year anniversary, it is the creation value of the trust which is tested against the current NRB. Where the creation value was within the NRB, this means that distributions made before the first 10-year anniversary can be made tax-free.

Taxation of non-bare trust investments

Most trusts (i.e. not bare/absolute or old-style, life-interest trusts) are subject to what is known as the rate applicable to trusts (RAT) and, as such, pay income tax of 45% on income arising (37.5% on dividend income) in excess of the trust personal allowance of £1,000 and 28% on capital gains tax (CGT) above the CGT annual exemption (which is half the personal annual exemption divided by the number of trusts created by the same person to a maximum of five).

The taxation of discretionary trusts is a complicated subject and beyond the scope of this book, but as a general rule dividend income is best avoided where this is being accumulated by the trustees. Alternatively, income can be passed directly to basic-rate taxpaying beneficiaries, so that it avoids higher-rate tax, without the underlying capital forming part of the beneficiary's own estate for IHT purposes.

The trustees could also invest in capital growth assets, which are taxed at a much lower rate than income. Another solution could be to hold investments within an insurance bond 'wrapper', as this is treated as being non-income-producing and not subject to income tax unless or until the bond is completely encashed or more than 5% of the original investment per policy year is withdrawn (the amount is cumulative so after ten years, say, up to 50% of the original investment could be withdrawn without an immediate charge to income tax). An insurance bond makes most sense where most, or a significant amount, of the total return arises from interest and/or dividends and the trustees wish to accumulate all returns.

An insurance bond (or parts of it) can also be assigned to a beneficiary, who would then be taxed on the gain within the bond when it is finally encashed by them. If the beneficiary is a non- or basic-rate taxpayer, they will pay less than had the trustees encashed the bond.

A discretionary trust will probably be suitable for those who:

- have not made gifts to a discretionary trust in the previous seven years which, when aggregated with the proposed gift, would exceed the NRB (currently £325,000)
- want a wide range of possible beneficiaries but also want to avoid any children having automatic access to capital at age 18
- will adopt an investment strategy for the trust that avoids dividend income where income distributions to children are not envisaged.

Practical uses of trusts

There are several ways in which you might use a trust as part of your wealth plan.

Flexibility for lifetime gifts

Where you want to make gifts now but don't want to make a decision on who gets what and when until some time in the future, a discretionary trust is ideal. The trustees usually have wide powers to invest, distribute, lend assets or borrow funds, depending on the needs of the beneficiaries. Although the trustees (who will usually include yourself in your lifetime) have the discretion to decide how benefits are provided, you can provide them with a side letter setting out some guidelines that you would like them to take into account. Although such guidance doesn't bind the trustees, it can provide a useful reference point where trustees are faced with competing demands or difficult decisions. Making lifetime gifts to a discretionary trust is also useful if giving assets directly to your chosen beneficiaries would exacerbate their own IHT position or where there is a concern about the beneficiary getting divorced or becoming bankrupt.

No immediate IHT charge will apply on gifts to a trust that:

- are within the available NRB (currently £325,000) every seven years
- are within the annual gift exemption of currently £3,000 (plus £3,000 for the previous year if not used)
- meet the test for gifts out of surplus income
- are exempt assets such as unquoted business shares or agricultural property
- are a bare trust for a minor beneficiary
- are derived from the death benefits from a UK or qualifying non-UK pension scheme.

Using trusts to diminish the value of jointly owned assets

If a property is owned by two people who are not married to each other or in a civil partnership, then each person's share is, for IHT purposes, subject to a discount in value. The discount is typically between 10% and 15%. If you are married or in a civil partnership you can take advantage of the joint property discount by ensuring that you have appropriate provisions in your and your spouse's/partner's will to deal with the ownership of your or their share of the home depending on who dies first. Under this arrangement a small part of the share of the house belonging to the first spouse/civil partner to die is placed in trust for your children or grand-children. The rest of the deceased's share of the property is held in a life interest trust for the surviving spouse/civil partner. This has the effect of reducing the value, for IHT purposes, of the share that is owned (both personally and via the trust) by the surviving spouse/civil partner. The joint property discount is shown in Figure 21.4.

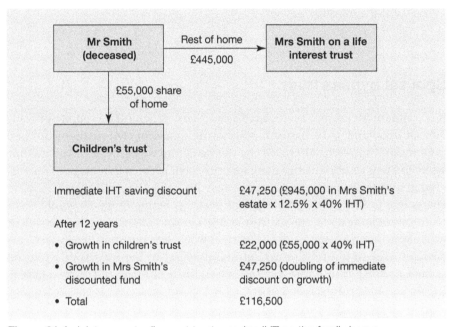

Immediate IHT saving discount	£47,250 (£945,000 in Mrs Smith's estate x 12.5% x 40% IHT)
After 12 years	
• Growth in children's trust	£22,000 (£55,000 x 40% IHT)
• Growth in Mrs Smith's discounted fund	£47,250 (doubling of immediate discount on growth)
• Total	£116,500

Figure 21.4 Joint property discount trust – saving IHT on the family home

Example

Andrew and Emily own a £1 million house in equal shares as tenants in common. Sadly, Andrew dies and his executors decide to transfer £55,000 of his £500,000 share to a trust for the benefit of his adult children. This uses up £55,000 of Andrew's NRB, with the balance (£270,000) available for Emily to carry forward to offset against her estate when she eventually dies. The balance of Andrew's share is passed to a life interest trust for Emily's benefit. Emily now owns £945,000 of the property by virtue of her own £500,000 share that she owned already and the £445,000 that is held in trust for her. Emily continues to be able to enjoy the use of all of the property and does not need to pay rent to the children for their share.

The immediate effect is that the value of Emily's share of the property will be reduced for IHT purposes on her subsequent death, to reflect the open market value of her share and the fact that a small element is owned by the children's trust. Using a discount factor of 12.5% on Emily's £945,000 share of the property, this represents an immediate IHT saving of £47,250. However, the potential savings are even higher depending on how long Emily lives and after, say, 12 years, this might increase to £116,500 based on the growth in the children's trust (£55,000 × 40%) and the growth in Emily's discounted fund (945,000 × 40%) in addition to the immediate savings.

Spousal bypass trust

It is common for exempt assets, such as business, agricultural property or commercial woodland, to be passed to a surviving spouse or civil partner who then disposes of it for cash. Alternatively, the executors will dispose of the exempt assets and pass cash to the surviving spouse or civil partner. In both cases the surviving spouse or civil partner ends up with cash that will potentially be chargeable to IHT on their subsequent death. A better approach would be to create one or more discretionary trust(s) either in your lifetime, or via your will, of which your surviving spouse or civil partner would be a potential beneficiary, and pass any exempt business or agricultural property to the trust(s) to avoid the exempt asset falling into your spouse's or civil partner's estate and thus avoid 40% IHT on his or her subsequent death.

In the case of a family business, agricultural property or commercial woodland that is to be retained after the death of the first spouse or civil partner, the surviving spouse or civil partner (or the trustees of any immediate post-death interest trust (IPDI) established by the first deceased spouse's will) could purchase the business or agricultural property from the trustees using their personal (or the IPDI) cash or assets, which ideally have no latent gains. This means that the surviving spouse/civil partner (or IPDI trustees) has swapped assets that would otherwise be subject to IHT on their eventual death, with business assets or agricultural property which will be IHT exempt once they have been held for two years. The bypass trust would then hold family assets that would be subject to IHT only at a maximum of 6% on the trust value to the extent that it exceeds the then applicable NRB (currently £325,000). Figure 21.5 illustrates graphically how this type of trust would operate in simplified form.

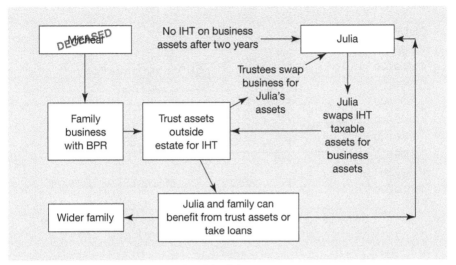

Figure 21.5 Spousal bypass trust (double dip)

Life insurance policies

Personally owned life policies should always be written under a suitable trust deed, to avoid the proceeds falling into your estate for IHT purposes and to speed up the distribution of assets. Assuming the life policy has no value or is a new policy at the time the trust is declared, there should be no immediate charge to IHT. Subsequent payment of premiums will be exempt from IHT as long as they are paid from 'surplus' income (and meet the conditions for expenditure out of surplus income) or are within the annual gift allowance of £3,000.

Where the life cover amount required is more than £325,000 (or whatever the IHT nil-rate exemption band is), and the intention is not to distribute policy proceeds immediately, the tax payable every ten years is currently a maximum of 6% on the amount in excess of the available nil-rate band. See Figure 21.6.

The pension bypass trust

As previously detailed in Chapter 20, a lump sum death benefit payment from a registered pension (and certain overseas pensions) is exempt from IHT. Depending on the type of trust under which the pension has been established, it can make sense to nominate a separate lifetime or will trust for any death lump sum payments, so that this can pass free of IHT and avoid falling into the estate of your surviving spouse or other family members. The trust should permit the trustees to make loans available to beneficiaries to further improve the IHT efficiency. See Figure 21.7.

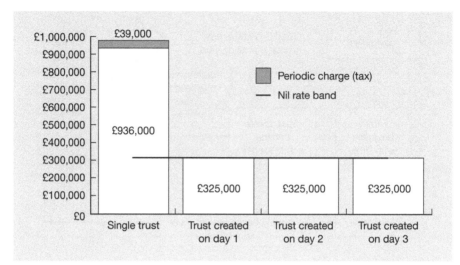

Figure 21.6 Life policy in trust and the periodic charge for settlements created on or before 6th June 2014

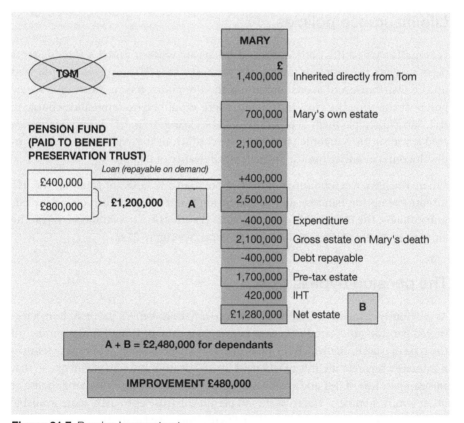

Figure 21.7 Pension bypass trust

The loan trust

As I briefly mentioned in Chapter 20, you could set up a trust (discretionary is usually best) for a nominal amount (say £10) and then loan capital, usually interest-free, to the trustees to invest as appropriate. Any future growth generated by the invested trust capital will arise outside your estate and also outside that of any of the beneficiaries if it is a discretionary trust. This allows you to freeze the value of the loaned capital, which remains in your estate, while retaining access to it by way of repayments on terms that you agree with the trustees. See Figure 21.8. The ten-year periodic tax charge is calculated on the value in excess of the available IHT NRB but after deducting any outstanding loan due to you.

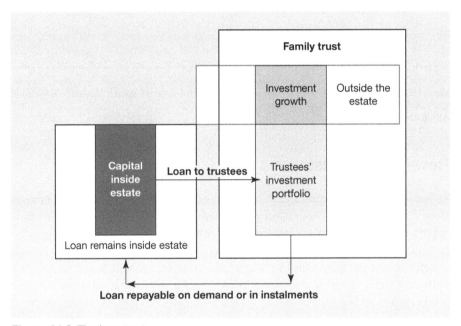

Figure 21.8 The loan trust

Discounted gift trust

A discounted gift trust allows you to give away capital that then qualifies for an immediate IHT saving, which would lead to the entire gift being outside your estate if you survive seven years. However, you have to agree a fixed amount of 'income' that the trust will pay you throughout your lifetime and it is not possible to vary or stop this amount. As such, it is important that you spend such 'income', otherwise the arrangement won't be as IHT-efficient as possible. The amount of immediate IHT saving, which is prescribed by HMRC and subject to medical underwriting by an insurance company, is obtained by applying a discount to the amount that is gifted to the trust. The discount will vary depending on your age and the amount of income taken, with the highest discount given to younger ages taking a high income. Table 21.1 sets out a range of discounts based on various levels of income and ages.

Table 21.1 Discounted gift factors

Age	% discount single	% discount joint lives
60	54.4	67
65	47.1	60.8
70	39.5	53.8
75	32.1	46.1
80	25.3	34.1

Note: The above figures are based on the basic discount. Slightly higher discounts may be available if the life assured is accepted on 'healthy' terms. In the case of joint lives, these factors assume both lives are the same age. Income is assumed to be 5% of the original investment.
Source: Sterling Assurance, May 2014.

Reversionary trust

Although the general rule is that you can't give away an asset and then benefit from it (the gift with reservation rule), there is a little-known exception[1] that applies to what is known as a 'reversionary trust'. This is achieved by creating a discretionary form of a reversionary trust from the gift[2] of the current value, death benefit or extension benefits of a single-premium, investment-based 'life' policy (although the underlying investment could be an investment fund if desired), but you benefit from the trust by way of regular maturities (reversions) of the policy.

The initial gift to the reversionary trust is treated as a CLT and as long as it is within the NRB (currently £325,000) there will be no immediate charge to IHT. The growth on the trust fund accrues outside your estate from day two and, as long as you live for seven years, the original gift will fall out of your estate for IHT purposes. The amount and frequency of 'reversions' must be selected at the outset

---

[1] 'In the case where ... the retention by the settlor (donor) of a reversionary interest under the trust is not considered to constitute a reservation' (see para. 7 of the Inland Revenue's letter to the Law Society dated 18 May 1987 at p. 518, in, *Tolley's Yellow Tax Handbook, 2013–14, Part 3*).

[2] This type of trust can be established only by a single settlor, not joint settlors.

and will if not spent fall back into your estate for IHT purposes. However – and this is the clever part – if you don't want to receive a reversion of the trust capital, you can disclaim this by advising the trustees before the reversion date and they will effectively defer it to a later date. The act of 'disclaiming' the reversion is not treated as a further gift and, as such, does not fall into your estate. Figure 21.9 illustrates how this arrangement works.

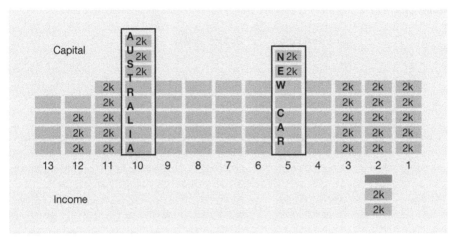

Figure 21.9 Reversionary trust and single-premium life policy
Source: Canada Life.

Combining a loan and reversionary trust

If you have substantial assets but want to make only a small commitment to estate planning initially, gradually protect your estate from IHT and preserve maximum flexibility for the rest of your life, you could consider combining a gift and loan trust and a reversionary trust. This involves first creating a trust (usually discretionary) with a modest gift, say £10, and then loaning capital to it. You can draw down the loan at any time and, as such, retain full access to that capital, although any growth arising occurs outside your estate immediately.

Shortly after creating the gift and loan trust, you then gift £325,000 (or whatever your available NRB is) to a reversionary interest trust and set this up to provide yearly optional 'income' by way of regular maturities. Any growth arises outside your estate immediately and, as long as you live for seven years, the gift will also fall out of your estate for IHT purposes. You then repeat this process every seven years, creating additional reversionary trusts equal to the NRB, while being able to benefit from the regular but optional 'income' reversions.

Table 21.2 illustrates how this would work with £1.5 million of capital where £1.2 million is lent to the first trust and £300,000 (i.e. below the current NRB) is gifted to the reversionary trust. If you are married or in a civil partnership, you could gift up to £650,000 to the reversionary trust if neither of you has made gifts to a discretionary trust in the previous seven years.

Table 21.2 Components of combined trust loan and gifts to reversionary trust

	Inside estate Assuming loan repayments are spent	**Outside estate**
At outset	£1.5m cash	Investment growth in Reversionary Trust plus investment growth on loan trust
7 years	£1.2m cash	£300,000 CLT to Reversionary Trust and investment growth plus growth on Loan Trust
14 years	£900,000 cash	£600,000 CLT to Reversionary Trust and investment growth plus growth on Loan Trust
21 years	£600,000 cash Loan fully paid	£900,000 CLT to Reversionary Trust and investment growth plus growth on Loan Trust
28 years	£300,00 cash	£1.2m CLT to Reversionary Trust and investment growth plus growth on Loan Trust

Source: Canada Life.

Everything should be outside the estate after 35 years while providing the individual with access to the £1.5 million during that period through a mixture of loan repayments and regular reversions of capital. Based on an assumed 6% p.a. investment return net of tax and charges, the amount held outside the estate would amount to nearly £8 million. Although each settlement would pay the periodic (ten-yearly) charge of 6% on the excess over the available NRB, this would still be much lower than the full 40% tax that would otherwise apply. See Figure 21.10.

Borrow and gift

Where you have a property or asset that could act as security, you could borrow capital against that asset and then gift it to an individual or a trust. As long as you, as the borrower, pay the interest arising on the loan (i.e. it is not rolled up), this is IHT-effective. This solution is particularly useful if you have an asset that is standing at a gain, as capital gains are washed out on death for CGT purposes, but the gifted monies will reduce your estate if you survive for seven years, providing that the original loan is actually repaid by your estate following your demise.

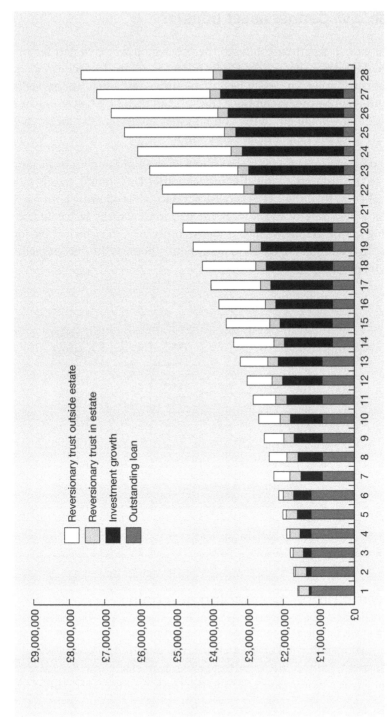

Figure 21.10 Projected value of combined £1.5 million loan and reversionary trust

Source: Canada Life.

Spouse/civil partner asset transfer

One spouse or civil partner could sell the other spouse or civil partner an asset (which could be their share of the family home) at full market value in return for an IOU of equal value. There will be no capital gains tax implications due to the CGT spouse/civil partner exemption. The IOU can then be gifted to one or more individuals and will fall out of the donor's estate after surviving for seven years. Figure 21.11 gives an example of how this works.

The only downside to this idea is that Stamp Duty Land Tax must be paid on the amount of the property sold to the other spouse. This should, in any case, be substantially less than the IHT otherwise payable, while allowing both parties to use or enjoy the property. In addition, the IOU must actually be repaid from the purchasing spouse's estate when they die, in order for it to be deductible for IHT purposes. This solution is useful where the family home is the only or main asset available for planning.

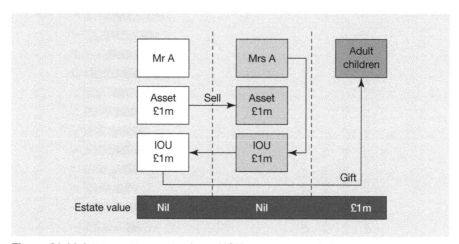

Figure 21.11 Inter-spouse asset sale and IOU
Source: Bloomsbury Wealth Management.

Investment property standing at a gain

Where you own an investment property that is standing at a gain but want to gift this to, say, your adult child or children, you can gift this to a special type of trust for their benefit, while at the same time making an election to defer the capital gains (known as a holdover election) to the trustees of the trust. This starts the seven-year IHT clock ticking and ensures that capital growth arises outside your estate, while ensuring that any future rental income is taxed against the beneficiaries. The trustees may, after a reasonable interval (at least four months is advisable), wish to transfer the property to the beneficiaries and at the same time defer (hold over) the latent capital gains to when the beneficiaries eventually dispose of the property. This would allow the trustees to hold over the gain to one or more beneficiaries, who can then dispose of the property at a time of their own choosing and potentially pay a lower rate of, or even no, capital gains tax. See Figure 21.12.

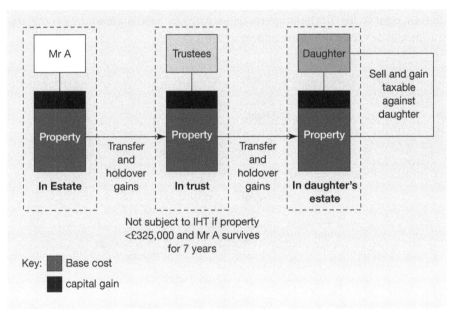

Figure 21.12 Gifting property standing at a gain
Source: Bloomsbury Wealth Management.

Gift and rent

With this idea you gift your home to your chosen beneficiaries and pay them a market rent for the right to live in the home. The rental income is taxable in the hands of the beneficiaries but the rental payments are immediately deductible from your estate for IHT purposes. It is vital to ensure that formal valuation advice is obtained, that the rental agreement is properly drawn up, that rental payments are physically paid to the new owner of the home and that the amount of the rent is periodically reviewed, otherwise it may not be IHT-effective.

Gift and buyback

A variation of the gift and rent solution involves you gifting your home to your chosen beneficiary and paying a market rent (see Figure 21.13). You may then offer to buy back a right to live in the property, rent-free, for the remainder of your lifetime. The value of the right to live in the home for the rest of your life rent-free is based on your life expectancy and the market rent applicable to the property.

The cost of buying the right to live in the home rent-free is immediately exempt for IHT purposes, as will be any subsequent increase in value. The value of the property gift will fall out of your estate after seven years. Although the value of the lifetime right to live in the property will remain in your estate for IHT purposes, this should be valued at nothing on your death.

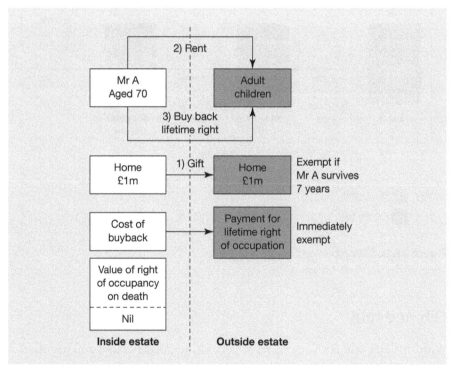

Figure 21.13 The gift and buyback home plan

Source: Bloomsbury Wealth Management.

Settlor interested trust

This idea works for gifts of cash or where an asset is standing at a loss of up to the available IHT NRB and where you need to retain access to rental or investment income from that asset. The gift is settled into a trust of which you are the life tenant, i.e. you have the right to income from it. However, you are prohibited under the terms of the trust from having any entitlement to capital, as this is reserved for your chosen beneficiaries.

The key benefit of this type of arrangement is to remove future capital growth from your estate from the outset and the original capital value if you survive seven years, a potential saving of up to £130,000 after seven years, while still allowing you to retain access to any ongoing income. See Figure 21.14.

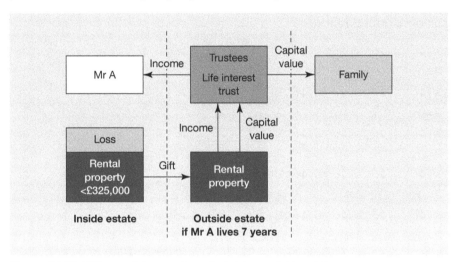

Figure 21.14 Gifting rental property and retaining rental income
Source: Bloomsbury Wealth Management.

Corporate trust

This idea works where there are shares in a company that do not (or may cease to) qualify for BPR (perhaps because it is an investment company) but it has significant value, whether or not there are unrealised capital gains on the shares. See Figure 21.15.

The company creates a special corporate trust with non-UK resident trustees. The shareholders then transfer some or all of their shares to the corporate trust. The corporate trust is intended to be a trust for the benefit of employees. The class of beneficiaries would be structured to exclude capital payments being made to the current shareholders of the company, in order to ensure that there is no IHT on the gifts to the corporate trust. Income payments would be permitted to ex-shareholders but will be subject to income tax in their hands.

The transfer of the shares to the corporate trust should avoid capital gains tax due to a special concession and the trust is treated as having acquired the shares at the original shareholder's base value, plus uprating for inflation. If the trustees of the corporate trust subsequently dispose of the shares and realise a capital gain, then no charge to CGT will arise, unless and until capital payments are made to UK-resident beneficiaries. If the beneficiaries can become non-UK tax resident, the gain can be avoided entirely.

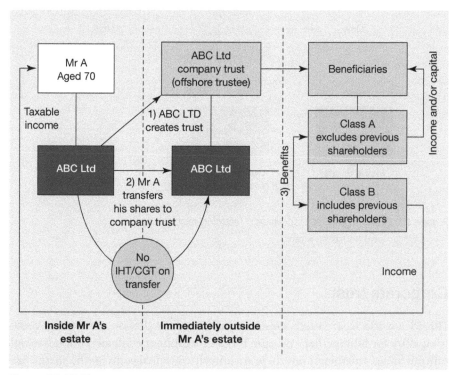

Figure 21.15 The corporate trust
Source: Bloomsbury Wealth Management.

Although 20% IHT would normally be charged on the gift of the shares to the trust, a special concession exists to exempt this charge when the gift is to a corporate trust. Although the tax rules on company trusts have changed recently, as long as it is correctly structured the transfer will immediately remove the shares from the original shareholder's estate for IHT purposes.

Wealth preservation trust

This solution allows you to obtain an immediate reduction in the value of your estate while retaining access to the capital without falling foul of the various anti-avoidance provisions that have been introduced over the years. It also avoids the 20% initial charge on gifts to trusts above the NRB (currently £325,000).

A trust is created by an unconnected person who is UK non-domiciled settling, say £1 million cash (see Figure 21.16). The trust has two interests, which are capable of being bought and sold. You then pay the trust £1 million to acquire both interests in it. The interests need to be acquired in a particular way to avoid falling foul of IHT anti-avoidance rules.

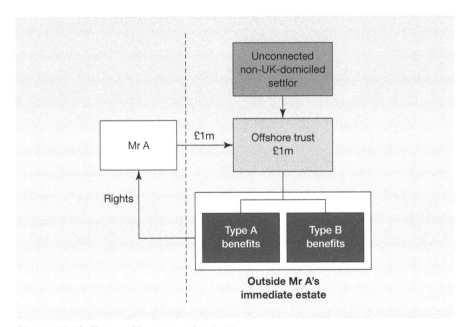

Figure 21.16 The wealth preservation trust
Source: Bloomsbury Wealth Management.

The trust does not form part of your estate for IHT purposes as you did not create it or settle the original value. The amount you paid for the trust interests is immediately removed from your estate for IHT purposes. If you require access to the trust funds, you can request a loan from the trustees at any time. This loan is also deductible from your estate for IHT purposes and repayable upon your death.

The capital in the trust is protected from unjustly being taken by various 'hostile' creditors and after your death the trustees can make a tax-free capital distribution to your chosen beneficiaries or another trust.

A word of caution. Using trusts to hold family wealth can help to avoid IHT and a range of other hostile creditors and also provide proper oversight of those assets so that they can be preserved within the family for their use. However, it is essential to make sure that you make decisions about the use of trusts within the context of your overall wealth plan. In addition, make sure that you have any trust correctly drafted, choose your trustees very carefully and check that they are aware of their responsibilities and duties. Finally, take personalised professional advice on the establishment, management and investment of trust assets. At the very least you need to ensure that the trustees know what they are doing and are well supported in the ongoing management and operation of the trust. That way, your family will reap the rewards of good planning without it becoming a drama.

CHAPTER 22
NON-TRUST STRUCTURES

'Each generation has a duty to commit to a contract between the past, the present and the future.'

Sir James Goldsmith, financier

There is a range of non-trust structures that might be used either in addition to or instead of a trust to hold and control wealth. In this chapter I explain the main non-trust structures,

Family investment companies

We looked at the use of a family investment company in Chapter 16 as a means of holding investments for the wider family and to obtain administration, cost and taxation benefits. However, an FIC also offers significant wealth succession and inheritance tax planning opportunities.

Capital structure

There is total flexibility in how the FIC can be structured in terms of the split of equity and loan capital. For example, you could subscribe a nominal £100 equity for 100 shares and have the main capital as an on-demand loan. If any of the FIC shares are to be gifted or not held jointly by a married couple, it will be necessary for you to receive a commercial rate of interest to avoid IHT issues.

As the shares would, in this scenario, be worth only £100 on day one, some or all of these can be gifted outright to other family members and/or transferred into a discretionary trust (or a number of discretionary trusts). This would enable the growth in the value of the shares to be captured by the other family members and/or the family trust(s) and therefore be outside your estate for IHT purposes. You could defer the decision on gifting any of the shares to a later date, but the longer you leave it, the more valuable the shares may become as the investment portfolio increases in value and any loan is repaid.

The benefit of funding the company with a significant loan is that you can receive loan repayments as you need them, without incurring tax that would otherwise arise on the payment of dividends or the disposal of shares to other shareholders or at wind-up of the company. It makes sense, therefore, to fund the company with a loan to the extent required by your likely lifestyle needs. Lifetime cashflow forecasting software, using reasonable planning assumptions, can be helpful in this regard.

Share structure

An FIC can have several classes of share, with different rights, which provides a number of interesting planning opportunities. For example, there could be A, B, C and D shares. While all shares would rank equally for the same treatment (*pari passu*) on the winding up of the company, only the A shares would have voting rights on all matters. In addition, the A shareholders would usually be directors of the company and so be able to control the investment and dividend-distribution strategy.

If all the voting shares are owned by the same person (for these purposes a married couple or civil partnership are considered one person), then for tax purposes their value is aggregated because the owner controls the voting rights. If, however, any of the non-voting rights were gifted to another family member and/or a trust, the A shares would be treated as being worth a premium to their actual cash value and the value of the gifted shares would be valued at less than their cash value due to the lack of voting rights. If, at a later date, the owners of the B, C or D shares received the A shares, perhaps via the A shareholder's will after their death, the B, C and D shareholders' shares would be subject to an immediate uplift in value due to acquiring the voting rights attaching to them.

Share valuation is a specialist area, but where the capital structure is relatively simple, the underlying asset of the company is a quoted, liquid investment portfolio and voting rights are concentrated in one class of shares owned by one shareholder, ascertaining a value should be less problematic. If some of the non-voting shares are gifted to a discretionary trust, this will trigger a chargeable lifetime transfer which means that HMRC would have to consider the values of all the share classes for inheritance tax. It would not have to do this if the gifts were made only to individuals and were potentially exempt transfers.

The FIC in action

It is perhaps easier to understand the key benefits of an FIC by looking at an example. What follows is just one example of how an FIC could be structured; there are numerous permutations possible.

Mike and Jackie are in their late 50s and they have £4 million of cash arising from the sale of a property, which they wish to invest in a diversified investment portfolio for the benefit of themselves and their wider family. Mike and Jackie both receive pension, rental and savings income, which utilises their personal allowances and basic-rate income tax bands. They have two children, Ben aged 32 and Matilda aged 29, who are both married with children, but they might have more in the future.

Mike and Jackie decide to create an FIC by subscribing £2 million of cash into four classes of share – A, B, C and D – of which only the A shares have voting rights, and appoint themselves as controlling directors. Mike and Jackie also make an on-demand loan to the FIC of £2 million and charge 4% p.a. interest (this being current market average for a mortgage). The exact allocation of capital is shown in Table 22.1.

Table 22.1 Capital structure of FIC

	Mike	Jackie	Totals
A shares	£100,000	£100,000	£200,000
B shares	£300,000	£300,000	£600,000
C shares	£300,000	£300,000	£600,000
D shares	£300,000	£300,000	£600,000
Total share capital	£1,000,000	£1,000,000	£2,000,000
Total loan capital	£1,000,000	£1,000,000	£2,000,000
Grand totals	**£2,000,000**	**£2,000,000**	**£4,000,000**

The FIC therefore holds £4 million of cash, which Mike and Jackie decide, as the controlling directors and sole shareholders, to invest in a diversified and fully liquid investment portfolio, of which 70% is allocated to equities and 30% to bonds via investment funds.

Mike and Jackie decide to retain the A shares but to gift the B shares to Ben, the C shares to Matilda and the D shares to a discretionary trust that includes Ben, Matilda and their current (and any future) grandchildren as potential beneficiaries. Mike and Jackie are also trustees of the trust.

The gifts of shares to Ben and Matilda will be treated as potentially exempt transfers and the gift to the discretionary trust treated as a chargeable lifetime transfer. On a practical note, the gift to the trust is made a day before the other gifts as this will minimise any inheritance tax that might become due if Mike and Jackie die before seven years have elapsed.

Value of gifts

Because the retention of the A shares means that Mike and Jackie can control the company, and therefore the value attributed to the other shares, the A shares will be deemed to have a value for IHT purposes that is more than the appropriate percentage of the company's net assets, i.e. the underlying portfolio. On the assumption (purely for illustrative purposes) that each of Mike's and Jackie's retained A shares would be worth, say, £225,000 rather than their respective £100,000 basic value, the total value of the other shares gifted for inheritance tax purposes would be £775,000, rather than their nominal value of £900,000 as set out in Figure 22.1.

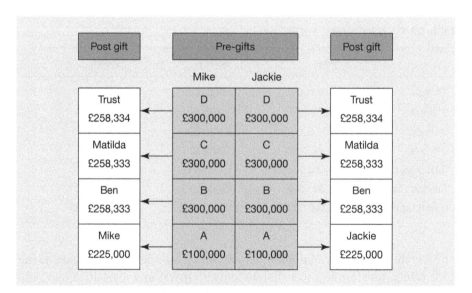

Figure 22.1 FIC shares – inheritence tax values

Extracting value

Mike and Jackie don't need to access their loan immediately, but the intention is to take ad hoc repayments to help meet their living costs in a few years' time when they stop their part-time consultancy business. In the meantime, Mike and Jackie receive annual interest on the loan of 4% (£40,000 p.a. each) on the basis that it is fully secured against the company's assets and repayable on demand. It would take 20 years for the loan to be repaid if repayments were taken at the rate of £100,000 per annum. As the loan reduces, so will the taxable interest that Mike and Jackie receive each year.

As controlling directors Mike and Jackie oversee the management of the company, including the investment strategy, in return for an annual pension contribution to their family self-invested pension (see Chapter 17 on family SIPP or SSAS) of £25,000. This avoids income tax and National Insurance and some or all of the contribution may be deductible for corporation tax purposes, while also avoiding IHT rules relating to reservation of benefit on gifts. Investment governance work, including the creation and updating of a formal investment policy statement (IPS) and the establishment and management of the investment portfolio, can be delegated to a wealth management firm. Figure 22.2 illustrates how Mike and Jackie and their family can take benefits from the FIC structure.

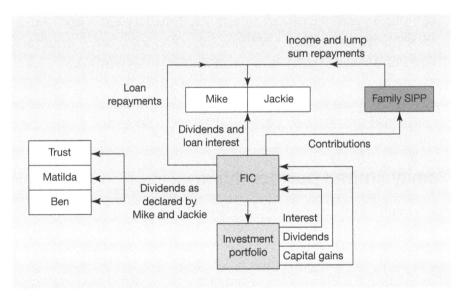

Figure 22.2 Extracting value from the FIC

The end result

By holding their investment portfolio via the FIC, Mike and Jackie have achieved the following estate planning outcomes:

- They retain access to the £2 million of capital loaned to the company and may take repayments as they need and investment conditions allow, without incurring personal taxation.
- They will receive reasonable taxable interest on the outstanding loan balance each year.
- They retain total control over the company, including the payment of any dividends.
- They could receive tax-free payments into their family SIPP.
- They have started the clock ticking on gifts worth circa £1.5 million and as long as they survive for seven years, these will fall out of account for IHT purposes.
- The value held by the discretionary trust and any future growth is sheltered from 'hostile creditors' and available for any of the wider family, including by granting loans.
- Although the value of the shares gifted to Ben and Matilda is lower than the face value, these would increase if Ben and Matilda received their parents' A shares upon Mike and Jackie's eventual demise. Although capital gains tax will be higher as a result, inheritance tax (which is charged at a higher rate than capital gains) should be lower as a result.
- They retain flexibility to invest in other asset classes in the future.

The use of FICs is a complex area and most suited to large-value estates that have already made maximum use of discretionary trusts. Expert advice should be sought from a legal and tax adviser who is familiar with this area.

Family limited partnerships

Family limited partnerships (FLPs) have been around in various forms for many years but have become more popular since the changes to trust rules in 2006. FLPs offer a structure that enables a family to bring together assets under common management, oversight and control of, say, the parents, but to obtain IHT and other benefits. An FLP is owned by its members, with designated members responsible for the governance and compliance matters. Usually the designated or controlling member will be either a general partner or a limited company.

Operation of the FLP is governed by the FLP agreement, which states how revenue profits/losses and capital gains/losses are to be treated. Because an FLP is transparent for tax purposes, income profits/losses and capital gains/losses arising each trading period will be taxed on each individual member, in proportion to their share as agreed in the FLP agreement. It is possible to vary how they will be allocated to different members from year to year. Capital contributions and capital profits can be the same as or different from each member's income profits.

An FLP can be useful where there are assets, such as property, that have unrealised capital gains and are to be introduced as a member's capital contribution, where profits need to be attributed differently to each member from year to year. In this respect an FLP is potentially more flexible than an FIC. However, if the FLP is a UK-constituted entity that establishes an investment portfolio, it will potentially be classed as an unregulated collective investment scheme and as such the FLP would need to be authorised and regulated by the UK Financial Conduct Authority. There are two ways to avoid the regulatory burden and expense associated with this obligation. First, the FLP could be established outside the UK, e.g. Jersey, or, second, the management of the investment portfolio could be delegated to a suitably authorised and regulated investment manager.

The use of FLPs is a complex area and most suited to large-value estates that have already made maximum use of discretionary trusts. Expert advice should be sought from a legal and tax adviser who is familiar with this area.

Inheritance tax portfolio services

Business property relief is a tax relief provided by the UK government as an incentive for investing in specific types of trading companies. It was introduced by the government in 1976 and has since been extended to investments in certain types of unquoted companies to encourage investment into this area.

Once assets qualifying for BPR (this also applies to the assets that qualify for agricultural property relief) have been held for two years, they are exempt from IHT (provided that they are still held at the time of death). In the event of your death within two years, BPR assets would be subject to IHT.

However, if the asset is transferred to your spouse or civil partner upon death, it would be treated as if they had held it from outset and they would need to survive for only the remainder of that two-year period for it to be exempt from IHT (i.e. the first death does not restart the two-year clock – see Figure 22.3). In this situation your spouse or civil partner would still retain full control and access to the capital.

It is possible to obtain immediate IHT exemption from investment into a BPR-qualifying asset if the amount invested is equal to, or less than, the proceeds of an asset (possibly a family business) that previously qualified for BPR and that was disposed of within the past three years.

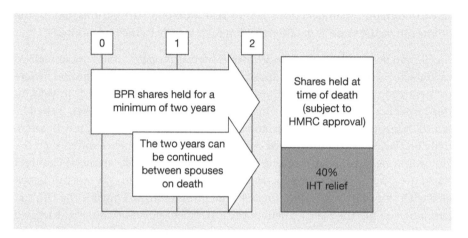

Figure 22.3 Inheritance tax relief in two years
Source: Bloomsbury Wealth Management.

A key benefit of holding an asset that qualifies for BPR is that it allows you to retain control of and access to it, meaning that you have flexibility should your circumstances change. The challenge is finding a BPR-qualifying asset that provides sufficient liquidity, capital security and investment return to make it attractive. There is clearly no benefit in saving 40% IHT if you've lost 50% of the value of your investment.

If you are at the stage in your life where investing into a new business is not appealing or you have neither the time nor the inclination to find a suitable BPR-qualifying business investment, there are well-tested solutions that can offer the benefits of BPR, while limiting the possible downsides.

The new breed of BPR investment

Over the past decade a number of investment solutions have been developed that give access to unquoted companies that qualify for BPR but that address the downsides of illiquidity and potential loss of capital usually associated with such investments. What follows is a description of how a typical (market-leading) BPR investment solution works.

You invest your money into an unquoted company, which deploys its money into a number of BPR-qualifying trades, which are managed and controlled by the BPR scheme provider's staff on behalf of you and the other investors. The only shareholders in these companies are the BPR scheme investors and their shareholdings are the only source of capital. The BPR scheme provider is, therefore, able to run these companies in a way that is best aligned with the interests of its investors. In particular, it can ensure that the companies only enter into transactions where it is able to mitigate the risks and maintain BPR treatment.

The types of trades in which the underlying companies engage are very carefully selected on the basis that they:

- are highly cash-generative and capital invested is continually returned to the wholly owned trading companies
- have minimum risk of capital loss due to trading activity and risk mitigation undertaken
- meet the qualifying criteria for BPR treatment
- can be closely monitored by the BPR provider.

See Figure 22.4.

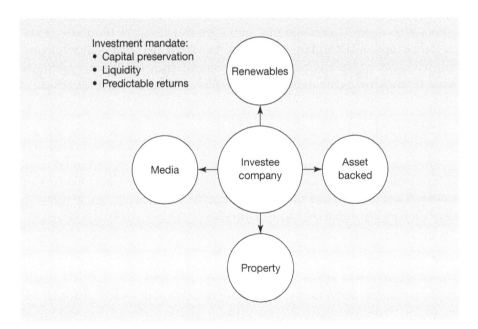

Figure 22.4 Business property relief qualifying investments
Source: Octopus Investments.

Underlying investments

Examples of typical investee companies' trades are as follows.

Property developer bridging finance

Typically, a developer needs to raise a loan against one property to enable them to fund development activity on another property. Traditional banks have become reluctant to lend, so this presents an opportunity for the BPR business to provide bridging finance, at a very good margin, secured by a first charge on the property. Usually the borrower will refinance the loan after 6–9 months, thus ensuring that the company is continually turning over cash. If the borrower does not repay the loan at the agreed time, the lender can sell the property. Since loans are usually less than 60% of the property value, anything short of a large fall in value or depressed sale value will not impede the ability to be repaid. The borrower will not want to lose their equity, so they are heavily incentivised to avoid foreclosure.

New car financing

Typically, finance of a new car is based on 100% of the purchase price, less a small deposit. However, a much lower-risk way of providing vehicles funding is to finance only the trade-in value of a new car, together with extremely strict underwriting of borrowers. This means that, in the event of default by the borrower, the car can be repossessed and sold at auction to recover the outstanding amount. With a low default rate and high asset cover on each loan, this is a very profitable business, which has been through three recessions and three stock market crashes.

Media

Providing financing of film and television production can be low risk when it is secured against pre-sold exploitation rights and/or government-backed tax credits, on a project-by-project basis. The typical media financing transaction lasts for between 6 and 18 months, although sometimes it can be longer, and this helps to maintain liquidity within the trading portfolio.

Solar energy

Financing commercial solar energy installations, which are underpinned by long-term government subsidies, provides strong cashflow at quite low risk, with the equipment protected against damage through insurance. Sometimes additional security is taken by way of a legal charge against the land or property on which the solar equipment is installed.

Expected return

Each of the underlying trades is highly profitable and generates continual cash-flow. The BPR investment provider manages the trades and cashflow with the aim of preserving the value of investors' capital (in nominal terms) and providing a return of 3% per annum compound (equivalent to 5% per annum for a 40% rate taxpayer) on the amount invested (after deducting initial and ongoing charges).

Although the underlying trades generate significantly more return than 3% p.a. compound, your return is unlikely to exceed 3% p.a. as the excess represents the BPR investment provider's margin (after costs borne in running the underlying company's business and paying corporation tax). Not benefiting from this excess return is the price that investors have to pay for the BPR provider's oversight, minimising of downside loss and obtaining BPR treatment on the holding.

Some of the BPR investment providers are so confident that they can preserve investors' capital and achieve, say, 3% annual growth that they choose to defer the payment of their annual management charges and will take them only at the time investors exit the BPR investment (or transfer the holding to a trust) and then only if the targeted annual return has been achieved after the deduction of the management fee. The company valuation is determined by reference to the principal amount invested plus whatever the target return is (typically 3% p.a.) compound, with ongoing oversight and advice from a major accountancy firm.

Access and liquidity

Although the BPR investment should not be operated like a bank account, investors can access their investment at any time. The minimum amount for a capital withdrawal is £1,000 and in the normal course of events withdrawals will be paid within a week or so, although under certain circumstances withdrawals may take up to 12 weeks. Because the leading BPR investment providers take in more cash from new investors than they pay out to exiting investors, withdrawals are facilitated by the provider transferring redeeming investors' shares to new investors (see Figure 22.5).

If there were more sellers than buyers (which has not happened to date with the largest providers), the BPR company would buy back shares using retained cash. In the event of major legislative changes, such as the removal of BPR by the government and where liquidity within the company is insufficient to facilitate a share buyback, the process could take much longer. For example, if every investor wanted their money back at once, most BPR investment providers estimate that about 50% could be provided within 6–12 months and the balance within 24 months.

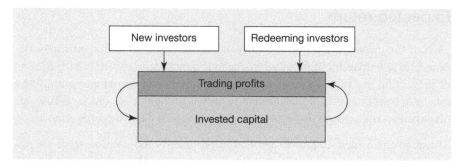

Figure 22.5 Managing liquidity
Source: Bloomsbury Wealth Management.

Taxation

Growth on the investment would be taxed only when investors withdraw money from the scheme. The investment return will normally be taxed as a capital gain when the redemption is a sale of shares to other investors (handled by the BPR company), but it will be subject to income tax (like a dividend) if, in order to achieve that withdrawal, the BPR company itself has to purchase the outgoing investor's shares. It is only the growth that is taxed in either circumstance, not the amount withdrawn.

Individuals are entitled to an annual CGT exemption limit (£11,000 for the 2014/15 tax year). If they are not utilising their annual CGT exemption and the 'gain' on any withdrawal falls within this limit, there is no requirement to declare this or complete a tax return. If the amount of the 'gain' is greater than this annual exemption, CGT is payable on the excess at up to 28%. In the event of the investor's death, there should be no liability to CGT on their investment.

A BPR investment solution is not a panacea and is unlikely to suit all individuals. However, if IHT is a concern (you have more years behind you than in front of you), you want to avoid the expense and complications of trusts and retaining control and access is important, it can be a useful planning tool as part of your overall wealth plan.

However, there are circumstances where it is not possible to obtain BPR. This might be because either you don't have BPR-qualifying assets or don't want to invest in the available BPR-qualifying investment arrangements. It may be the case that, whether or not you are prepared to invest in a BPR-qualifying investment, you might not be confident that you will survive the necessary two years for it to be exempt from IHT. This is where the next solution might be useful.

The discounted value arrangement

Until a few years ago there were a number of so-called 'death bed' planning arrangements which used a specially modified excluded property trust to remove value from an individual's estate immediately. Such planning was popular with people who were in very poor health and who wanted to avoid 40% of their estate disappearing in IHT upon their eventual demise.

Immediate IHT reduction

Help is at hand, however, for those with a short life expectancy but who want to secure an immediate and sizeable reduction in their IHT exposure while also retaining some access to their capital. A discounted value arrangement (DVA) is an offshore investment bond which has special policy conditions that have the effect of immediately reducing its value for IHT purposes. No trusts or other complicated legal structures are involved and the investor does not need medical assessment.

An individual invests cash into a special offshore bond, of which they are deemed to be the legal owner. As well as the investor being the life assured, they appoint several other younger individuals from their family (although it could be anyone) as lives assured. The younger these people are, the better the planning (more of which later).

The policy conditions are such that the bond has no surrender value during the original policyholder's lifetime, but they retain the right to take an annual withdrawal of up to 10% of the original investment, with any unused withdrawals being available to carry forward to future years. On the death of the original policyholder, the policy does not at this stage come to an end due to the existence of the other lives assured. However, the annual withdrawal right reduces to either 1%, 2% or 3% per annum and the surrender value remains suppressed.

The ownership of the bond passes according to the terms of the deceased owner's will or codicil. For probate and IHT purposes the value of the policy, which will depend on the underlying investment, is subject to a substantial discount to reflect the fact that the only benefit is the limited annual withdrawal facility that the bond provides as a right until the death of the youngest life assured. The amount of discount applied to the policy upon the death of the original owner depends on the age of the youngest life assured and typically varies between 40% and 65%, as set out in Table 22.2.

Table 22.2 Example discounts to policy value on original owner's death based on age of youngest living life assured with a 1% withdrawal right

Age	Discount	Age	Discount
16	64.9%	40	56.1%
25	62.2%	45	51.4%
30	60.3%	50	47%
35	58.3%	55	41.9%

Source: Watson Wyatt.

Encashing the policy

Although the policy terms would not provide a surrender value to the subsequent new owners of the bond, there is nothing to stop them approaching the insurance company at some stage in the future, possibly a few years after the death of the original owner, and requesting a non-contractual encashment of the policy. While each case will be assessed on its own merits, the standard operating position of the insurance company is to consider requests to surrender on a case-by-case basis where the contract does not include a surrender option.

This type of policy has been around for several years and all policies that have been subject to probate have successfully obtained the types of discounts suggested earlier. An additional benefit is that the disclosure of tax avoidance schemes (DoTAS) rules that have recently been extended to IHT planning arrangements do not extend to this policy because it was available prior to the introduction of the DoTAS IHT rules.

There are a few important points about this planning that need to be considered:

- The investor must not alter their will to make specific mention of the DVA at the time at which they invest.
- The insurance company is under no obligation to offer an early surrender value after the original owner's death.
- This type of planning should be considered only once all other conventional planning has been considered.

Example

Take the example of Glenda, who is 85, in declining health but still mentally capable. As well as her house worth £650,000 she has about £1 million of capital in savings accounts, ISAs and funds (with minimal capital gains). Glenda wants to stay in her home but needs to fund care fees, living costs and property upkeep. In addition to her annual pension income of £30,000, she therefore needs at least £30,000 per annum from her capital. Glenda wants to hold all her capital on deposit and is not keen on investing in 'business schemes' or complicated trusts, but she is keen to minimise IHT on her eventual death.

Glenda decides, with the help of her daughter, Carrie (55), and son, Michael (52), to invest all her available liquid capital in a discounted value arrangement. As well as herself, Carrie and Michael, she includes her grandchildren, Luke (24), Maddy (21) and Ben (16), as lives assured on the policy. She invests the bond into a range of cash deposits that yields about 2% gross and no income tax is due on this interest as it rolls up tax-deferred within the bond. Glenda has an immediate option to withdraw up to £100,000 per annum from the bond, of which £50,000 will be tax-deferred. She decides to take just £30,000 per annum in arrears, which means that each year she can carry forward £70,000 to withdraw in a future year, of which £20,000 will be tax-deferred.

Glenda's death about a year later occurs before she has taken her first annual withdrawal. At this stage the bond is worth £1 million after accounting for gross interest earned and policy charges. The bond, however, is valued for probate purposes at £350,200 due to the application of a 64.8% reduction factor based on the fact that the youngest life assured is Ben, who is 17 by then. Glenda's executors claim a carry forward of her deceased husband's nil-rate band and when aggregated with her own NRB the only taxable value left in her estate is the discounted bond value of £350,200. The IHT payable is therefore £140,080 rather than the £400,000 that would have applied had she done nothing – a saving of £260,000.

This type of policy is useful where BPR assets are not desired or not appropriate, or there is some doubt that the investor would survive the necessary two years for the BPR IHT exemption to apply. It does, however, need to be carefully considered in the light of the individual's and their wider family's views, needs and circumstances. In this regard the help and assistance of a caring, diligent and knowledgeable wealth planner familiar with such structures is essential.

The A&M plan

Up to the 2006 Budget, accumulation and maintenance (A&M) trusts offered a very effective way of giving capital to younger generations of the family, without either the underlying beneficiaries having an automatic right to the capital at age 18 or the capital in the trust forming part of their estates for inheritance tax purposes.

Typically, income and capital would be advanced to fund school fees and help with other expenses, such as gap-year trips. While the income and gains arising on the A&M trust were subject to 40% income and capital gains tax, if income were distributed to a beneficiary paying no or basic-rate tax, the beneficiary could reclaim all or some of the tax paid by the trustees. At least one beneficiary needed to have a right to trust income by the time they were 25.

Another useful feature was that the gift to an A&M trust was treated as a potentially exempt transfer for inheritance tax purposes. As such, there was no immediate charge to inheritance tax at the time the gift was made and after seven years the gift was outside of the donor's estate. In the meantime, growth arising on the trust assets arose outside the donor's estate.

Since 2006 new gifts to A&M settlements have been treated in the same way as those to discretionary trusts and are subject to an immediate charge of 20% if the gift, including gifts made to discretionary trusts within the previous seven years, exceeds the NRB (currently £325,000).

As we saw in Chapter 21, individuals who wish to gift assets to minor children now have the choice of gifting to a bare trust or to a discretionary trust. While for many these trusts will be perfectly acceptable, for some people they will not, for a variety of reasons including not wanting the beneficiary to have outright access to the capital at 18 or because they have already made the maximum gift into a discretionary trust within the last seven years.

An alternative approach

However, there is a way of making a gift to minor or adult children which:

- is treated as a potentially exempt transfer and thus avoids an immediate tax charge
- avoids the £100 income tax rule on parents who gift capital to their children via a bare trust
- provides virtually tax-free roll-up of income and gains

- provides access to some of the gift to fund education and other maintenance costs as required
- does not allow the child access to the capital automatically at age 18 but instead at a later age specified by the person making the gift.

Enter the accumulation and maintenance plan (see Figure 22.6). The basic concept is that the person making the gift invests in an offshore investment bond with multiple lives assured, ideally including the young person for whom the capital is intended. This should avoid the bond becoming subject to tax on the gain on the death of the person making the gift. The bond is then assigned to one or more people (this could include the person making the gift), who own the bond as bare trustee/s for the minor child. This is treated as a potentially exempt transfer and leaves the NRB untouched in lifetime. As long as the donor survives for at least seven years, the gift will fall out of their estate.

The child will become absolutely entitled to the policy at age 18, as is the case with any gift to a bare trust. However, the bond has special policy provisions that are specified at outset and have the effect of suppressing the surrender value of the bond until a certain date of the donor's choosing. This could be when the recipient is, say, 25, or any other age the person gifting the money deems appropriate.

All income and gains arising in the bond roll-up are virtually tax-free (depending on the assets held) until 'chargeable event' occurs (see Chapter 15 – single-premium bonds). Such an event arises when the bond is totally encashed, a withdrawal is made of more than 5% per annum (cumulative) of the original capital, the death of all the lives assured on the bond or assignment of the bond for money's worth. Currently, gains are taxed at the owner's highest marginal rate, i.e. up to 45%, with no allowance for non-reclaimable withholding taxes. In certain cases it might be possible to time the chargeable event to arise when the beneficiary is either UK non-resident or pays only basic-rate income tax.

As the bond technically comprises lots of smaller segments, it is possible to time encashments over a number of years to minimise or defer tax. This type of arrangement works best for higher-rate taxpaying parents who wish to make substantial gifts to minor children who have a fair chance of becoming UK non-resident or basic-rate taxpayers when the relevant policy acquires an encashment value (top slicing relief may prove useful too, as may time apportionment relief for any periods of ownership while UK non-resident).

In the intervening period between the date the policy is gifted and the date that the full value of the bond becomes available, it is possible to specify that the policy can provide regular withdrawals to meet expenses such as education and other maintenance payments. As long as these are within the 5% annual allowance

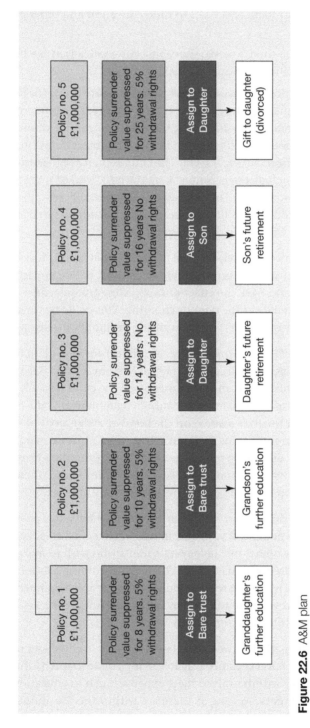

Figure 22.6 A&M plan

Source: Lombard International.

(with unused amounts from one year able to be carried forward to use in future years), no immediate tax charge will arise.

The flexible legacy plan

The A&M plan is taken a step further with the incorporation of additional policy features that make it even more flexible and potentially more tax-effective. These features include:

- the right to create an entitlement to part or total surrenders and to switch off or amend the entitlement after its creation
- a similar provision in respect of assignment of some or all of the policy for value.

These policy features are then assigned by the investor to the trustees of a discretionary trust, together with the right to appoint a discretionary investment manager. The investor who creates this trust is precluded from future benefit.

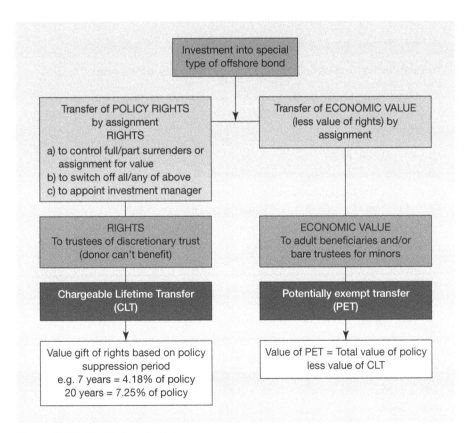

Figure 22.7 Flexible legacy plan
Source: Bloomsbury Wealth Management.

Once these policy features/rights have been assigned to the trust, the policy itself (including full economic value) can then be assigned directly to adult beneficiaries or to bare trustees to hold on behalf of a minor. Because the policy rights that have been assigned to the discretionary trust have a value, they serve to reduce the value of the potentially exempt transfer arising from the gifted policy. The exact value of the rights transferred to the trust will depend on the period for which surrender rights on the policy are suppressed, with longer periods giving rise to higher values. See Figure 22.7 above.

Example

The flexible legacy plan in action

Max and Cindy, who have not made any previous gifts, wish to make gifts of £1 million from each of them (i.e. £2 million between them) to each of their children, Mandy (23), Sam (20) and Josh (18). They each invest £1 million into three investment bonds, which are subject to the following terms:

- Each child can have full access to the capital in their policy at age 35.

- Each child is to be paid £20,000 p.a. from their policy in the interim.

- Consideration should be given to future requests for an advance of some or all of each child's policy proceeds before their 35th birthday, to cater for changing circumstances.

Of the total gifts of £3 million from each parent, £180,000 will be treated as a chargeable lifetime transfer from each of them, representing the value of the additional policy features gifted to each trust based on the time period between now and when Mandy, Sam and Josh each reach age 35. The economic value of each policy, after deducting the value of the rights transferred to the trust, will be treated as a potentially exempt transfer to the adult children of £2,820,000 from both Max and Cindy, i.e. £5,640,000 in total.

No inheritance tax is due at outset and all future growth will arise outside Max's and Cindy's estates. If they survive the gift by seven years, the CLT and the PET gifts will fall out of their respective estates completely. Otherwise the gift of policy rights to the trust and part of the policy values gifted to the children will be deducted from Max's and/or Cindy's nil-rate band at the time of their death. An excess gift over the NRB will be subject to IHT at 40% on subsequent death unless death occurs between three and seven years, when it will benefit from a sliding-scale reduction in tax from 80% to 20% of the full amount due.

The A&M plan or flexible legacy plan will be suitable for those who want to make significant gifts and who:

- want to avoid the capital passing to the child automatically at age 18, but instead at an older age
- wish to make more substantial gifts
- want the bulk of the gift to be a potentially exempt transfer to avoid the 20% lifetime charge applicable to discretionary trusts
- have already made gifts made to discretionary trusts in the last seven years which have utilised the current £325,000 nil-rate band
- wish to pursue an investment strategy that balances capital growth and income with virtually no tax on an arising basis
- as parents, want to avoid the £100 income limit applicable to a bare trust or the additional tax that applies to dividends distributed under a discretionary trust
- think that there is a good possibility that the recipient child will be either a non/basic-rate taxpayer or a non-UK resident on encashment.

Foundations

A foundation is a legal entity that combines the features of a trust and a company. It is similar to a company, in that it is a distinct corporate legal entity managed by a board of directors in accordance with its charter and regulations, but it has no shareholders. It is similar to a trust in that it has one or more objects that may be a purpose (charitable or non-charitable) and/or be for the benefit of one or more beneficiaries.

The primary use of a foundation is for private wealth management, including:

- as an alternative to a traditional trust where international families are not familiar with the concept of a trust or find them complicated to understand
- a more acceptable vehicle than a trust in certain jurisdictions that require a higher degree of transparency for wealth-holding structures
- to control global charitable assets and giving
- as a means of holding 'orphaned' special purpose vehicles
- to carry out general commercial transactions.

Foundations are therefore a truly international legal structure that can be used to create sophisticated inter-generational and charitable planning and are usually based in places such as Jersey, Latin America, Liechtenstein, Luxembourg and Malta.

Foundations are unlikely to be suitable for most families, unless the wealth is substantial (in the tens of millions of pounds' worth of assets) or where a sophisticated tax structure is in place, such as an international purchased life annuity.

CHAPTER 23
YOUNG PEOPLE AND MONEY

'Continuous effort – not strength or intelligence – is the key to unlocking our potential.'

Winston Churchill

In this chapter I want to give an overview and some practical ideas on how to help young people become good at managing their own and possibly, in due course, family money. The issues discussed in this chapter are the product of what I have learned from working with clients over the past 25 years. They are not meant to be prescriptive but to give young people and their parents, grandparents and wider family a greater perspective on developing a healthy and effective relationship with money.

Despite the essential role that money plays in our lives and the serious challenges presented by increasing life expectancy, students graduating with more than £25,000 of debt, unaffordable housing and the subsequent austerity arising from the global credit crisis, recent research[1] suggests that about two-thirds of young people have never received any formal education on personal financial planning. The same research found, however, that half of the young people surveyed said they find personal finance 'interesting' and:

- nearly all still visit their bank branch at least occasionally
- nearly three-quarters have never used mobile banking – and many of those are worried about security considerations
- many don't really consider student debt to be debt at all – apparently, because it is taken directly from their gross pay

[1] Robson, S. (2012) 'GENERATION Y: the (modern) world of personal finance', July.

- most are virtuous – nearly two thirds pay off credit and store card debt within a month to avoid interest payments
- women generally tend to have lower savings than men and are less likely to take investment risks
- more than four in ten of those who contribute to a pension do not know what type of pension they have – money purchase, final salary, etc.

Another recent study[2] into the attitudes of people aged between 20 and 29 found that they estimate their lifestyle in retirement will cost them about £42,000 per annum in today's terms. Despite this, 37% cited their main priority being to save sufficient capital to fund a deposit on a house or flat, although worryingly 24% were not saving at all. A 2014 estimate[3] suggests that those in the 16–24 age group save £95 per month (11% of their average income) and those in the 25–34 age group save £118 (about 8.5% of their average income).

Money values and beliefs

While we could debate the relative importance and influence that money has in society, the fact is that it is central to our existence and wellbeing. Much of our approach to dealing with money in general, and personal financial planning in particular, is learned from our parents, wider family and peers as we are growing up. This leads to a number of money styles, which we discussed in Chapter 2 and are summarised again in Figure 23.1.

Early influences in relation to money

When I first meet new clients, one of the questions I ask them is how money was handled in their family when they were growing up, because that gives me a good idea of the key influencing factors on their own money style and values. Examples of these influences include:

- which parent handled the family finances and the messages that they gave to their children about money
- whether money was tight or plentiful
- whether there was/is tension between parents about financial matters
- whether their parents struggled to fund their education

[2]   MRM London (2014) 'Generation austerity', January.
[3]   NS&I's Quarterly Savings Survey, April 2014.

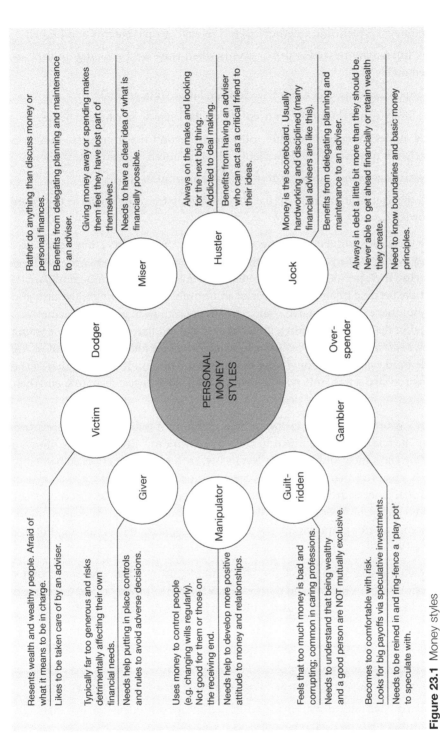

Figure 23.1 Money styles

Source: Created from data in Hallowell, E. and Grace, W. (1989) *What Are You Worth?: Coming to Terms with Your Feelings about Money*, Weidenfield and Nicolson.

- if money was plentiful, whether this was created by their parents or inherited
- any financially related issues or events when they were growing up that are memorable
- the approach to pocket money, working and rewards in general
- the lifestyle that the family enjoyed – frugal, lavish or somewhere in between
- role models, mentors or other individuals beyond the immediate family (a teacher or parents of friends perhaps), who influenced their attitude to money
- the messages about money that they picked up from their peers
- the messages and influences that they picked up from the media as they were growing up.

While these early influences do affect your financial 'personality', they do not necessarily define how a young person relates to money, nor how good they will be at managing their personal finances. A real challenge for parents and grandparents who have become financially successful and/or inherited meaningful wealth, and as a result have enjoyed a good standard of living, is how to avoid this demotivating and/or disincentivising their children or grandchildren as they become young adults. *Made in Chelsea* is a 'reality' television series that follows the lives of young people from wealthy families living in Chelsea in London. It is telling that of the dozen or so characters, only two have a regular job and the rest seem to spend their time meeting for coffee and planning their social lives.

When a young person has known a nice standard of living as they were growing up, has not had to do much in the way of work to earn money (or obtain a monthly allowance) and has made few (if any) sacrifices or experienced hardship, there is a real risk that they will not develop the resilience, purpose and sense of self-worth from 'running their own race'. My experience is that teaching their children and young people the value of money comes through the application, by parents and/or grandparents, of a number of approaches including, but not limited to:

- showing restraint and modesty – for example, using public transport, flying economy class one way and business class the other, buying the young person an older first car and them using this for at least the first few years of driving
- continuing to work and/or be involved in business activity even though there may not be a financial need to do so, in order to demonstrate a work ethic
- matching what the young person earns from part-time, temporary or vocational work, or paying them an allowance based on unpaid voluntary work
- making charitable donations conditional on the young person also making a contribution from their own resources

- encouraging them to carry out fundraising activity to fund a trip to carry out voluntary work in a developing country

- providing a monthly allowance that is less than the young person needs, but topping this up with variable payments linked to additional agreed positive activity or outcomes

- talking about money in a positive way and stressing the importance of regular saving and making good long-term financial decisions

- expressing gratitude for the family's financial success, wealth and standard of living and appreciating that not all people have the same financial capability and resources

- not giving children and young people everything they want, but giving them what they need

- giving the child or young person the cash amount of any savings in school fees that may arise from achieving a scholarship

- providing a small amount of capital to enable them to invest this as they see fit, but not for spending

- explaining key terms and concepts in an age-appropriate and engaging way, possibly using graphical examples, stories, analogies and real-life examples

- not making love and acceptance conditional or linked in any way to material and financial success

- expressing how important it is to not be motivated solely by financial and materialistic reward.

Passion and purpose

Having something that one is passionate about leads to a strong sense of purpose, which in turn provides the necessary motivation to pursue those ideals and dreams. This is particularly important where financial incentives are not strong (or even non-existent) because wealth already exists in the family. Psychologists advise that a strong sense of purpose is essential for individuals to build a sense of self-worth, identity and character. It is also essential to enable a young person to define themselves without reference to their family's financial status (whether poor, affluent or wealthy).

For example, my family was poor, we lived in a tiny house and we never had very much in the way of comforts. However, I never accepted that that was how I was going to live when I grew up. While clearly I had an economic incentive to work hard to improve my lifestyle, many of my peers who also lived in poor households seemed to resign themselves to the same fate as their parents and accepted that being poor and having limited choice was their destiny. One of my childhood friends did, however, live in a very large house, with extensive grounds, tennis courts, horses and a swimming pool, and his parents were clearly wealthy. Unfortunately he was a lazy, spoilt and greedy individual who, I believe, went on to cause a trail of upset, destruction and drama when he became an adult. Clearly, the financial success of his parents didn't make him either a nice person or financially capable.

It's not where you've come from that matters but where you're going.

Human capital

Developing a sense of identity from having a passion and purpose can help young people to decide on the direction they want to take their life. Human capital is our ability to generate wealth and other positive outcomes from our own endeavours. Regardless of whether a young person starts out with any inherited wealth, they do start out with potentially a very high amount of human capital.

Many people consider a good education to be a stable foundation for happiness and success. Education means different things to different people. Some see it as a means to develop a love of learning in the broadest sense; some see it in terms of acquiring intellectual skills, knowledge and academic capability to enable the pursuit of a profession; while others see it as a means of developing social skills and taking part in character-building experiences. For many people a good education involves all of these elements.

It is common for first-generation successful people to want to give their children a better formal education than they had themselves. Parents who went to an independent school and/or went to university are, understandably, often keen for their children to do the same. Whether this leads to better financial outcomes for those young people is debatable, particularly if the things they are learning do not equip them to make good financial decisions, or be able to cope with adversity, or develop a vision and purpose for which they have a passion and some flair.

Parents often have strong ideas of what is right for their children's future and how they should best develop their talents. For many young people, university will be a rewarding and enriching experience that helps them to develop their character, skills and independence. For others, whether or not they do well at school, sometimes university is not right for them, regardless of what aspirations their parents might have for them or the fact that they can afford to support them financially.

Basic literacy and numeracy skills are a prerequisite for anyone. However, many of the most well-known entrepreneurs, such as Bill Gates, Richard Branson and Steve Jobs, either dropped out of or never attended higher education, but went on to build multi-billion-pound businesses.

'Press on. Nothing in the world can take the place of persistence. Talent will not; nothing is more common than unsuccessful men with talent. Genius will not; the world is full of educated derelicts. Persistence and determination alone are omnipotent.'

Ray Kroc built McDonald's into the most successful
fast-food company in the world

Higher education funding

Higher education funding in England changed quite significantly in 2012/13. As a result universities are now permitted to charge students much higher tuition fees. A summary of the new funding system is set out in Table 23.1. Scottish and EU (excluding those from England, Wales and Northern Ireland) students studying in Scotland do not pay tuition fees, nor do they pay any form of graduate tax. While students in Northern Ireland have to pay tuition fees, these are a much lower fixed amount (£3,685 p.a. at the time of writing) for courses taken at Northern Irish universities.

The key changes under the new system are as follows:

- As in the past, students are entitled to take out a government-backed loan, which they do not have to repay until after graduation. However, students requiring loans must now borrow substantially larger amounts to meet higher tuition fees.

- Under both old and new systems, graduates must repay 9% of their gross income above a certain level of annual income. This threshold was £15,795 (in 2012 prices) under the pre 2012/13 system and this threshold increased in line with the RPI. The 2012/13 + threshold is higher (£21,000 in 2016 prices) and rises in line with average weekly earnings (which tend to rise faster than prices). Graduates must make repayments either until they repay their loan in full or until 30 years has elapsed (it was 25 years under the old system), after which any remaining debt is written off.

- Under the new system, graduates are charged a real (above-inflation) interest rate of 3% while studying and 0–3% after graduation (compared with interest equal to inflation as measured by the RPI – i.e. 0% interest in real terms), depending on their income.

Table 23.1 Higher education funding system in England for students first enrolled in 2012/13

Students first enrolled in 2012/13	
Tuition fees	Up to £9,000
Fee loans	All students may get a loan from the Student Loans Company (SLC) to pay the fees and must repay SLC after they graduate.
Maintenance grant	In 2012, £3,250 if household income less than or equal to £25,000 p.a. Tapered away at around 18% withdrawal rate thereafter. No grant available when parental income exceeds £42,600. The maximum grant increases slightly in subsequent years.
Maintenance loan	The maximum loan is £4,375 for students living at home, £5,500 for others outside London, and £7,675 for those away from home and in London. The maximum loan is lower for the final year of study. Students lose 50p maintenance loan for every £1 they receive as maintenance grant. The loan is tapered away at 10% for household income above £42,875. All students are guaranteed at least 65% of the maximum loan. The parameters did not change in cash terms between 2012 and 2013.
Other student support	The National Scholarship Programme (NSP) was introduced to give at least £3,000 each to low-income students. Eligibility requires household income to be no more than £25,000. The award may be given as fee waivers. Universities determine the detailed criteria. Not all eligible students are guaranteed an award. The NSP has since been abolished for undergraduates.
Accumulation and repayment of student loans	
	Real interest rate (relative to RPI).
During study	3%.
After graduation	0–3% depending on graduate income: 0% if below the repayment threshold, linearly increasing to 3% for income at or above the higher repayment threshold.
Repayment rate	9%.
Repayment threshold	£21,000 in 2016 (above which 9% of income is to be paid).
Higher repayment threshold	£41,000 in 2016 (at which point the real interest rate is 3%).
Threshold indexation	Annually in line with national average earnings from 2017.
Repayment period	30 years.

Source: Payback Time? Student Debt and Loan Repayments: What Will the 2012 Reforms Mean for Graduates?, Institute for Fiscal Studies, April 2014. **http://www.ifs.org.uk/publications/7165**

The combination of threshold and interest changes makes the system more generous in some respects and less generous in others. Recent research[4] into the financial implications of the new English higher education funding system has drawn some interesting conclusions:

- Students will graduate with much higher debts than before, averaging more than £44,000, compared with about £25,000 under the old system.
- The lowest earners will actually pay back less than under the old system, whereas the highest earners will pay back much more.
- Only 5% of students will have repaid their student loans by the time they are 40 compared with about 50% under the old system.
- About 75% of all students will not earn enough to repay their loans within the first 30 years, leaving an average debt of £30,000 to be written off by the state.

For a graduate employee with earnings of more than £21,000 p.a. (in 2016 terms), the combination of tax, National Insurance contributions and student loan repayment means a combined marginal rate of 41% (20% + 12% +9%) until they hit real higher-rate tax (currently 40%), when the marginal rate rises to 51% (40% + 2% + 9%). That is not a pleasant prospect, especially as the research analysis referred to earlier suggests that it will cover most of the family-raising period. Yet repaying the loan early could mean in about three-quarters of cases removing the benefit of the 30-year loan write-off. For most families, rather than funding to meet student loan costs, the idea should be to fund to meet graduate living costs.

Many universities in other European countries offer similar courses taught in English, but charge much lower tuition fees than English universities. This cost saving needs to be weighed against the potential higher living and travelling costs and the quality of the degree obtained.

Learning about business

Where a family runs a business, regardless of whether the young family member goes on to higher education, it offers the potential for younger family members to gain work experience. Learning to communicate, collaborate and understand other people are key life skills that will serve any young person well in the future. Where there is an aspiration to pass on the family business to the younger generation, this will enable them to gain a good understanding of and appreciation for the business's fundamentals.

---

[4] *Payback Time? Student Debt and Loan Repayments: What Will the 2012 Reforms Mean for Graduates?,* Institute for Fiscal Studies , April 2014.

I learned the principles of hard work, getting on with people, good organisation and delivering good customer service from working in the public house that my parents managed when I was a teenager. I didn't always agree with my parents' way of running the business, but at least I was in an environment where I could learn whether or not running a business was for me. Those early experiences laid the foundation for the skills that I developed later on when I started my own business – Bloomsbury – in 1998 and which I continue to lead to this day.

Financial capability

Financial capability refers to the basic skills we all need to make wise choices about money. Without these basic skills, the odds of having good financial outcomes are greatly reduced due to poor decision making and the higher likelihood of financial services organisations exploiting their customers' lack of financial capability.[5] In this section I set out the main basic financial planning concepts and offer some rules of thumb and practical principles and practices for managing money.

Budgeting

In the course of my career I have met many high-earning and wealthy people and in the early years I assumed that a high earner would become wealthy and a wealthy person would be able to stay wealthy. However, I learned that if someone spends more than they (or their wealth) earns, they will never become (or stay) wealthy. Learning to spend less than you earn, possibly by deferring certain spending, using cheaper alternatives, or earning higher income through increased work, involves more effort than having what you want whenever you want it. This is particularly the case if you always had a nice lifestyle as you were growing up and never had to make sacrifices.

Budgeting is one of the key skills to learn early on and is the foundation upon which financial freedom, choice, security and independence are based. Look at the range of monthly savings required to accumulate £1 million shown in Figure 23.2. At 5% p.a. investment returns and a ten-year time horizon it requires monthly savings of £6,600, compared with over the 30-year time horizon which

---

[5]   The UK financial services regulatory structure, which is recognised as one of the most comprehensive and stringent in the world, has developed over the past 25 years or so in large part because there is usually an asymmetrical (opposing) relationship between the knowledge, understanding and financial skills of financial services firms and that of their customers. Without strict regulations and oversight, history shows that some firms are likely to exploit their superior knowledge, to the detriment of their customers.

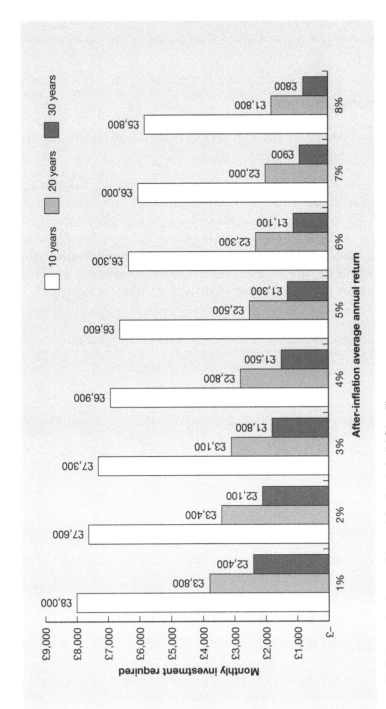

Figure 23.2 Approximate monthly contribution to build £1 million

requires £1,300 p.m. at the same rate of return. This is the classic trade-off that we all have to make each day between consumption now and deferring gratification to the future.

Compound interest

'Compound interest is the eighth wonder of the world. He who understands it, earns it ... he who doesn't ... pays it.'

Albert Einstein

When we earn interest or other investment income and retain this with the principal capital, it is available to earn further income. Earning interest (or returns) on interest is a fundamental financial planning concept, which is illustrated in Figure 23.3. The higher the rate of return achieved and the longer the time horizon, the greater the effect this compounding will have, as illustrated in Figure 23.4.

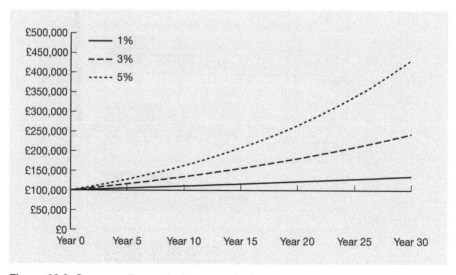

Figure 23.3 Compounding works best over the long term

The Rule of 72

A really simple but highly useful and quick rule of thumb for working out compound investment returns, without having to do complicated calculations, is

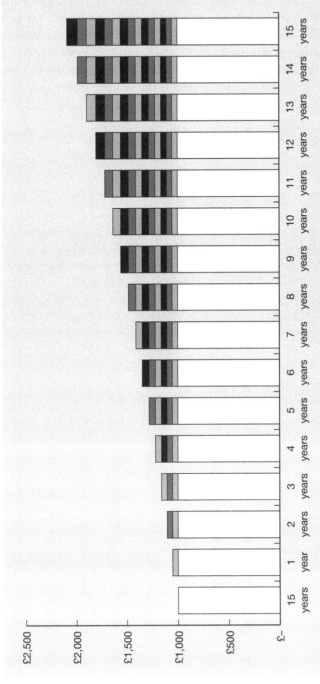

Each block represents the interest earned on the previous year's capital and accumulated interest. So for example, the first small shaded block is the interest that is earned on the original capital (the large block) from year two onwards. The second small shaded block is the interest that is earned from year three onwards on the original capital and the existing interest that was added to the capital previously. And so on.

Figure 23.4 How compounding works

called the 'Rule of 72'.[6] If you take the compound (geometric) rate of return and divide it into 72, you can estimate the number of years it will take for you to double your money, as illustrated in Table 23.2. For example, 72/7 is about 10, so with 7% p.a. investment returns it would take roughly 10 years for capital to double. The higher the return, the less time it takes. The rule can also be used to estimate the annualised return required to double the value of money over a given time period, by dividing the time period into 72, as illustrated in Table 23.3.

Table 23.2 Years to double your money at different rates of return

Return (pa)	1%	2%	3%	4%	5%
Years	72	36	24	18	14

Table 23.3 Rate of return to double your money over a specified time horizon

Time	5 years	10 years	15 years	20 years	25 years
Return required (pa)	14%	7%	5%	4%	3%

Inflation and the Rule of 72

The price of goods and services can stay the same, fall or rise from year to year. The most common position is that the price of the majority of goods and services will tend to rise over the long term. This rise, known as positive inflation, is measured by ongoing monitoring of the prices of a broad range of goods and services. Thus the inflation rate refers to the average rise in that basket of prices over the previous 12 months.

Because the impact of inflation is felt most acutely over the long term, it is a particular threat to savings that are accumulated or earmarked to fund lifestyle in older age when one can't, or no longer wishes to, work. Even low rates of inflation can have a devastating effect on the purchasing power of money and the Rule of 72 can also be used to understand this, as illustrated in Table 23.4.

6 The 'Rule of 72' is only a reasonable approximation.

Table 23.4 The erosion of purchasing power of capital by inflation

Inflation (pa)	1%	2%	3%	4%	5%
Years to halve capital	72	36	24	18	14

If we take a look at the longer-term historical returns that different investment asset classes have delivered, such as equities (owning a part share in a company), bonds and cash (lending to governments and companies), the mantra that comes to mind is *'get (or stay) rich slowly'*. Attempting to *'get rich (or richer) quick'* is no different to gambling. Over the past 114 years cash has delivered a return of around 0.80% p.a. above inflation, government bonds around 1.2% p.a. and UK equities a shade over 5% p.a.[7] Figure 23.5 illustrates the significant fall in the purchasing power of cash over the past 15 years.

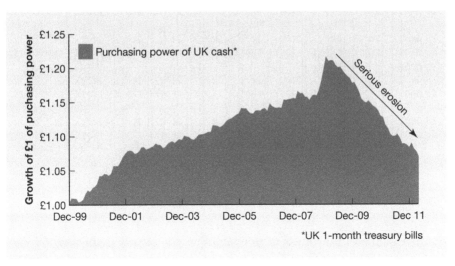

Figure 23.5 Cash is not a good long-term investment strategy for long-term goals
Source: Albion Strategic.

Borrowing

Compounding also works in reverse where one borrows money and pays interest. The longer the time horizon and the higher the interest rate, the more total

---

[7] Barclays Equity Gilt Study, 2014.

interest will be paid. Perhaps the best example of this is a repayment mortgage. Figure 23.6 shows a typical 25-year mortgage. Initially, the majority of the repayments relate to interest arising, with the balance being part-repayment of the loan. The loan does not reduce much in the first few years but then starts to reduce as compounding works in reverse. Clearly, the lower the interest rate charged and/ or the higher the monthly repayments, the faster the loan will be repaid. It's very easy to think that small percentages don't matter but, as the example shows, this can amount to a significant cost over the life of a mortgage.

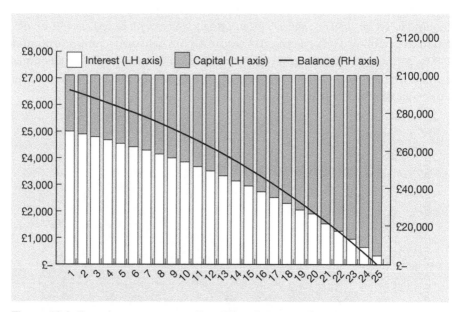

Figure 23.6 Repaying a mortgage with a 5% pa interest rate

Another example of the effect of compounding on debt is a credit card. A credit card offers a convenient means of buying goods and services and as long as the balance is repaid in full each month, there is no charge (although some cards do impose a small fixed annual fee for the card facility). To the extent that there is any outstanding balance each month, after deducting any partial repayment made, the card issuer will charge a relatively high rate of interest on the outstanding balance. The credit card company is keen for its customers to repay only the minimum amount necessary to meet the monthly interest costs arising, and this is typically set at 3% of the outstanding balance each month. Figure 23.7 shows how long it would take to clear a credit card debt with a typical 20% annual interest charge assuming different repayment levels.

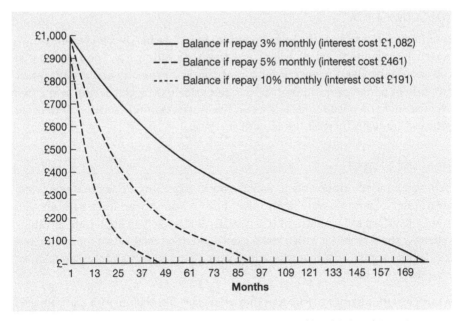

Figure 23.7 Time to repay a £1,000 credit card balance with a 20% pa interest

Principles and practices

The following principles and practices are a simple summary of what I have learned from many other financially successful people, researching and studying what works and from my own experience of managing money.

Principles

Watch your spending

It doesn't matter how much you earn. If you spend all, or more than, you earn, you'll always be poor. While it is easy to be seduced into buying what you want, rather than what you need, deferring gratification and living within your means is the cornerstone of financial success. It's a good idea to track your spending for a week or a month to get an idea where your money goes. Small but regular changes in expenditure can free up cash that you can use to build financial security. As the old saying goes: 'Fools work for money and money works for the rich.'

Pay yourself first

Your financial security is the most important priority when it comes to devising a personal expenditure budget, before rent, travel, socialising, etc. I don't mean that you should live like a pauper in pursuit of saving for the dim and distant future but rather change your mindset so that you prioritise regular saving as the first expense that you need to meet. It's a bit like fitness training: start small to begin with and gradually increase the amount you save.

The devil of debt

Debt can be used responsibly to enable you to buy things today that you really need, such as a home in which to live, but for which you don't have enough money to afford to buy outright (particularly if it is likely to appreciate in value). Whatever the reasons for which you borrow money, remember two things: interest is a definite regular cost that will reduce your ability to save and the capital must eventually be repaid.

While current interest rates are low, they won't stay like that for ever and you need to think carefully about the impact on your expenditure if interest rates were, say, three times higher than at present (as they have been in the past). For this reason, even though buying a home with a mortgage can be a good long-term use of funds, make sure that you don't overstretch yourself. There's more to life than paying a mortgage. Also, avoid at all costs any form of borrowing on credit/store card or payday loans.

Keep it simple stupid (KISS)

The technology company Apple has made a virtue out of simplicity and it drives everything it does. You should adopt the same mindset in your personal financial planning and keep things as simple as possible.

If it looks too good …

If anyone tells you that they have a sure-bet investment that is virtually risk-free and will generate a 20% p.a. return, and it looks as though they actually mean or believe what they are saying, you need to give them a wide berth. If it looks too good to be true then it probably is.

Talking tax

You need to avoid becoming obsessed about avoiding tax. There is a whole industry dedicated to feeding off the greed and stupidity of people who hate paying tax and the authorities are increasingly attacking contrived and aggressive planning.

You need to have achieved a degree of financial success to pay tax in the first place. In addition, a certain amount of tax is necessary for any decent society to operate in a fair and equitable manner. Minimise your tax bill by using all the legitimate and tried and tested products and solutions available, but not to such an extent that you don't have enough money to live on today.

The media is not your friend

The media, in the form of newspapers, 24-hour news, websites or magazines, is not designed to help you to make good decisions. It focuses on what personal finance professionals call 'noise' or 'financial pornography' in the form of negative stories or sensationalist 'get rich quick' ideas because they are newsworthy. People who participate in such media comment are chosen because they make the media outlet more marketable, not because of their insight. In general, the news is not the truth but a form of entertainment, so remember that when forming your opinions about money.

Keep costs low and diversify

As a general rule with long-term investing you get everything that you don't pay for. There is no evidence to support the commonly voiced (usually by those with an interest in the outcome) assertion that it is better to buy an expensive investment fund than a similar lower-cost one. Costs are certain whereas investment returns aren't.

Practices

Build a cash reserve

Having a cash reserve available is essential to enable you to cope with the inevitable ups and downs that arise in life. Your cash reserve should represent at least three months' expenditure, plus any funds that you will need to spend within the next few years, such as a house deposit or education/training costs. A cash ISA will usually offer better interest than standard savings accounts and is free of income tax, but avoid accounts that lock you in to a fixed term or charge a high transfer fee. You need to be able to access your cash should the need arise.

Protect your income

At the beginning of your working life your greatest asset is your ability to earn an income. If you were unable to work due to disability or illness for the medium to long term, it could consign you to poverty for life. Income-protection insurance will keep paying you a proportion of your income until you can return to work or reach a certain age (usually when you expect to retire). Healthy young people can usually get this type of cover easily and at relatively low cost, so if your employer doesn't offer cover (as most don't), buy your own personal policy. Do not confuse this with the (justifiably) much-maligned 'payment protection insurance', which pays out (if it does at all) for a short period only and does not provide any long-term protection.

Invest in yourself

In addition to a positive mental attitude, increasing your relevant skills and knowledge is the best way to increase your earning power. Therefore, looking for ways to invest in your capability, whether that's night school, distance learning or day release by your employer, makes a lot of sense.

Join a pension plan

If you are offered the chance to join an employer-sponsored pension plan, then do so. Over the next few years (the exact dates depend on the size of the employer) all employees will be automatically enrolled in a pension plan through their employer unless they actively opt out. Whatever you do, *do not* opt out because the employer has to make contributions in addition to your own and the taxman also contributes. If you are self-employed, contribute to a low-cost pension with a choice of index funds and limit your risk by spreading your contributions across global markets, whether via one fund or several. The earliest contributions make the most growth and can make the difference between a decent retirement income or not. Although these funds can't be accessed until age 55, that might actually be a good thing.

Don't rush to buy property

Although buying your own home generally makes more sense than renting over the long term, avoid rushing in to buy a house until you have established your earning power, know where you want to live (which may be dictated by your work) and have a clearer idea of who, if anyone, will be your life partner. Buying and selling properties is an expensive business and if you have to sell at a time when the value of the property has fallen and your equity is reduced, it can set you back years.

Repay debt

An interest-free loan from your family is the cheapest form of borrowing and payday loans are the most expensive. As a general rule you should avoid, or repay, debt as fast as possible, starting with the most expensive debt first.

Below is a simplified list of borrowing types in broad order of interest costs, with most expensive first. Typical annual interest rates are shown in brackets:

1 Pay day loans/doorstep lending (400–2,000%)
2 Pawnbrokers (130–500%)
3 Storecard (20–35%)
4 Credit card (8–55%)
5 Secured personal loan (6–23%)
6 Unsecured personal loan (5–15%)
7 Residential mortgage – 95% of property value (6%)
8 Residential mortgage – 85% of property value (5%)
9 Residential mortgage – 70% of property value (3%)
10 Student loan – pre-2012 graduates (1.5%)
11 Borrowing from family (nil to 4%)

Invest most of your long-term money in equities and property

Assuming you have followed all the suggested actions above, you should invest the bulk of any surplus income, plus your pension fund, into worldwide equities. A rough rule of thumb is to take your age from 100 and the answer is the amount to invest in equities. Don't worry about volatility (the value moving up and down) because, with an asset class which is expected to rise over the long term (20 years +), regular savings benefit from something called pound cost averaging. This means that the average price you pay for the investments should be less than their average price over time. As you get older you may need to reduce your exposure to equities, but by then the compounding of returns (earning returns on previous returns) over time will have worked its magic and reduced the relative risk of price fluctuations because your capital should be worth many times what you invested.

CHAPTER 24
PHILANTHROPY

'We make a living by what we get, but we make a life by what we give.'

Winston Churchill

In Chapter 1 we looked at Maslow's hierarchy of needs and the fact that, as our own and our immediate family's needs are met, it is natural to seek a higher level of fulfilment, meaning and purpose: the process of self-actualisation. Giving time or money to causes from which neither you nor your family can directly benefit is clearly an altruistic and selfless act and may help you to achieve that feeling of greater meaning and purpose in your life.

Giving time

Helping people or causes doesn't have to mean giving away your wealth. Giving your time can be equally valuable and, in many cases, more fulfilling. There are numerous organisations throughout the UK that offer ways for people to volunteer their time and expertise across a diverse range of roles, examples of which are:

- magistrate
- special police constable
- school governor
- working with prisoners or detainees
- hospital visitor
- advocate for vulnerable individuals
- visiting elderly people
- education support
- National Trust, RSPCA, RSPB, etc.

Sometimes, particularly in poorer countries, sharing your skills and knowledge can be extremely valuable. Voluntary Service Overseas (VSO) is one of the world's largest independent international development organisations, which works through volunteers to fight poverty in developing countries. 'VSO's high-impact approach involves bringing people together to share skills, build capabilities, promote international understanding and action, and change lives to make the world a fairer place for all.'[1] There is high demand for teachers, engineers and health workers, as the provision of education, infrastructure and health services is sparse in many developing countries.

An acquaintance of mine, who is very successful and wealthy, derives great meaning and pleasure from supporting the building and upkeep of schools in Africa. As well as making cash donations, he and a few friends go to Africa to provide hands-on help with the building and painting. This has the added benefit of enabling him to see the real difference that he is making on the ground by meeting the staff and pupils of the schools he has helped, thus motivating him to continue his support.

Giving money

While philanthropy is something that is well understood and practised in the United States, it less so among wealthy people in the UK. A study found that only 18% of wealthy individuals in the UK said charitable giving was one of their top three spending priorities, compared with 41% of their US counterparts.[2]

This reticence to give certainly doesn't seem to be related to wealth. Over the years I've met modestly affluent people who give 10% of their earnings to charity, even though they have not achieved financial independence themselves. In other cases I've met multi-millionaires with far more wealth than they or their family could ever spend, but they make only modest charitable gifts. Research shows that the poorest 10% of donors give 3.6% of their total spending to charity, whereas the richest 10% give only 1.1%.[3]

---

[1]   www.vso.org.uk/about/

[2]   Ledbury Research and Barclays Wealth (2010) 'Global giving: The culture of philanthropy'.

[3]   Cowley, E., Smith, S., McKenzie, T. and Pharaoh, C. (2011) *The New State of Donation: Three decades of household giving to charity, 1978–2008*, Cass Business School and University of Bristol.

A common barrier to higher giving is that wealthy people often feel they can't afford to give much to charity until they feel financially more stable. A 2010 study found that 71% of wealthy people give only when they feel financially secure.[4] It is natural for people to feel less secure when the economy has suffered a downturn, such as the recent global credit crisis. But this is unlikely to be the only or even the main reason for reticence to gift more meaningful amounts to charity.

It is probable that some people see giving to charity as complicated, or worry that it will unleash a rush of begging letters. Others see charities as inefficient and think that very little of their gift will be used to make a real difference, once administration charges have taken their share. In my experience, the biggest reason that charitable giving isn't a bigger priority among affluent and wealthy individuals is because they haven't given it any real thought or consideration. While they might respond to disaster requests or TV appeals, it is the exception, not the norm, for people to seriously consider how charity fits into their wealth planning.

Let's go back to that question in Chapter 1: 'What's important about money to you?' If you can identify a cause with which you really connect and develop a passion for, then you are much more likely to be motivated to make more meaningful gifts in your lifetime and/or through your will. This is where a good wealth adviser can add value, by helping you to work out what causes are important to you and selecting charities – possibly by engaging a charitable giving specialist – and determining how to give easily and tax-efficiently and, more importantly, to monitor the impact of your giving.

Financial giving can be done in your lifetime on a planned or ad hoc basis and/or left for the executors of your will to deal with after your death. Clearly, if you give in your lifetime, you can derive some personal satisfaction from the outcome. I use a philanthropy questionnaire with clients to help them identify what, if any, philanthropic aims they have and this is reproduced in Figure 24.1 should you wish to use it.

Reasons for giving

There are six key reasons why you might want to make charitable giving a serious part of your wealth plan, as set out in Figure 24.2 and discussed further below.

---

4   Bank of America Merrill Lynch (2010) 'Study of HNW philanthropy: Issues driving charitable activities among affluent households'.

Philanthropy survey: an act of kindness, a generous gift

Name: Date:

1. Charities or causes into which I feel a need to invest my time and energy:

2. Charities or causes to which I currently contribute:

3. Causes that I would like to support on a perpetual or annual basis:

4. Charities that I would like to provide for in my will:

5. Endowment funds I would like to establish:

Figure 24.1 Philanthropy survey

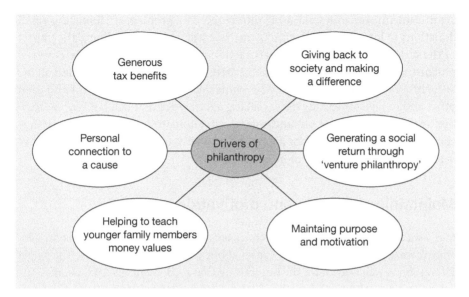

Figure 24.2 The main drivers of philanthropy

Giving back to society and making a difference

Bill and Melinda Gates and Warren Buffett have given billions of dollars to the Bill and Melinda Gates Foundation, which is the largest transparent, managed independent foundation in the world, with an endowment of $36.3 billion. The Foundation aims to advance education and technology use in the United States and to eradicate malaria, polio, HIV/Aids and poverty in the developing world, and has distributed $25.36 billion to date.[5] Gates and Buffett announced that more than 50 prominent businesspeople have made a public pledge to make more substantial charitable donations. Warren Buffett said:

'Were we to use more than 1% of my claim checks (Berkshire Hathaway stock certificates) on ourselves, neither our happiness nor our well-being would be enhanced. In contrast, that remaining 99% can have a huge effect on the health and welfare of others.'[6]

While you may not be able to make donations on the same scale as the Gateses and Buffett, you could almost certainly make donations that would have a

---

[5] Gates Foundation factsheet, as at 30 June 2011.

[6] Bill and Melinda Gates Foundation website – Just Giving pledge, **http://givingpledge.org/**

significant impact and make a big difference. The problem with making small donations to lots of charities without any real strategy is that it dilutes the impact of the donations and erodes the satisfaction derived from giving. The power of philanthropy comes from the focus and drive of the philanthropist. It also allows affluent and wealthy families to stay connected with the wider world and each other and to give something back, making a difference that will last beyond their lifetimes. The purpose of philanthropy is, therefore, to make an impact, change things about which you are not happy and, to a large extent, pass on these positive values to your wider family – more of which later.

Maintaining purpose and motivation

Many successful people maintain a strong sense of purpose and motivation by generating wealth to fund charitable causes about which they care deeply. The singer Elton John is well known for the fundraising that he does for his AIDS charity. The singer and actor Roger Daltrey has been a keen supporter of the Teenage Cancer Trust, which he helped to establish in 2000, and he speaks with passion and conviction about how this helps him to stay positive and enthusiastic about his life purpose, as well as keeping in touch with those much less fortunate than himself.

Successful businesspeople are increasingly making sizeable gifts to their own charitable foundations or established charities, at the expense of leaving a larger legacy to their family and friends. Sometimes this provides a business owner with the motivation to continue in business and defer, indefinitely, any notion of 'retiring'. Tom Hunter, the Scottish entrepreneur, is a good example of a self-made person who keeps working to fulfil his higher calling in life. After selling his business, Sports Division, to JJB Sports for £290 million in July 1998, Sir Tom moved to Monaco for tax reasons. At the same time, he established a charitable foundation – The Hunter Foundation – with £10 million, initially as a tax-mitigation tool.

Hunter explained that he had realised making money was 'only half the equation' and announced, after setting aside enough money to keep him and his family comfortable throughout their lifetimes, he would return to live in the UK and continue to invest in and nurture new businesses via his private equity company, West Coast Capital. He intends to channel gains and profits arising from his private equity investment into charitable causes in what he calls 'venture philanthropy'. In 2011, the foundation had invested £50 million.[7] Hunter said in an interview:

---

[7]   **www.thehunterfoundation.co.uk**, as at 30 June 2011.

There is more great wealth in fewer hands than ever before in history. My own personal belief is that with great wealth comes great responsibility ... all the material goals have all been settled some time ago, so now the philanthropy is the real motivator to continue to make money. The aim is to redouble our efforts in wealth creation in order that we can, over time, invest £1 billion in venture philanthropy through our foundation.[8]

Helping to teach younger family members money values

Teaching young people the value of money and a sense of responsibility in terms of how to manage wealth sensibly can often be made easier by engaging family members in the process of giving. While this could be as elaborate as a family 'board' to guide giving by a dedicated family charitable trust, it can also be a simple matter of making sure that giving is a regular part of family dialogue.

In my family, for example, once a year, each of us has to choose one large and one small charity to which we would like to make a charitable donation and explain why. In the case of my daughters, they each have to donate £1 of their own savings for every £10 given by my wife and I. This achieves a number of objectives:

- My daughters know that planned charitable giving is a key priority for my wife and I.

- By each supporting a large and a small charity, we strike a balance between those organisations that may have a high impact in terms of results but are not as well funded as the more visible and established charities that are well funded, proven and have economies of scale.

- Making our own donation subject to our daughters also making their own contributions causes them to make a small sacrifice of their own money and to appreciate what they have compared with others.

- The act of actively choosing our charities gives each of us a sense of ownership and engagement in the giving process.

- Talking and thinking about charitable giving causes us as a family to think more about others and less about ourselves, which also helps to give us all a greater sense of meaning and purpose in life.

- It gives us all more motivation to do our best in our lives and share the financial fruits of our efforts.

---

[8]   Sir Tom Hunter, announcing his philanthropic intentions in an interview with Robert Peston, *BBC News*, July 2007.

Just as it's never the 'right' time to start a family, it's never the right time to start charitable giving. If you wait until you feel wealthy enough, the opportunity to make a real difference to others is likely to have been missed.

Personal connection to a cause

The reason that cancer and heart disease charities are well funded is because almost everyone knows someone who has been affected by those conditions. I have a particular interest in education and parenting, as they are both issues that I feel go to the heart of many of society's problems and my own experiences of both were less than ideal. The more you connect with and feel passionate about a cause or issue, the more likely it is that you will be motivated to support it. In addition, you will probably derive more pleasure and satisfaction from charitable giving to that cause, particularly if you are clear what your gift is being used for and can see tangible results.

I suggest that you widen your net a bit more than the usual charities and think carefully about whether there are less mainstream, but equally worthy, causes with which you connect and that are important to you personally, as a gift to one or more of these might have a much higher impact and social return. I have known clients who feel strongly about the value of a good education and they have provided funds for free or subsidised education for disadvantaged pupils at some of the best independent schools. Although not a charitable gift, I've also known people agree to fund some or all of the educational needs of their relatives' or friends' children, sometimes requiring a matching contribution, pound for pound, to ensure a sense of ownership and responsibility on the part of the child's parent.

Generous tax benefits

The government is keen to support charitable giving and wants to encourage a more giving society. One of the ways that giving is encouraged is by offering a number of very generous tax benefits. These include income tax relief, freedom from capital gains tax on assets gifted and exemption from inheritance tax on lifetime gifts or those made on death, as summarised in Figure 24.3.

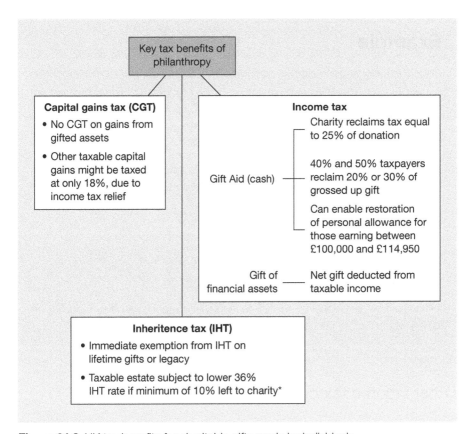

Figure 24.3 UK tax benefits for charitable gifts made by individuals

Gift Aid

For cash gifts it is better for all concerned to make a gift that falls within the Gift Aid scheme. Gift Aid allows a charity to reclaim basic-rate tax on donations from UK taxpayers and enables higher-rate and additional-rate taxpayers to claim 20% or 30% tax relief, respectively, on the amount of the gift grossed up for basic-rate tax. If the amount of UK tax (income tax and/or capital gains) paid by the donor is less than the amount of basic-rate tax that the charity can reclaim, the shortfall has to be repaid by the donor to HMRC, although in practice this is rarely done.

Example

Claudia is a higher-rate taxpayer and gives £8,000 to a recognised charity. Under the Gift Aid scheme, this will be treated as a gift of £10,000 (£8,000 grossed up by 25%), from which the basic-rate tax of £2,000 has been deducted at source. The charity can reclaim the basic-rate tax of £2,000 directly from HMRC, so it will receive a total of £10,000.

As Claudia is a higher-rate taxpayer with taxable income of £45,000, she may claim higher-rate tax relief on the gift. This is calculated as follows:

Grossed gift	£10,000
Tax relief at 40%	£4,000
Less: tax deducted when gift made	(£2,000)
Reduction in Claudia's tax liability	£2,000

If Claudia were an additional (45%) rate taxpayer, the corresponding reduction in liability would be £2,500 (i.e. 25% of £10,000).

Other income tax benefits

The reduction in higher/additional-rate tax is given by an increase in the basic-rate income tax band equal to the grossed-up gift. In the example, Claudia's basic-rate band would be increased from circa £32,000 to £42,000 for the tax year 2014/15. This means that any dividend income otherwise taxable at 32.5% (less the 10% credit) could fall within the extended basic-rate band with no extra tax payable.

If Claudia had taxable income of £20,000 and, as such, had lost her personal income tax allowance,[9] then a gift of £16,000 would gross up to £20,000 and extend her basic-rate income tax band by the same amount. This would bring Claudia's taxable income down to £100,000 and enable her to retain her personal

---

[9] The personal income tax allowance is reduced by £1 for every £2 that taxable income exceeds £100,000 until the allowance is nil and, as a result, the effective marginal rate of income tax on taxable income between £100,000 and £120,000 can be as high as 60%, depending on the source of income ((£20,000 × 40%) + (£10,000 × 40%) = £12,000) so (£12,000/£20,000) × 100 = 60%).

income tax allowance, thus providing effective personal tax relief of 50% on the net cash donation and 75% including the tax reclaimed directly by the charity.[10]

It is also possible to make a gift and carry this back to the previous tax year, subject to you having paid sufficient income tax in that tax year to meet the tax claim by the charity. The deadline for carrying back a gift is on or before the time you make the donation but no later than 31 October (if you file a paper tax return) or 31 January (if you file an online tax return) in the year that the gift is made.

Gift Aid and chargeable events on insurance bonds

It is important to note that the basic-rate tax band is not extended for the purpose of computing relief on top-sliced gains under a life assurance policy.[11] For example, if Claudia had taxable income of £31,000 after allowances for the tax year 2014/15 and the top-sliced gain under a single-premium bond was, say, £2,000, then higher-rate tax would usually be calculated on £1,000 (i.e. £32,000 – £31,000).

Were Claudia to make a gross Gift Aid payment of £1,000, then, although the basic-rate threshold would be increased to £32,000, for top-slicing relief it would be held at £31,000, so the higher-rate tax would still be based on a chargeable gain slice of £1,000.

Capital gains tax and Gift Aid

Taxable capital gains (after deducting losses and/or the annual capital gains tax exemption) are taxed at 28% unless the taxable gain falls within your unused basic-rate income tax band of, currently, circa £32,000, when it will be taxable at 18% to the extent that it falls within the basic-rate band.

For example, Stephen has total taxable income after personal allowance of £32,000 and taxable capital gains of £25,000.

---

[10] The effect of the gift is that Claudia would receive £4,000 as a tax reduction on the grossed-up gift of £20,000 and avoid £4,000 of higher-rate tax due to the reinstatement of her personal allowance of £10,000. This equates to marginal tax relief of 50% on the net cash donation (£8,000/£16,000). When combined with the tax reclaimed at source by the charity of £4,000, this equates to total tax relief equivalent to 75% (£12,000/£16,000).

[11] For an explanation of top-slicing relief, see Chapter 15.

Gains that fall within basic-rate tax band	Nil
Gains that exceed the basic-rate tax band	£25,000

All of the gain will be taxed at 28%, resulting in a liability of £7,000. If, however, Stephen made a charitable donation under Gift Aid of £20,000, his basic-rate income tax band would be increased by the amount of the grossed-up gift (£25,000), to be £57,000. After deducting his taxable income of £32,000, this means that he has £25,000 of unused basic-rate income tax band and, as such, the entire taxable capital gain will be taxed at 18% – i.e. £4,500 rather than £7,000 had he not made the contribution. See Chapters 14 and 16 for more on capital gains tax planning.

Non-cash gifts to charities

Although the Gift Aid scheme does not extend to non-cash gifts, it is also possible to obtain tax relief at your marginal rate(s) of income tax, as well as exemption from capital gains and inheritance tax, by donating 'qualifying assets' to a registered charity or foundation, including one created by yourself.

Such 'qualifying assets' include:

- quoted shares (on a recognised exchange)
- units or shares in a unit trust or OEIC
- shares or units in an offshore fund
- a freehold interest in land in the UK or a leasehold interest in such land for a term of years absolute.

Relief is given by way of deduction against income otherwise subject to tax. The amount that can be deducted is broadly the market value of the asset gifted plus the incidental costs of disposal, e.g. commission, costs of transfer. So, if a donor with a taxable income of, say, £125,000 gave qualifying shares worth £50,000 to a charity, the donor's taxable income would be reduced to £75,000, resulting in an income tax saving of £20,000 (40% of £50,000).

In addition:

- there would be no capital gains tax to pay on the gift, even if the shares had appreciated in value since their acquisition, and
- there would be no inheritance tax on the gift.

It is also possible to sell an asset to a charity at below its market value and, in this situation, the proceeds are deducted from the gift value for the purposes of determining exemption from capital gains and reducing taxable income.

Charitable legacy IHT reduction

Where at least 10% of your taxable estate is left to a registered charity, the remainder of your taxable estate will be taxed at 36% rather than the standard 40% IHT rate. If you were not going to leave money to charity on your death, this rule will not motivate you to do so, but it's nice to know that it is costing the estate only 60% of the gross gift, as shown in Table 24.1.

Table 24.1 Effects on net estate of charitable legacy rule

	No charitable legacy	With charitable legacy – before 06/04/12	With charitable legacy – on or after 06/04/12
Taxable estate	£1,000,000	£1,000,000	£1,000,000
Charitable legacy	NIL	(£100,000)	(£100,000)
Net taxable estate	£1,000,000	£900,000	£900,000
IHT charge	(£400,000)	(£360,000)	(£324,000)
Net estate for beneficiaries	£600,000	£540,000	£576,000

Increase of 6.7%

Ways to give

There are four main ways to give to charities, as set out in Figure 24.4. The receiving entity must, however, have a charity reference number issued by HMRC.

Direct to charity

This means that you gift cash or a financial asset directly to your chosen charity. This is simple and is best if your overall level of giving is modest, ad hoc and you are good at keeping on top of paperwork for when you come to complete your tax return.

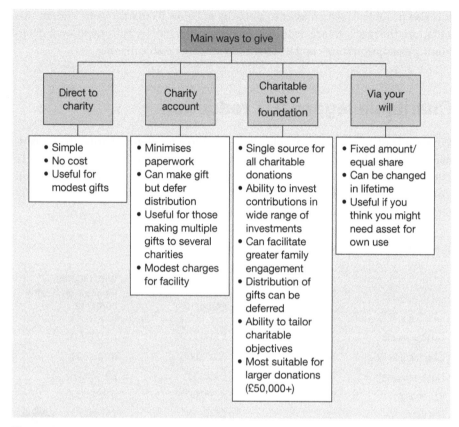

Figure 24.4 Main ways to give

Charity account

If you want simplicity, particularly if you make gifts to lots of charities each year, and/or you want to obtain the tax benefits now but defer a decision on which charities to support, a charity account can be very useful. These accounts are similar to a normal bank current account, in that you pay cash donations into the account, which usually earns a modest amount of interest. Withdrawals are permitted only in order to make donations to your chosen registered charities and these can be done electronically or by issuing cheques. Charity accounts are offered by a number of organisations, including the Charities Aid Foundation (CAF) and Charities Trust, although they do make a small charge on each contribution and a small annual charge.

Charitable trust or foundation

This is a personalised type of trust that attracts charitable status and provides a high degree of flexibility over how funds can be deployed, although neither you nor your family may benefit from the trust personally. Like a charity account, a charitable trust allows you to make substantial donations but defer deciding which charities are to benefit. Alternatively, you could build up capital, of which you could delegate the management to a professional investment manager, which will fund ongoing charitable giving long after you've ceased to make contributions. In addition, there is greater flexibility to invest in businesses, whether social or normal commercial enterprises, that you think will have a high social impact and/or generate significant profits or capital gains that can be distributed to charities.

The Charity Commission,[12] however, is getting hot on making sure that charities *do* distribute funds rather than leave them to stockpile. So, you could have problems if you set up a charitable trust and then contribute funds to it for a period of years without ever paying anything out. The best approach is probably to ensure that you start to make distributions within a few years of setting up the trust and to keep making distributions, even if these are less than the ongoing contributions and any investment growth.

Because the costs of setting up and managing a charitable trust are higher than for a charity account, they are most suited to those making a more substantial gift – usually £50,000 or more. In practice, however, contributions to this type of structure are usually in excess of £250,000. Although a charitable trust or foundation is usually set up by a lawyer, organisations such as CAF can provide you with your own charitable trust that is pre-approved with HMRC and for which they handle all ongoing administration and compliance for a competitive price. In addition, they have a range of external investment options at preferential rates. However, if you have specific needs and objectives, or you like the idea of having a bespoke charitable trust, go ahead and have your legal adviser create the entity for you.

Via your will

Leaving a legacy to one or more charities via your will is easy. It can be changed at any time while you are alive and avoids you having to give away cash or assets that

---

[12] The Charity Commission regulates charities in England and Wales.

you might need to call on for your personal use in your lifetime. You could stipulate a fixed amount or specific asset or give all or part of your residue estate. There can be issues with each, particularly where confusion can arise if you have a list of gifts in your will, some of which are tax-free and some of which are not. You need to make clear your intentions – i.e. whether they each receive the same amount net or the charity receives more because it's tax-free.

In the next and final chapter we'll go back to where we started in Chapter 1, when I asked: 'What's important about money to you?' I'll share with you a few final thoughts on living a life with a purpose to help with the motivation needed to ensure that your wealth helps to achieve all that is important to you.

CHAPTER 25
NO REGRETS

'I am successful today because someone believed in me and I didn't have the heart to let them down.'

Abraham Lincoln

One of the most important attributes of those who enjoy a long and fulfilling life is having a strong sense of purpose. As I said in Chapter 1, the more you know what is important to you and why, the easier it will be to determine an appropriate wealth strategy and associated solutions. If you've read the entire book and got this far, then well done, but before you go I just want to give you some of my personal perspectives and pose some thought-provoking questions.

Are you inspired by your life?

Do you appreciate the people you've met and experiences you've had so far? You might find it useful to keep a journal of what you've learned and keep updating it. We are a product of our thoughts and feelings and we usually get what we expect or tolerate in our lives. The two biggest excuses in life are 'I'm too young' and 'I'm too old'. Why believe that you have arrived; why not keep growing? There are people becoming first-time authors in their sixties, starting businesses in their seventies, taking exams in their eighties and running marathons in their nineties!

The standards that we set for ourselves will usually be in a comfort zone that is well below our potential. Personally, I am grateful for what I have experienced and achieved so far, but I'm also very excited about what the future holds. How excited are you about your future and those of the people you love and care about?

The power of knowing your 'why'

Passion comes from enthusiasm and enthusiasm comes from belief. Knowing what's really important to you and what your higher calling is are key elements of belief in yourself. While you might think that leaving a financial legacy is important, what about leaving a legacy of character? By character I mean that unique combination of human attributes of integrity, principles and authenticity.

Was there someone who acted as your mentor, who helped you to become the person you are today? If you aren't already, could you be a mentor to others to provide inspiration, support and encouragement? My view is that our example is the only thing that influences others. Think about your actions, deeds and messages. What impact do these have on your family, friends and colleagues and are they the impacts that you want?

If you are clear what is important to you and how you define success, fulfilment and happiness, then there is a higher chance that you'll achieve it. The old saying of 'being careful what you wish for' comes to mind.

Happiness is not the same as pleasure

Pleasure can be sustained only by the activity that produces it, whereas happiness is a state of mind that comes from a series of actions, thoughts, feelings and attitudes. If you find it hard to be happy and contented, try acting happy for the first two hours of every day and eventually it will become a habit.

The news is mainly negative and not intended to make us happy. For most of us, 90% of life is great and 10% is not so great, so why not focus on the 90% that is great and forget the other 10%? Control what you can control and don't worry about what you can't (investment returns, taxes and politicians!). Instead focus on what you have, not on what you don't have or may have lost. Silence is the key to contemplation and wisdom, so try to avoid being stimulated and electronically connected all the time.

At the end of each week in my firm, we ask each member of the team to score their happiness on a scale of one to ten. Our current average is about eight, but we are aiming for ten. What's your happiness score and why is that so? Each week at the dinner table, I ask my family what's the best thing that happened to them that week. The idea is to focus on the good rather than the negative things and we find it helps us to stay positive and appreciative of the good things in life.

Financial happiness

Experiencing bad days, sadness and disappointment are all part of being human, but feeling happy the majority of the time is something most of us would aspire to achieve. As the old adage goes, money can't buy you love, happiness or good health (with health more influenced by genetics, lifestyle and environment), but it can give you choices. However, we can't spend our way to happiness – or can we?

'Money is better than poverty, if only for financial reasons.'

Woody Allen

A new book[1] on the subject of financial happiness suggests that how we spend our money, rather than how much money we have, determines our overall level of happiness. The authors are behavioural science experts who have researched how spending influences human happiness and they have found five core principles that increase happiness. Here's a quick overview of their findings.

1. Buy experiences, not things

The excitement and satisfaction we derive from buying material things – a new car, clothes, jewellery, gadgets, etc. – soon wears off. Yet we remember things we've done, people we've met and places we've visited long after we forget the price we paid.

For example, when I was on holiday recently, we decided to hire a boat for the day to explore the coast and beaches. Instead of hiring the small boat that I would have had to captain, we decided to pay a bit more for a larger boat that came with a skipper. As well as avoiding the stress of me having to be responsible for the craft, it was more comfortable and had a longer range. We remember the day but have quickly forgotten the cost.

2. Make it a treat

If you set yourself a goal or give yourself conditions for acquiring material possessions or buying experiences, you'll enjoy them more. When I started writing the first edition of this book I told myself that, once it had been published, I would buy myself the acoustic guitar I'd been promising myself for several years.

---

[1] Dunn, E. and Norton, M. (2013) *Happy Money: The new science of smarter spending*, Oneworld.

Although I could afford to buy the guitar anyway, linking its acquisition to the achievement of another goal gave me greater satisfaction and a sense of achievement. I've promised myself an electric guitar when this edition is published.

3. Buy time

Life is too precious and short to waste it doing things we aren't good at, don't love or that get in the way of us spending time on things that are more important to us. For example, I hate gardening, completing my tax return, ironing and paperwork. I therefore spend money to delegate these tasks to people who are paid to do them and are better at them than I am. I also hate queuing, so I will pay a premium to avoid doing so, wherever possible.

Spending money to save time, avoid delays or achieve things quicker leads to greater happiness. What can you pay to delegate or avoid to free up your valuable time?

4. Pay now, consume later

Deferred gratification increases happiness. Research suggests that saving up for something and then buying it makes us feel much better than buying something on credit. Even if you have the money to buy something, why not defer it and save up the funds to buy it? For example, instead of paying my tax in two big lumps each year, I now pay it monthly in advance, to avoid the pain I felt every time I had to send off a payment every January and July. Now I don't notice the tax liability quite as much as I did.

5. Invest in others

Helping others financially makes us happy. Whether it's sponsoring someone for a charitable event, making a small loan to help them achieve something, paying for them to have a meaningful life experience or buying them something special, it improves how we feel.

Our level of happiness is influenced by many things, but the research in this book suggests that how we spend our money can have a big impact. Have a good look at what you spend your money on to ensure that you really are getting the most happiness for every pound that you spend.

Who do you have around you?

We are judged and affected by the company we keep. If you have negative and unpleasant people around you, that can rub off and make you the same as them. My experience (and I've interviewed in excess of 1,000 people over the past 25 years) is that people are either drains or radiators. Drains sap you of energy and enthusiasm, so avoid people who are drains and those who have no love of life. Radiators, meanwhile, are usually warm, giving, enthusiastic, passionate and inspiring. Who do you have around you and are they the right people?

Just do it!

An acquaintance of mine works in a hospice and as a result she regularly comes into contact with people who are at the end of their lives. Her experience is that when someone knows that they are going to die, they rarely regret the things they have done in their life but they do regret the things that they didn't do, say or become.

It was, therefore, with this thought in mind that I finally bought myself the guitar that I'd promised myself several years ago. While I do play the piano and can read music, I couldn't play the guitar or read guitar music. So, having bought the guitar, I am now learning to play it, under the guidance of a gifted young musician who lives near to me (the first tune I learned was an old blues classic, 'No one knows you when you're down and out').

There is no doubt in my mind that eventually I'll be able to play the guitar at least to a level where others can recognise what I'm playing. I have thought about how I will think and feel when I can play really well and what that will mean to me. This gives me the motivation and discipline to do the practice. I'm focused on the outcome, not the process.

I did a similar thing when I taught myself to play the piano when I was 12. My first piano was an ancient, hand-painted, clapped-out upright, which was untenable, had missing notes and sounded like it had a duvet stuffed down between the strings. Despite the limitations of the instrument, I eventually learned how to play the Scott Joplin piano composition 'The Entertainer'. Now, more than 30 years later, never a week goes by when I don't sit down to play my beautiful, and perfectly tuned, Yamaha baby grand piano.

All those years ago I started with my piano dream, continued with hard work and eventually had sufficient wealth to enable me to buy a lovely instrument. I hope my guitar dream is equally as successful and who knows, I might eventually be playing a Fender Strat or Gibson Les Paul in years to come. Either way I try to live my life so that when my time is up, I will have as few regrets as possible about the things I haven't done in my lifetime.

So what about you? If you knew you had only weeks to live, what regrets would you have about what you hadn't done, become or said? Once you can answer that question, you are well on your way to living a life that is truly rich, rewarding and meaningful.

A thought to leave you with

Your life isn't defined by money or your net worth but by the things that you do, see and experience on a daily basis and that make you happy and fulfilled. It's not my job to tell you what's important to you or how to live your life. I do hope, however, that you are clear on your life's purpose so you know the 'why' (the mission, vision, values and goals) of your wealth plan. If you understand those, then the 'what' and 'how' of your wealth plan (the strategies, tactics and tools set out in this book) will fall neatly into place. In that context I hope that the future for you and the people you care about will be even bigger and more exciting than your past.

What did you think of this book?

We're really keen to hear from you about this book, so that we can make our publishing even better.

Please log on to the following website and leave us your feedback.

It will only take a few minutes and your thoughts are invaluable to us.

www.pearsoned.co.uk/bookfeedback

USEFUL WEBSITES AND FURTHER READING

Websites

Wealthpartner: dedicated website for readers of *The Financial Times Guide to Wealth Management*. You can download a range of templates, tools and questionnaires to assist you with creating your own plan. You can also sign up for a free wealth planning update service.

Institute of Financial Planning: official website for the professional body that awards and monitors the international Certified Financial Planner CM (CFP) and Accredited Financial Planning Firm accreditations. Online searchable registry of Accredited Financial Planning Firms in the UK is available at **www.financialplanning.org.uk/wayfinder**

Findanadviser: consumer website of the Personal Finance Society – the professional body that awards and monitors the Chartered Financial Planner designation. Online searchable database of Chartered Financial Planners can be found at **www.findanadviser.org/**

The Money Advice Service: a government-backed, comprehensive, independent and free source of information and guidance on a wide range of personal finance issues. Includes access to an online personal finance 'health check' analyser, interactive money planners, in-depth money guides and a product-comparison tool for insurance, annuities, pensions and other financial products. Free general advice is also available via telephone or face to face. **http://moneyadvice-service.org.uk/default.aspx**

Which? Savings rates booster comparison tables. www.which.co.uk/money/savings-and-investments/guides/saving-rates-booster

BBC Radio 4 Moneybox: website of the long-running Radio 4 personal finance programme with a range of articles, videos and links to other websites on personal finance issues. **http://news.bbc.co.uk/1/hi/programmes/moneybox/default.stm**

The Pensions Advisory Service: useful source of independent information and guidance on pension-related issues. **www.pensionsadvisoryservice.org.uk**

HM Revenue & Customs, Pensioners Portal: useful information and guidance on a range of tax-related issues affecting those receiving pension benefits. **http://hmrc.gov.uk/pensioners/index.htm**

Directgov: a wide range of information on money, tax, pensions, education funding and state benefits. **www.direct.gov.uk/en/index.htm**

Disability Law Service: free information and guidance for people with disabilities. **www.dls.org.uk**

Schmidt Tax Report: subscription-based online and printed tax-planning newsletter aimed at successful individuals and business owners. **http://schmidtreport.co.uk/index.htm**

Registered Pension Schemes Manual (RPSM): HMRC comprehensive, in-depth technical guide to registered pension schemes. **www.hmrc.gov.uk/manuals/rpsmmanual/index.htm**

Books

Financial DNA: Discovering your unique financial personality for a quality life by Hugh Massie (ISBN-10: 0471784206)

The Energy of Money: A spiritual guide to financial and personal fulfilment by Maria Nemeth (ISBN-13: 978-0345434975)

Money and the Meaning of Life by Jacob Needleman (ISBN-13: 978-0385262422)

The Seven Stages of Money Maturity by George Kinder (ISBN-13: 978-0385324045)

Man's Search for Meaning by Viktor E. Frankl (ISBN-13: 978-1844132393)

The Millionaire Next Door by Thomas J. Stanley and William D. Danko (ISBN-13: 978-0671015206)

3 Dimensional Wealth by Monroe M. Diefendorf, Jr and Robert Sterling Madden (ISBN-13: 978-0976901402)

Wealthy and Wise: Secrets about money by Heidi L. Steiger (ISBN-13: 978-0471221418)

Smart Couples Finish Rich: 9 steps to creating a rich future for you and your partner by David Bach (ISBN-13: 978-0767904834)

Values-based Financial Planning: The art of creating and inspiring financial strategy by Bill Bachrach (ISBN-13: 978-1887006033)

Enough!: True measures of money, business, and life by John C. Bogle (ISBN-13: 978-0470398517)

The Number: A completely different way to think about the rest of your life by Lee Eisenburg (ISBN-13: 978-0743270311)

Sudden Money: Managing a financial windfall by Susan Bradley (ISBN-13: 978-0471380863)

A Random Walk Down Wall Street by Burton G. Malkiel (ISBN-13: 978-0-393325350)

Against the Gods: The remarkable story of risk by Peter Bernstein (ISBN-13: 978-0471295631)

The Little Book of Common Sense Investing by John C. Bogle (ISBN-13: 978-0-470102107)

The Investment Answer by Daniel C. Goldie and Gordon S. Murray (ISBN-13: 978-0982894705)

Smarter Investing: Simpler decisions for better results by Tim Hale (ISBN-13: 978-0273708001)

Winning the Loser's Game: Timeless strategies for successful investing by Charles D. Ellis (ISBN-13: 978-0071545495)

No Monkey Business: What investors need to know and why by Stuart Fowler (ISBN-13: 978-0273656586)

Investor Behavior: The psychology of financial planning and investing by H. Kent Baker and Victor Ricciardi (ISBN-13: 978-1-118-49298-7)

Guide to Investment Strategy: How to understand markets, risk, rewards and behaviour by Peter Stanyer (ISBN-13: 978-1-78125-072-3)

Preparing Heirs: Five steps to a successful transition of family wealth and values by Roy Williams and Vic Preisser (ISBN-13: 1-931741-31-X)

The entrepreneur's tax guide by Alan Pink (ISBN-13: 978-2-781-85612-3)

The Rational Optimist by Matt Ridely (ISBN-13: 978-0-00-726712-5)

INDEX

Note: Page numbers in *italic* indicate entries in figures or tables